KLEIN

LONDON AFTER RECESSION

London After Recession

A Fictitious Capital?

Edited by

GAVIN POYNTER, IAIN MACRURY AND ANDREW CALCUTT

University of East London, UK

ASHGATE

Published by
Ashgate Publishing Limited
Wey Court East
Union Road
Farnham
Surrey, GU9 7PT
England

Ashgate Publishing Company
Suite 420
101 Cherry Street
Burlington
VT 05401-4405
USA

www.ashgate.com

British Library Cataloguing in Publication Data
London after recession : a fictitious capital?. -- (Design and the built environment series)
1. London (England)--Economic conditions--21st century.
2. London (England)--Social conditions--21st century.
3. Global Financial Crisis, 2008-2009.
I. Series II. Poynter, Gavin, 1949- III. MacRury, Iain.
IV. Calcutt, Andrew.
942.1'08612-dc23

Library of Congress Cataloging-in-Publication Data
Poynter, Gavin, 1949-
London after recession : a fictitious capital? / by Gavin Poynter, Iain MacRury, and Andrew Calcutt.
p. cm. -- (Design and the built environment)
Includes bibliographical references and index.
ISBN 978-1-4094-3102-2 (hardback) -- ISBN 978-1-4094-3103-9 (ebook)
1. London (England)--Economic conditions--21st century. 2. London (England)--Social conditions--21st century. 3. Global Financial Crisis, 2008-2009. I. MacRury, Iain. II. Calcutt, Andrew. III. Title.
HC258.L6P69 2012
330.9421--dc23

2012007224

ISBN 9781409431022 (hbk)
ISBN 9781409431039 (ebk)

MIX
Paper from responsible sources
FSC www.fsc.org FSC® C018575

Printed and bound in Great Britain by the MPG Books Group, UK.

Contents

List of Figures — *ix*
List of Tables — *xi*
List of Contributors — *xiii*
List of Abbreviations — *xv*
Preface — *xvii*

Introduction: A Fictitious Capital? — 1
Gavin Poynter

PART 1 GLOBAL CITIES AND RESPONSES TO RECESSION

1 The Global Recession — 15
Gavin Poynter

2 New York City's Economy: More than Wall Street? — 37
Sean Collins

3 The Glittering Prizes of Shanghai — 51
Alan Hudson

4 Finance and Culture: Twin Towers in London's Lightness of Being — 67
Andrew Calcutt

PART 2 FINANCIALISATION AND LONDON'S ECONOMY

5 Historic Transitions and Circuits in London's Financial Services — 83
Richard Sharpe

6 Opening and Closing Spaces for Fictitious Capital: The State and Finance Capital in London — 101
Richard Sharpe

7 London's Financial Services: After the Credit Crunch — 115
Daniel Ben-Ami

8 The Apprentice: Realities and Fictions for the London Skyline 127
Iain Macrury

9 A Tale of Two Journalisms: Counteracting Tendencies in London's Media 147
Andrew Calcutt

10 The Real Economy and the Regeneration of East London 161
Alvaro de Miranda

11 Energy 177
James Woudhuysen

12 Carbon Trading in the City of Undoing 199
Maxine Newlands

13 Music from the Storm Clouds: The Continuing Troubles of the Music Business 213
Andrew Blake

14 Farewell Nathan Barley? The Rise and Decline of the Freelance Creative 227
Graham Barnfield

PART 3 MOBILITY AND SOCIAL POLICY IN LONDON

15 Overcoming the Limits to Travel 249
Alastair Donald

16 Immigration and London's Economy 267
Gavin Poynter

17 The Housing Crisis 283
Penny Bernstock and Gavin Poynter

18 The Health Service of the Future 295
Justine Cawley

19 Hard Times for Higher Education: Knowledge Economy, Economies of Knowledge 305
Karina Berzins

PART 4 LONDON'S FUTURE

20 The Crisis of Fictitious Capital 317
Michael Rustin

21 Toward a New Urban Economy? 337
Gavin Poynter and Michael Rustin

Index *351*

List of Figures

1.1 Chinese GDP at constant prices, annual Change 1990-2010 (in per cent) 21
1.2 Manufacturing as percentage of GDP globally and across comparator countries 25
1.3 Financial Services Output Selected Countries 2000-2005 (2000=100) 26
1.4 Financial and Business Services Output as share of GDP 1970-2009 26
2.1 US industry GDP as % of total US GDP 1947-2010 42
5.1 The Hierarchy of Profit Realisation Built on the Base of Profit Generation: The Higher up the Hierarchy, the Greater the Risk 87
8.1 The Apprentice dramatises individuals in competition, judgement, justification and business practice but it is also highly conscious of place – London's city skyline is both figure and ground for the show 137

List of Tables

1.1	Rates of GDP Growth (annual average compound growth rates) Selected Countries 1950-1998	20
1.2	Top Five Foreign Holders of US Securities (June 2006)	22
2.1	Employment by Industry in New York City	45
7.1	Financial Services Employment in Central London (in thousands)	118
7.2	Financial Services' Share of GDP in Major Economies (% Share of GDP)	119
8.1	Ideal Types of business 'cities': Criteria for status and justification	140
11.1	Final energy consumption, Greater London and UK, 2008, TWh	178
11.2	Main components of London energy use, by sector and by energy source, 2008, TWh	179
11.3	Energy use, London, 2004-2008, and as projected to 2011 and 2015; TWh	180
11.4	Fuel poverty in London, thousands of homes	181
11.5	Projected GVA, investment and jobs through the Mayor's climate change mitigation programmes by 2025	192
13.1	Music Venues and Performances in Five Global Cities	213
16.1	Migrants to the United Kingdom by Decade of Arrival	271
16.2	Total Migrants to London Boroughs from pre-1970 to 2008	272

List of Contributors

The Editors

Gavin Poynter is Professor of Social Sciences, University of East London and a member of the London East Research Institute management board.

Andrew Calcutt is Principal Lecturer in Journalism at the University of East London, editor of *Rising East* and Chair of London East Research Institute.

Iain MacRury is Associate Dean, School of Arts and Digital Industries and Director of London East Research Institute.

Contributors

Graham Barnfield is Senior Lecturer in Journalism, University of East London and a member of the London East Research Institute management board.

Daniel Ben-Ami is a finance and economics journalist. His articles have been published widely including for *Fund Strategy*, *The Australian* and *The Guardian.* See http://danielbenami.com/.

Penny Bernstock is programme and field leader in Sociology at the University of East London and Vice-Chair, London East Research Institute.

Karina Berzins is a Research Fellow with Continuum, the Centre for Widening Participation, Policy Studies at the University of East London, and a Senior Research Fellow with London East Research Institute and a member of its management board.

Andrew Blake is Professor in Cultural Studies and a member of London East Research Institute management board.

Justine Cawley is a freelance health consultant, visiting fellow of London East Research Institute and also holds honorary appointments at London South Bank University and Buckingham New University.

Sean Collins writes about American economics and politics for *Spiked* and other publications. He is based in New York.

Alastair Donald is Associate Director of the Future Cities Project and an urban designer, researching mobility and space at the Martin Centre for Architectural and Urban Studies, University of Cambridge.

Alan Hudson is Director, Leadership Programmes for China, University of Oxford, Department for Continuing Education.

Alvaro de Miranda is Senior Research Fellow, London East Research Institute and member of its management board.

Maxine Newlands is Senior Lecturer in Journalism, University of East London, a member of London East Research Institute management board and of the editorial board of *Rising East Essays*.

Michael Rustin is Professor of Sociology at the University of East London, Visiting Professor Tavistock Clinic and a member of London East Research Institute management board.

Richard Sharpe is Lecturer in Journalism at the University of East London, a member of London East Research Institute management board and of the editorial board of *Rising East Essays*.

James Woudhuysen is Professor of Forecasting and Innovation, De Montfort University, Leicester.

List of Abbreviations

AIM	Alternative Investment Market
BoE	Bank of England
DCLG	Department of Communities and Local Government
DCMS	Department of Culture, Media and Sport
EiP	Eco-Industrial Park
ETS	Emissions Trading Scheme
EU ETS	European Union Emissions Trading Scheme
GATT	General Agreement on Tariffs and Trade
GLA	Greater London Authority
GP	General Practitioner
GVA	Gross Value Added
HBOS	Halifax, Bank of Scotland
HCA	Homes and Communities Agency
HSBC	Hong Kong Shanghai Banking Corporation
IBRD	International Bank for Reconstruction and Development
IMF	International Monetary Fund
IPCC	Intergovernmental Panel on Climate Change
LDA	London Development Agency
NEPIs	New Environmental Policy Instruments
NYSE	New York Stock Exchange
OBR	Office for Budgetary Responsibility
OPLC	Olympic Park Legacy Company
PCT	Primary Care Trust
PFI	Private Finance Initiative
PPP	Public, Private Partnership
RSL	Registered Social Landlord
RBS	Royal Bank of Scotland
SROI	Social Return on Investment
SiP	Sustainable Industrial Park
TIF	Tax Increment Financing
TfL	Transport for London
UNCED	United Nations Conference on Environment and Development

Preface

This book is the latest of the publications that have emerged from discussions, seminars and events held by London East Research Institute, University of East London. Our publications on East London commenced in the 1990s, charting the impacts of de-industrialisation on that part of the city. In more recent times, Ashgate Publishing, especially Valerie Rose, has kindly supported us in publishing our work on the Thames Gateway project: *London's Turning* (2008) edited by Philip Cohen and Michael Rustin and *Olympic Cities* (2009), edited by Gavin Poynter and Iain MacRury. The momentous events arising from the credit crunch and subsequent global recession, pressed us into a series of further discussions about London's role in creating the deepest economic crisis for more than 70 years. This book is the product of those discussions.

We wish to record our deepest thanks to all the contributors for working so hard to complete to deadlines and to address complex contemporary issues but always with an eye on their long term implications for London and for those who live in this city. There are many individuals within and outside the university to thank for their views and comments provided to the authors. In particular, we would like to thank all the policy advisors and experts from city-wide, local and national government who provided their views on recent developments, especially Richard Derecki, Graham Kinshott and Ralph Ward. Warmest thanks are also due to friends and colleagues for spending informal hours talking over ideas that informed the chapters in this book. Special thanks also to the UEL staff who contributed to internal seminars at which our ideas were tested and developed.

Finally, all our contributors owe a debt of gratitude to their friends and family for their patience and support while writing the chapters for this book – often within tight time frames and at the expense of normal life. We hope, however, that the book makes a real contribution to the collective understanding of what really are abnormal times.

Gavin Poynter, Andrew Calcutt and Iain MacRury

Introduction: A Fictitious Capital?

Gavin Poynter

Boris Johnson, Mayor of London, on London and the financial crisis 2007-2011:

> To the banker bashers, I say, what's your ideal economic model? We can't ignore and hate the bankers. What would that achieve? Show me how reducing financial services boosts manufacturing. London attracts the brightest people from around the globe – it serves the global economy. It's one of the best places in the world in which to raise money. Why should harming that provide a boost to other parts of the economy?[1]

Karl Marx on London and the financial crisis 1837-1839:

> An enormous quantity of these bills of exchange represents plain swindle … (and) cannot be remedied by having some bank like the Bank of England, give to all the swindlers the deficient capital by means of its paper and having it buy up all the old depreciated commodities at their old values…everything here appears distorted. Particularly in centres where the entire money business of the country is concentrated, like London, does this distortion become apparent … it is less so in centres of production.[2]

In an interview recorded in January 2011, the Mayor's spirited defence of London's financial services sector and its special role in the global economy was designed to counter the 'banker bashing' that arose in the UK and across the world in the wake of the credit crunch (2007-2009). Financial institutions, located particularly in London and New York, were widely blamed for a crisis whose origins lay in the highly technical character of the 'toxic' products spawned in the financial world of intermediation and risk management. As the crunch progressed from financial crisis to global economic recession, its impact spread from the US housing market to western financial markets and to most nations and sectors of the international economy. In his defence of the London's pre-eminent role in global financial

---

1 Blackhurst, C. (2011) 'The MT interview, Boris Johnson', *Management Today*, 1 January 2011. Available at http://www.managementtoday.co.uk/features/1047368/the-mt-interview-boris-johnson/#, accessed 10 January 2011.

2 Marx, K. (1972). *Capital: A Critique of Political Economy*, Volume 3. London: Lawrence & Wishart, 470.

intermediation, Boris Johnson was reminding a readership of British managers of the sector's significant contribution to the British economy as a whole.

In his reference to London's banking crisis of 1837-1839, Karl Marx was also reminding his readers that London was the centre of the 'money business' of the entire country (and Empire), and that the Bank of England was the credit guarantor of last resort. The failure of three banks in March 1837, led the Bank of England to provide advances to other banks to prevent panic. The Bank's actions did not remove the threat of bankruptcy, so the state raised the discount rate and borrowed from France and the German principalities. Marx's analysis of this relatively localised banking crisis, used in his explanation of the distinctions between money and real capital, has perhaps some resonance today. It highlights the flaws arising from attempts by a central bank to buy up all the old depreciated commodities (today's 'toxic' assets) at their old values; the social and economic 'distortions' that arise in those financial centres whose activities, in the world of circulation, are distanced from the 'centres of production' and, perhaps most importantly, how the development of interest-bearing capital and the credit system gives rise to capital re-appearing in various forms, where 'the greater portion of this 'money capital' is purely fictitious' (Marx 1972: 470).

The subtitle of this book, Fictitious Capital, is taken from Marx's (and Engels's, mainly in the form of footnotes) incisive study of bank capital and the role of the credit system. This book's focus is London (as was theirs). Our analysis takes up the Mayor's challenge to find an alternative economic model, and follows Marx's instruction to reveal the contemporary forms of socio-economic and cultural 'distortions' expressed in the credit crunch and subsequent recession.

Just as it was in the mid-nineteenth century, the City today is a centre of the 'money business' ('the City' with a capital C, is used to designate the financial districts of London, now extended to include Canary Wharf as well as the 'square mile' to which 'the City' was previously tantamount). As Boris Johnson reminds us, London's financial and business sectors serve the global economy. The purpose of this book is to examine the impact of this global role on London's society, culture and industry. This analysis is undertaken in the wake of the most significant international financial crisis since the inter-war years; a crisis that arguably provides an important opportunity to reassess the 'post-industrial, services led' approach which has been the model for London's growth since the 1980s.

In the economic sphere, London's recent reputation as a 'global city' has been concentrated on the spectacular growth of financial and business services industries. London and the South East of England have accounted for a very significant proportion of Britain's GDP growth over recent years, with several sectors apparently benefitting from the successes (and excesses) of the finance sector, including retail, housing, business services and the cultural and creative industries. The credit crunch and its aftermath have raised important questions about this model of urban social, economic and cultural development and the pattern of economic growth on which it is founded.

Our starting point is that the financial crisis makes necessary a re-thinking of what is meant by 'the economy', the activities it involves and the value it creates. Contributors seek to develop new approaches to the urban economy that challenge current assumptions concerning the benefits arising from London's financial and business services. Contrasting the 'disembedded' character of these and associated industries with those sectors whose roots lie in the 'embedded' world of production, this book examines the impact of the recession and discusses London's future trajectory as an entrepreneurial city and as capital of the United Kingdom. While recognising the enduring capacity of London to 'reinvent' itself – from being the centre of a vast Empire to becoming a global centre for financial and business services – contributors evaluate different dimensions of this city's current and future development through analyses derived from sociological, economic, cultural and urban studies perspectives.

We hope the title of this book captures the ambiguities of meaning and interpretation that contributors expose in examining the future of a 'capital' city which has come to rely on its role in the international traffic of money, *en route* to productive investment elsewhere. Similarly, our title is intended to suggest the air of unreality which pervades London's relationship with the rest of Britain, now that this national capital – the capital city of the original industrial nation – has re-oriented itself financially and internationally.

Theorising Cities

According to the United Nations, by 2007 more than half of the world's population lived in cities and by 2030 over five billion of the projected world population of eight billion will be city dwellers (UN-Habitat 2006). It was the rise of urban spaces, characterised by 'the money economy and impersonal social relations' (Haussermann and Haila 2005: 44) and their separation from rural life in late nineteenth century Europe, that prompted Georg Simmel (2004) to develop a social scientific approach to the study of the city and modernity at the turn of the twentieth century. Densely populated cities such as Berlin, produced new forms of social relations based upon the specialisation of industries, the rise of new divisions of labour, and the creation of a competitive economic environment that spurred industrial innovation and cultural creativity. In parallel, the individual in metropolitan life, according to Simmel's analysis, developed a new self-awareness and a heightened capacity to withstand the intensity of the modern city. The rise of the modern metropolis corresponded with an enhancement of human capacities albeit within spatial structures generated by a highly competitive, money economy.

Influenced by Simmel's work, the theorisation of urban life shifted in the inter-war period to the United States of America where what became known as the Chicago School argued that urban living generated competition between ethnic and social groups which in turn led to the creation of the segregated city. The concepts used to identify this universal pattern were of Darwinian origin. That the trajectory of urban development contained, according to the Chicago School, a ubiquitous character conflicted with studies of cities which suggested that specific cultural and social contexts generated diversity in patterns of urban development. From the 1960s a new form of urban studies emerged that sought to explain the relation between city structures and civic life in the different interactions occurring in each, particular conurbation.

The urban studies that developed in the second half of the twentieth century crossed disciplines – art, architecture, planning and design, urban sociology, political economy and the fledgling cultural studies – to establish different and critical ways of thinking about and engaging with the city as a site of theory and praxis. Some of the most interesting movements, reflecting the rise of a New Left radicalism in the 1960s, were relatively short-lived and not 'mainstream'. For example, in writings on urbanism and architecture produced in the 1960s and early 1970s, the Situationist International (SI) conceived a radical project through which the city could move from the 'site of alienated labour and passive consumption' to becoming 'the crucial spatial stake of any project of radical social transformation' (McDonough 2009: 3). Meanwhile, other, more mainstream intellectuals began to explore the role of world cities, such as London, in their exercise of political, financial and economic power (Hall 1966), in ways that, as Hamnett has argued, were initially largely historical in content and descriptive in character (Hamnett 2003: 24). The turn of radical or critical urban studies to new theorisations of the city arose from attempts to examine the social and cultural consequences of urban development and planning, and to analyse the significant changes taking place in western economies from their internationalisation in the 1960s, to de-industrialisation in the 1970s/1980s, and on to the post-industrial in the 1990s. In examining these developments, theorists of the urban sought to challenge orthodoxies and explore new ways of conceptualising the city, weaving together, in particular, the cultural and sociological with insights offered by critical political economy.

The Cultural Critique

In her critique first published in 1961, Jane Jacobs focused upon the failings of urban planners working in the great cities of the USA to appreciate the importance of sidewalks, corners and neighbourhoods as spaces that fostered creativity and diversity in urban life. For Jacobs, the great American cities were much diminished by post-1945 developments that generated low income neighbourhoods which emulated the slum conditions they were intended to replace, while fostering middle-income housing that was dull and uniform, and luxury housing that was simply vulgar (Jacobs 1961: 4). Cities were losing their intimate, casual and diverse character as monolithic shopping malls and monumental cultural centres began to dominate the rhythms of urban life. For Jacobs, cities required districts that had more than 'one primary function', where different modes of commerce and leisure generated outdoor activity across the day, where blocks or streets were short, and new vistas appeared at each turn. Neighbourhoods should mix new and old buildings and all districts should have sufficient population density to ensure that a solid residential community exists (Jacobs 1961: 150).

Jacobs' writings and activism in New York were catalysed by her concerns with forms of urban decline produced by dock and factory closures, and the poor quality and large scale responses arising from state-led re-development schemes. Whilst she was primarily defending the communal character of traditional neighbourhoods under threat from development, her writings informed subsequent cultural theorisations of space and place in which responses to urban change amounted to a crisis of authenticity, as Zukin describes it (2010: 222-3); a crisis reflected in the 'conflict between the corporate city and the urban village', where the former threatens to destroy the embedded character of the latter. For Zukin the response to the decline of the great western cities that Jacobs had identified in the 1960s, came from gentrifiers, immigrants and entrepreneurs in cities like New York and London who from the 1970s and 1980s were to create neighbourhoods that were clean, modern and creative, generating communities of (post-industrial) consumption shaped by the upper middle class and supported by politicians, the media and new entrepreneurs. For Zukin, such neighbourhoods produced an *apparent* reconciliation of the conflict between the corporate city and the urban village but to make such a resolution really possible, she argued, it would be necessary to harness the attributes of authenticity and align it to a greater democracy, thus extending the sense of ownership and rootedness beyond the upper middle class to all sections of society (Zukin 2010: 246).

The cultural critique of urban change in the second half of the twentieth century, briefly illustrated here by reference to the original text by Jacobs and the subsequent writings of authors such as Zukin, was also addressed by social geographers and sociologists who sought to explain the new patterns of social relations that were emerging initially in London and the cities of America's east coast in the 1950s and 1960s (Lees, Slater and Wyly 2008: xv).

Cities and Social Change

A significant theme addressed in these studies has been the process of gentrification, a word used by sociologist Ruth Glass (1964) to describe developments taking place in London in the late 1950s and early 1960s which involved 'the rehabilitation of old housing stock, tenurial transformation from renting to owning, property price increases and the displacement of working class residents by the incoming middle classes' (Lees, Slater and Wyly 2008: 5). The concept has evolved as urban sociologists have explored the wider effects and responses to de-industrialisation in western cities in the decades after Glass coined the term. Smith (1986), for example, expanded the concept beyond housing to incorporate the redevelopment of post-industrial western cities as centres for leisure, hotel accommodation, conferences, events and retail and restaurant areas; in short, incorporating many of the attributes of the late twentieth century service-oriented and consumption-driven city (Lees, Slater and Wyly 2008: 5).

The review of gentrification produced by Lees, Slater and Wyly (2008) usefully reminds us of some important insights into the relationships between urbanisation and historical conjunctures or crises that inform the themes in this book. Periods of significant economic turbulence may, in turn, generate important changes of status within and between social classes and throw up new strata within society. Gentrification, as Hamnett (2003) has argued, was deployed by Glass with a hint of irony. Her use of 'gentry-fication' was derived from an historical reference to changing class structures in the countryside in sixteenth and seventeenth century England, in which there emerged a new social class, situated between the landed nobility and yeomanry. Gentrification was a term also used by Martin Weiner (1985) in his study of the cultural struggle between financial and industrial elites in late nineteenth century England – a struggle that was resolved, according to Weiner, in the favour of the former with 'the entrenchment of anti-industrial sentiments in the financial and professional classes' having significant implications for British society throughout the twentieth century. In gaining the upper hand, the City, with its close historic ties to the aristocracy and English gentry, secured a social status that industrialists (mainly located in northern England) never enjoyed (Weiner 1985: 128).

Inspired by the writings of authors such as Glass, sociologists have sought to explain and debate recent changes in urban social structures in the wake of de-industrialisation and the increased dominance of service-based industries in western cities. For Sassen (1991) cities such as New York and London where financialisation is most advanced, have generated highly polarised social structures through the creation of vastly increased numbers of high and low income earners. Hamnett, however, has challenged Sassen's analysis by drawing upon data on London and other cities that reveals an increase in the proportion of professional and managerial workers relative to middle and low income earners, but not the evidence, between 1961 and 1991 at least, of decisive growth in the proportion of low earners (Hamnett 1994; Lees, Slater and Wyly 2008: 93). For Hamnett, the professionalisation of large parts of the urban labour market was the precondition for gentrification in cities such as London. Whilst Hamnett's analysis contains echoes of Bell's description of the post-industrial society (Bell 1973), other sociologists and geographers have created a variety of new labels aimed at capturing and defining the essential features of city economies whose wealth is increasingly based upon human rather than industrial capital, where knowledge-based workers provide the core of what the US author Richard Florida has called a new 'creative class' (Florida 2004). The creative class would typically be found in the financial and business services sectors and the cultural industries, being attracted to clusters of economic activity that are reliant upon complex communication technologies and advanced divisions of labour in which higher economic value-added arises from the input of knowledge rather than from the process of manufacture.

Whilst many urban sociologists have focused upon the rise of a knowledge-based 'gentry', others have examined the coin's other side: the relative decline of traditional working class communities and manual occupations; changes in the gender and ethnic divisions of labour; and how such changes increasingly interacted with the global movement of labour in the last half of the twentieth century. In the USA, the implications of these changes were first revealed in the 1960s, in the Harlem (1964) and Watts (1965) riots, and continually expressed in subsequent social unrest throughout the black ghettos of major American cities. Whilst the riots were connected to endemic patterns of discrimination across America, and to the broad, political struggle for civil rights and against racism, their occurrence in major inner cities also reflected a deep crisis in the urban social order. White flight to the suburbs, the relative deterioration of inner city housing stock, rising levels of property tax and property depreciation combined to create inner city decay; and over several decades the recovery from this has been only partial and piecemeal, as recorded by such authors as Castells (1980) and Davis (1990). While Federal intervention provided mass transit systems and other infrastructural improvements in major US cities in the 1970s and 1980s, and home ownership opportunities were expanded to relatively poor communities, the continuing fragility of the urban American social order was again made explicit in the pitching of 'tent cities' for those made homeless by foreclosure during the credit crunch and subsequent recession.

On the other side of the Atlantic, London – and East London, in particular – has been an important source for the analysis of inner city social change in Britain. For most of the past two centuries, East London was the city on the outside or the 'other' side; the poor east in stark contrast to the rich west. It was and remains the gateway to Britain for successive waves of immigrants and its industry traditionally focused upon the making and the movement of the materials from which those in London's City offices and trading floors profited. The closure of the docks in the 1960s and 1970s and the decline in the industries that depended upon them, hastened the demise of the traditional white working class communities whose experiences of everyday life were captured by Young and Wilmott (1957) in their famous study of *Family and Kinship in East London*. The authors describe life through the microcosm of Bethnal Green where extended families lived together in tight-knit communities, occupations were passed from father to son, and self-reliance enabled East Enders to survive largely without the welfare state (Dench, Gavron and Young 2006: 1).

Subsequent studies of East London have focused upon the impact of welfare state policies on employment, housing and immigration (Dench, Gavron and Young 2006), patterns of gentrification (Butler 1997), and successive waves of urban regeneration projects that have transformed parts of East London since their commencement in the early 1980s (Butler and Rustin 1996; Imrie, Lees and Raco 2009; Cohen and Rustin 2008). Such studies have examined the governance of urban regeneration projects in London, the impact of major regeneration schemes, the expansion of the City's international financial and business services sector into Canary Wharf, replacing the derelict docks area, and more recent developments associated with the vast regeneration programme designated as Thames Gateway (an area that extends eastwards along the Thames estuary incorporating the coasts of south Essex and north Kent), and, latterly, the implications of East London hosting the 2012 Olympic and Paralympic Games (Poynter and MacRury 2009).

The most recent studies discuss, amongst other dimensions, London as a global city in which the spectacle of the mega-event is allied to programmes of urban renewal (Rustin 2009; MacRury and Poynter 2010). In examining successive rounds of urban regeneration, their authors have charted London's move eastwards and the impact of successive central government policies driven both by the trickle-down, 'neo-liberal' model of city-building implicit in the Docklands development (New York's Manhattan was its blueprint), and by the more directly interventionist approach subsequently adopted by the Labour government with regard to London 2012 investment.

Regeneration and development to the east of London has been accompanied by a changing skyline in its centre and City, major new developments along the river and new luxury housing to the west. Areas that were once sites of an industrial port city have been 'revalorised' (Hamnett 2005: 248) in their re-creation as part of a post-industrial city – a pattern of development evident in other major western cities and one with profound impact upon urban social structures, rupturing old class divides and yet creating new ones. But can this revalorisation and the social relations upon which it rests be sustained in the wake of the deepest recession in 70 years?

The Economy and the Global City

Perhaps the most influential framework for theorising cities in recent decades has been provided by those authors whose studies of the city have been grounded within a wider exploration of the transformations in the international economy. In the course of his interview for *New Left Review* published in August 2000, David Harvey recounted his intellectual journey as a geographer, from Fabian socialism in the 1960s to the leading, Marxist 'social geographer' by the end of the twentieth century. He undertook this odyssey in the attempt to explain the relationships between cities, urbanisation and capitalism. He explored the relationships between money flows, the concentration and accumulation of finance capital and their spatial dimensions (Harvey 1982, 2001: 10), and demonstrated that the trajectory of growth and expansion in capital accumulation is paralleled by the 'growth path of urbanisation' (Harvey 2008). The necessity for capital to create a surplus product, the basis of surplus value, also generates the need for the surplus to be absorbed and the focus of its absorption is the city.

Harvey draws upon historical examples, such as Haussmann's reconstruction of Paris in the mid-nineteenth century, and contemporary illustrations of this point, arguing, for example, that the expansion of urban centres in the USA in the 1990s and immediate pre-credit crunch period absorbed considerable amounts of surplus capital through the construction of city centre offices and homes, and suburban housing developments, partially steadying the world economy in the wake of successive regional crises in the 1990s, but also, in doing so, generating an unsustainable domestic US market for mortgages and 'huge trade deficits with the rest of the world' (Harvey 2008: 4). A similar process of urban redevelopment took place in countries like Spain and the United Kingdom. For Harvey, however, perhaps the most significant feature of the urbanisation process over the last two decades has been its internationalisation, with China, since 1997, leading the way. The vast infrastructural projects in China, the creation of huge metropolitan centres of population and industry and their construction via debt-financing, have been facilitated by China's special economic relationship with the USA, innovations in international financial markets, and the development of the necessary credit facilities to support them. While China has, at least in part, taken over from the USA in the wake of the credit crunch in sustaining the dynamic behind the global urbanisation process, other nations have joined in, 'Chile booms thanks to the high price of copper, Australia thrives and even Brazil and Argentina have recovered in part because of the strength of Chinese demand for raw materials' (Harvey 2008: 4). In the global cities created through this urbanisation process, 'urban life has become a commodity', as has the city itself.

The conceptual basis of Harvey's recent analyses lie in his earlier works, in which he develops a spatial dimension to his interpretation of Marx's understanding of capital, explaining accumulation on a geographical scale (Harvey 2001: 265). The creation of value is dependent upon the capacity for realising it through circulation. The sphere of circulation expands as a result of accumulation and as its precondition. Understanding this process is the prerequisite for studying the historic development of capitalism in the twentieth century and its more recent manifestations. In making this connection, Harvey provides insights into the respective roles performed by global cities in the twenty-first century. The physical landscape of the city is created via capital investments in buildings, transport and infrastructure which are appropriate to their time, more-or-less; but in due course the infrastructure and built environment are no longer adequate to the changing needs of capital in all its forms and its swift movement around the globe, especially in the latter part of the twentieth century. Entrepreneurial western cities had to 'negotiate a knife-edge path between preserving the values of past capital investments in the built environment and destroying these investments in order to open up fresh room for accumulation' (Harvey 2001: 247). A growing proportion of social wealth is, according to Harvey, spent on the means of transportation and communication, thus reducing rates of profit while at the same time being a precondition for their future increase. Whilst conventional location theories seek to identify the conditions that give rise to harmonious and virtuous cycles of regional economic growth and urban development, Harvey identifies a dynamic to urbanism that constantly expresses tension and contradiction.

The Structure of this Book

London, perhaps, is the global city whose recent growth exemplifies the tensions of destruction and creation: the destruction of its main centres of manufacture and the creation and consolidation of its role as a centre of international financial intermediation. London's trajectory as an urban economy has shifted decisively toward the roles it performs in the world of circulation. In facilitating this shift in the period since the 1970s and 1980s, the City and London's riverside have experienced major re-developments; the City has also expanded eastwards. Financial power, in the form of international developers supported by the state and city-wide government, have sought land to secure the 'highest return' on developments; land and property values have soared; and established residents in lower price and social housing are being progressively displaced as legal rights and welfare support are diluted.

The social habits and cultural forms of the post-industrial city, project an air of affluence reflected in the development of shopping malls, artisan markets and niche stores. Choice is extensive for those who can afford it; for the rest it is, according to Zukin, 'pacification by cappuccino' (Zukin 2010: 231). For Harvey, this new urban environment reflects a process of 'accumulation through dispossession' (Harvey 2008: 5-9), a process that has arguably gathered momentum in London in the wake of the credit crunch and the implementation of the social and economic policies adopted by the Conservative/Liberal Democrat coalition government since its election in May 2010.

The period since the credit crunch is the focus of this book. The book draws upon the analyses of the cultural, social and economic dimensions of urbanisation outlined in this chapter whilst also re-examining and re-thinking them in the wake of the credit crunch and subsequent global recession. Is it possible, for example, to re-imagine the city without reference to the imagined community of the country examined so eloquently by Raymond Williams in *The Country and the City* (Williams 1975)? Is Jacobs's invocation of the urban village with its attributes of small scale and social intimacy now so thoroughly compromised as an ideal by its commodification, that a new form of urban social embeddedness needs to be conceived? Are revalorisation and 'gentrification' irresistible trends in the global city or can a new form of democratisation and value creation be achieved? Contributors explore these and other aspects of London, and question whether the future trajectory of this city's economy and society is likely to be characterised more by 'business as usual', or whether the financial crisis has necessitated profound change in the way that London lives and works.

The book divides into four parts. In Part 1, the opening chapter discusses the genesis of the credit crunch and the resulting global recession. It goes beyond explanations that primarily blame the bankers, and explores the structural problems which emerged in London from the collapse of the market-oriented, national model of productive growth and social development. In the light of the structural issues identified here, subsequent chapters in Part 1 examine contemporary New York and Shanghai, while Chapter 4 highlights the distinctive strengths and weaknesses of London as a global city. Part 2 provides detailed case studies of some key sectors of the London economy, illustrating their 'embedded/disembedded' character and their contributions to the creation of economic 'value' and social well-being in the city and beyond. Part 3 provides insights into immigration and the provision of energy, education, transport, housing and health, and explores current provision in the context of London as both a global city and an unbalanced economy. Part 4 draws upon the arguments presented by contributors to make the case for new approaches to understanding the urban economy and, in particular, using these to review London's future within the UK and beyond.

References

Bell, D. (1973). *The Coming of Post-industrial Society*. London: Penguin.

Butler, T. (1997). *Gentrification and the Middle Classes*. Aldershot: Ashgate.

Butler, T. and Rustin, M. (eds) (1996). *Rising in the East*. London: Lawrence & Wishart.

Castells, M. (1980). *The Economic Crisis and American Society*. Oxford: Blackwell.

Davis, M. (1990). *City of Quartz*. New York: Basic Books.

Dench, G., Gavron, K. and Young, M. (2006). *The New East End*. London: Profile.

Florida, R. (2003). *The Rise of the Creative Class*. New York: Basic Books.

Glass, R. (1964). 'London, Aspects of Change'. London: Centre for Urban Studies reprinted in Glass, R. (ed.) (1989). *Cities of Urban Doom*. Oxford: Blackwell.

Hall, P. (1966). *The World Cities*. London: Weidenfeld & Nicholson.

Hamnett, C. (2003). *Unequal City*. London: Routledge.

Hamnett, C. (2004). 'Social polarisation in global cities: Theory and evidence', *Urban Studies*, 31(3), 401-24.

Harvey, D. (1982). *Limits to Capital*. Oxford: Oxford University Press.

Harvey, D. (2000). 'Interview', *New Left Review*, 4, Second Series, July-August, 2000, 75-97.

Harvey, D. (2001). *Spaces of Capital*. Edinburgh: Edinburgh University Press.

Harvey, D. (2008). 'The right to the city', *New Left Review*, 53, September-October 2008, 1-9, available at http://newleftreview.org, accessed 25 February 2011.

Haussermann, H. and Haila, A. (2005). 'The European City: A Conceptual Framework and Normative Project, in Y. Kazepov (ed.) (2005). *Cities of Europe*. London: Blackwell, 43-64.

Imrie, R., Lees, L. and Raco, M. (eds) (2009). *Regenerating London*. London: Routledge.

Jacobs, J. (1961). *The Death and Life of Great American Cities*. New York: Vintage.

Lees, L., Slater, T. and Wyly, E. (2008). *Gentrification*. London: Routledge.

Marx, K. (1972). *Capital: A Critique of Political Economy*. Volume 3. London: Lawrence & Wishart.

McDonough, T. (ed.) (2009). *The Situationists and the City*. London: Verso.

Poynter, G. and MacRury, I. (eds) (2009). *Olympic Cities: 2012 and the Remaking of London*. Farnham: Ashgate.

Poynter, G. and Macrury, I. (2010). 'Team GB and London 2012, the paradox of national and global identities', *International Journal of the History of Sport*, 27(16-18), November 2010, 2958-75(18).

Rustin, M. (2009). 'Sport, Spectacle and Society, Understanding the Olympics' in G. Poynter and I. MacRury (eds) *Olympic Cities: 2012 and the Remaking of London*. Farnham: Ashgate.

Sassen, S. (1991). *The Global City: London, New York and Tokyo*. Princeton, NJ: Princeton University Press.

Simmel, G. (2004). *The Philosophy of Money*. London: Routledge.

Smith, N. (1986). 'Gentification, the frontier and restructuring urban space', in Smith, N. and P. Williams (eds) *Gentrification of the City*. London: Allen & Unwin, 15-34.

UN Habitat (2006). Urbanisation, A Turning Point in History. Available at http://www.unhabitat.org/documents/media_centre/sowcr2006/SOWCR%201.pdf, accessed 23 June 2011.

Weiner, M. (1985). *English Culture and the Decline of the Industrial Spirit 1985-1980*. Harmondsworth: Penguin.

Williams, R. (1975). *The Country and the City*. London: Paladin.

Young, M. and Wilmott, P. (1957). *Family and Kinship in East London*. London: Routledge and Kegan Paul.

Zukin, S. (2010). *Naked City*. Oxford: Oxford University Press.

PART 1
Global Cities and Responses to Recession

Chapter 1
The Global Recession

Gavin Poynter

Introduction

In 2008, the credit crunch progressed from financial crisis to global economic recession, its impact spreading from the US housing market to western financial markets and, by the end of that year, to most nations and sectors of the international economy. Its apparent origins, in the highly technical character of the 'toxic' products spawned in the financial world of intermediation and risk management, informed a hesitant and, in turn, managerial analysis of its development. This hesitancy was reflected in the statements expressed by politicians and business leaders throughout much of 2008 as they oscillated between inaction and reaction, and expressed fears, in turn, about the crisis realising uncontrollable inflationary or deflationary trends.

For much of 2008, American and British politicians and business leaders continued to downplay the problems created by the credit crisis until the financial world reached the brink of collapse. The UK government spent much of the year in denial about the weakness of the British economy – it was sound in its essentials – blaming American and wider, international developments for the position the UK economy was in,[1] while the US government dithered over a bailout plan which was initially designed to buy up all the worthless, toxic assets of the finance sector but eventually took the form of buying shares in US banks.

The combination of denial, hesitancy and indecision that characterised responses to the early stages of the economic crisis had its origins in the political and business world's interpretation of the recent performance of the western, mainly Anglo-American, model of capitalism. Those who sought to manage it created a rhetoric laced with words such as stability, expansion, and globalisation, when, in reality, the leading western nation, the USA, and its junior partner, the UK, were seeking to manage economies whose productive dynamism had waned and which, particularly in the case of the UK, relied increasingly upon servicing productive activities occurring elsewhere in the world. A thin veil of respectability

---

1 The (then) UK Prime Minister, Gordon Brown, repeatedly blamed the credit crunch and subsequent recessionary trends on international or external factors rather than acknowledging any problems inherent in the UK economy. See Poynter, G. (2008) 'The Credit Crunch and London's Economy' *Rising East*, Issue Number 8a, July 2008, http://www.uel.ac.uk/risingeast/currentissue/academic/poynter.htm.

was lent to this perception by the theorisation of knowledge as the intangible, magical ingredient of a new type of western economy that lives by its wits rather than by what it makes.[2] The hollow nature of these ideas and policies is now perhaps exposed, creating the opportunity for a more considered and reflective view of what is really happening in London, the west and the wider world.

This chapter focuses upon the origins of the credit crunch and the subsequent international recession. It argues that the most serious economic crisis in 70 years arose from the underlying structural weaknesses of western economies, weaknesses that first came to the fore in the late 1960s and early 1970s, particularly in the USA and Britain. The Anglo-American response to the end of the post-1945 'golden age' was to embark upon a process of financialisation, a process whose impact has extended far beyond the financial centres of the cities in which such activity is concentrated.

For Epstein (Epstein 2005: 3) financialisation refers to a broad trend by which financial motives, markets, actors and institutions come to play an increasing role in national and international economies. Other authors refer more specifically to the ways in which profit making arises increasingly from 'financial channels rather than through trade and commodity production' (Krippner 2005: 14), and many use the concept to examine ways in which enterprises have come to privilege shareholder value over longer term investment in productive capacity. In this chapter, the understanding of financialisation has three main dimensions. First, its origins are traced back to the international economic crises of the late 1960s and early 1970s; crises marked by decline in profit rates and a consequent rise in liquidity, as capital searched for profitable investment, and the internationalisation of production by advanced economies. These were the pre-conditions for finance to regain its centrality in global economic affairs (Brenner 2002; Harvey 2011; Epstein 2005: 25). Second, financialisation is used to refer not only to the world of financial institutions but also to the increasingly finance-focussed behaviour of ostensibly non-financial corporations. Put simply, over recent decades many companies whose origins lie in the world of production have come to behave like financial enterprises (Crotty 2005: 77-110). Finally, this chapter begins to address the negative effects of a highly financialised economy, which have spread inexorably into wider society through their impact upon industries (further explored in Part 2 of this book), state welfare and social policies (further investigated in Part 3 of this book), and via their severe effects upon the citizen, for whom debt-driven patterns of consumption (systemically encouraged to artificially maintain demand)

2 There is an extensive literature on 'creating' the knowledge-based economy from the academic and policy-making worlds of UK, European and American government institutions in particular. For an overview of EU policy development, see, for example, Rodrigues, M. (2003). *European Policies for a Knowledge Economy*. Aldershot: Edward Elgar. For a brief, concise critique see Jessop, B. (2000) 'The State and the Contradictions of the Knowledge-driven Economy' in Bryson, J. et al. *Knowledge, Space, Economy*. London: Routledge, 63-78.

have become unsustainable. These are the dimensions of financialisation which are discussed below.

The Origins of the Credit Crisis

Credit crises are not unusual events. The expansion of credit in the 1970s and early 1980s in western economies helped stave off recessionary trends arising from the weak performance of the production sector, but eventually led to debt-inflation that was only addressed in the mid-1980s by governments who curbed public spending and tightened credit controls (Brenner 2006: 159). The 2007 credit crunch and subsequent crisis had different origins in the service sector, arising from a credit squeeze in the US housing market. Andrew Palmer, explaining in *The Economist* how 'Paradise' was 'Lost', suggested that bankers and finance houses had forgotten the maxim, 'know your customer' (Palmer 2008). They lent to people who did not have publicly available credit histories and who were, therefore, classed as 'sub-prime' rather than belonging to the primary market (Palmer 2008: 7). Only a small number of financial institutions seemed to have been adversely affected by exposure to the high risk, sub-prime market, when, in the summer of 2007, the US housing market dipped and large numbers of sub-prime borrowers defaulted on their loans. Pain spread rapidly throughout the financial world because the institutions which sold sub-prime mortgages had also re-packaged the debts and sold them on to other institutions in the sector. What was designed to make the system more resilient by spreading risk, became instead the source of contagion. In Palmer's words, 'the risks flowed back to the banks as toxic assets' (Palmer 2008: 6). Whilst the site of the bubble was initially the housing market, the credit crisis had its origins in the process of financialisation.

In turn, the origins of financialisation may be traced to the 1950s and 60s with the emergence of new types of consumer credit, supported by the development of the now ubiquitous credit card, the development of institutional finance (pension funds, insurance and mutual funds), and the expanding practice of professional fund management. Credit provision in the second half of the twentieth century became a very important part of the activities of many industrial sectors, not just the banking and finance world. For example, by the end of the twentieth century, General Motors secured most of its profits through the operations of its financial arm, GMAC, rather than through the making and selling of automobiles.[3] In turn, from the mid-1960s

3 Amongst a wide range of financial service products, GMAC has provided General Motors (GM) with vehicle financing deals typically channelled through GM car dealers in the USA. At the end of 2008 it was owned by GM (49 per cent of shares) and Cerberus Capital (51 per cent of shares), and it was considering an application to achieve bank holding company status in order to access the US government's financial relief package. To do so, GMAC was required to increase its capital base and reduce the share holdings of its two owners. Access to the relief package would provide the basis for raising the level

the activities of international finance institutions were furthered by the development of computer-supported, risk management models, and the emergence of new market mechanisms designed to track share performance over time rather than simply recording current prices. The focus on performance assisted investors in tracking share values, adjusting their expectations against short term movements in prices, and facilitating the diversification of investment portfolios to take account of changes in inflation, currency and interest rates, and other risk factors.

Taking such risks into account, the diversification of investment gave rise to 'hedging', in which those who took higher risks for potentially greater rewards achieved 'leverage' by mortgaging their existing assets in order to buy additional assets through the options market or by taking a 'short position' (a short-term bet on the value of the additional assets purchased). Legislative changes in the UK and subsequently the USA further aided the expansion of the role of corporate finance in London and New York. As discussed below, such developments reflected the underlying lack of investment in the 'real' economies of each nation. The process of financialisation masked the underlying weaknesses of these economies but as long as financial institutions expanded their transactions with each other (what became known as 'over the counter' transactions), it seemed possible to turn even the least attractive assets into tradable commodities.

This process, which came to be called 'securitisation', was initially designed to enable banks to share risk with other investors by passing on loans as if they were assets. In this process, the original credit note arising, or derived, from the transaction with the customer, is sold on in the form of bonds or securities (hence the description 'derivatives'). In turn, these asset-backed securities were invested in by others such as hedge funds, i.e. privately owned investment companies that engage in complex investment portfolios designed to secure high returns for wealthy individuals and institutional investors (Blackburn 2008; Schiller 2008). The consequence of the massive expansion in securitisation, whereby an original value is resold many times over, was that banks and other financial institutions were unable initially to identify the extent of their exposure to the credit crisis that commenced in the US housing sector, and, in turn, the international character of these institutions ensured a rapid spread of the contagion. Banks and other institutions stopped lending to each other – the wholesale money markets in the USA and UK effectively closed down, causing the US Federal Reserve and, subsequently, the Bank of England to step in to inject liquidity. Whilst in the UK, Northern Rock was saved by the Bank of England and the (then) Labour government, many other prestigious institutions were forced to undertake write-downs in their values, to the tune of around $200 billion in the US alone. An estimate produced by the US Monetary Forum in February 2008 suggested that a write-down of this magnitude would mean massive contraction of the credit made

---

of credit available for customers and in turn, it was hoped, stimulate demand for GM cars. See Bullock, N. (2008) 'Questions hang over GMAC's future', *Financial Times*, Tuesday 30 December 2008, 17.

available by US financial institutions to US households and companies, to the tune of $910 billion by the end of that year (US Monetary Policy Forum 2008).

This estimate proved to significantly understate the problem as 2008 unfolded. Investment banks in the US began to collapse as the year progressed. Bear Sterns, the fifth largest US investment bank, collapsed in March 2008, with the Federal Reserve insisting it be sold to JP Morgan. But, the greatest shock came from the failure of Lehman Brothers in September 2008, an investment bank that served institutional shareholders. The Lehman *debacle* triggered the deepest crisis of confidence in the financial world because Lehman Brothers had dealt extensively with a range of financial institutions whose exposure to its collapse would take a long time to unfold. Although between June and August 2008 Lehman Brothers wrote down the value of its residential property and mortgages section by $700 million, its over-exposure to the sub-prime sector was its undoing (estimated at $54 billion at the time of closure). When Lehman Brothers collapsed, the hedge fund industry also suffered a huge blow. To some pundits Lehman Brothers seemed too big to be allowed to fail. But the Federal government, which had already bailed out AIG, the largest insurance company in the USA, and nationalised Fannie Mae and Freddie Mac, the largest mortgage providers, did not extend its rescue programme to Lehman's, which went to the wall in September 2008.

By that time, the finance sector had given up its role as primary financial mediator in the US and UK, with lending between banks grinding to a halt as they pursued programmes designed to lick wounds, rationalise costs and re-capitalise. In their place, the US and UK governments were forced to intervene; the US with a $700 billion bailout, and the UK with a package of financial support that resulted in partial nationalisation of the UK banking sector. By early 2009, the UK and USA administrations were preparing further packages of action designed to kick start their respective economies. But despite this woeful tale of banking excess, it would be wrong to place the primary responsibility for the creation and consequences of the credit crunch upon financial institutions alone.

The Real Cause of the Credit Crisis: Loss of Dynamism in Western Economies

Since the early 1970s western economies have experienced a long downturn, with only brief periods of respite such as the superficial 'New Economy' boom of the late 1990s. The main characteristics of the downturn have been the loss of the dynamic pattern of economic growth experienced in the post-war 'golden age', and increasing reliance on services and especially financial services as the primary contributor to economic expansion in countries like the USA and UK. The growth of bank capital has expanded as commercial and industrial capital has shifted into the business of banking; conversely, the contribution of ostensibly non-financial services enterprises to the expansion of financial services has reflected widespread

Table 1.1 Rates of GDP Growth (annual average compound growth rates) Selected Countries 1950-1998

Country	1950-73	1973-98
US	3.93	2.99
Japan	9.29	2.97
Germany	5.68	1.76
Euro 12	4.65	2.03
UK	2.93	2

Source: Statistics selected from Maddison, A. (2002). *The World Economy: A Millennial Perspective*. Paris: OECD, 262.

attempts to raise shareholder value rapidly, without investment in long term research and productive activities (Itoh and Lapavitsas 1999: 96; Crotty 2005).

GDP growth between 1970 and 2000 rose at half the rate achieved in the 1950s and 1960s in most developed industrial nations (See Table 1.1). Over the last two decades, the economies of the USA and UK, in particular, have remained relatively stable without undertaking significant investment in production industries, apart from some parts of the IT sector. In short, production industries have tended to engage in a constant process of rationalisation. But this has occurred in the absence of any significant destruction of 'old' capital and its replacement by 'new', and with only brief exceptions to this trend, e.g. in the US manufacturing sector in the mid-1990s (Brenner 2006: 297). The consequence of this unspectacular but stable growth, and the underlying lack of investment in productive capacity, has been a rise in the amount of liquidity available for circulation in financial markets (Mullan 2008: 3). Thus decline in the performance of the real economy has facilitated the rapid expansion of the role of corporate finance in the US and UK economies in particular, with finance performing an increasingly important role in stimulating growth in these economies. An input/output analysis of UK economic performance published in 2005 recorded that:

> Financial and business services continue to form the largest single sector of the UK economy in 2003, accounting for 31.7 per cent of total gross value added (GVA) up from 27.6 per cent in 1998 … manufacturing industry contributed less than 15 per cent of total economic output in 2003. The sector's contribution was more than 20 per cent of GVA till 1998, but it has fallen to 14.8 percent in 2003. (ONS 2005)

Accompanying rapidly growing dependence upon financial services and the loss of productive dynamism in western economies, has been the parallel process of dynamic, productive expansion within developing economies, particularly China, over recent years.

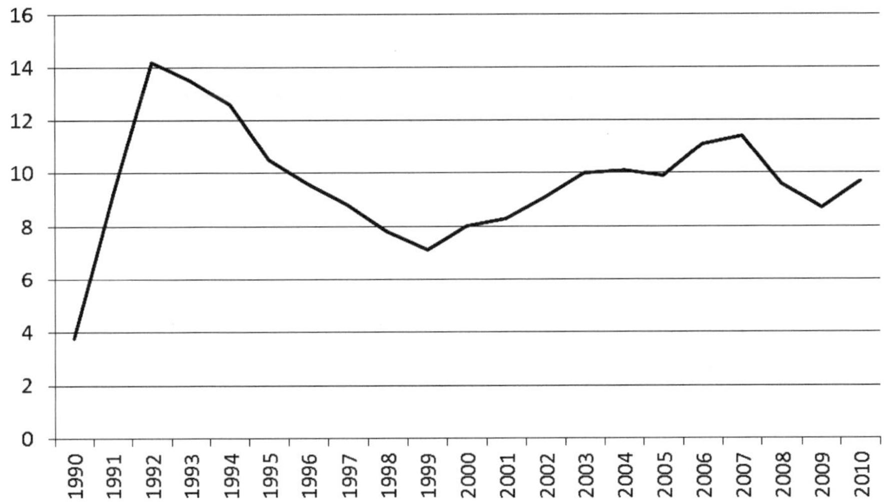

Figure 1.1 Chinese GDP at constant prices, annual Change 1990-2010 (in per cent)

Source: China National Bureau of Statistics.

China's spectacular rate of economic development enabled it to become the new workshop of the world, especially in relation to the US economy, to which it has exported increasing volumes of manufactured goods (Figure 1.1). For example, between 2003 and 2004 alone, China's annual exports to the USA expanded by some 57 per cent to reach approximately $70 billion. At the same time, China sustained high foreign exchange reserves, significant proportions of which were used to purchase US securities and especially treasury bonds which helped suppress long term inflationary trends.[4] By September 2007, it was estimated that China's holding of US securities had reached $1 trillion (see Table 1.2 and CRS 2008: 5).

The 'special economic relationship' between China and the US enabled the latter's economy to act as a vast market for the consumption of manufactured goods which helped to stave off international recessionary trends in the early years of the new century, and helped the US to sustain consumption at levels that reached new heights, fuelled by easily available credit to private consumers. This US consumption-led boom – in practice, an example of a society living beyond its means – started to collapse in 2007 as a result of the housing crisis, and collapsed further in 2008 as difficulties which first surfaced in sub-prime housing became a general crisis of credit. Unlike earlier credit crises, this one started in financial

4 Another source of liquidity from developing economies over recent times has been Sovereign Wealth Funds, government supported funds drawn from foreign exchange reserves and used for overseas investment. They were valued at about $4 trillion in 2008. See Mullan 2008: 3.

Table 1.2 Top Five Foreign Holders of US Securities (June 2006)

	Total	Long Term (LT) Treasury	LT Government Agency	LT Corporate	Equity	Short term
Japan	1,106	535	184	108	195	85
China	699	364	255	59	4	17
UK	640	47	28	249	300	16
Luxemburg	549	52	38	233	193	32
Cayman Islands	485	19	50	111	178	31
World Total	7,778	1,727	473	2,021	2,430	615
China's Holding as a % of World Total	9%	21.1%	53.9%	2.9%	0.2%	2.8%

Source: U.S. Treasury Department, Report on foreign portfolio holdings of US securities as of June 2006, May 2008, 8 in CRS 2008, 5.

services and rapidly spread to other parts of the economy via, for example, the curtailing of credit facilities for enterprises and the dramatic curbing of private consumption, especially in the USA.

A broadly similar process unfolded in both the USA and Britain, leading one prominent commentator to suggest that:

> … what is happening in credit markets today is a huge blow to the credibility of the Anglo-Saxon model of transactions-oriented financial capitalism. (Wolf 2007: 1)

The failure of US and UK administrations to recognise the underlying weaknesses of their respective economies for much of 2008 (and arguably to identify any worrying trends during the preceding decade) tended to exacerbate the problems initially generated by the collapse of the US housing market. Even when the US administration introduced its troubled assets relief programme in September 2008, there was no clear strategy behind it:

> Congress scared everyone by failing to hammer out a deal showing the world that the US political class did not understand the depth of the crisis. The Treasury launched the plan with no clear idea of what it would do, then twice changed its mind over how to use the money.[5]

5 Authers, P. (2008) 'Four strong contenders for mistake of the year', *Financial Times*, 13-14 December 2008.

By comparison, the Labour government's bailout of the UK banking sector to the tune of £50 billion in October 2008, primarily through the provision of new capital in the form of preference shares and the introduction of the Bank of England's new liquidity scheme designed to provide short term loans to encourage banks to start lending again, looked like decisive action. Prime Minister Gordon Brown implied that such measures comprised a strategic approach which could be replicated in other countries whose banking systems were also suffering. But Catherine Meyer of the US magazine, *Time*, remained sceptical of the suggestion that Brown and his Chancellor of the Exchequer, Alistair Darling, were acting strategically:

> Their emergency rescue plan was hatched over weeks but finalized in such a hurry that bleary officials labored overnight to finish it before the skittish markets opened. At a morning press conference, both men maintained that the problem started with the US sub-prime crisis; Brown refused to answer questions about how Labour policy over more than 10 years in office might have contributed to the situation. 'This is the time to talk about the future,' he said. (cited in Meyer 2008)

By the end of 2008, US and UK governments intervention had staved off the outright collapse of the banking sector, but the sector remained in intensive care, with little real evidence of any capacity to provide the kind of lending and credit facilities required by other sectors of the economy. During the autumn, while the US and UK governments were introducing their bailouts, the global nature of the crisis really began to take effect, with financial institutions in several developed nations coming close to collapse.

Tightening credit conditions, falling consumer demand, and increases in world commodity prices (especially energy prices), jointly ensured that the US economy moved rapidly and dramatically toward recession. In November 2008 alone, over half a million jobs were lost in the US, the highest monthly rise in the jobless total since 1974. As the US appetite for cheap, imported, manufactured goods fell, so did estimates of the growth rates of export oriented nations such as China. By the end of a tumultuous year, the economies of the advanced and the most rapidly developing nations moved toward major recession in the former and significant slowdown in the latter. The US, UK and other economies showed varying degrees of resilience to these recessionary trends, but the Anglo-Saxon model was not all right in its fundamentals. Indeed, its 'fundamentals' illustrated a major, relative decline in dynamism, an historic shift away from productive activities toward the transient fruits of financialisation, and, in the immediate wake of the credit crunch, a dependence on public finance to stabilise domestic economies. This dependence, according to Turner, was exacerbated by the failure of policy makers to reduce interest rates during 2008, so that by 2009, when central banks began to pump liquidity into the markets, they were also creating the basis for next phase in the crisis – a rising public debt burden (Turner 2009: 66-7).

In 2009 and early 2010, the course of public discussion in Britain moved rapidly from truncated criticism of the economy and especially the finance sector, to concern about how and when to cut state spending.[6] In the months leading up to the UK general election in May 2010, all the major political parties expressed their commitment to reducing public debt, with, initially at least, Labour and Liberal Democrat leaders arguing for a slower pace of reduction than the Conservatives. The negotiations that eventually gave rise to a Conservative/Liberal Democrat coalition government hinged, in particular, on the Liberal Democrats conversion to the Conservatives' approach to deficit reduction, as later indicated by Vince Cable, the Liberal Democrat Treasury spokesperson who became Secretary of State for Business in the coalition government. His Damascus moment was catalysed by the sovereign debt problems facing Greece, which came to the fore almost as soon as the UK coalition was formed; Britain had to tackle its debt sooner rather than later in order to avoid a similar experience:

> If deficit reduction comes too rapidly there is a danger of deeper recession and even bigger deficits. But like the governor of the Bank of England, and like the OECD [Organisation for Economic Co-operation and Development], I have changed my view on this. I have been persuaded that early action is absolutely necessary, and that is what we are doing. (Allen 2010)

The trajectory of discussion since the general election has merely reflected the shifting expressions of the problem – from credit to financial to sovereign debt crisis – without examining its underlying causation. Failure to debate the structural conditions which generated the deepest crisis for capital in 70 years, has inevitably given rise to narrow definitions of what must be done. The focus of the UK coalition government during its first year in office was to restore stability by introducing policies designed to reduce public spending and shift the bill for the recession away from finance and business towards the rest of society. The structural problems associated with a slow/no growth economy have not been addressed. Curbing the excesses of the public sector has been touted as the way out of recession, while underlying weaknesses and over-reliance on a highly financialised economy, are largely ignored. It is to these problems and their origins that the next section turns.

---

6 Marjorie Smith succinctly recorded this political shift in the *Tribune*, 30 September 2010: 'in recognizing the coalition government's success in shifting the focus of public discussion. It should not be forgotten that the one irredeemable economic fact of the recent and present crisis is that responsibility and blame lie with the private sector. Public finances have taken a massive hit due to the cost of bailing out the banks and the related measures of economic stimulation. This has nothing to do with public sector profligacy. However, the prevailing wisdom among the mainstream media and the chattering classes is that, in order to put the public finances back on track, levels of public spending must be drastically reduced to lay the foundations for a sustainable recovery. This is the big achievement to date of David Cameron and George Osborne. They have succeeded in redefining the political landscape so that cutting the deficit is now the be-all and end-all of policy'.

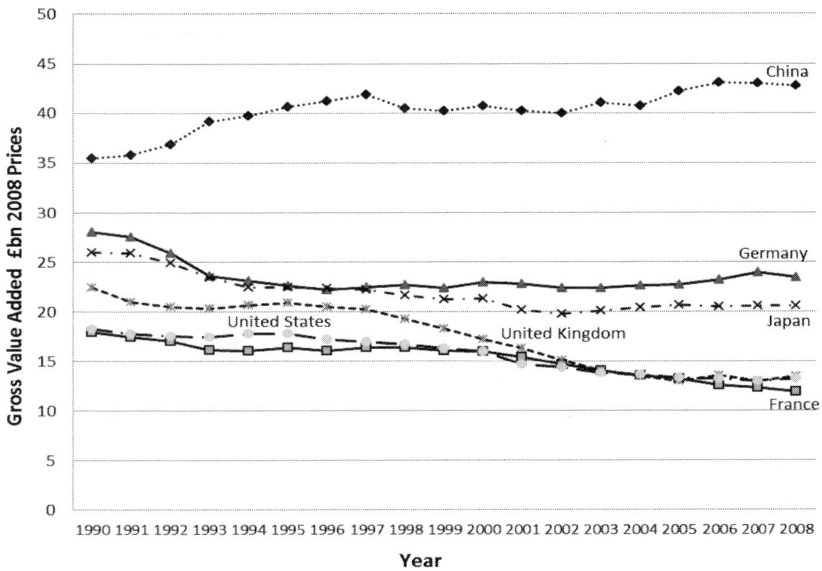

Figure 1.2 Manufacturing as percentage of GDP globally and across comparator countries

Source: Department for Business, Innovation and Skills (2010), Economics Paper 10b, Manufacturing in the UK Supplementary Analysis, 2.

Financialisation in Britain

On the surface Britain's structural crisis has arisen from its over-reliance on a narrow range of industries, particularly finance and business services. In 2009, financial services and related business activities (legal, accountancy, maritime services) provided 14 per cent of UK Gross Value Added (GVA) and the wider business and consultancy services sector 24 per cent, a total of around 40 per cent of GVA as compared to manufacturing which contributed about 12 per cent. The same services generated a surplus of £40 billion in foreign trade, while the deficit in traded goods stood at £82 billion in 2009 (NESTA: 2010). Financial services output significantly increased in Britain in the period 2000-2006, immediately before the credit crunch; a significant rise comparable to the USA and well above other leading European economies (Figure 1.3). All major western economies, with the exception of Germany, have experienced a similar pattern of manufacturing decline as a percentage of total GDP (Figure 1.2), though the growth in importance of finance and business services in Britain has outstripped most other nations.

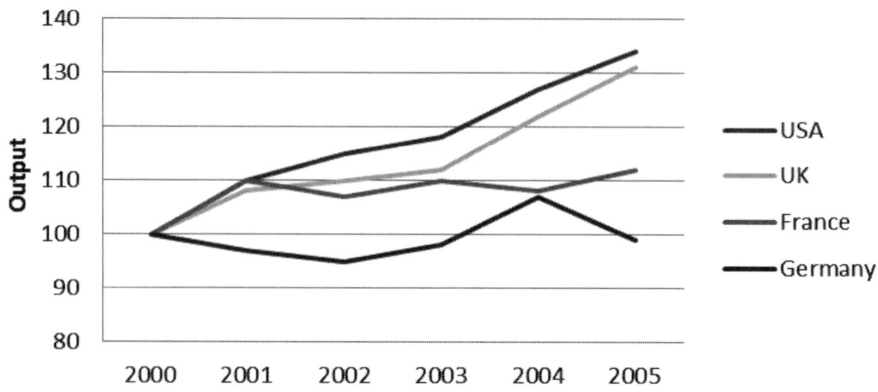

Figure 1.3 Financial Services Output Selected Countries 2000-2005 (2000=100)

Source: Oxford Economic Forecasting (2007) *London's Role in the UK Economy*. London: City of London Corporation/Oxford Economic Forecasting.

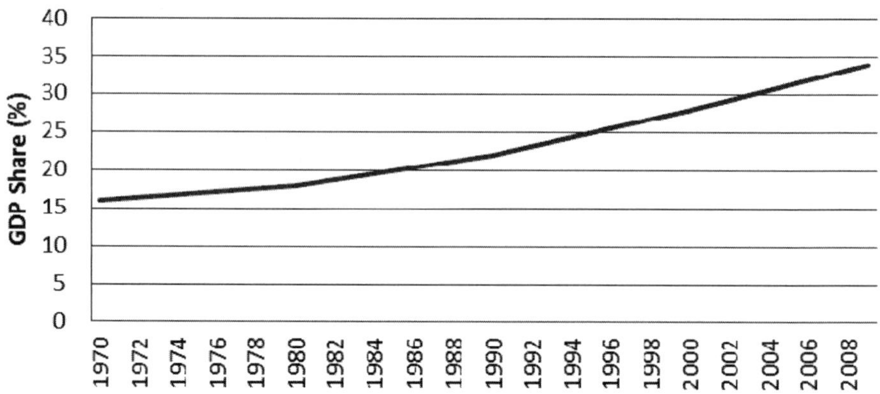

Figure 1.4 Financial and Business Services Output as share of GDP 1970-2009

Source: Office of National Statistics.

It might be argued that Britain has achieved a competitive advantage in these services, so that the sectoral imbalance in the UK's economy is not a real problem. This chapter challenges this view. Whilst acknowledging London's prominence in global financial markets, it is suggested that this is simultaneously a source of strength and a sign of weakness, facilitating the uneven expansion of capitalism globally and at the same time acting as a barrier to the recreation of economic dynamism in Britain. Three reasons for this are outlined below (other reasons are explored in future chapters). First, the rapid growth in lending arising from financialisation has been to the detriment of investment in productive industries in the UK. Second, financialisation has fuelled the global imbalances that tend to reinforce Britain's *entrepôt* role; and, finally, policy responses to the credit crunch and subsequent recession in the UK, have tended to reinforce the negative social effects of the crisis by giving added momentum to the financialisation of society.

Financialisation and De-industrialisation

The rapid growth in the financialisation of Britain's economy was addressed by Adair (Lord) Turner, chairman of the Financial Services Authority, in 2010. One measure, as he records, is the total value of the balance sheet of the UK banking system as a percentage of GDP:

> The total balance sheet of the UK banking system, defined to include all legal banking entities operating in London, had by 2007 reached around 500% of GDP, compared with 34% in 1964, and was dominated not by the banks' relationship with UK households and companies, but by a complex mesh of intra-financial system claims and obligations. (Turner 2010: 10)

Since the 1960s there has been a huge expansion in financial intermediation, with open markets providing opportunities for banks and non-bank, financial institutions (enterprises, pension funds, hedge funds, equity funds and so on) to enact a multitude of transactions and take fees in a world of circulation which is increasingly remote from the 'real' economy. This expansion is tantamount to the process of securitisation discussed earlier. The estrangement of these transactions to the real economy, was also indicated by Lord Turner: 'the vast majority of net lending to the corporate sector is explained by lending to commercial real estate with, for instance, manufacturing only a marginal net borrower from the banking system, and indeed borrowing less (in 2010) in nominal terms than in 1998' (Turner 2010: 20).

Within the UK, the process of financialisation has tended to crowd out the banking system's historical role in providing credit for investment in productive capacity and new technologies. Non-financial corporations have tended to raise funds through open financial markets, becoming themselves an important part of the financial services sector, and acting to raise immediate shareholder value rather than increase profitability from the long-term development of production. At the same time, larger UK enterprises have increasingly fallen prey to foreign ownership; and the combination of all these trends has resulted in the 'hollowing out' of British (and US) manufacturing industry (Lapavitsas 2010; Orhangazi 2008).

Global Imbalances

Financialisation, exemplified by the growth in bond markets, has fostered major difficulties in international financial markets. Whilst the emergence of finance capitalism took place in the late nineteenth century when the gold standard provided the universal peg for currencies, in the twenty-first century, exchange rates are unstable, thus making borrowing by one country from others somewhat hazardous unless it takes place in the borrower's currency. Being the 'world's borrower of last resort' (Wolf 2009: 194), the USA has used this position to great effect. Since the early 1990s, exporting countries such as China and Germany have generated huge current account surpluses by lending to nations such as the USA and allowing them to run large current account deficits. The exporting nations and developing countries (the latter under pressure from the International Monetary Fund) have sought to protect their own currencies and maintain stability in their exchange rates; and this, in turn, has given rise to a significant accumulation of foreign exchange reserves held in US dollars and used, in part, to buy US bonds.

In the wake of the global recession, the problem of global imbalances remains unsolved; quantitative easing within the USA has pushed down the value of the dollar denominated against other countries and, in turn, generated beggar-my-neighbour responses from other nations, including capital controls and currency protection measures. While full-blown protectionism remains a real possibility, renewed growth in the global economy has already slowed. Nations such as the UK which are unable to achieve significant growth in export-led manufacturing, are thus more than ever reliant on the international performance of their financial and business services.

The continued failure of the world's leading industrial economies to adopt multilateral policies designed to address global imbalances, leaves the UK's capacity for economic recovery much diminished, while, paradoxically, its reliance upon international intermediation in finance and business services, has increased. In this sense, Britain's, especially London's, engagement with the massive expansion in international intermediation, facilitated by a notable tradition of mercantile and imperial activity, remains the main source of economic growth in the UK; but it also indicates the limits to expansion across the British economy.

From the 'Socialisation of Finance' to 'the Financialisation of Society'

For John Maynard Keynes, one of the most influential economists of the twentieth century, the state's role in economic affairs consisted mainly in taking the necessary steps 'to adjust the propensity to consume and the inducement to invest' (Keynes 1973: 379-80), primarily to avoid wastage of resources such as unemployment. If these goals were achieved, the advantages of individualism would 'still hold good'. The state's role was to ensure that government did enough to enable the 'free play of economic forces' and to reduce the scarcity value of capital with low and stable levels of interest, thereby ensuring the eventual demise of the *rentier* – the functionless investor (ibid.). Keynes maintained that to restore the confidence of entrepreneurs during a depression, it is necessary for governments to ensure that the nominal rate of interest remains low over the long term. To do so they buy up bonds, driving down their price. To secure recovery, Keynes argued, 'the state may also be directed to increasing and supplementing the inducement to invest' (Keynes: 1973: 377). Keynes translated this conceptual framework, set down eventually in his General Theory, into specific policy proposals in his evidence to the 1931 Macmillan Committee,[7] where he called for loan-financed public works (Clarke 1988: 236). This 'socialisation of investment' was perhaps the only means to ensure a return to (near) full employment; yet Keynes was also concerned to indicate the limits beyond which public/private cooperation should not go:

> But beyond this no obvious case is made out for a system of State Socialism which would embrace most of the economic life of the community. It is not the ownership of the instruments of production which is important for the state to assume. If the state is able to determine the aggregate amount of resources devoted to augmenting the instruments and the basic rate of reward to those who won them, it will have accomplished all that is necessary…the necessary measures of socialization can be introduced gradually and without a break in the general traditions of society. (Keynes 1973)

Today, the role performed by the state is rather different to that envisaged by Keynes. Whilst it has retained the vestiges of what came to be known as the Keynesian welfarism of a post-1945 'golden age', in many other ways the economic activity of the British state has changed significantly over the last three decades. Continuing to act in a truly Keynesian mode would have meant responding to the slowdown in accumulation that became evident in the crises of the 1970s by socialising some aspects of the financial world, if only to prevent 'a break in the general tradition of society'. Instead, during recent decades, the state has helped to financialise the social world, reinforcing rather than diminishing the role of the *rentier*. In Britain, the state has facilitated this through, for example, creating an 'independent' role for the central bank (the Bank of England), extensive legal and regulatory reform, and fostering a web of direct relationships between financial institutions and the citizen.

The British state sits behind the Bank of England, the UK's central bank. While since 1997 the central bank has been institutionally independent, nonetheless it is required to reconcile the interests of private finance with the public interest, as defined by the government of the day. Thus the state, with the central bank as its intermediate agent, is the guarantor of last resort for the banking and finance

7 The Macmillan Report was published on 13 July 1931. It report arose from a group of leading economists who had been brought together by the UK government to investigate the causes and consequences of the 1929 Wall Street Crash.

sector – as revealed during the credit crisis. The Bank of England, meanwhile, attempts to focus primarily on monetary policy; but it is also concerned with the supply of credit and other facets of the economy. Its contradictory roles have been accentuated by financialisation. It seeks to protect financial institutions while also attempting to enact its interpretation of the public interest; asking, for example, banks to reduce leverage (the proportion of liabilities to assets), while at the same time increasing credit to their customers. The Governor of the Bank of England captured the dilemmas facing the institution in a speech made to Midlands industrialists in January 2009:

> Some say that because the massive increase in indebtedness contributed to the crisis, the right response is to save and repay debt. Others argue that the only way out of our present difficulties is to borrow and spend more. Who is right?
>
> Both are – up to a point. We cannot avoid the necessary long-term adjustment. To pretend otherwise would only store up problems for the future. But we can try to slow the pace of the adjustment to domestic demand, in order to limit its impact on output and employment. So we need to take actions now that will dampen the adjustment in the short term while recognising that the adjustment will ultimately need to be made. This is the paradox of policy at present – almost any policy measure that is desirable now appears diametrically opposite to the direction in which we need to go in the long term. Spending now supports the economy, but in the long run we need to save more and borrow less. Public borrowing sustains spending, but in the long run needs to fall. Banks are encouraged to run down their capital to enable them to absorb losses while continuing to lend, but in the long run they will need more capital. Interest rates have fallen to unprecedented levels, but in the long run will need to rise to more normal levels.[8]

More than two years on from the governor's speech, we now know how the paradox of policy was at least partly resolved. Banks secured more capital with much help from the tax payer, a programme of extensive public spending cuts was introduced, and financial collapse averted, with the public interest (employment and public services) firmly subordinated to the quest for financial stability. This episode has shown how the institutional independence of the central bank thinly obscures its highly political function. The coalition government has used the Bank of England, especially the Monetary Policy Committee and the recently formed Office for Budget Responsibility (OBR), to present its own political judgements as if it were only following expert financial advice.

The financialisation of society, of everyday life, has assumed new dimensions over the past 30 years. Private consumption has rapidly accommodated to its

8 Mervyn King, Governor of the Bank of England, speech made to a CBI dinner, Nottingham, 20 January 2009. http://www.bankofengland.co.uk/publications/speeches/2009/speech372.pdf.

mediation by financial institutions. The pre-conditions for this process may be traced back to the 1970s and 1980s, when it was facilitated by advances in information technology, the emergence of international banking institutions with the capacity to override national regulation, and the passing of legislation such as the UK Building Societies Act, 1986, and the Financial Services Act, 1986, which ushered in the de-regulation of the City known as 'Big Bang' (later modified by the Financial Services and Markets Act, 2000, which introduced the Financial Services Authority as a timid regulator of the sector). Legal and regulatory change affirmed the separation of the spheres of finance and productive capital, and the state provided the framework for a direct relationship between financial services and the individual, enabling this relationship to assume new dimensions. Easy credit became available to additional sections of society as formerly illiquid assets, such as mortgages, were used to provide security against personal loans. The credit card became the day-to-day source of debt as well as a means of payment, and non-bank financial institutions and enterprises began to develop an extensive range of new financial products for the individual consumer.

In 2007, the Social Justice Policy Group (a Conservative think-tank, then under the leadership of Ian Duncan Smith, MP) published a report, *Breakdown Britain*, which revealed that Britain's personal debt to income ratio had risen from below 50 per cent in the 1970s to reach over 140 per cent by 2007, with average household debt rising that year to over £54,000. Unsecured debt, not pegged to owning a home or another significant asset, had risen dramatically: the UK accounted for one third of all such debt throughout Western Europe; and the debt trap extended to the poorest sections of Britain's population (Social Justice Policy Group 2007: 11-13). In addition to providing the legal and financial framework for the huge expansion of personal debt in the UK, the state had extended debt-driven modes of consumption into new areas that were once the hallmark of social, non-marketised provision; and this trend is now set to accelerate with, for example, the shifting of the cost of early years and nursery provision, care for the elderly and higher education, away from the state and toward the individual. In the case of higher education, debt is secured against the future earning power of the graduate. Increasingly driven by its attempts to sustain consumption in a period of weak accumulation and now austerity, the role of the state has significantly changed. Welfare capitalism and the form of social democracy fostered in the post-1945 'golden age' has been incrementally replaced by a different mode of financialised and individualised social relations which monetise not merely the appropriation of current 'living' labour but also extracts an ever increasing range of promissory notes from the labour power of the future.

Conclusion

The slowdown in economic growth since the 1970s in western economies was the condition that accelerated the process of financialisation in the British economy, which ran at a faster pace than in many other western states. Britain's historic role in international financial intermediation and its ready adoption of the legal and regulatory frameworks required to underpin London's global advantage, have hastened de-industrialisation and affirmed a growing reliance upon the tradability of financial and business services. The emergence of finance capital with a life separate to and distinct from the real economy, served to modify the creative and destructive trends evident in 'production driven' capitalism, ameliorating them temporarily. Despite several warning signs provided by the Asian crisis and the west's new technology bubble, the credit crunch came as a surprise to most politicians and many economists. In turn, the coalition government over its first year in office has settled for policies that may, at best, secure a slow and painful recovery with, in Keynesian terms, a considerable waste of resources (especially in the form of worklessness and unemployment).[9]

The coalition government's policies and the muted response from the opposition Labour Party, have at least two sources in common: first, the prevailing perception of the credit crunch and its aftermath, which has ignored the underlying structural issues facing capital and the serious imbalances arising from such structural deficiencies; second, collusion with the process of financialisation by previous governments, Labour and Conservative, through their adoption of 'liberal' regulatory regimes and social policies that strengthen the tendencies toward social fragmentation and the privatisation of social provision. The result to date has been a much diminished society and considerably lower expectations of what the future holds for the UK. Whilst the state is still widely conceived and debated in Keynesian-sounding terms, its purpose has significantly changed. The change began in the 1970s, when it also faltered; but over recent years it has gathered pace, accelerated by significant shifts in global patterns of production and wealth creation. In the UK, what became known as the Anglo-American model of capitalism served mainly to subordinate the public interest to the financial interest, privileging short term shareholder value over longer term capital investment in several sectors of the economy and encouraging economic growth through domestic consumption based on easy credit.

9 Turner expresses the failure of policy makers to grasp the underlying issues facing the UK economy very clearly in his book *No Way to Run an Economy*: 'As Marx warned, the inability to understand the true source of the profit renders policy makers unable to see the scale of the underlying crisis. The failure to distinguish between returns from fictitious capital and real value presents them from acting swiftly. The very nature of capital accumulation at the top of economic booms, with the huge rise of fictitious capital, and the intoxicating success this brings for many afforded power and influence, blinds them from taking even the basic remedies advocated by Keynes' [Turner, G. (2009). *No Way to Run an Economy*, pp 144-5]. For a critique of contemporary scepticism concerning economic growth as a counter to stagnation, see D. Ben-Ami (2010) *Ferraris for All: In Defence of Economic Growth*. Bristol: The Policy Press.

The financialisation of the everyday has had significant social consequences, including the inversion of Keynes's call for the socialisation of finance. It has also served to mask the relative stagnation in wage levels experienced in the UK over recent years, modifying for a period the social impact of losing much of the collective capacity to defend pay and working conditions. Second, the workplace as the main source of disposable income for many sections of society has been 'supplemented' by a more direct form of exploitation based upon private debt; and, finally, the state has incrementally transferred to the individual the responsibility for meeting the costs of major areas of social provision, such as pensions and, more recently, higher and further education.[10] By reducing the prop of public spending, coalition government policies have exposed the underlying weaknesses of Britain's national economy whilst failing to address the structural problems that gave rise to it.

Financialisation was enacted through the finance sector but has, this chapter suggests, much deeper origins and far wider implications for industry and society in Britain. It has produced an economy that is severely unbalanced in its spatial (regional) dimensions and social relations. The following chapters examine the implications of these underlying problems both in relation to London and by comparison to other cities such as New York and Shanghai, where finance currently enjoys a different kind of relationship to production.

References

Allen, K. (2010). 'Cable admits U-turn on public spending cuts', *The Guardian*, Thursday 3 June 2010, available at http://www.guardian.co.uk/business/2010/jun/03/vince-cable-pledge-to-help-business, accessed 12 October 2010.

Authers, P. (2008). 'Four strong contenders for mistake of the year', *Financial Times*, 13-14 December 2008, accessed 18 December 2008.

Ben-Ami, D. (2010). *Ferraris for All: In Defence of Economic Progress*. Bristol: Policy Press.

Blackburn, R. (2008). 'The Credit Crunch', *New Left Review*, 50, March/April 2008, 63-108.

Brenner, R. (2006). *The Economics of Global Turbulence*. London: Verso.

Bryson, J., Daniels, P., Henry, N. and Pollard, J. (2000). *Knowledge, Space, Economy*. London: Routledge.

Clarke, S. (1988). *Keynesianism, Monetarism and the Crisis of the State*. Aldershot: Edward Elgar.

Crotty, J. (2005). 'The Neoliberal Paradox: The Impact of Destructive Product Market Competition and Modern Financial Markets on Nonfinancial

10 This process is likely to gather a new momentum in many areas of social policy as a result of Prime Minister David Cameron's 'Big Society' initiatives by which public/state provision is being displaced by an assemblage of local 'community-based' projects.

Corporation Performance in the Neo-Liberal Era', in G. Epstein (ed.) (2005). *Financialisation and the World Economy*. Aldershot: Edward Elgar, 77-110.

CRS Report for Congress (2008). 'China's Holdings of US Securities: Implications for the US Economy', updated February 2008, Washington: Congressional Research Service.

Epstein, G. (ed.) (2005). *Financialisation and the World Economy*. Aldershot: Edward Elgar.

Itoh, M. and Lapavitsas, C. (1999). *Political Economy of Money and Finance*. Basingstoke: Macmillan Press.

Jessop, B. (2000). 'The State and the Contradictions of the Knowledge-driven Economy' in *Knowledge, Space, Economy*, edited by Bryson J. et al. London: Routledge, 63-78.

Keynes, J. (1973). *The General Theory of Interest and Money*. London: Macmillan.

Krippner, G. (2005). 'The Financialization of the American Economy'. *Socio-Economic Review*, 3, 173-208.

Lapavitsas, C. (2010). 'Financialisation and Capitalist Accumulation: Structural Accounts of the Crisis 2007-2009' Research on Money and Finance, Working Paper no. 16, London: School of Oriental and African Studies, available at http://www.scribd.com/doc/54655712/Research-on-Money-and-Finance-Lapavitsas.

Meyer, C. (2008). 'Flash Gordon Brown', 15 October 2008, *Time*, available at http://www.time.com/time/magazine/article/0,9171,1850562,00.html, accessed 28 December 2008.

Mullan, P. (2008). The truth about the 'credit crunch', *Spiked*, Monday 7 January 2008, available at http://spiked-online.com/index.php?/site.

NESTA (2010). *Rebalancing Act*. NESTA research Report, June 2010, available at http://www.nesta.org.uk/library/documents/rebalancing_act_080610.pdf, accessed 20 October 2010.

Office of National Statistics (2005). News Release 'Business and financial services economic impact is double manufacturing', ONS 19 August 2005, available at www.statistics.gov.uk, accessed 28 December 2008.

Orhangazi, O. (2008). 'Financialisation and capital accumulation in the non-financial corporate sector: A theoretical and empirical investigation of the US economy 1973-2003', *Cambridge Journal of Economics* 2008, 32, 883-6.

Palmer, A. (2008). 'Paradise Lost', *The Economist*, 17 May 2008, 3-10.

Poynter, G. (2008). 'The Credit Crunch and London's Economy' *Rising East*, Issue Number 8a, July 2008, available at http://www.uel.ac.uk/risingeast/currentissue/academic/poynter.htm, accessed 15 July 2011.

Rodrigues, M. (2003). *European Policies for a Knowledge Economy.* Aldershot: Edward Elgar.

Schumpeter, J. (2010). *Capitalism, Socialism and Democracy*. London: Routledge Classics.

Schiller, R. (2008). *The Subprime Solution*. Princeton, NJ: Princeton University Press.

Social Justice Policy Group (2007). *Breakdown Britain*, available at http://www.centreforsocialjustice.org.uk/default.asp?pageRef=180, accessed 23 September 2010.

Turner, A. (2010). 'What Do Banks Do? Why Do Credit Booms and Busts Occur? What Can Public Policy Do About It' in *The LSE Report, The Future of Finance*. London: LSE.

Turner, G. (2008). *The Credit Crunch*. London: Pluto.

Turner, G. (2009). *No Way to Run an Economy*. London: Pluto.

US Monetary Policy Forum (2008). Available at http://research.chicagogsb/edu/igm/events/conferences/2008-usmonetaryforum.

Wolf, M. (2007). 'Why the credit squeeze is a turning point for the world', *Financial Times*, 12 December 2007.

Wolf, M. (2009). *Fixing Global Finance*. London: Yale University Press.

Chapter 2
New York City's Economy: More than Wall Street?

Sean Collins

Introduction: Staying on Top of the World

With a population of approximately eight million, New York City remains America's largest city, more than twice the size of Los Angeles, the next-biggest. Home to Wall Street, Broadway, Woody Allen, Jay-Z, and baseball's Yankees, the Big Apple looms larger-than-life in the country's imagination. While Americans in other parts of the country can be dismissive or critical of New York, they can also embrace it as their own, as many did following the 9/11 attack in 2001.

New York is not the most populous city in the world – that would be Tokyo, according to most measures. Nevertheless, New York is sometimes referred to as 'the world's capital', or, as one *New York Times* writer (Kristof 2005) put it, 'the unofficial capital of planet Earth'. One reason for the designation is the city's cosmopolitanism: a long-time entry-point for immigrants, the population today is still heavily comprised of outsiders, with one in three people today having arrived from abroad. New York claims to have the world's largest financial centre (though London might dispute that), the world's largest stock exchange, the world's top advertising agencies (think *Mad Men*), some of the world's most valuable real estate, and the world's largest mass-transit system.

Many close followers of New York's economy over the past decade have debated why the city's growth decelerated over the course of the late 20th century. For example, the city's population dropped significantly during the 1970s, and it took until 2000 before it regained its 1970 peak of 7.9 million. But in comparison with other big northeast and midwestern cities, New York has withstood economic pressures rather well. As Edward Glaeser (2005) notes, of the 16 largest cities in those regions, New York is the only one with a higher population today than 50 years ago.

In many respects, New York has survived and prospered since the 1980s because it was able to re-focus its economy around financial and other service industries. In adopting this strategy, New York has been at the vanguard of the US economy generally, which has also relied more on services rather than goods-producing industries for its economic output. Yet, just as New York was at the forefront of the upswing, so too it has been prominent on the way down: Wall Street was clearly at the heart of the financial meltdown of 2008 and the concomitant recession. The downturn has called into question an economic model that puts finance in a central role. In turn, a financial sector that has shown itself to be vulnerable raises serious concerns about the viability of New York's economy, given its dependence on that sector.

This chapter will examine the historical trends in New York's economy, including the growth in financial services. In particular, it will consider the main sources of employment and income in recent decades, and situate the city's economy in the wider US economy. It concludes by considering the consequences of the crash for the city's future development.

Becoming King of the Hill

There has been a longstanding association between New York and finance. In the late 17th century, Wall Street – named for the street where a former wall fortified the Dutch settlement of New Amsterdam – was a site where merchants traded shares and bonds. A century later, traders and speculators met near a buttonwood tree on Wall Street, and their 'Buttonwood Agreement' in 1792 led to the formation of the New York Stock Exchange.

It is therefore understandable if many assume that finance has always been central to NYC's economy – understandable, but wrong. Over most of New York's economic history, finance has played a peripheral role compared with other industries.

New Amsterdam was a trading post under the Dutch. The city was an important port for maritime trade, especially for trading furs with Europeans. Following the British takeover in 1664, the city was renamed New York. Under British rule, trade continued to be the primary activity, and food products such as bread and flour became the key exports.

While a significant and growing port, New York was not the largest in the US in the 18th century; Boston and Philadelphia were busier. However, New York held certain geographical advantages over these cities, such as its water depth and the superiority of the Hudson River as a means of transportation inland. Furthermore, as Epstein (1995) emphasises, New York's 'polyglot origins' meant that, unlike Boston and Philadelphia, it was more welcoming to people of all persuasions (including Catholics and Jews), and allowed more freedom to improvise economically. As Epstein says, the openness that attracted 'early freebooters to Manhattan seems to have become a permanent feature of New York's culture and attracted their energetic successors as well' (ibid.).

These advantages came to the fore during the American Revolution, as Boston and Philadelphia suffered. Unlike those cities, New York remained under English control and was not as disrupted by the war. British troops entered and left the country via New York, and it became the main port for British imports. New York continued to grow, and following the War of 1812 – which again was more disturbing for its rival cities – it became the nation's largest port. Its relative advantage then increased enormously with the construction of the Erie Canal in 1825. The canal linked New York all the way to the Great Lakes and the country's Midwest hinterland, which provided New York with unparalleled access to markets and the interior of the US. By 1830, 40 per cent of the country's trade passed through New York.

The Rise and Fall of Manufacturing

At the start of the Civil War in 1860, New York was clearly the dominant city in the US economy, with more people located there than anywhere else in the country. Manufacturing was present in the city from colonial times, and even before the Civil War it had grown to the point that the large majority of the city's workers were involved in production. As of 1850, manufacturing employed 43,340, compared with 11,360 in commerce (Glaeser 2005). But following the Civil War, this shift towards manufacturing really took off.

New York's manufacturers focused on the production of non-durable goods for mass consumption: garments, refined sugar, printed materials, leather goods and tobacco products (Drennan 2010). The city was an ideal place to locate a plant, as there were already transportation links to move raw materials into the city, while the city's manufacturers had a close knowledge of the consumer's buying preferences. Having a centralised site of manufacturing also brought economies of scale: capital was accumulated in a concerted way in the city, and re-invested in more advanced machinery. New York also had a large pool of immigrant labor to draw from. For most of the late 19th century this meant there were sufficient workers to meet the expanding demand for labor. But from 1890 and the boom in immigration, this abundant supply provided a further advantage to employers, since competition for jobs held wages down.

Manufacturing would remain the bedrock of New York's economy into the early 20th century. At the turn of the 20th century, the leading industries were still garments, sugar refining and printing/publishing. These would remain the city's main sectors for another hundred years. And as of 1910, about 40 per cent of total NYC employees were in manufacturing (U.S. Bureau of Census, Census of Population, cited in Drennan 2010), by far the biggest proportion.

After 1910, the number of employees in manufacturing declined as a proportion of total New York City workers. Employment in manufacturing was still growing in the first half of the 20th century; it was just that the pace of growth was eclipsed by that in other occupations, namely clerical, professional services, and trade and transportation. Compared to other major industrial cities, New York was more diversified. As corporations grew in size and complexity, more of them made New York their headquarters than any other city.

However, manufacturing would eventually decline further. After continuing to grow through the Great Depression and World War II, employment in manufacturing began to fall in absolute terms: it peaked in the 1950s at about one million employees. The number of Fortune 500 companies calling New York home also began to drop. This decline was the result of a number of factors. The costs of transporting goods were reduced over time, first by the railway, and then by the truck. Access to a waterway was less of an advantage, as there were alternative methods of transportation to and from the hinterland. And manufacturers could now more readily base themselves outside the city, since transportation costs were relatively low, and employees could drive cars to work rather than rely on public transportation within the city. At the same time, New York was becoming less of an ideal environment for manufacturing. The physical fabric of manufacturing plants was deteriorating, the costs of real estate and labor increased, and traffic congestion delayed the movement of people and goods. New York was also losing out to foreign competitors, who were introducing more efficient machines and/or paying lower wages.

Gradual decline in manufacturing became a sharp decline in the economic crisis of the 1970s. Employment overall fell from 3.8 million in 1969 to a low of 3.2 million. Manufacturing jobs were hit hardest, falling by 35 per cent from 1970 to 1977 (Drennan 2010). Of course, New York was not the only part of the US to experience the trend towards deindustrialisation. But the impact of two recessions was felt especially hard in New York, and there were issues in play which were particular to NYC. New York's infrastructure was decaying, and a crime explosion made it seem that society was unraveling. The general sense of crisis crystallised in the city's fiscal crisis in 1975. New York appealed to President Gerald Ford and the federal government for assistance to avert bankruptcy. Ford initially refused, which led to the famous *New York Daily News* headline: 'Ford to City: Drop Dead!' But a second effort was successful, and the federal government lent money to the city. In return, New York's government was streamlined and its budget was put on a sounder footing.

A Reinvention Based on Finance and Other Services

The late 1970s was a period of deep pessimism for New York and the country. The economy was mired in a slump, and there was no obvious way out. Ronald Reagan was elected in 1980 promising renewal ('Morning in America'), but the US economy fell into another recession in 1981-1982.

However, the thorough shake-out of manufacturing industry during the period from the mid-1970s through to the early 1980s eventually restored profitability and paved the way for the national economy to recover. At the same time, this unstable period of downturn and recovery ushered in a structural shift: a move away from manufacturing and towards services. Many professional services are best-suited to be located in cities, given the need for concentrated populations of educated labor and face-to-face business interaction, among other considerations. Consequently, as the country's largest city, New York was well-placed to benefit from these national trends.

At the start of the 1980s, manufacturing employment represented 17 per cent of all New York City jobs; by the end of the decade, that proportion fell to 11 per cent. This process continued, in dramatic fashion: by 2008, only three per cent of all New York jobs were in manufacturing. New York was no longer a top manufacturing centre, nor the country's largest port – those honors now went to Los Angeles.

The decline in manufacturing has had a dire effect on communities, especially in the four boroughs outside of the island of Manhattan (the Bronx, Queens, Brooklyn and Staten Island). In a much-cited article in the *New York Review of Books*, Jason Epstein (1992) noted how manufacturing bolstered social cohesion: 'It was mainly by means of these manufacturing jobs and jobs in shipping and wholesaling, many of them associated with the port ... that most of the city's newcomers supported their families, and through which many of them accumulated bits and pieces of capital, set up businesses of their own, and educated their children'. However, the demise of manufacturing has led to social decay. Referring to a neighborhood in Brooklyn, Epstein writes: 'By 1990, 41 percent of Bushwick's population depended on public assistance. Only 5,000 of the original white population were left. Like the rain forest or Florida's coral reef, Bushwick, which had been growing for three hundred years, is dying or already dead, its streets dominated by a dozen teen-age drug gangs... . Other New York neighborhoods are just as bad'.

But the contraction of manufacturing in New York since the late 1970s has been overshadowed by the expansion of other industries. Coming out of those gloomy years, New York reinvented itself, and shifted from a blue-collar to a white-collar orientation in the process. A variety of 'post-industrial' businesses came to the fore, in industries such as finance and insurance; professional services (lawyers, accountants, advertisers, business consultants); information services (publishing, broadcasting and other media); tourism; and retail. Many of these largely white-collar jobs were generally higher-paying. In turn, these incomes supported a luxury retail sector that took on a more upscale flavor, nearly exclusively in Manhattan.

Financial Services

The 1980s marked a watershed in the composition of the US economy. It was in the middle of that decade that, for the first time in the country's history, financial services represented a higher proportion of total output (Gross Domestic Product) than manufacturing. As Figure 2.1 shows, this trend has continued since.

Armed with rhetoric extolling the 'free market', the Reagan administrations of the 1980s introduced a series of policies that directly or indirectly benefited the financial sector, including dollar devaluation, tax cuts, reduced regulation and fewer restrictions on mergers and acquisitions. At the same time, the Reagan years saw a cultural shift in which money-acquisitiveness and luxury became more acceptable than before. As Steve Fraser notes in his excellent study of how Wall Street has affected American culture, *Every Man a Speculator* (2005), what was

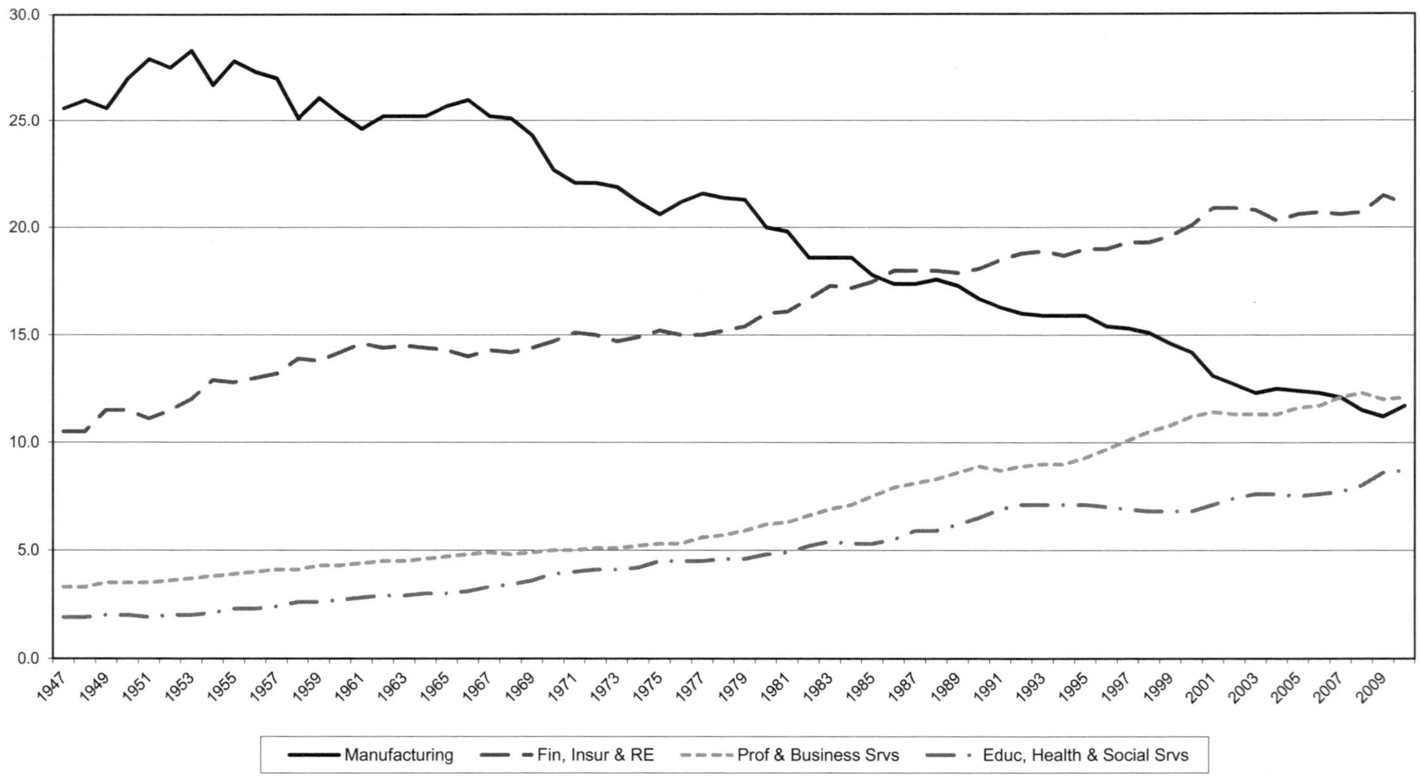

Figure 2.1 US industry GDP as % of total US GDP 1947-2010

Source: U.S. Department of Commerce, Bureau of Economic Analysis.

distinctive about this second Gilded Age was that the so-called 'corporate raiders' – junk-bond kings and other financiers, presented themselves as rebels against the establishment old guard. Michael Milken, Ivan Boesky and Carl Icahn were not just aiming to get rich; acting in their self-interest, they were also attacking sclerotic, bloated corporate bureaucracies and making them leaner, meaner and in better shape to face the competition. The era's ideologues viewed 'shareholder value as a form of liberation theology with global implications', Fraser writes.

But these favourable government policies and cultural trends were not the whole story. Underlying these was a more fundamental driver: the spontaneous movement of capital. Specifically, as profitability in manufacturing industry stagnated, capital was freed up and flowed into other, more promising areas. For the most part, the new areas were not populated by other manufacturers or technology firms, but rather companies in financial and other services. In addition, the spreading 'financialisation' of the economy meant much more than just the growth in finance firms. It also was evinced in the increasing reliance of non-financial firms on financial methods as a source of profits – ranging from developing credit subsidiaries, e.g. General Motors and its lending arm GMAC, to growing dependence on pension fund investments and other treasury reserves.

In such an era, New York – home to Wall Street, the financial capital of the US – was bound to be at the forefront. In the 1980s, Wall Street itself became a cultural icon, summed up by Gordon Gekko in Oliver Stone's 1988 film Wall Street. (It was ironic that while Stone intended audiences to condemn Gekko, many found him an attractive figure). Over the decade, employment in New York City's financial sector grew from about 350,000 to 400,000.

Of course, finance was far from a new feature of city life. Wall Street was established in the process of sharing risk on sea voyages (Glaeser 2005). As mentioned above, the New York Stock Exchange and other financial institutions were established in the 18th century. From the Civil War onwards, New York was clearly the country's leading center of finance and business services. However, the role of financial services in the broader economy had fundamentally changed over time. In the past, financial services grew alongside the wider growth of productive industry and the economy generally. In the 19th century's Gilded Age, finance in New York (and elsewhere) oiled the wheels of the expanding industries: railroads, steel, oil, electricity and chemicals. Finance took its cut, but it was secondary; productive industry was in the driving seat.

From the 1980s and after, it became clear that finance had become more of an economic catalyst in its own right. In 1950, finance jobs represented seven per cent of all jobs in New York; by 1990, that had increased to 12 per cent. Moreover, the financial world was now seen as a key area for investment and profit-generation: in mergers and acquisitions; in asset-stripping companies; in loading companies up with debt and taking them private. It was, in Kevin Phillips' phrase, 'paper entrepreneurialism' (2002). From the perspective of the economy as a whole, this form of finance is a less healthy, more parasitical type.

The rise of new finance faced its first major setback on 'Black Monday' in October 1987, when the stock market crashed. In the fallout from it, Milken and other financiers were put behind bars. A slew of books and movies were produced in the late 1980s that ridiculed the one-time 'masters of the universe', including *Liar's Poker*, *Predators' Ball*, *Bonfire of the Vanities*, *Barbarians at the Gate*, *American Psycho* and *Wall Street.*

But another Great Depression did not follow, as some (such as John Kenneth Galbraith) had predicted. And generally, the finance train kept chugging along. As the finance writer Michael Lewis (2009) has pointed out: 'At the time [1987], to a lot of people, it felt like the end of something. In retrospect it appears more of a beginning'. Indeed, it was the start of a substantial increase in credit and speculative activity. Further blows to the sector's credibility that later emerged – for instance, the 1997-8 Asia crisis, the crisis which ensued after the bailout of the hedge fund Long-Term Capital Management, the busting of the internet bubble, and the downturn following 9/11 – did not derail this on-going development.

Various ideas have been put forward to try to explain why Wall Street was never thoroughly de-legitimised during the 1990s and 2000s. One is the idea that the masses have become shareholders themselves, and more interested in getting rich in the stock market than in condemning it – the so-called 'shareholder nation' thesis (Fraser 2005). While clearly there are a variety of contributing factors, two of the most important are: (1) the political and business establishment's on-going support for finance during that period, as they believed it is one of the few areas of dynamism in the economy; and (2) the lack of a thorough critique of financialisation and a persuasive alternative to it.

For the past two decades, finance has been the main face of New York's economy. And yet, for all its prominence, city-based employment in the finance sector (defined broadly as finance, insurance and real estate) has steadily declined over this period: it fell by six per cent in the 1990s, and by a further five per cent between 2000 and 2008. (n.b. Years cited refer to annual averages, and, as such, 2008 data does not highlight the decline in employment that began in earnest in September 2008; that decline is clearly evident in the 2009 data in comparison with 2008 data). A sub-sector associated with Wall Street, namely, Securities and Commodity Contracts, bucked the overall trend in the 1990s and did show a 22 per cent increase in employment in that decade; but jobs in that area also declined in the 2000s.

As of 2008, finance represented 12 per cent of total employment in New York City; not insignificant, but not huge either; and other industries are bigger employers. But its stamp on the economy is larger than employment data indicate. For instance, while employing 12 per cent, finance generates 35 per cent of total wages – a key determinant of consumer demand and economic activity. The sub-category Securities and Commodity Contracts, associated with investment banking, shows an even starker contrast: with only five per cent of the city's employees, it (amazingly) generates nearly a quarter of its total wages. Such data on income give an indication of the extent that the New York economy is reliant on the finance sector.

Table 2.1 Employment by Industry in New York City

	1990		2000		2008		% Change	
	# Employed	% of Total	# Employed	% of Total	# Employed	% of Total	1990-2000	2000-2008
Educational and Health Srvs	476	13%	615.2	17%	719.0	19%	29%	17%
Prof. and Bus. Services	466.9	13%	586.5	16%	602.9	16%	26%	3%
Government	607	17%	568.9	15%	564.1	15%	-6%	-1%
Trade, Transp & Util	600.7	17%	570.5	15%	574.5	15%	-5%	1%
Financial Activities	521.4	15%	488.8	13%	465.0	12%	-6%	-5%
Leisure & Hospitality	218.1	6%	256.7	7%	310.2	8%	18%	21%
Information	169.2	5%	187.3	5%	169.5	4%	11%	-10%
Other Services	124.8	4%	147.4	4%	160.8	4%	18%	9%
Nat. Res, Mining and Cons	114.4	3%	120.5	3%	132.7	3%	5%	10%
Manufacturing	265.2	7%	176.8	5%	95.6	3%	-33%	-46%
Total	**3,563.7**	**100%**	**3,718.6**	**100%**	**3,794.3**	**100%**		

Source: New York State Department of Labor.

Other Service Industries

Financial services by no means exhaust the story of the 'post-industrial' trend in New York City's economy since the 1970s. As mentioned, there are other industries that represent a higher proportion of the city's workforce. Table 2.1 shows the employment numbers in 1990, 2000 and 2008 by industry. As it indicates, as of 2008, four industries exceeded 'Financial Activities' as sources of employment.

'Professional and Business Services' is one of those industries. This category includes services in the fields of law, accounting, architecture and engineering, computer systems, management consulting, advertising, and company management. In the 1990s, employment in this industry grew solidly, in contrast to declining employment in financial services. However, between 2000 and 2008 this sector's employment was essentially flat, growing by only three per cent over a 10-year period. A notable sub-industry is computer systems design: its total number of jobs more than tripled in the 1990s, reflecting the dot.com boom and the emergence of 'Silicon Alley' in lower Manhattan. But the data for the next decade shows how gains in that once-promising industry did not materialise: following the internet bust, job growth in that sector was stagnant between 2000 and 2008.

Like financial services, professional and business services encompass generally higher-paying occupations. In 2008, it represented 19 per cent of the city's total wages. It is truly remarkable that these two industries (financial and professional services) combined generate over half – 54 per cent – of the total wages in New York City.

Obviously, there are linkages between finance and professional services, and many associate the two together under the 'white collar' rubric. But the services industry with the most employees in the city is 'Education and Health Services', and it has little direct connection with the world of finance.

This industry has seen solid and consistent growth in employment since 1990. Its share of total employment has increased from 13 per cent in 1990 to 19 per cent in 2008. More than three-quarters of the jobs in this category are health-related. One sub-industry, 'Home Health Care Services' has experienced stunning growth: the number of jobs quadrupled from 1990 to 2008. Unlike financial services, jobs in the education and health services industry are generally lower-paying: in 2008, the sector's 19 per cent of the total jobs produced 11 per cent of the total wages. The typical profile of a home health worker is a black or Hispanic woman who is 45 years of age or older, with a high school diploma (equivalent) or less, and who earns $26,000 a year, which is slightly above the minimum wage (NYC LMIS 2009).

This growth in employment in education and health services is part of a national trend, as this industry's share of total national jobs has steadily increased since 1990. What's behind this growth? There are a number of potential contributing factors: the ageing of the population; sustained levels of state spending; the general tendency towards cost inflation in the US health sector; the growing preference for home care rather than institutional care.

But, given prevailing perceptions, most people would probably be surprised to learn that healthcare outstrips finance in terms of NYC's job creation. When people think of the Big Apple's economy, it is still Wall Street bankers, not home health workers, which spring to mind. There is also a geographical dichotomy between the two: financial services are dominant in Manhattan, while education and health services predominate in the outer boroughs. Despite their distance, there is perhaps a symbiotic relationship between them, as tax receipts from financial services are then used to support public spending on education and health services.

The Crash and Its Aftermath

The US has arguably been a 'financialised' economy for at least three decades, and despite crashes and downturns over those years, its supposed dynamism was taken for granted by many. Nevertheless, for those inclined to notice, there were certainly early signs that the financial crash of 2008 was on its way. The housing sector turned down in 2007, and banks began to take large write-offs for 'toxic' mortgages on their books. The economy entered recession at the end of that year. Then, in March 2008, the investment bank Bear Stearns collapsed, and the government stepped in to arrange a fire-sale to JPMorgan Chase. In September 2008, the bottom dropped out: the stock market went into free-fall, and the government let Lehman Brothers go to the wall; but then, in a panic, rescued AIG.

Wall Street was clearly implicated in the financial meltdown, which was most immediately triggered by the pricking of the housing bubble in the US. Wall Street firms were able to convince rating agencies like Moody's and Standard & Poor's to apply their highest rating (triple A) to their complex packages of subprime mortgages (that is, mortgages with a high likelihood of defaulting), and then sell them on to unsuspecting investors who thought they were buying something safe, thus garnering massive fees in the process. Wall Street's securitisation of mortgages directly affected Main Street's lending. Securitisation created demand for new mortgages, especially subprime mortgages, and facilitated a new class of loan originators in firms like Ameriquest and Countrywide. These new companies shunned traditional methods of assessing creditworthiness, doing away with documentation of income (when not deliberately falsifying income) and interviews, because they didn't have to: they could simply turn around and sell the mortgages on to Wall Street. When these dodgy assets were marked down, however, the 'contagion' spread globally.

All parts of the US were affected by the recession that followed the crash. Yet, being the location of Wall Street, New York was especially impacted by the financial retraction. Financial services employed approximately 470,000 just before the September 2008 crash; at its low point, in January 2010, the sector had lost about 50,000 jobs, an 11 per cent decline. Related jobs concentrated in Wall Street such as securities and commodity contracts, fell even further (by 20 per cent) during that same timeframe. Unemployment generally in the city jumped up; a rise of 10 per cent occurred between September 2009 and January 2010.

From its low point in early 2010, the total number of city jobs has increased by about 125,000, a modest three per cent rise. Financial services employment has also recovered, growing by the same percentage and maintaining its share at 12 per cent of total New York employment. In contrast, manufacturing has not picked up. Indeed, since its peak in the 1950s, manufacturing employment has been mercilessly slashed: from approximately one million to about 75,000 today.

In May 2011 NYC's unemployment rate was 8.6 per cent, or 0.5 per cent lower than the national average. It transpired that New York recovered a more quickly and robustly than the rest of the country. As the *New York Times* noted in August 2011, 'The city has regained jobs lost since the financial crisis of 2008 at twice the rate of the country as a whole' (McGeehan 2011). It is perhaps ironic – or perverse – that Wall Street has recovered faster than Main Street; but this has been, at least in part, the outcome of the strategy adopted by President Obama's administration, in which financial services have taken top priority.

Whither NYC?

In July 2011, New York City Mayor Michael Bloomberg addressed a 'Future of New York City' conference. Bloomberg noted problems he inherited, including ageing infrastructure and an economy that was 'too dependent on Wall Street'. He said that his administration had created a five-borough diversification strategy 'that included not only finance, but also film and television, bio-tech, fashion, arts and culture, tourism, modern manufacturing, and small business of every kind'. And Bloomberg used the occasion to announce a new initiative: an offer to assist a top university in building an engineering and applied sciences campus in the city, as a means of spurring technology businesses.

The desire to diversify beyond Wall Street is understandable. The sector has lost about 100,000 jobs over the past two decades. The crash has certainly revealed that the city's economy is vulnerable if it remains so reliant on financial services. As fears of a double-dip recession emerged in mid-2011, Wall Street was already retrenching, announcing a round of big layoffs.

New York has many legacy advantages that make it likely to retain its hold on financial services. However, there is the possibility of erosion. For example, the need for regular face-to-face contact may be diminishing, especially given technology (already we see more financiers based outside of New York, such as the hedge funds operated out of Stamford, Connecticut, or Warren Buffett out of Ohama, Nebraska). Looking ahead, as a global financial center, New York is increasingly challenged by London as well as the upstarts Singapore, Hong Kong and Shanghai.

In the aftermath of the crash, with many blaming Wall Street, there is a tendency to focus attention on regulating financial services. While there are no doubt sensible regulations that should be introduced, there is a danger that the discussion over new rules will distract from growth priorities. Expand productive industry, and finance will be restored to a less prominent role.

But it remains a big question as to whether New York can execute and succeed with a diversification strategy. The idea of linking universities and science-based entrepreneurs has existed for some time (Epstein, for instance, discussed it in his 1992 article). And many of the industries Bloomberg mentioned as part of the diversification strategy have not grown in employment numbers over the past decade – an exception being tourism, which mostly involves lower-paid work.

A different story is told in a 2011 report issued by the New York State Department of Labor on 'significant industries' in New York City (NYS DOL 2011). The authors identify 12 key industries. Of these, two of the highest in terms of expected job growth through 2016 are 'ambulatory health care services' (+34 per cent) and 'social assistance' (+21 per cent). Given the recent trend we mentioned regarding the growth in health and social services jobs, future growth might seem a reasonable assumption.

The other highest projected job gainers are 'professional and technical services' (+24 per cent) and 'securities and commodities contracts' (+22 per cent). But how confident should we be in these projections? Professional services employment growth has been flat over the past decade, and investment banking jobs have declined in number. Also, it is interesting to see that these economists' projections indicate an expectation that not much will change – they still expect Wall Street and other professional jobs to drive employment. None of the industries identified by Mayor Bloomberg for his diversification strategy are listed as likely ones to see job growth in the next five years.

One author (Siegel 2011) accurately described New York as having an 'hourglass economy': 'all the action on the top and bottom, and not much in the middle'. A Drum Major Institute report found that more than half of all new jobs since the recession were in the city's two lowest paid industries – retail and hospitality – while 31 per cent of New York adults are now employed in low-wage labor (Drum 2011). These are not jobs that can sustain a thriving working class. New York's population has been boosted by immigration, but has remained roughly constant overall, as the newcomers are offset by leavers, who depart as they get older and want to raise families in suburban towns or smaller cities.

New York is faced with severe challenges. Both its fragile financial services sector and its state-dependent health services sector are showing real signs of age. But at the same time, the city has tremendous legacy resources to draw upon, and it is continually renewed by immigrants who, as Frank Sinatra has it, 'want to be a part of it' and 'make it there'. There are many ideas for renewal, but the first step is to gain acceptance about the nature and scale of change needed, and an agreement that a major shift in economic orientation is required.

It's up to you, New York.

References

Drennan, M.P. (2010). 'Economy', in *The Encyclopedia of New York City*, 2nd edition, edited by K.T. Jackson. New Haven, CT: Yale University Press.

Drum Major Institute (2011). 'Report: Low-wage jobs dominate NYC job growth'.

Epstein, J. (1992). 'The tragical history of New York', *The New York Review of Books*, 9 April 1992.

Epstein, J. (1995). 'Metropolitan life', *The New York Review of Books*, 16 November 1995.

Glaeser, E.L. (2005). 'Urban colossus: Why is New York America's largest city?' Harvard Institute of Economic Research, Discussion Paper Number 2073.

Kristof, N. (2005). 'China, the world's capital', *The New York Times*, 22 May 2005.

Lewis, M. (ed.) (2008). *Panic: The Story of Modern Financial Insanity.* WW Norton & Company.

McGeehan, P. (2011). 'Divining New York's fate should a double-dip recession hit', *New York Times*, 15 August 2011.

NYC Labor Market Information Service. 'Industry group profile: Employment in New York City Home Health Care Services'. May 2009.

NYS Department of Labor, Bureau of Labor Market Information (2011). 'Significant Industries: A Report to the Workforce Development System. New York City'.

Phillips, K. (2002). *Wealth and Democracy: A Political History of the American Rich.* New York: Broadway Books.

Siegel, F. (2011). 'Goodbye, New York State Residents Are Rushing for the Exits', *New Geography*, 28 May.

Chapter 3
The Glittering Prizes of Shanghai

Alan Hudson

Introduction

On a recent visit to Shanghai, in the spring of 2011, I was taken to the penthouse bar of a five-star hotel, just off the Bund. The special feature of the 32nd floor bar was a rooftop Jacuzzi. It was warm and sultry, the bar was heaving, but the Jacuzzi was empty. Perhaps because there was too much business to do: in the lobby there were directions to a Citroën sales conference, and the Shanghai Motor Show was about to open; hence the mixed Chinese and international crowd. But this bar is also a popular hang-out for wealthy young Shanghainese, and for the growing population of ambitious westerners who have gone east to make their fortune.

The smallest Tsingtao beer that the hotel could put its hands on, set you back 50RMB. If you could have found such a small bottle in a nearby supermarket (and they do not usually stock such small bottles), it would have cost a maximum of 5RMB. Advice to travellers on a normal budget: do not use the mini-bar, there's always a small retail outlet nearby. Meanwhile, back on the 32nd floor, the waiters moved eagerly and observantly among the guests, ready to offer thimble-sized refills. This is boom time Shanghai, the reborn Pearl of the Orient.

At these giddy heights the view of Pudong, and especially the Huangpu River, almost vertically below, are spectacular. Looking down, one seemed to bestride the world beneath – both physically and figuratively. On the river an uninterrupted line of working barges trundled downstream to the Yangtze, the new deep water port at Yangshan, and the East China Sea; another turned upstream on the Yangtze to the great river ports of Wuhan and Chongqing, deep in the Chinese hinterland. Two days later I was in Wuhan, where Mao swam the Yangtze, and watched, perhaps the same barges, move raw materials and finished goods up and down the river.

What struck me then, as it had done in Shanghai, was the almost forgotten feature of Shanghai's emergence as nearly everyone's favourite for global city status: production. Whatever might be in the minds of the gilded youth in downtown Shanghai, whose dads might have made it big in the Zhejiang business expansion, or in the heads of the marketing boys for the sleek luxury car models now enjoying record sales, the precondition for the Jacuzzi and the cocktails, as well as my humble Chinese beer, was making stuff.

By 2020, just as China's economy is expected to be approaching the size of the US economy, Shanghai's economy will be matching that of New York, currently the richest economic region of the world (Schifferes 2007). The year, 2020, though something of an arbitrary choice, has been given a special significance for Shanghai. In 2007 the State Council, the highest policy-making body of the Chinese government, declared that by 2020 Shanghai would become a Global Financial, Trade and Shipping Centre. The underlying message of this declaration, as issued by the leadership of the People's Republic, is that China's industrial pre-eminence will now be translated through Shanghai and other mediating centres; and China taking on more of this mediating role will have huge implications at home and abroad.

In the rest of this chapter I assert the centrality of production, both in general, and in relation to Shanghai's re-emergence. I then outline the policy framework put in place by the government of Shanghai to sustain and enhance the city's development. The chapter concludes by situating Shanghai in a global, national and regional context, with comments on some of the more pressing problems facing the city and its citizens, now and in the coming period.

Production Matters

There are, of course, many new features to Shanghai's recent development, but it is worth recording one parallel with its historical antecedents, London and New York. Though this economic basic was almost buried until the financial crisis of 2007-8 brought the 'weightless economy' down to earth, the development of all three global cities – London, New York and Shanghai – testifies that production is historically and logically prior both to consumption and to the secondary structures of the financial apparatus (Heartfield 1998, 2000; Leadbeater 2000). Financial services, however useful they may be in bringing production to the point of consumption, do not spring like Venus from the waves; but emerge and develop as a result of new zones of productive strength. Similarly, the liberation of financial centres from the strict laws of production – their freedom to speculate – is not in itself a new stage of economic life but a secondary effect of productive dynamism elsewhere (perhaps on the doorstep of the global city, but possibly on the other side of the world). Thus the framing narrative for contemporary Shanghai is that production matters.

In the literature on global cities, the vitality of productive services features frequently. Thus: 'One of the key properties of the current phase is the ascendance of information technologies and the associated increase in the mobility and liquidity of capital' (Sassen 2009: 3).

But the above remains a descriptor, more or less adequate, of a particular moment of capital accumulation; it does not have sufficient analytical weight or explanatory power. On the other hand, the following formulation, though written in the nineteenth century, does more to explain the further development of the 'global city' in the twenty-first:

> Thus, while capital must on one side strive to tear down every spatial barrier to intercourse, i.e. to exchange, and conquer the whole earth for its market, it strives on the other side to annihilate space with time, i.e. to reduce to the minimum the time spent in motion from one place to another. The more developed the capital, therefore, the more extensive the market over which it circulates, which forms the spatial orbit of it circulation, the more does it strive simultaneously for an ever greater extension of the market and for greater annihilation of space by time. (Marx 1973: 539)

Scholars of the 'global city' would do well to make this their starting point. As deployed in the recent discourse, however, 'global city' is one of a growing number of terms ('globalisation' is its immediate precursor), which represent phenomenal forms but explain little (Lewis and Malone 1996: xxxvi-xlv). To the contrary, 'global city' often serves to elide the distinction between production and circulation; and the effects of this elision are not confined to academia. As they are bedazzled by Prada and Ferrari (Cadwalladr 2007), the bright young things of Shanghai are also plugged into this unhelpful discourse; so too are those among the Party economists and policy makers who have followed the line that designer shopping on the Bund is the cause rather than the result of economic prosperity.

In the same vein, the Chinese officials who arrive (via Oxford) at Bicester Shopping Village, where they do their best to strip the shelves of designer goods, return home with plans to brand their own cities in a quick shift towards a service economy; forgetting, if only temporarily, that the very existence of these cities is typically the result of production, production and more (much more) production.

This is not to deny the importance of the economic cycle as a whole, or more particularly, the significance of productive services, as the lubricant of a dynamic economic entity such as Shanghai. The emerging role of this sector, and in particular the construction of the Hongqiao Central Business District will be discussed later as an expression of Shanghai's potential. But reasserting the primacy of production, serves to avoid the one-sided, and even other worldly incantation that 'globalisation is to blame'. In such a reading, agency is denied to the individual, the corporation, and the nation state, each of which can only be buffeted by the *deus ex machina*, globalisation, which manifested itself, first brightly and now frighteningly, on the computer screens of international markets. Seen from this restricted viewpoint, the present economic order, the structure which is the methodological alter ego of agency, becomes a natural, eternal phenomenon, largely preordained and barely susceptible to any form of human intervention.

Of course, terms such as 'globalisation' and 'global city' were coined in an attempt to explain how we got where we are today. But their logic is disarmingly simple, i.e. its simplicity disarms those who subscribe to it. When we observe, correctly, that human beings did not *decide* on the current state of affairs, it is self-defeating to ascribe current conditions to an autonomous force called 'globalisation'. We might as well capitalise the 'g' and shorten its five syllables to one: God. Alternatively, and this is why even a cursory view of Shanghai is so valuable, it is possible to establish how today's global economy is the expression of the economic decline of a hegemonic power, and, not without problems (some of which are nothing short of disasters), the emergence of new centres of productive and financial activity, such as Shanghai, whose leaders and business people can either repeat the mistakes of the declining economies, or feel out new processes and test out new institutions which may become the instruments in a new configuration of economic and political power.

Shanghai's Second Coming

Shanghai's recent emergence is all the more spectacular if we consider its recent history. Although Shanghai was the key centre of China's first encounter with modernity, in the period after the 1911 revolution, the city effectively became closed off from the world: first through the Japanese invasion and then as a result of Maoist doctrine (Hudson 2008: 162-3, Mitter 2008, Wasserstrom 2009: 77-94). The emblematic city, both of China's modern intelligentsia and the centre of its most powerful working class, was stigmatised under Mao. Stigmatising Shangai chimed in with promoting the petty industrialisation of rural areas in a perverse, inverted elimination of the gap between town and country. Shanghai contributed 350 billion yuan (US$40 billion) in revenue to the central government from 1949 to 1985 but got back only 3.5 billion yuan (US$44 million) for building municipal infrastructure (Chen 2009: xvii).

In the inter-war years Shanghai was already a city of international significance, not only in terms of size and economic development but also with regard to its social energy and cultural production. This legacy of intellectual endeavour, social liberalism and political action, is what made it so alarming to the regime after 1949 (Mitter 2009). To this day, the inter-war experiment in urban living has yet to be reproduced in Shanghai. Indeed, it is striking how much present day Shanghai still harks back to the earlier period in search of its identity. It reproduces the form rather than the innovative content of its most exciting era in the pastiche bar area of Xintiandi and the ubiquitous TV gangster soaps, replete with borsalinos and split skirts.

The economic opening up of Shanghai and the Yangtze Delta took place as much as a decade after the first Special Enterprise Zone, which was announced during Deng's famous southern tour in 1978. Much later, Deng regretted this lost opportunity as his biggest mistake. Shanghai got the green light to get rich in the late 1980s, but the real take off took place in the 1990s, when former Shanghai mayor Jiang Zemin took pole position in Beijing. Jiang's elevation initiated the domination of the party by the Shanghai clique, which came to an end with the arrest on corruption charges, in October 2006, of Shanghai party secretary Chen Liangyu (Chen 2009, Schifferes 2007).

Although Shanghai no longer has the privileged position which it enjoyed for nearly 20 years, its economic position is assured. The Shanghai region, including the adjoining parts of Jiangsu and Zhejiang, accounts for 30 per cent of China's foreign exports and attracts 25 per cent of all foreign investments into the country, while 20 per cent of manufacturing output is produced here. The GDP of the Shanghai region alone is $450 billion, equivalent to half the size of the entire economy of India. Each year more foreign investment flows into Shanghai alone than to any other developing country (Schifferes 2007).

More than 500 multinational companies, ranging from General Motors to Volkswagen, have their regional corporate headquarters in Shanghai. Between 2003 and 2009, more than 50 multinational companies set up regional headquarters in Shanghai. In 1998 Shanghai did not rank in the world's top ten ports, in 2003 it had become the world's third busiest port behind only Hong Kong and Singapore. In 2007, it passed Hong Kong in the number of containers, and is now the world's biggest port (Chen 2009: xix).

Planning the Future

The peculiar feature of Shanghai, and China as a whole, is the close association of both a centralised Five Year Plan, written in considerable detail for application at national, provincial and municipal level, and, at the same time, a capitalist market, red in tooth and claw, ring-fenced by state authority. Translated into inter-personal terms, the quintessential relationship is between a party official and a property developer, though they may turn out to be the same person.

What is intended is therefore, at one level, transparent. It is contained in the 11th Five Year Plan (2006-10), whose overarching rubric was for Xiaokang or balance, between economic development and social justice (reference); and the 12th Five Year Plan (2011-15), whose insistent message is for improvements in social management, or 'strong government and strong society'. The bridge between the two FYPs and the chosen symbol of Shanghai's emerging brand, was Expo 2010, with its associated phrase 'Better City, Better Life' (Hudson 2008: 162, 168).

Both the Five Year Plan and the track record of Expo 2010, present an unambiguous story of consistent success. Here in the UK, or anywhere else in the West, it is only sensible to be sceptical, even cynical, about government claims for economic expansion. In China, however, you can believe the hype (in this respect, at least). Given the terrible historical precedent for the use of the term (Dikotter 2011), it is unfortunate that each section of the 'General Report on the Follow-up effects of Expo 2010 Shanghai China' is described as a 'Great Leap Forward'. But, however turgid, insensitive and dispiriting the official prose may be, it achieves a measure of justification in the reality of the productive economy (Development Report 2011, General Report, Expo 2010, 2011).

The eight 'Great Leaps Forward' can be grouped into two broad themes: economic and social. In the economic sphere success is reported in the internationalisation of the city, with emphasis on cooperation in science and technology, education, culture, economy and trade and tourism. This is linked to upgrading research and development and assimilating new technologies as displayed in the pavilions of the contributing nations. Particular attention is paid to the low-carbon economy. There is a commitment to shift quickly to a service economy but in the context of accelerating new industries 'to form a modern service industry chain'. And finally, an issue to which we will return, the impetus to the regional integration of the cities of the Yangtze River Delta region as the sixth largest core city group in the world.

In the social sphere the emphasis very much follows the tone and content of the 12th Five Year Plan – 'strong government and strong society'. This was further borne out in conversations on the purpose of Expo which I had, in the course of 2009-10, with senior officials and policy makers in Shanghai. Memorable among these was the official who reported that experiencing the logistics of Expo – 'urban security management, volunteer organisation, social mobilisation systems, event organisation, and traffic management' – had helped to engender a sense of society across Shanghai.

It has also, the official report suggests, stimulated innovation in the social management model, prompting Expo volunteers to contribute to social management and community building. Finally, there is an assertion that it has greatly boosted the promotion of Shanghai's soft power.

Better City, Better Life

Shanghai Expo 2010 was a public stepping stone in this development but a step designed primarily to give the world a favourable vantage point on Shanghai. Expo was a public declaration of Shanghai's significance. Apart from the integration of the Expo site into plans for the long-term economic development of the area, it was also engineered to train its citizens in a manner the government thought would be appropriate for international status; though this is not how it is presented in the official summary of its success.

I conducted a three-stage, informal survey of 80 volunteers, citizens and civil servants: first, during the autumn of 2009, about six months before Expo began; again, at the beginning of Expo in the spring of 2010; and, finally, toward its end in the autumn of 2010. I also conducted detailed interviews with leading policy makers and planners, a workshop with Shanghai students, and street interviews around Shanghai.

The dynamic economic development of Shanghai means that the government can put trains, housing and employment all in the same place. Shanghai now has more skyscrapers than New York and a public transport system bigger than London's. The Expo site was at the heart of the urban redevelopment of both the city region and the city core. The plan was also to green the old industrial areas along the Huangpu river. All of this could be seen in a scale model, the size of a basketball court, on public exhibit in downtown Shanghai. But Shanghai's boom years were already well underway, so why have the Expo at all?

This was my first question to thc planners. To which the unanimous first response was that it would help to build up the infrastructure. Senior planners suggested that this was an integral part of the 11th Five Year Plan. In response to my observation that the Shanghai government seemed perfectly capable of building an effective city infrastructure without recourse to such a huge demand on resources, the replies became more interesting and nuanced. The planners argued that the pressure of the deadline and the scale of the enterprise would stimulate the human resource capabilities of the thousands of administrative and technical experts involved in the planning and execution of Expo. Moreover, the fact that this could be done would be indicative that Shanghai had arrived as a Global City. The oft repeated mantra was: 'Let the Chinese see the world; and the world see China'. The success of the human resource exercise and the global branding are both reported as successes.

Making Citizens

But this was often only the preamble to a much more telling explanation. Expo 2010 was, both planners and volunteers insisted, a powerful instrument for educating the citizen. The argument was that Shanghainese had to be moulded into acceptable inhabitants of a new global city.

The mechanisms and processes through which this may be achieved are of great interest to Chinese policy makers. One side of the answer is immediately in their own hands: economic growth. The second component – social justice – is the element which eludes them, and for which they seek practical and technical answers such as consultative procedures. Beyond this and in accord with the two traditions of Chinese thought and Western sociology, the aim is to manipulate of the environment in such a way as to educate citizens and improve the quality of their citizenship. The Chinese call this *suzhi* or 'population quality' (Murphy 2004: 1-20). The idea is that individuals carry with them a capacity and a responsibility to be good citizens. The word can be used in common speech but it also features in central government discourse where it serves to assign responsibility for poverty to individual failing rather than to the erosion of the national welfare system. The government, in turn, must find ways to encourage and inculcate good behaviour. Those without 'quality' must be educated, or trained, in citizenship.

However, it is far from clear how much of an impact, or long term effect, this may have. This particular response was almost entirely absent in the interviews with ordinary citizens. It was more pervasive in the volunteer response. It is clear that this rubric was a significant element in volunteer training, where it is a familiar technique: instil the appropriate attitudes in a new cohort, at the entry point, who will then transmit the new culture to a wider audience. But for most of my volunteer interviewees, Expo was a disappointing experience. It was hard work, the whole event was not of the quality they had expected, and at the end they would return to being unemployed graduates.

Furthermore such fixations have already proved difficult to translate into new social habits. In my autumn 2009 stay I was struck by a municipal campaign to end the habit of the local population wearing pyjamas to the shops. Again young volunteers were primed with lines from a script: 'Dear Auntie, do you think it reflects well on our city to go outside in your pyjamas?' In the past, and still in the old city, this was the habit because the shops were, quite literally, on your doorstep. Pyjamas were also a status symbol: they prove that you can afford unique sleepwear! And as such the campaign had little impact.

The social role of Expo was to integrate the citizen as a component part of the plan, with the citizenry appearing as a distinct but ultimately controllable factor. Not quite the engineering of souls, but, in the historic spirit of urban sociology, adjusting the responses of the citizen in alignment with the plan and, allegedly, the best interests of both. This theorisation of the city, derived from both Chicago city planners and the Chicago School of sociologists, is attractive to Chinese academics – not least since the agent of progressive change remains the planner rather than the unpredictable citizen (Hudson 2008: 162, 168).

Chinese officials are very much aware of the erosion of the citizens' trust in them as individuals, the question mark over the legitimacy of their institutions, and the potential for civil dissatisfaction and opposition. However, all this is perceived as a technical problem with a technical solution. Thus for this group also, the priority for the 12th Five Year plan becomes social management. Shanghai Expo 2010 offered an interesting example of how Chinese planners understand urbanisation and how the city works. If there were a model, it might be described as 'efficient corruption', in that the hard infrastructure gets built and public facilities are improved via state intervention but with windfall profits, to put it mildly, for developers. But with the hollowing out of the core city, no one will yet say what will happen on this huge site. There is no wider understanding that the separation of economic growth from public engagement may not only be problematic but actually detract from the vitality and ambience of the city.

Hongqiao Central Business District

Shanghai was, and still is, a major production centre. Its economy is more diverse now and much of the heavier and dirtier industry has been displaced to the city region and beyond. But it is still the locus and the designated focus of the productive dynamism of the lower Yangtze Delta, embracing the Shanghai Municipality itself, as well as crucial areas of the rich provinces of Zhejiang (and its capital Hangzhou); Jiangsu, including the historic capital city of Nanjing; Suzhou, and also Ningbo, in the province of Anhui. The Yangtze connects Shanghai to Wuhan, in Hubei province, and through the Three Gorges to Chongqing and even into Sichuan.

In order for the whole of this economic region to be integrated it has to be linked in terms of transport and other key elements of infrastructure. This is the driver for the restructuring of the Shanghai economy within the context of the productive capacity of the region. While manufacturing's percentage share of regional GDP fell from 77.4 per cent in 1978 to 50.1 per cent in 1997, in 2006 it was still 50.6 per cent. The parallel figures for services, as a percentage of GDP were 18.6, 47.8 and 50.6 per cent respectively (Chen 2009: xxviii). This figure reflects the myriad small retail outlets of old Shanghai. The municipal state, the active agent and driver of the shift to services, intends to boost the productive service sector and attract more international companies through discretionary terms and attractive living conditions for foreign companies (Wu 2009: 125-45, Zhang 2009: 167-91).

What has been described to me as the last major infrastructural project in Shanghai, the Shanghai Hongqiao Central Business District (CBD) is designed to re-balance the service sector away from low grade facilities and employment (Wholesale, retail and catering as percentage of Service Sector GDP, 21.4 per cent in 2003, the last year for which the whole breakdown is complete) to Transport, Storage and Communication, 13.9 per cent in 2003 and Finance and Insurance, 20.6 per cent in 2003 (Chen 2009: xxviii, Liu and Chiu 2009: 93-125). The 'rebalancing' of the economy is seen as crucial by Shanghai's policy makers since although the city is regarded as having a competitive advantage *vis-à-vis* Hong Kong in its traditional industrial sectors Hong Kong still leads in sophisticated service industries: financial services, investment banking and logistics.

A new executive authority has been established by the Shanghai Municipality to supervise this project. This is no small beer since it involves coordinating the activities of 22 government and para-statal agencies, including five police forces. Nevertheless, the research phase will be completed in 18 months, the plan presented by 2012, and the project will be completed in the following five years.

Hongqiao is already developed as a transport hub. It is the site of Shanghai's second and more domestically oriented airport and will be the terminus for the high-speed rail link to Beijing (4.5 hours), Hangzhou (38 minutes), Nanjing (42 minutes). The multidirectional high speed network will create the fusion of the Yangtze River Delta's 'half-hour circle'. The projected daily human traffic flow is 1.4 million.

The current population of the core CBD area of 3.7 square kilometres, is 50,000; and 650 000 in the entire designated area of 26 square kilometres. By 2020 the core area will have a population of 150,000 and the wider area a population of 1.2 million. So with a projected population growth of nearly 600,000, there is no shortage of energy and ambition (interview with project director, in Shanghai 4 April 2011).

Low carbon technologies and high-speed communication for a smart city are already *de rigeur* in Chinese cities. Shanghai already has 12 metro lines, five of which pass through the transport hub. Early reports of the content of Shanghai's 12th FYP indicate IT infrastructure as a key priority. Shanghai's mayor, Han

Zheng, has pledged to invest 100 billion yuan (circa £10 billion) in support of the city's key industries: IT, bio-tech industries, high-end equipment manufacturing, new energy and the new materials sector (China Analytics 2010). The low carbon city is already built into the Hongqiao CBD plan. Not as a green argument against growth or as an apologetic rationalisation of lack of funding, but as capital investment for the twenty-first century (Yang 2010).

Noticeably absent was any discussion about the involvement of the people who are and would be living there. This is not because the planners had no concern for the population. The whole idea was through economic growth to realise the slogan of Expo 2010: 'Better City, Better Life'. In an interview, a senior member of the project team, told me: 'Of course construction companies can build in the core area where former residents have moved to a large residential district nearby'. While the overall population will increase, it will involve the displacement of the present residents and their replacement by a population geared to the central function of the new CBD: 'We expect the area will grow into a high-end innovation business center for the Yangtze Delta Region and that urban development of suburban Qingpu and Songjiang districts can be fostered as well', he continued (Wang 2009).

This ambitious project opens up exciting commercial prospects. As one happy development company announced, having won a slice of the action:

'The New Central Business District will be an energy efficient and environmentally conscious development characterised by its highly pedestrian-friendly environment. Located next to what will become the world's largest intermodal transit facility, the development will focus on reducing carbon dioxide emissions through a series of sustainable strategies, such as integration of highly efficient transportation systems, rain water collection and on-site water treatment, on-site renewable energy generation, and energy efficient building envelopes and systems' (Skidmore, Owings and Merill 2009).

The autonomous activity of the citizen is not part of the formula. The citizen is designed to be the passive recipient of an impressive plan, materially better off, displaced from the much of the old city, but disengaged from the city's future except as a factor to be managed. Since the urbanisation of China is acknowledged policy and has to take place to facilitate economic growth and social justice, then the creativity of the urban dweller necessarily requires an outlet. This much is recognised in the official discourse; but it has yet to find a recognisable form, either officially or even unofficially.

Situating Shanghai

The emergence of Shanghai, as a leading player but by no means the only Chinese player on the world stage, also reposes the discussion between economic power and political control in the international, national and regional environment: China in the world, Shanghai in China, and Shanghai in the Yangtze Delta.

The historical development of the first tier of global cities (London, Paris, New York) suggests that although manufacturing need not remain dominant either inside thc city walls nor even within the immediate vicinity, nonetheless it will have been a crucial factor in the first attainment of international status. The recent development of Shanghai only serves to affirm that any city in the running for such status is likely to have been forged through the productive dynamism of the surrounding area. This means that the expansion of production is a necessary precondition for such development, though not a sufficient basis for it.

If anyone needs reminding that the financial crisis occasioned a step change in global economic relations, then the following examples will serve to illustrate the changing relationship between the Chinese and the US economy:

- The eastern, replacement, span of the San Francisco Bay Bridge is to be built in Shanghai and transported the 10,500 kilometres to Oakland for the opening in 2013. The total cost of the whole project (the western span is merely being renovated), is $7.2 billion. The contract with Shanghai Zhenhua Heavy Industries is estimated to save $400 million on the cost of having the job done in California. In Shanghai there is a low cost, but also highly skilled workforce, often working seven days a week from 7.00am until 11.00pm, sleeping in company dormitories – and all this for $12 a day. Besides the cost savings, it is equally important that this labour force works in enormous, modern steel fabrication facilities, which have won further contracts for Congolese copper mines, high speed rail links in Brazil and apartment complexes in Saudi Arabia. All this is backed up by the full financial weight of the Chinese government, which supports infrastructure companies who take on work of this monumental scale (*The New York Times* 2011).
- In a different and emerging market, *The New York Times* reports that the 'Chinese Eclipse America's solar future' (Woody 2010). Chinese solar panel makers now supply about 40 per cent of the Californian market, itself the largest in the United States. A JAS Shanghai executive stated: 'At the end of the year (2011), we will have 1.8 gigawatts of capacity and will have grown from 4,000 employees at the beginning of the year to more than 11 000' (ibid. At the same time a leading Silicon Valley company, Solyndra, reported an expected total production capacity of 300 megawatts by the end of 2011 – a figure which is dwarfed by the activities of their Chinese counterparts. The USA still has an innovative edge, but a drop in silicon prices, access to the key material, government subsidies and mass production keep Chinese companies ahead of their smaller US competitors.

The result of such development is that Shanghai in particular, and China in general, are becoming more attractive to those high status activities, such as the 'creative industries', which still mark out the superior position enjoyed by successful western economies. It is also notable that these industries seem to have a unique appeal to the contemporary imagination, East and West. If in this respect there is something of a convergence, in the way that status is handed out (and taken back), significant discrepancies remain between the two hemispheres. Clark Marcus, a partner in a US West Coast architecture firm, and president of the American Institute of Architecture, told *The New York Times*: 'The US political establishment is mostly attorneys. In China, the highest ranking officials tend to be engineers. They see a problem, they allocate money and effort toward a solution' (*The New York Times* 2011). Whereas in the USA and Europe, lawyers are typically drafted in to securitise a problem – ratify distribution of the risks it is thought to contain – rather than solve it.

Nonetheless, the acolytes and senior employees of just this kind of western company are now making their presence felt in the fashionable bars of Shanghai. It remains to be seen whether, on the one hand, Shanghai's cultural capital and cachet will fully capture them; or more importantly, how long it will take Chinese companies to take over the 'creative work' for themselves.

Shanghai in the World

Shanghai cannot follow the exact historical trajectory of London and New York because those cities will remain powerful players and their orbit and gravitational pull must affect developments in global economic arrangements. Nevertheless, with its manufacturing prowess, infrastructural and technological innovation, alongside its trading, shipping and now financial ambition, Shanghai is set to be at, or near, the top of many global league tables.

A key moment for Shanghai, and for China as a whole, will be full convertibility for the RMB (Brown 2007, Gao 2009, Leung 2007, Roubini 2009). This has been the subject of intense discussion across the world in the last few years, and especially since the financial crisis when Chinese holdings of US government debt became crucial to global economic stability. It is itself a signal of how the world has changed that the discussion is at its most intense in the highest policy making circles in Beijing; and here, and only here, will the decision be made.

For the People's Republic to nail its economic emergence, and potentially relegate the dollar, as the dollar previously sidelined sterling, then the RMB must be open to global trading and become an insurgent reserve currency. So far Beijing has merely mooted a basket of currencies, moving to diversify its currency holdings and establish the RMB as a regional currency *vis-à-vis* some of its ASEAN neighbours. The limits to the progress of the RMB are not economic, however; they are largely political. Beijing, true to its political tradition, is fearful of full convertibility, with the corresponding loss of total and central control. Yet it can only be a matter of time before the pressing need of the Chinese economy to transform raw muscle into more sophisticated policy instruments, impels a conversion in Beijing.

Shanghai in China

Such a move would not only suit Shanghai but also the other significant economic powerhouses in the Chinese economy, notably Beijing/Tianjin and Hong Kong, and the Pearl River Delta. Insiders in Shanghai are still circumspect about whether Shanghai is really seen in Beijing as China's most valuable asset, this despite the State Council directive we have discussed. It is in the nature of Chinese politics to keep even the most illustrious guessing, and even the favoured can fall from grace. The idea that the personal is political, has a special meaning in China.

There is also a serious argument in favour of Hong Kong as the best vantage point for the next stage of China's economic and financial growth, especially in the light of Hong Kong's international outlook, its recent history and reputation for conviviality. But this is not how it looks in Beijing. Hong Kong is too far away; it is an unwelcome reminder of political disintegration earlier this century; it is not yet part of the same political and administrative system; and it is Cantonese. So despite Shanghainese concerns born of the experience of the arbitrary nature of life at the top of the greasy pole, Shanghai is still the best bet to become the most rounded citadel of Chinese economic power.

Shanghai and the Yangtze Delta

We can expect the economy and culture of the Shanghai region, if not the politics, to undergo a disjuncture with its own hinterland and nation state. In the same way that New York and London have more in common with each other than with Iowa and Macclesfield respectively, such are the characteristics of global cities. This is much more akin to the relationship that Hong Kong now has to the Pearl River Delta and the rest of mainland China, rather than the city state of Singapore with which Shanghai is often compared. (Ho 2009: 73-93)

In Shanghai's case this is a disjuncture more to do with the cultural experience of the poorer, western provinces, such as Yunnan. The whole of the Yangtze Delta is economically developed, although there are political tensions. True to the conceptualisation of the global city as a city-region, Shanghai is now the epicentre, or as Shanghai's own public officials and policy makers dub it, 'the big brother' of a network of cities including Hangzhou, Suzhou and even Nanjing (cities which are in their own right, significant economic and political players).

When Shanghai describes itself as a big brother it does not go down well with representatives of such historic and powerful cities such as Nanjing and Hangzhou, respectively the capitals of Jiangsu and Zhejiang provinces. The administrative divisions across the Yangtze Delta make for political conflict in aspects of economic policy such as the distribution of cutting-edge industries, from nanotechnology to bio-engineering. These industries find the universities, and especially the ambience, of Hangzhou and Suzhou, very attractive; and unsurprisingly, the governments of Jiangsu and Zhejiang do not see themselves merely as the next destination for Shanghai's displaced heavy (and dirty) industries.

At the time of writing (September 2011), the only regional political mechanism for discussing and resolving such potentially antagonistic situations is a quarterly meeting at mayoral-governor level. This is important but it also points to the limitations of effective discussion in all Chinese policy-making and communication. This is a barrier at all levels of Chinese society.

Conclusion

Critical commentators (Hutton 2008, Jacques 2009) have argued that China's political system presents an insuperable barrier to sustained economic progress. Nolan has claimed that China is still economically subordinate to the multinationals. Whatever view is taken of China's authoritarian regime, and of the domestic danger of holding too many dollars, this is a serious misreading of capitalist development, at least since the days of Bismarck's Germany and Meiji Japan.

Shanghai's economic development is as secure as anywhere in the world, if not immune either to the inherent instability of the global system or its own real estate bubble; and not forgetting the typical avarice of its new elites. There is also little doubt that Shanghai's own, world-class universities can provide the talent to sustain economic diversification. A generation ago the brightest young things would have made for Silicon Valley and Wall Street (or they would have wanted to); now it is possible to fly high without flying the coop.

But how exciting and livable will the new Shanghai be? Will it taste blandly homogenous in the manner of international airport terminals, up-market hotels and conference centres? Or will it be a city in which its own sensibility, creativity and urban excitement speak of a new and appropriate tale of the way we live? At the very least can it again be the Shanghai of the 1930s, let alone the New York of the Jazz Age? These are wide-open questions, which can only be answered by the people of Shanghai themselves.

References[1]

Brown, K. (2007). *China goes Global*, Open Democracy, available at http://www.opendemocracy_power/china/foreign_investment, 10 October 2007.

Cadwalladr, C. (2007). *The Great Leap Forward*, *Observer* Magazine 21 January 2007, 33-41.

Chen, X. (2009). *Rising Shanghai, State Power and Local Transformations in a Global Megacity.* Minneapolis, MN and London: University of Minnesota Press.

1 All websites last accessed 31st July 2011.

Dikolter, F. (2011). *Mao's Great Famine: The History of China's Most Devastating Catastrophe, 1958-62.* London: Bloomsbury.

Gao, V.Z. (2009). *China's Heart of Gold, The New York Times* Op. Ed. Contributor, available at http://www.nytimes.com/2009/05/14/opinion/14gao.html?pagewanted=print, 16 May 2009.

Heartfield, J. (1998). *Need and Desire in the Post-Material Economy.* Sheffield: Sheffield Hallam University Press.

Heartfield, J. (2000). *Great Expectations: The Creative Industries in the New Economy.* London: Design Agenda.

Ho, K.C. (2009). 'Competitive Urban Economic Policies in Global Cities, Shanghai through the Lens of Singapore', in Chen Xiangming, *Shanghai Rising.*

Hudson, A. (2008). 'Mr Science and Mr Democracy, the pursuit of modernity in China, *CITY*, 12(2), July 2008, 161-70.

Hutton, W. (2008). *The Writing on the Wall: China and the West in the Twenty First Century.* London: Abacus.

Industrial Policy in China and the 12th Five Year Plan (2011-2015). China Analytics, 12 October 2010.

Jacques, M. (2009). *When China Rules the World: The Rise of the Middle Kingdom and the End of the Western World.* London: Allen Lane.

Leadbeater, C. (2000). *Living on Thin Air: The New Economy*, London: Penguin.

Leung, A.K.P. (2007). *The Chinese Dimension of the Global Credit Crunch*, available at www.andrewleunginternationalconsultants.com, 27 August 2007.

Lewis N. and Malone, J. (eds) (1996). Lenin V.I. *Imperialism the Highest Stage of Capitalism*, London: Junius/Pluto Press.

Lui, T.L. and Chiu, Stephen W.K. (2009). 'Becoming a Chinese Global City Hong Kong (and Shanghai) beyond the Global-local Duality' in Chen Xiangming, *Shanghai Rising.*

Marx, K. (1973). *Grundrisse.* London: Penguin.

Mitter, R. (2005). *A Bitter Revolution: China's Struggle with the Modern World.* Oxford: Oxford University Press.

Mitter, R. (2008). *Modern China: A Very Short Introduction.* Oxford: Oxford University Press.

Murphy, R., 'Turning peasants into modern Chinese citizens: "Population quality" discourse, demographic transition and primary education', *The Chinese Quarterly*, March 2004, 1-20.

Observer/New York Times 30 January 2011, 8.

Observer/New York Times, 3 July 2011, 4.

Roubini, N. (2009). *The Almighty Renminbi?* A The New York Times Op-Ed. Contributor, available at http://www.nytimes.com/2009/05/14/opinion/14Roubini.html?pagewanted=print, 16 May 2009.

Sassen, S. (2009). 'The Global City Perspective Theoretical Implications for Shanghai', in *Shanghai Rising, State Power and Local Transformations in a Global Megacity*, edited by Xiangming Chen. Minneapolis, MN and London: University of Minnesota Press.

Schifferes, S. (2007). 'Shanghai creating a global city', *BBC News*, available at http://newsvote.bbc.co.uk/mpopps/pagetools/point/news.bbc.co.uk/1/hi/business/6618163, 27 December 2007.

Shanghai Municipal Government (2011). *Development Report of Shanghai International Economic, Financial, Trading and Shipping Centers*, available at www.hibooks.cn.

Shanghai Municipal Government (2011). *General Report*, follow up effects of Expo 2010.

Visser, R. (2010). *Cities Surround the Countryside: Urban Aesthetics in Post-Socialist China.* Durham, NC: Duke University Press.

Wang Zhongwei, speech as head of the publicity department of CPC Shanghai, 16 September 2009.

Wasserstrom, J.N. (2009). *Global Shanghai, 1850-2010: A History in Fragments.* London and New York: Routledge.

Woody, T. (2010). *China Eclipses America's Solar Future, Observer/New York Times*, 31 October, 3.

Wu Fulong (2009). 'Globalization, the Changing State, and Local Governance in Shanghai', in Chen Xiangming, *Shanghai Rising.*

Yang Wenyao, *Practice and Innovation of Low-Carbon Concept in the Planning of Hongqiao Business District.* 46th ISOCARP Congress 2010.

Zhang Tingwei (2009). 'Striving to be a Global city from below, The Restructuring of Shanghai's Urban Districts', in Chen Xiangming *Shanghai Rising.*

Chapter 4
Finance and Culture: Twin Towers in London's Lightness of Being

Andrew Calcutt

Between the Royal Wedding at the end of April 2011 and the opening of the Olympic Games in July 2012, London's status as global city of culture received further confirmation in the hit movie of summer 2011. *Cars 2*, which defied critics to gross $476m worldwide sales in its first month on release (Richwine 2011), is a Disney Pixar film about animated cars struggling to save the world from a dastardly plot to discredit alternative fuel and revert to Big Oil. When the conspiracy reaches its climax, the scene shifts to the most evocative location on earth: London; complete with two sets of royalty – the centuries-old English monarchy and the 50-year-old court of British popular culture.

As worldwide audiences call on Pixar to animate their interests and concerns, so Pixar's storytellers called on London as the universal location – the place that everyone in the world already feels connected to. While cities such as Beijing have recently entered the world stage by staging the Olympics (2008), London has no need to make such an entrance; it is already centre stage. Hence its Olympiad (2012) has been an attempt not to win worldwide attention but to avoid losing it.

London's place in the real world rests on its position in the collective imagination; and the role of the imagination is as real for capital as it is for human beings. In finance – the kind of economic activity which London excels in, capital imagines its own actualisation and conjures up an advance on its own potential growth. Meanwhile, humanity receives belated recognition in the other sort of activity which London is renowned for – the composition of art and culture. As the home of both sets of imaginings, London really is the fictitious capital of the world.

But what accounts for London's capital status? What does the rest of the world see in London? How does the world see itself reflected in a city which has been in something like decline for almost a century? As capital of a country which has been losing economic power and political authority for a hundred years, what is it about London that outsiders readily identify with, even from inside fast-growing conurbations whose political and economic development is diametrically opposed to Britain's long-term decline?

This chapter addresses such questions with the suggestion that something more than mere proximity connects London's current cultural role with its contemporary financial function. London's twin towers – finance and culture – exist not only alongside each other: the one is already inside the other; inherent in what is also its opposite. However, what goes on inside each of these structures now takes place largely outside the general relation of capital and labour in production, and beyond the first of its economic laws – the law of value. Up to a point, London has lived well from such law-breaking. But the city which lives beyond its means, which has taken the opportunity to live beyond what capitalism generally means, is also blighted with a peculiar lightness of being.

London-lite is easily unnerved. In recent years, this city has undergone two dramatic episodes – the credit crunch of 2007-9 and the phone-hacking scandal of 2011, in which its propensity for living on thin air thickened overnight into a crisis of self-confidence. These episodes had much in common. Each represented a reaction to unchecked escalation: first of personal debt; then of personal disclosure. Each was something of a reality-check; but in both instances, the descent into crisis turned out to be as unchecked as the prior escalation. In these moments, when lightness of being became suddenly unbearable, London glimpsed its own estrangement from the rest of the world, and acknowledged the extent to which it has flouted the standards that the rest of the world is expected to live by, even while continuing to perform as the greatest show on earth.

But if London is the city that the rest of the world can identify with, not all Londoners feel the same way about it. In early August 2011, the riots that took place across London were led by young men who displayed, not least for the benefit of iPhones, Facebook pages and TV cameras, extreme alienation from this city, its representatives, and all that it represents. Though extreme, their estrangement can hardly have been absolute or the rioters would not have cared about being seen (by others) to be alienated. Instead, they performed a riotous spectacle partly in order to gain the world's attention. Conversely, in the attention economy their value increased along with successive images of their disaffection.

Though the rioters were unanimously condemned by London's politicians and police (*The Sun* 9 August 2011), their actions had much in common with the way London operates in today's world economy. The riots were an eruption of contempt for the law of property; London's inflated markets – in the City, but also including the housing market, are equally contemptuous of the law of value. Aside from their financial gains, the rioters were, above all, a spectacle; similarly, for billions of people throughout the rest of the world, London is a spectacular rendition of the seemingly unfettered life that they themselves are unable to lead.

At the time of the riots, concerns were expressed about the damaging effect on London's reputation. But London's cultural reputation partly depends on its capacity to represent disaffection, and the riots only confirmed its capability. London could not be cool without this, the essential complement to the city's other role as the ancient embodiment of common purpose and social cohesion – old-fashioned qualities which may seem anachronistic to today's Londoners, yet millions of outsiders are prepared to come to London in order to experience them as tourists (GLA Economics 2011). By selective reference to both its past and its present, for the benefit of the outside world London is able to *do* alienation and integration at the same time; while for many of its inhabitants the city they live in does next to nothing.

Again, there is a correspondence between the duality of London's cultural dimension (integration and alienation as represented in the selective curation of London past and present), and the ambiguous character of the financial services which the city also provides. In that capitalist finance is ultimately the financing of (future) production, and, similarly, at however many steps removed, it is also derived from previous rounds of such production, in these aspects it represents continuity in productive activity. But in that it is not production – moreover, as it becomes increasingly bound up in its own circuits, it is also the suspension and eventually the negation of production, so finance also represents alienation from productive activity, to a degree in keeping with the spectacular estrangement displayed by London's rioters in August 2011. Hence finance itself is variously integrated with and alienated from capitalist production; and its shares this ambiguity with London's culture, past and present.

Neither the distance between finance and production, nor the proximity of one to the other, is fixed for all time and in all places. Thus, even between the covers of this volume, chapters on Shanghai and New York reveal that the social position of finance is different in each of these two cities, and different again from its position in London today.

Similarly, at different times in one and the same city of London, finance has been both integrated with production, and, as it is now, further removed from it. Moreover, such is the level of correspondence between financial activity and cultural activity that at any given time, the current relation of finance to production, i.e. whether these two are less integrated and more alienated from one another, finds an echo in contemporary culture. Taking three points in time – 1811, 1911 and 2011 – this chapter will indicate how on each occasion contemporary cultural formulations have kept time with the financial activity of the day and its characteristic relation to production. Furthermore, by forming these three points into a guideline, it will be suggested that alienation has become the overriding feature of London's culture at the same time that its financial activity has come to be defined by increased estrangement from productive activity, much of which has moved out of the UK altogether, in a long march East (Poynter 2010).

This movement has not only changed the nature of London's financial activity; it has also affected the contemporary cultural experience of Londoners. Though judicious deployment of past and present allows London culture to stand for both harmony and dissonance in the eyes of the rest of the world, this does little for the millions of Londoners who are commonly alienated from the harmonious (re)construction of London's past – its so-called heritage. When so many of the city's inhabitants are only at home with the present-day culture of alienation, their experience tends to be as imbalanced as London's over-reliance on financial services. Accordingly, while London's economy has become strongly identified with a particular form of finance that is peculiarly estranged from production, so alienation has become almost a whole way of life for London. The flash mob riots of August 2011 were an especially intense expression of this, but by no means out of character with the life course of many Londoners. Rather, widespread estrangement is the necessary complement of London's disembodiment. Being alienated pervades a city that exists on thin air and persists in lightness of being. How different this is from earlier times when both finance and culture were grounded in the original development of capitalist production (1811) and its subsequent extension into Empire (1911).

Some Enchanted Evening (1811)

The airiest of airs, gracefully extended into a symphonic movement; throughout this particular movement, there is no sound that does not bear some relation to the opening cluster of notes, however fleeting they may have seemed on first hearing. Yet in all its 11 minutes and more, there is barely an instance of straightforward repetition. Instead, these first notes are drawn into a process of continuation, transition and transformation. The process is complex but not obtuse. During its development, successive, related motifs are revised, diverted and asserted; divided and multiplied – doubled, tripled and quadrupled; dissolved and resolved; inverted and reformulated. No wonder the sections of a symphony are described as its *movements*.

The symphony is Beethoven's, and the movement referred to is the first of his sixth, the *Pastoral* (1808). It was first heard by the London public on 27 May 1811, in a concert at the Hanover Square Rooms given by a Mrs Vaughan (Grove 1903: 224). We can only imagine the scene as the (small) orchestra began to play, illuminated by a mixture of candlelight and the evening sunlight of England's early summer. With hindsight we can see that the dynamic form of Beethoven's composition, heard for the first time in London that evening, complemented what was going on at that very moment, both inside and outside the concert rooms, namely, the immediate composition of a single audience from the various individuals in attendance, and, more widely, the original composition of the first-ever capital city based on capitalist production.

In the following paragraphs, this chapter shows how each of these different compositions – musical, convivial, societal – entailed abstraction from that which previously existed, and the precise formulation, the bringing into existence, of something new. Thus there are three movements to be considered, each of them different but all of them related. Subsequent sections of this chapter will consider how such movements, in all their variations, may have become equally restricted, to the detriment of London and its people.

Beethoven's *Pastoral* symphony is an evocation of country life. The opening movement expresses joy at being in the country, as expressed by someone coming to it on a visit. Having extricated himself from the village, in this symphony the urbane man goes on to describe country life for himself. Far removed from the peasant farmer, Beethoven's position resembles that of Capability Brown (1716-

83), who landscaped the enormous gardens of great English houses to look like the countryside. In their abstraction from the rural, both men formulated a new experience of it.

In this instance, Beethoven's orientation to his particular subject matter is consistent with the general position of the nineteenth century composer in relation to his music. In a period of extensive, formal development, each symphony was expected to offer a new experience of music, actualised in the continuous development of symphonic form. Great innovators such as Beethoven forced themselves past all existing formulations in almost every piece they wrote.

Accordingly, in nearly all his compositions, Beethoven sought to arrive at a new point in the developing history of music. In order to establish this, his original position, he was first obliged to engage with all the music that already existed. Though he was to become profoundly deaf, in his composer's ear Beethoven was still listening to everything that everyone else had ever played or written (as far as he could retain it), and struggling to extricate himself from all their previous particulars. As he composed each work, Beethoven's inner ear became the site of a general relation between musical components already formulated by other musicians. In his abstraction from their particulars, he was also addressing other people's work in order to supersede it. Yet the only way to hear what lay beyond their work, was to write down that general relation in the form of a new piece of music; to give musical form to that moment of abstraction from already existing music. Thus Beethoven arrived at his music by dancing between the particular and the general, abstraction and formulation; all the bars in each movement of his every *opus*, originate in this dialectical movement.

The composition of Beethoven's audience contained something of the same dance moves. Not that his listeners were dancing, literally; and without wishing to equate the concert-goer's leisurely activity with Beethoven's gargantuan efforts, nonetheless it was by their active engagement with the movements entailed in his music, that the various individuals who took their seats in the Hanover Square Rooms, were transformed into a single audience. Out of many, particular persons, they composed themselves as one, general relation – the audience. Their unity was both a particular formation and an abstraction from the particular individuals who had earlier entered the concert hall. In this *pas de deux*, their composition was an echo of Beethoven's.

In Hanover Square on 27th May 1811, audience members moved from being particular persons to become part of a whole. The general whole – the audience – was an abstraction from its particular constituents. Yet while it was *the* audience – in general, it was also *an* audience, i.e. the audience particular to a specific concert on a designated day. Thus the movement entailed in forming an audience was both an abstraction from personal particulars and the formulation of a further particular. Again, these (sedentary) activities resembled the movements undertaken by Beethoven in the act of composition – abstraction from the old and specification of the new.

There was yet further correspondence between the composition of Beethoven's audience and the contemporary composition of a new, capitalist society. During the seventeenth and eighteenth centuries, when capital was mainly deployed to finance trade, capitalist society was largely confined to trading centres such as London. But in the late eighteenth and nineteenth centuries, capital was increasingly exported from London into the regions in order to finance manufacturing (Rubin 1979); hence London was transformed from a merchant city into the executive head and trading arm of the world's first manufacturing nation (Brown 1991). Not that industrial capital supplanted merchant capital entirely – certainly not in London, the capital city that contained them both. But their relationship changed; and with this change came unprecedented change in social relations – the ways in which people relate to each other.

As they entered into a nationwide system of newly built factories, each, particular group of labourers was transformed into an equivalent portion of labour – productive human activity in general. Each labourer was now also part of a new relation between all labourers – a general relation which had not previously existed. These people now existed in two forms at the same time: once as their personal selves; and again as their social or societal selves, in their capacity as part of the general relation between productive human beings.

Out of many was composed one labour.

The composition of the general relation of labour entailed a process of abstraction from particular labourers. Labour in general was brought into being by productive capital, the privately owned formulation of previous social activity, now used to purchase labour power employed in the next round of productive activity. (The term 'productive capital' is not meant to suggest that capital is productive on its own; only labour – the general form of human activity, has this capacity. 'Productive capital' is used here to designate capital deployed in production, to distinguish it from capital which continues to move through financial circuits).

Productive capital generated specific activities (manufacturing) in order to generate an even bigger claim on human activity in general. This claim was realised as value, and partly redeployed as capital, i.e. re-invested in another round of manufacturing. Thus the general relation as a whole, came into existence as a combination of capital as well as labour; yet capital values are privately-owned claims on a particular portion of social activity – labour. In nineteenth-century Britain, therefore, the emergence of labour was the actualisation of the general relation in its social form, while the establishment of capital amounted to the general relation, privatised.

Conversely, both parties – labour and capital – were generalities. As generalities, neither labour nor capital was directly tangible; they could only be encountered in the form of many capitals and as many groups of particular labourers, each deployed by one of many capitals and employed by the person(s) who happened to own it. But this does not mean that labour and capital, at that time, were only vague phenomena; or that they are only a mental construct of ours. Labour and capital were real generalities (like the audience for the first London performance of the *Pastoral* symphony), which came into existence at a specific period in history (just as that audience came into being on a particular evening); and their coming into existence gave that period its precise definition, namely, the development of generalised commodity production. In other words, the new historical reality of labour and capital – the general, social relation – was also the composition of a mature capitalist society.

As in Beethoven's music and the composition of his audience, the construction of capitalist society occurred in a kind of dance between abstraction and formulation. The general form of productive activity, labour, came into existence as an abstraction from particular branches of production (in pre-capitalist epochs, these branches were never so readily comparable nor so accurately calibrated); but the generalisation of human activity was also oriented to the formulation of specific products, which were themselves transformed into particular values, i.e. proportionate claims on human activity in general. And so the dance went on – swerving from the abstract to the concrete and *vice versa*; sweeping the old ways aside in a new social movement; and encompassing the arts and 'society' – Mrs Vaughan's concert-goers as well as their Beethoven, alongside production and finance.

The Weight of Empire (1911)

This symphony begins with a restless swirl of notes, like the folds in a lady's silk dress as she moves, or the swell of the sea. The second movement manages to contain its melancholy, but only just: it includes a dangerously slow march (the Emperor is dead, the whole city poised to mourn him in the caesura between one footstep and the next). The third is excitable, unputdownable, always climbing, but where? In the fourth movement there is resolution, at last, only for it to be qualified and dissolved. We are swirling again; the restlessness of previous movements has made an unwelcome return. In the final minute, the last chord rises to a crescendo – a fat blast of sound, before falling away to the merest sliver. Will the centre hold, it seems to be asking.

The scale of this music is as vast as the British Empire. It is Elgar's second symphony (1911), first performed as pat of the London Music Festival at the Queen's Hall, London, in May 1911 (Moore 1984). But during its first performance, there was something not quite right. The hall was not full, and of those in attendance by no means all were prepared to give themselves over to the music. Some did not recognise themselves in what Elgar was offering; hence they were unwilling to offer themselves up as part of his audience. They may have remained inside the concert hall, but they were sitting outside the dance (as described above).

Elgar's second did not enjoy unreserved success until after the First World War, when it was revived by the young Adrian Boult. Only then were listeners more readily attuned to it. Perhaps they could hear something of their wartime experience, even though the symphony itself predated what it now seemed to be echoing.

Elgar's second symphony (1911) is a soundtrack to the pressures of Empire, which seem to press down upon the composer as they would soon impress themselves on the millions caught up in the Great War of 1914-18. In all their pomp, as they awaited the coronation of George V later that year, it is hardly surprising that London's pith-helmeted imperialists did not warm to this symphony at its first performance in 1911. At that moment, only a minority was ready to hear the pressing uncertainties it contains.

Instead of Beethoven's confidence – arrogance, even – in riding the waves of sound, Elgar's symphony is a study in difficulty. The composer constructs a wall of orchestration, which he himself is then obliged to withstand. He is not sending a message – it is not that kind of work; but in formal terms alone, he has introduced the possibility of being overwhelmed. Similarly, the symphony contains numerous innovations, but they do not tend towards resolution, as Beethoven's had tended to do. Again, the sound of the orchestra seems almost too heavy for the composer to bend it to his will. Inside his own music, Elgar withholds resolution; and his listeners duly held out on him, until such time as their own experience caught up with the music which he had already advanced.

It had not fully entered the consciousness of the imperial elite, but by May 1911 the vast expanse of the British Empire – the continuous stretching entailed in it – was already a source of considerable strain. Furthermore, every inch of Empire seems to have been be marked out by a high level of ornamentation – the triumph of what Cannadine (2002) calls 'ornamentalism'. From military medals to neo-Gothic buildings, London rested on a bed of baubles; but the sheer weight of them also acted as something of a depressant. Though the British Empire depended on the proliferation of almost everything, this means it was also on the point of being stuffed.

Empire was an extension of national capitalist production, now operating at a volume and density which threatened its own velocity (Lenin 1996). The latter could only be maintained by injecting more finance: a great deal more; not once or twice, or sometimes; but continuously, as part of the deck furniture (or else the ship might turn into the Titanic). Though fanciful, it is plausible to suggest that Elgar's second symphony finds the composer in a similar position. Encumbered, if not overwhelmed, by the texture of the orchestra, he eventually charts his way forward through his own music; but only by recourse to extraordinary, formal developments – the same formulations which some of his first audience found so disagreeable in May 1911.

In the advanced capitalist economies of the late-nineteenth and early-twentieth century, the extraordinary development was the new level of intimacy between finance and production (Lenin 1996: 27-43). Not only was there more financial activity in London at that time, but more of it was closely linked to the expansion of manufacturing, partly in Britain but especially in new centres of production scattered across the Empire. Via expanding financial institutions, never before was so much capital moved so rapidly into production; but the volume and the rate of this deployment came about in the attempt to buttress Britain against the weight of its own, productive activity. Newly intensified at the end of the nineteenth century, the romance between finance and British-owned industry was born of economic necessity.

When capitalist production became more reliant on the involvement of financial institutions, it could not but confirm the importance of financial activity. But besides affirming the role of finance as catalyst to production, the confirmation of finance also suggested that it might outgrow secondary status and come into its own. This suggestion was taken up in the speculative boom of the 1920s; and speculation has been an especially dirty word since 1929, when the boom ended suddenly and the Great Depression began. But before rushing to condemn all financiers for their speculative habits, please note that without some degree of speculation, the capitalist economy would be even more thoughtless and random than it has been until now. Similarly, we should note that most art and much culture consist of speculation about what we have made of ourselves: they are the accountancy of who we are. That both finance and art are secondary activities is not, in itself, cause for concern. But problems arise when their engagement with primary activities is at best intermittent or verging on the non-existent, as is the case in London today.

A Ballad of Estrangement

The Brill Building, songwriting factory of 1950s New York (chord sequences); Smokey Robinson, singer (vocal *timbre*); John Johnson, Tamla Motown rhythm section (bubbling bass); Bob Dylan (stance); The Stooges/Clash/Guns'n'Roses (power chords, riffs and guitar sounds); Norman Whitfield (string arrangements); Eminem (white man rapping).

The musical influences upon East London's Plan B, aka Ben Drew from Forest Gate, include all of the above (and more). Their influence upon Plan B's *The Defamation of Strickland Banks* (2010), the album which won him the 2011 Brit Award for male solo artist, is remarkably direct. Although Plan B did not sample them, i.e. incorporate elements from their previous recordings into his own production, nonetheless he used their signature sounds almost as clip art to be pasted into his own work. If this means that, compared to other, earlier composers, Plan B's work is source-dependent, this does not mean that he is individually lacking in creativity. Curating such elements, re-deploying these found objects in a way that retains their cultural *cache*, and, by acting as their broker, recouping a unique return on their original worth, requires considerable skill and imagination. Associated with the development of 'remix culture' observed by Hebdige (2004) and Lessig (2008), this kind of creativity is akin to that of the finest financial minds who design increasingly rarefied derivatives from a shrinking base (relatively speaking) of primary value (Tett 2009).

Music critic Simon Reynolds observes that we are in the grip of 'retromania – pop culture's addition to its own past' (2011); but reliance on previous cultural forms, i.e. the tendency to derive today's culture from forms which originated in earlier times, is not primarily to do with the past. Rather, it is largely a measure of London's current estrangement from origination, i.e. primary productive activity, conducted through the general relation of labour and capital, in which new value originates.

As London has come to depend more on the operation of financial derivatives, so it becomes unhinged from the general relation which has been its underpinning since the onset of generalised commodity production in the early nineteenth century. For the best part of two centuries, British society was precisely defined by this generality, with London at its head. But, as defined above, the general relation was more than a set of contractual arrangements between many capitals and millions of workers. It is the relation from which society as a whole is composed – the societal relation, the relation that specifies *capitalist* society in human historical development; and diminished involvement in it can only lead to local forms of association which are as much alienated from this general relation as they are associative in their own, particular terms. Thus in London today, finance-oriented culture is also a culture of alienation. Similarly, when a city is as alienated from production as London now is, it finds itself so cut off from *doing* that it is substantially undone. Instead of being the general relation in its urbane form, London has become a city of undoing; and its own undoing is collated in contemporary culture.

In this setting, the dance of abstraction and formulation is severely restricted. Plan B, for example, is tied in to existing formulae – musical traits as previously specified by his diverse influences. At the same time, he is continually abstracted from that originating process in which new musical forms have often been arrived at – the very same process which his influences were immersed in when they arrived at their signature sounds. Some of them made their characteristic breakthrough in circumstances which seem less than promising. Both the Brill Building and the Tamla Motown studio, for example, adopted an assembly-line approach to music making. This was mass production of culture in factory-style conditions. Yet, staff employed in this setting were also expected to produce new models of music, using existing song structures as their raw material. They were spurred on to originate; and what they originated, it seems that Plan B can only curate. In relation to the opposite but complementary aspects of musical composition – the dance, he is contained within what we might have wanted him to escape from; but stands slightly aside from that which we would have hoped he could fully engage with. His positioning has much in common with most of the financial activity currently routed through London. As ever, finance is reliant on the prior production of value elsewhere, but now it is unusually distant from production – hence also estranged from the general relation of labour and productive capital, and the concomitant process of origination; and thus condemned to be derivative.

In *The Defamation of Strickland Banks*, the theme of alienation is echoed in the storyline itself (man betrayed, then sent to prison where he betrays himself); but similarly intense alienation was equally audible in love songs as sung by the late Amy Winehouse, whose death in July 2011 might be also described as a tragic case of self-estrangement. Moreover, even when today's Londoners come together to listen to music, their alienation from each other pervades the venue as much as their togetherness. Locally, at least, producing a general relation via cultural experience, now seems fraught with difficulty, just as the general relation of labour and productive capital remains stubbornly absent from London's financial activity. As in 1811, there is close correspondence between musical, convivial and societal composition; but in London today their common theme is alienation rather than integration.

Conclusion: Local Limitations and Global Vision

In London's current culture, the steps between abstraction and formulation are halting and difficult. Similarly, in the city's economic activity there is less of a dance between finance and production; more of a stand-off between them. Whereas Beethoven needed only the briefest reference to rustic dances in order to transform them into something altogether original, neither Plan B nor the London economy is currently capable of such wholesale innovation.

For the most part, today's Londoners find it hard to envision anything beyond the limitations inherent in London's present form. If they continue to construct this place as a city of alienation, in keeping with the estranged character of today's financial activity, it follows that they themselves will behave in an alienated manner towards their own construction. In which case, daily life in London will default to a sort of slow rioting – the slow-motion, less violent continuation of early August 2011.

Informed by the particular experience of London (how could it be otherwise?), the local world view tends to reproduce the particulars of London's current role in the world, especially its diminished association with the general relation comprised of labour and productive capital. In global terms, however, the general relation has never encompassed as many people as it does now. As a force for generalisation and socialisation, capitalist production has never ranged so widely, even if it is also acquisitive, domineering and partly alienating; hence the worldwide attraction of London, past and present, as a monument to socialisation as well as atomisation.

While many locals tend to view themselves and others within the narrow terms of London's recently restricted activity, the visitors' view, coming from the wider world and their active participation in it, is often more generous. While we had better watch out for readings of the past which are absurdly positive, it would be pitiful if Londoners were condemned to repeat only those aspects of their own past which lend themselves to a mean-spirited version of contemporary alienation. Whether imported from overseas or fostered within home-grown, humanist institutions, it would be better for London if more Londoners acquired some of that generous and generalising perspective in which this city cannot be reduced to a single, self-alienating dimension. We may yet find ourselves looking East, not only for manufactured goods, but also in an effort to end the restricted gaze of the financial economy, and re-open London's horizons.

References

Beethoven, L. van (1808). Symphony No 6 in F, *Pastoral*, op. 68, recorded (1994) by the Royal Liverpool Philharmonic Orchestra (cond. Sir Charles Mackerras).

Brown, R. (1991). *Society and Economy in Modern Britain, 1700-1850.* London: Routledge.

Cannadine, D. (2002). *Ornamentalism: How the British Saw their Empire.* Oxford: Oxford University Press.

Elgar, E. (1911). Second Symphony in E flat, Op. 63, recorded (1945) by the BBC Symphony Orchestra (cond. Sir Adrian Boult).

GLA Economics (2011). Local Area Tourism Impact Model Results for 2008 and 2009, available at at http://www.thesun.co.uk/sol/homepage/news/3741843/PM-David-Cameron-condemns-riots-after-jetting-back-to-deal-with-riots.html, accessed 20 August 2011

Grove, G. (1903). *Beethoven and his Nine Symphonies.* London: Novello.

Hebdige, D. (2004). *Cut'n'Mix: Culture, Identity and Caribbean Music.* London: Routledge.

Lenin, V.I. (1996). *Imperialism: The Highest Stage of Capitalism (A Popular Outline)*, introduced by Norman Lewis and James Malone. London: Pluto Press.

Lessig, L. (2008). *Remix: Making Art and Commerce Thrive in the Hybrid Economy.* London: Bloomsbury Academic.

Moore, J.N. (1984). *Edward Elgar: A Creative Life.* Oxford: Oxford University Press.

Plan B (2010). *The Defamation of Strickland Banks*, London: 679 Recordings, released by Atlantic Records.

Poynter, G. (2010). London's Economy in the Long Recession, *Rising East Essays* 2(1), 4 March, available at http://www.uel.ac.uk/risingeast/essays/2010-03-10.htm, accessed 20 August 2011.

Reynolds, S. (2011). *Retromania: Pop Culture's Addiction to its Own Past.* London: Faber & Faber.

Richwine, L. (2011). 'Box Office Heading Toward Record Despite Economy', *Los Angeles Times*, 17 August, available at http://www.latimes.com/entertainment/sns-rt-us-boxoffice-summertre77g4qn-20110817,0,6275363.story, accessed 20 August 2011.

Rubin, I.I. (1979). *A History of Economic Thought*, translated and edited by D. Filtzer. London: Pluto Press.

The Sun (2011). '16,000 cops to reclaim the streets: Cameron vows to restore order', 9 August, available at http://www.thesun.co.uk/sol/homepage/news/3741843/PM-David-Cameron-condemns-riots-after-jetting-back-to-deal-with-riots.html, accessed 20 August 2011.

Tett, G. (2009). *Fool's Gold: How Unrestrained Greed Corrupted a Dream, Shattered Global Markets and Unleashed a Catastrophe*. London: Little, Brown.

PART 2
Financialisation and London's Economy

Chapter 5
Historic Transitions and Circuits in London's Financial Services

Richard Sharpe

Introduction

London as a centre of financial mediation is a centre of the realisation of profits. Profits are *generated* by people extracting commodities from nature and from transforming these in agriculture or production into other commodities; profits are *realised* in market transactions as these commodities are sold, then consumed. London has tapped into ever wider sources of generated profits in order to build and retain its roles as a centre of realisation. It has been through various transitions, some forced upon it and some of its own making. It arrived in 2008 at the pinnacle of global realisation, along with New York, only to be challenged by issues which had constantly been central to its role as a mediator: what are the risks and, therefore, what should be the price? This chapter deals with the period before the 2008 crash as these earlier events laid the foundations of its role in the early twenty-first century and created the circumstances and methods by which it worked; and the 2008 crash has been narrated and discussed elsewhere extensively. London has crashed before as a centre of financial mediation and recovered. It could do so again if it knew its own history. The history of London as a centre of financial mediation, therefore, has direct relevance to the 2008 crash and to attempts to alleviate its affects.

To sustain its role as a centre for the realisation of profit, London has had to successively tap into wider sources of profit generation. It has also had to reinvent itself as a centre through changes in its internal structure and methods of operations. Banks also branched out from their core businesses such as retail banking or financial trade and became involved in multiple forms of financial mediation. Amalgamations made the London banks larger and more concentrated. These last two tendencies made individual banks, eventually in 2008, too large and too central to all financial operations to be allowed to fail. Yet, banks have constantly failed in the history of London, causing the weak to be culled and others to focus on securing closer ties with the generation of profits. The profits realised in London financial markets have often not been used to reinvest in the generation of profit but have been used to continue the realisation of profit by investments in the state and other financial trading activities. In other words, stepping away from generation and more towards the realisation of profit and then taking the next step, speculation in financial instruments themselves.

London has tapped into ever more distant sources of capital, first domestic then international in its attempts to realise profit. It has been hit by successive waves of over enthusiastic credit expansion as its financial class repeatedly lost track of the essential link between the generation of profits and their realisation, as it speculated increasingly generated fictitious rather than real capital. These are the internal crises inherent in the capitalist banking system. London has consistently tried to re-establish itself as a centre of financial mediation after crises brought on internally or externally. It has been able to draw in more financial mediation from a wider domain, some domains bringing with them risks which London could not and cannot measure. Financial mediators must have confidence in other parties and the financial instruments they trade in. The methods of judging risks and therefore gaining or lessening confidence have changed over time. But the central questions about risk and price remain. London has at times got both answers about risk and price wrong, as it inevitably will in a market engaged in realising not generating profit. This chapter will examine the circuits of financial mediation successive generations of London's financial class have created. The space in which they have been allowed to operate in by the state is discussed in the next chapter.

The First Modern Circuit of Financial Mediation in London: 1680s to 1840s

Many of London's bankers in the latter seventeenth century had been goldsmiths. They were in the City of London close to where merchandise was landed and merchants operated. Central to the merchants was the Royal Exchange [1]also known as 'Change', a central exchange for all types of goods and services which had been established in 1571 through Royal Charter. The total English import trade was worth £6 million in 1700 (£814[2]million in value in 2008 [Officer]): London's share of 40 percent was worth £2.4 million and its exports were worth £6.5 million. By 1770 imports were £12 million (£1.3 billion [ibid.]); exports were £14.3 million; London's share of this trade had fallen to under 30 percent; but that still translates into £4.3 billion worth of exports in 2008 values. (ibid.) The City banks were the first line of financing this trade. They accepted deposits from successful merchants; they issued notes on these deposits; and they discounted bills and gave cash for a bill which was due in the future for a discount, therefore, generating credit for more trading. Some banks also traded in commodities on their own behalf. All of the larger cities of England and Scotland also had their own banks. In the west of London there were also 'country' banks, banks set up to service the needs of clients outside the City of London. These 'country' banks

1 See Addison's laudatory description of the Royal Exchange in 1711 in Mackie, Erin (ed.) (1998). *The Commerce of Everyday Life.* Bedford, St Martin's

2 All contemporary values are calculated using the retail price index.

then dealt with the established City banks, linking agricultural profits with the merchant interests of London. By 1750 there were 12 'country' banks in London; by 1797 there were 290 (Porter 1990: 189).

An essential component of the late seventeenth and eighteenth century financial circuit focused on London was the Bank of England (Bank), established in 1694. It was established as a private company to fund the state. The Bank issued shares to the public and raised initially £1.2 million (£157 million in value in 2008 [Officer]) which it lent to the government at 8 percent per annum (Rowe 1997: 82). The directors of the Bank were not initially bankers but merchants so the Bank was called by the established bankers of the City 'the merchants' bank' (Kynaston 1994: 83). Two of the Bank's roles in the circuit of capital were, therefore, established: supplying credit to the government and issuing notes. The first notes issued by the Bank with proper monetary banking were issued in 1695. They were £10 (£1,356 [Officer]), £20, £30, £40, and £50 notes (Miller 1970: 4). These high denominations show that the notes were not intended for retail trade but for settling larger accounts.The Stock Exchange (SE), originally operating within the Royal Exchange until stock buyers and sellers were ejected for rowdiness in 1698, traded in the shares of the Bank, the government's other debts, and the shares of trading companies, those of which who issued shares like the East India Company.

The transition of London's financial interest from a local funding mechanism was established by this circuit: agricultural rents and profits from sale deposited locally; these deposits moved in part to London; and used to fund government expenditure and the markets in commodities. The other part of the circuit was merchants accumulating through trade depositing profits in City banks and starting to speculate through the SE. This was the circuit which continued through the eighteenth century. As agriculture grew more productive so did this circuit; as extraction from primary sources of materials grew in the merchant part of this circuit, through the ventures of explorers and traders, so the circuit expanded.

How did London's financial powers in this period assess risk and so the correct price? They largely depended on reputation: the reputation of individuals, partnerships and companies. They did not have publically available accounts of companies or partnerships, they just had the transactions on the various markets to guide them. They inspected samples of goods and graded them. They had extensive networks of correspondents with whom they exchanged information through the posts going out of and into London three times a week. Part of this reputation was because the other party to the transaction was perhaps a member of the same family. Another part was created by what the agents had done before and this information was gathered in ledgers, day books and diaries. Another part of reputation was an assessment of what the individual agent was worth and when a crash of an agent came it was often revealed that they were worth much less than others had assumed. They had boosted their standing by extravagant spectacle and consumption well beyond their ability to fund it in order to give the impression of wealth before realising that wealth. Some of the information was gathered directly and some through the media of newspapers and magazines. The lists of bankruptcies were closely monitored. All of this information was formalised in "character books' which individual firms kept, in effect representing finely tuned credit ratings of other City houses (Kynaston 1994: 80). In Barings' character book of the late 1820s there are references such as 'In all his dealings he is scrupulously honest and there is not a Merchant in the City of London whose Character in every respect stands higher'. And of another: 'Their business is executing Orders for the Shipment of Colonial Produce to the Continent, but their Connexions are not first rate' [ibid.]. As a matter of security, most of London's banking institutions kept to their own narrow field of business, whatever they chose, and did not try to build universal banks along the lines of some US and European continental banks. That is, until the 1970s (Cottrell 1994: 1137).

The virtuous circuit that emerged in the late seventeenth and early eighteenth century drew into it increasing volumes of cash, seeking profits. It made the fortunes of many speculators. This expansion of credit inevitably led to a crash, one of the world economy's big ten according to Kindleberger and Aliber (2005: 9) (Kindleberger died before the 2008 crisis). The crash focused on the heavy speculation in the South Sea Company, which had a charter from the King of Spain to trade in the Southern Atlantic. The company used the prospects of this trade to bid for the government debt in competition with the Bank. The shares of the Company became an object of speculation, regardless of its underlying profitability. Here we see the financial mediation of London losing sight of the generation of profit and focusing only on its realisation. There was, in fact, little actual trade done, only trade in its shares and the Company did not win the business for government debt. South Sea Company shares topped £2,000 in June 1720 (Andréadès 1966: 131). The success of these shares brought other company promoters into the market. Some were sound companies such as the London Assurance Company. Others were high risk, such as a company that sought to make a perpetual motion machine, and one that would not even reveal what it would do until it had the money. The bubble burst when 86 companies were officially named as bubble companies.

If we follow the path of the South Sea Bubble collapse we shall see the dynamics of all bubbles and crashes. There were no profits paid and no capital growth as there was no underlying value being generated by extraction or production nor realised in trade: there was just the share price which rose and rose as more investors were drawn in by the previous rises. Some of the owners of these high-priced shares used them as collateral for loans, releasing more money for the purchase of other financial instruments or commodities. This created an excess of credit, of fictitious capital separated from the generation of profits; such an excess always precedes a crash, but not every excess of credit leads to a crash. Through this fictitious capital, trade in many sectors increased. Some potential investors stood aside and refused to trade in the shares, denying themselves short-term profitability but probably ensuring their survival when the crash came. Some investors realised there was no real value in the shares and sold: if enough sell at the same time then the shares start to drop and panic sets in. Banks and individual lenders called in the credit

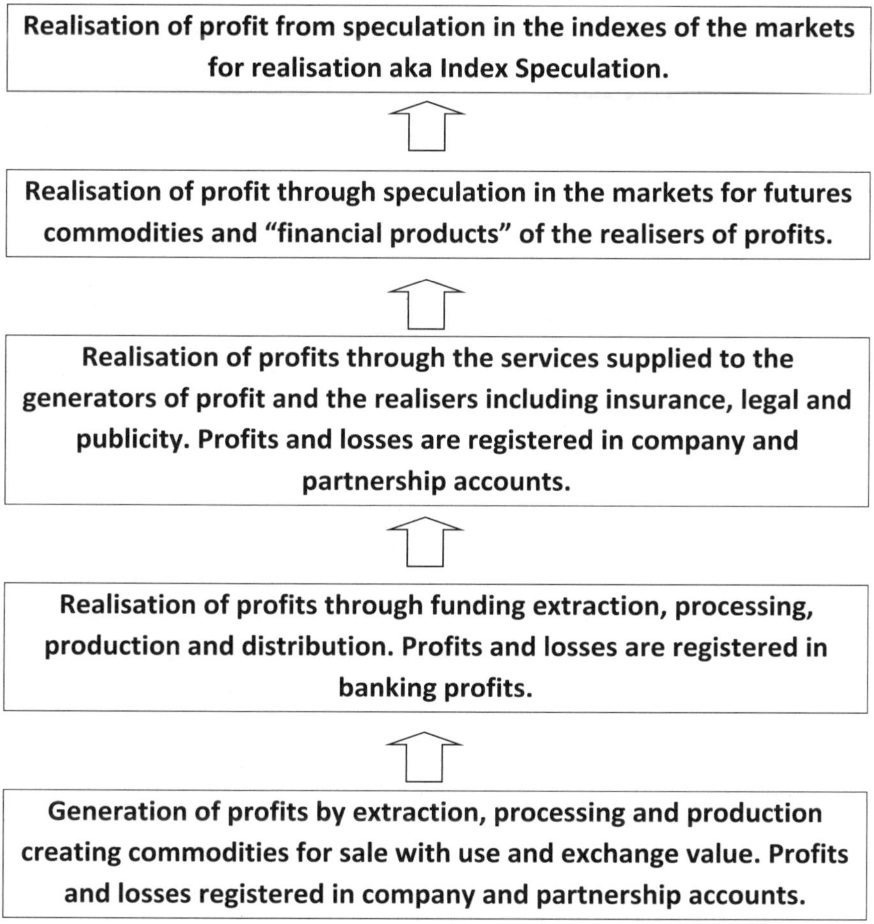

Figure 5.1 The Hierarchy of Profit Realisation Built on the Base of Profit Generation: The Higher up the Hierarchy, the Greater the Risk

they had extended on the value of the shares as the price of the shares dropped. This further squeezed individuals who owned shares and the whole market went into a dive. Credit, a function of trust in value, froze up, confidence evaporated. The fictitious capital evaporated. As it did so fraud was exposed, as it often is at the bursting of a bubble: many founders of the Company were involved in an early example of what subsequently became known as a 'Ponzi scheme' (Kildenberger and Aliber 2005: 109).

As is shown in Figure 5.1, layers of speculation in the realisation of profits are founded on the base of profit generation in extraction and production. In times of speculation in fictitious capital layer is piled upon layer as more schemes, or what became called 'financial products' to realise profit, are created. When the crisis breaks, the top layers collapse and are no longer a means of realising profit. This collapse reduces the gap between generation and realisation. But those activities generating profits are often deeply affected by the collapse of the top layers as credit is in short supply, starving the base generating profits of the oxygen of investment capital. As a banker at Coutts wrote as the South Sea Bubble burst 'not a shilling to be borrowed'(Healey 1992: 49).

The names of the investors may change, the financial instruments/products they are speculating in may change, their values may change, but the mechanism is the same, as Kindleberger and Aliber show. When investors trade just on the price of a financial instrument as if it had intrinsic abilities to generate rather than to realise profits, and they lose sight of its connection to the generation of profits through extraction and production, then crisis is not far away. Economic growth stuttered in the 1720s and 1930s as a result of the restricted credit following the bubble. It started to revive in the 1750s, and continued to grow, apart from a brief interval in the 1790s. Industrial production, in this early stage of the industrial revolution, still rested on small works and the putting-out system. The changes which fuelled the expansion of both infrastructure and industry were privately funded, not funded by London's financial institutions. These included, first, the turnpike roads; then the canal expansion from the end of the 1750s; and continued with agricultural development – bringing more land under cultivation and improving methods of production. These developments were fuelled by a rising population – 5.7 million in England in 1751 to 8.7 million in 1801 (Porter 1990: 206-7).

Outside London banking expanded and contracted in regular waves with each subsequent wave typically exceeding the previous high point. This pattern persisted from the middle of the eighteenth century through to the first quarter of the nineteenth century. There were 12 formal banks outside London in 1750, many of them set up by merchants with spare cash. This grew to 120 in 1783 and 280 in the 1790s. In comparison, by 1800 there were 70 London banks, either 'country' or City banks. In the crash of 1825-6, 80 of the banks based outside London in England closed (Cottrell 1994: 1139). These banks either collapsed, were bought by London banks, or, like Barclays and the Midland, moved their operations to London. The remaining banks outside London were welded into the London-based circuit as they dipped into the London money market for investments or loans, and used London banks to discount their bills.

There were many runs on the Bank during this phase of mediation. None was more important in its effect than the run in 1745 as the Jacobites got as far as Derby in attempts to unseat George II and, if victorious, would have dissolved the Bank. The Bank paid out those demanding cash slowly, in sixpences. It also 'seeded' the queue for withdrawals with its supporters being the highest seeds (they paid the cash back in) while delaying payments to genuine withdrawers and creating an illusion, overall, of payments entering into the Bank. But the most significant event in this crisis was a manifesto signed by London merchants and fundholders which said the signators would accept the Bank's notes and would pay up when presented with them. In one day 1,140 signed, quieting the speculation (Andréadès 1966: 151). The Bank had come through the crisis, becoming, in its course, the focus for London capital and adding to its roles as supplier of credit to the government and as the issuer of notes.

In another run on banks, in 1837, the Bank took on its fourth role as lender of last resort partly as a result of a US crisis. Some American houses in London needed assistance: 'they were solvent but unable to meet the demands made upon them at the moment' (Kynaston 1994: 108). The great trading centre of Liverpool and the cotton-goods manufacturing industry of Lancashire, both dependent on American trade, urged London's financial class to help. At first it was reluctant but eventually the Bank advanced the American companies £6 million (£455 million [Officer]). 'A terrible crash was avoided …' (Andréadès 1966: 266). But the shock waves meant that many small banks outside London went bust (Cottrell 1994: 1140). That is, all but the National Provincial bank which was formed in 1833 and set out, unlike other banks at the time, to build a branch network. In the same year, the London and Westminster was formed in London as a joint-stock bank. Those making profits from transport improvements and industrial development may have deposited some of their profits in London, but London was not, at that time, a direct source of funds for these developments.

The Second Circuit – Politicians, Financiers and Merchants Find a Policy in Free Trade: 1840s to 1914

In this second circuit which led to the golden years of London's financial intermediation, the methods for assessing risk available in the first circuit were augmented first by the telegraph in the 1850s; then by the offer of credit insurance in the 1880s; followed by the creation of specialist daily papers *The Financial News* (1884) and the *Financial Times* (1888); by the creation of credit-rating agencies; and then by the telephone. Both the telegraph and the telephone speeded up the delivery of information, often squeezing out the delays in information through which speculators could gamble.[3]

The telegraph had an impact in three ways. First, prices of commodities were more linked to the actual supply as news of crops, ship loadings etc. were swiftly relayed to London. In other words, the base of production and distribution was more closely linked to the speculation in the prices of these commodities. Second, taking mediation in the opposite direction towards speculation, it led to the arbitrage market, trading on the differences in prices between different markets, particularly the US markets and London. Traders on the London SE continued to trade after the market closed every day in Throgmorton Street, outside the official bounds on the SE. Third, merchants in London, with more knowledge of what

3 See Engel's notes to Fictitious capital in Marx, K. *Capital*, Volume 3, chapter XXV, 543.

was being bought, loaded and shipped to them, no longer needed to keep in their London warehouses large volumes of commodities. This undermined the role of the older merchant houses which increasingly turned to finance, giving rise to the term merchant banks. The first of the existing credit rating agencies started in the 1860s in the USA as a report by Mr Poor on railroads. In 1906 Standard and Poor's viewed the credit level of non-railway companies. Moody's was founded in 1909. All of the early railway developments were funded by local capital, not London capital. It was not until the early 1840s that London financiers were involved.[4]

From 1842 the Bank supplied funds to the markets for railway expansion by offering loans of up to £250,000 (£19.2 million in value in 2008 [Officer]) for railway debentures (Kynaston 1991: 37). It continued this policy for well over a decade, creating a circuit from general deposits at the Bank into capital for the growing transport infrastructure. This led to a crisis in 1847 which was exacerbated by the failure of the potato crop and increase in corn prices in 1845 and 1846. Free trade was firmly established by the repeal of the Corn Laws in 1845. The spectre of revolution engulfed many continental capitals in 1848. In England it proved to be the 'last flame from the candle of Chartism' (Postgate 1955: 214-8). The relative stability of England in this year of continental revolution and then counter revolution made London more attractive as an international financial centre.

From the 1850s the London SE was increasingly used by foreign countries to finance their national debt and by foreign-owned companies to raise capital. By the mid-1850s, it is estimated by Morgan and Thomas (1969) that overseas investments were over £200 million (£13.6 billion in 2008 [Officer]). To the mid-1870s this increased more than fivefold. Between 1860 and 1876 150 foreign government loans were issued in London with a nominal value of over £720 million (£49.2 billion in 2008 [ibid.]). South and Central America were particular favourites. It was not only foreign states which saw London as a potential centre of finance, it was also foreign private banks. By the middle of the nineteenth century London was such an attractive centre that foreign and colonial banks either appointed agents to or established offices in London (Ashworth 1960: 169). This tapped the London banking system into yet more sources of international capital and profit.

The crisis of 1857 in the London financial markets was another triggered by events in the USA. In the USA, railway speculation, the discovery of gold deposits and the development of an unregulated banking sector caused a crisis. This rippled through to London as New York banks pushed up interest rates to attract depositors and shield themselves from bad debt. This drained gold from both London and Paris, causing some UK banks to fail (Andréadès 1966: 343-

4 For example, the chair of the Eastern Counties Railway, the London to Colchester line completed in 1843, was Henry Bosanquet, also chair of the London and Westminster Bank (Vaughn 2009: 75). Bosanquet was a member of a long standing family of London bankers; his father had been a governor of the Bank; one brother was a partner in the bank Bosanquet, Salt & Co; and another brother championed West Indies trade and was a governor of the South Sea Company (Stephens and Lee 1917: 874-6).

52). It seemed as if the Bank especially was subject to a 10 years cycle of crisis; 'From 1819 to 1870 the Bank came to the verge of bankruptcy every ten years' (Andréadès 1966: 404). During this time some of the profits from the growing industrialisation in the North of England and Scotland were being recycled into speculation in London. For example, John Foster and Sons, owners of the Black Dyke Mills in Bradford, West Yorkshire, was a client of P Cazenove and Co, the London stockbrokers. In late 1859 and early 1860 Cazenove regularly wrote to Fosters proposing investments on the London Exchange (Kynaston 1991: 49-52).

This growing industrialisation was encouraged by the development of the concept of limited liability which was sanctioned in 1862. Now companies could extend their credit way past the limits of the individual shareholders. This led to a strong burst of speculation until the crisis of 1866, partly induced by the US Civil War. 'The disorganisation of the cotton trade, the confusion due to the export of gold, the fall in the rate of interest and the accumulation of capital resulting from the extension in the use of machinery, very soon gave a feverish and speculative character to the English money market ...' (Andréadès 1966: 354). When the 1866 crisis abated, the 1870s recession set in with collapsing agricultural prices as a result of the growing international nature of food production.

There was also a change in the type of banking undertaken. Retail banking was growing as the profits accumulated by the new middle class were deposited and became a source of capital for the growing branches of the joint stock banks. National and Provincial, a leader in this retail banking sector, had over 100 branches by the mid-1870s; Lloyds have over 100 in 1890; the Midland by 1893; Barclays by 1896; and London and Westminster by 1909 (Cottrell 1994: 1146). Between 1870 and 1914 the number of bank offices increased four-fold in England and Wales (Ashworth 1960: 167). By the early 1870s, Walter Bagehot recorded that 'all the petty cash of private persons down nearly to the end of the middle class' was used as credit by the English banking system, (Bagehot 1873: 81). These bank offices were now processing more cheques which began to replace bills of exchange for retail customers. Banks also expanded into providing overdrafts and offered extra services such as trustee and executor departments. They became wider in their offerings and, therefore, more a centre of risk. Banks could gain some economies of scale in these transactions: they could also take the many small transactions and accumulate them into sizable capital. Hence there was a pressure to consolidate created by the joint stock banks. Private banks fell away in importance and the number of joint stock banks diminished with takeovers. This was particularly accelerated in the last three decades of the century: in 1873 there were 121 English joint-stock banks: by 1913 there were only 43 (Ashworth 1960: 167).

From the mid-1870s the Bank provided a more coherent lead to the London banking system by systematic and frequent changes in the bank rate:

> The Bank began to adjust its rate more promptly, in anticipation of changing conditions rather than in response to changed market rates, and it was less tempted to delay because, by agreeing to discount for its regular customers at the

> prevailing market rate and charging the published bank rate only to the rest of the market, it no longer risked a loss of business by raising Bank rate. (Ashworth 1960: 171)

In the 180 months from 1884 to 1898 the Bank changed the interest rate 89 times. The longest period of stability was from March 1894 to August 1896 when the rate stayed stable at 2 per cent. The largest changes were in 1890 when the rate was changed every month. (Whitaker 1900: 309) The decline of the need for warehouses as a result of better information about crops and loading of ships led in the 1880s to the development of forward dealing, or what we would now call futures trading. It started on 1st May 1888 in coffee and then expanded to sugar. (Kynaston 1995: 19) This method of trading, pioneered here on commodities, was in the twentieth century extended to financial instruments of all kinds.

London's financial class had an early opportunity to plug itself into the potential generation of profits from the emergent electrical engineering industry and provide capital for it; it got it wrong. In 1882 there was a boom in the shares of the Brush Company then a leader in the field of electrical engineering. About £7 million was subscribed to share offerings, 'few of the ventures survived' (Kynaston 1974: 342). London, with burnt fingers, withdrew its confidence in electrical engineering: 'the confidence of the [investing] public in electricity was almost destroyed, and could only be regained by years of patient work' Alexander Siemens said that year (Kynaston 1994: 340-2). Another industry to get the attention of investors was armaments. The growing armaments budgets of the later 1880s and 1890s brought this industry to the attention of London. But investment in industry was unusual business as banks were, in the main, not raising capital for industry apart from railways, docks and public utilities. Yet the securities of industry and commerce as a whole did grow: government gilt edged securities grew to £1 billion (£73 billion [Officer]) in 1913 from £800 million in 1873. In contrast, 'the volume of quoted nominal capital in industrial and commercial companies rose from a mere £50 million in 1890 to over £1 billion in 1913' (Thomas 1986: 9). But home securities were still only 40 per cent of the market in 1914. American railway stocks were a favourite: overseas railway stocks rose to £2.9 billion in 1913 from £300 million in 1870 (ibid.). The importance of the international circuits linking London to other areas where profit was generated in the late Victorian/Edwardian period is seen by the capital passing out of London to British possessions and foreign countries in 1911-13. Some 46 per cent were for foreign countries; 37 per cent for 'British possessions'; and 16 per cent for UK issuers (Lavington 1934: 194).

This second Victorian/Edwardian circuit shows that spates of speculation based often not on profits from production or extraction continued even in the high age of Britain's Imperialism and financial dominance. More sources of capital were drawn into London, more markets opened for its investments. Sometimes they were opened by force, as in China; sometimes by merchants, as in Egypt. It was buttressed by a Bank surviving a range of crises every decade to 1870 and the continued policy of free trade and reliance on the gold standard. By the end of the first decade of the twentieth century, a wider crisis was to engulf this circuit of mediation.

War, the Battle to Regain 'Normalcy' and War Again: 1914-45

A cash crisis soon erupted on the declaration of war in August 1914. It was assumed, rightly, that the Government would need large amounts of cash to continue the war and borrowers in enemy countries stopped paying. The Government stepped in by printing Treasury notes, calling a temporary moratorium on some debt payments, and the Bank provided exceptional loans with the backing of the Government. 'By these means the financial crisis was resolved before the end of 1914' (Ashworth 1960: 266). Much of the international trade and financing which London depended on stopped during the war. But shipping was needed and with shipping came insurance, which boomed. And the German overseas territories were now under Allied control because of the reach of the Royal Navy and so were open for business to London capital. (Ashworth 1960: 267) After the war London was keen to restore 'normalcy', as it was called. One trend which continued was amalgamations. Banks were getting bigger through drawing in the cash from retail depositors and their international business. A group of 12 dominated by the end of the nineteenth century. Then there was a frenzy of amalgamations which shrank this to five by 1918: Barclays, Lloyds, the Midland, National Provincial, and the London and Westminster. The Bank started to be worried and made it known that it did not want any more mergers or takeovers (Cottrell 1994: 1149).

London did not just look back but also forwards: the financial mediators of London were focused on creating new circuits through which to realise profits. The new ones included the colonies taken from Germany in Africa and the Pacific. But the main activities of the SE focused on domestic stocks (Thomas 1986: 11). As a result, the number of industrial companies quoted on the SE rose from 569 in 1907 to 1,712 in 1939 with a combined market value five times greater (Cain and Hopkins 2001: 417). The Bank was urging the City to finance industry. The Governor of the Bank, Montagu Norman, wrote in 1930:

> I believe that the finance which for 100 years has been directed by them [City bankers] abroad can be directed by them into British industry, that a marriage can take place between the industry of the North and the finance of the South [of Britain]. (quoted in ibid. 414)

The boom of 1928 in the London SE was described by Kynaston as 'the last of the old style nineteenth century booms, producing a few good companies but a lot of rubbish that quickly perished once the market had turned. It gave the SE a thoroughly bad name' (Kynaston 1991: 109). The SE went through three phases from 1932-39 – a gradual recovery to 1935; two years of boom 1935-7; and from January 1937 gradual decline (ibid.: 134). Gilt-edged stocks to support

Government funding were the dominant part of the market: over a quarter of the 5,629 stocks listed in March 1938 were industrial and commercial; in terms of market value Government funds were 40 per cent with industrial and commercial stock only 14 percent (ibid.: 135).

From the early 1930s the attempt to regain 'normalcy' on London financial markets lost its energy as London tried to defend itself against the impact of the 1930s recession. International finance seized up as a source of realising profits as reparations were not paid, liquidity disappeared and trade shrank. 'From the 1930s until the late 1960s, international finance and the idea of globalisation slumbered – some even considered it dead' (Ferguson 2009: 306). Capital movements were severely controlled. London's financial powers, in effect, turned their back on the world and focused on the UK and the Empire. The SE continued to function at a lower level during World War II. It had a central role in raising Government debt. Government regulations made issues of stock for companies difficult but during 1939-45 the top six stockbrokers in the City made 109 issues for companies (Kynaston 1991: 168-9).[5]

Reconstruction and Slow Growth: 1945-79

The Labour government, elected in 1945, nationalised the Bank and many parts of the UK economy. The focus of the London SE remained on domestic issues and the funding of government debt in the gilt-edged market for well into the late 1940s. The first public offering on the SE after the war was for the steel maker John Summers in December 1945. (ibid.: 185) A lot of smaller companies were launched by brokers on the market as a result of their need for capital and the low interest rates.

In the early 1950s London found a new source of capital in which and with which to speculate: the Eurodollar. These were US dollars, some collected by the USSR and other communist countries, which they did not want to deposit in New York in case they were seized by the US authorities. The Bank adopted a '*laisser-faire, laisser-passer*' attitude on specific large financial transactions, providing that the transactions were not expressed in pounds. By the end of the 1950s the Eurodollar was created and the 'development of modern-day international banking began in earnest' (Wright and Pauli 1987: 19). This pool of dollars which could be traded in an unregulated way was enhanced with the Petrodollars the OPEC countries started to deposit, especially in London, in the 1970s. A third source of capital became available as Japan started to seek better returns for the profits it had made from manufacturing than it could gain at home. Japanese households saved at a much higher rate than the households of other industrialised countries. In 1974, Japanese personal savings as a percentage of disposable income was above 25 percent; in the

5 Some were for companies supported by the Government during the recession now generating profits: the Lancashire Cotton Corporation and the shipyard Harland and Wolff, among them. (Kynaston 1991: 169-70)

USA it was about 8 percent; and UK about 10 percent. For example, the Japanese post office, in which many Japanese put their savings, had by the mid-1980s $600 billion, 'making it the largest body of savings in the world, greater than the four largest commercial banks in Japan combined' (ibid.: 48). Japanese banks set up in London and they favoured investments in bonds (ibid.: 57).

September 1958 saw a new development in the financial circuit: the contested takeover of a UK company by US capital. British Aluminium (BA) became the target of takeover by two US companies: Reynolds and Aloca. The fight was public and intense. Eventually 'the Reynolds-TI camp had amassed 80 percent of the issued share capital of BA and some of the oldest and most revered institutions in the City had suffered an embarrassing defeat' (Blakey 1997: 50-51). From the late 1950s, private investors in stocks who had dominated the market were challenged by investing institutions. In 1957 investing institutions held 19 percent of ordinary shares on the market; by 1978 this rose to 47 percent and to 55 percent by 1983 (Thomas 1986: 17). These investing institutions were the focus of appeals by competing parties in the contested takeover bids.

Contested bids became the rage. In 1959 Harrods was taken over after a long battle by The House of Fraser; Charles Clore failed to take over Watneys but in the battle revealed how undervalued property was in the books of many publically-listed companies. This led to a scramble to find these undervalued assets and strip them out. There were also a growing number of floatations. The Polly Peck floatation was one of the first of a new type of company: built by financial operators and spanning many sectors of business they relied on a range of businesses to keep share prices high through generous dividends. These companies eventually flourished in the early 1960s and included Slater Walker (1964-75), Lonrho, Hanson, and Trafalgar House (1963-96). Many, like Polly Peck, collapsed in the 1990s. 'The rise and fall of Polly Peck ranks as the most spectacular of all booms and busts in SE history, going from zero to £1.5 billion in nine years and then back to zero in five weeks' (ibid.: 346).

As the Bretton Woods arrangement for the structuring of international capitalist finance broke down in the early 1970s so currencies were allowed to float and offshore markets such as the Eurodollar market in London achieved another spurt of growth. This led to a revival of non-government capital export, and London turned to an old favourite Latin America. Between 1975 and 1982 Latin American governments pushed up their lending from foreign capital sources to $315 billion from $75 billion (Ferguson 2009: 309). This level of lending was unsustainable leading to yet another crisis when in August 1982 Mexico declared it could not finance its debt.

At the Top Again: 1979-2008

The election of the Thatcher government in 1979 and her appointment and backing for her first Chancellor Geoffrey Howe provided the platform on which

London transformed itself yet again: from the financial hub of a nation struggling to find its path to an international centre to rival New York. Extraction may be closed down with the slaughter of the coal mining or oil extraction punitively taxed in order to generate government funds to cut the deficit; production may be axed as the safety net of government support was withdrawn from major industries including steel and motor manufacturing: but London could emerge as a world centre of profit realisation.

As a result of this domestic loosening of the corset and the wider international loosening, new markets emerged and old ones changed. The structure of international financial mediation was rapidly evolving: it had been dominated by the activities of larger banks cycling the surpluses of, for example, the oil-producing companies into financial support for national and international trade and production and government debt. It was now to be dominated by trade between financial mediators of an ever growing array of financial instruments which bankers decided to call financial products and to which spawned a finance industry. 'This [new] activity goes beyond the servicing of investors and savers traditionally fulfilled by the banks. Utility originally was attached to the actual need for what was traded: that is, a loan satisfied the need for money. Today, tradability is utility' (Sassen 2001: 84). One new market to emerge was hedge funds. The old market that changed rapidly in London was the SE through the 'Big Bang' (described in the next chapter). Both new and old markets sought new fields of realisation. The 'production' of new financial instruments flourished as a result of these searches. The first was a currency swap between IBM and the World Bank worth $210m over 10 years in 1981 executed by Salomon Brothers. 'This new form of trade spread fast across Wall Street and the City of London, mutating into wildly complex deals that seemed to give bankers godlike powers' (Tett 2009: 13).

If they were complex deals then traders needed to know the risks that entailed. The financial press, on which they often relied for analysis, failed to give any concrete warning about the outcome of such speculation as it flourished. Investors and traders turned increasingly to two sources of information: the credit ratings agencies and their own mathematicians who modelled risk. The increasing use of credit ratings agencies is shown by the growth of Standard & Poor's, a subsidiary of McGraw-Hill. In 1998 S&P had a turnover of $1 billion: this rose by 193.7 percent to its peak in 2007 at $3.1 billion; all this while McGraw's total turnover rose only 71 percent.

The other source of information on risk was the models built internally by financial mediators. These models could be run swiftly on the higher performance computers increasingly and increasingly cheaply available. A very public warning that such models could be fatally flawed came in the collapse in the USA of Long Term Capital Management: it has used 'computing power and mathematical skills to hunt for trading opportunities all over the world' (Tett 2009: 85-6). None of these models, it seemed, looked at the underlying generation of profits in extraction, agriculture and production but they did look at the 'generation' of profits in their realisation during market transactions in the processes of financial mediation. In other words, they were divorced from profit generation and only focused on realisation.

Eventually a toxic element entered into this mix: the financial 'products' which represented combinations of US consumer household debt which had grown to help the US economy absorb the increasingly productive industrial capacity of world capitalism, especially China's expanding consumer product industries. As McGraw stated in its annual report for 2008:

> We take little comfort from the fact that virtually all market participants—financial institutions, ratings firms, homeowners, regulators and investors—did not anticipate the extreme and ongoing declines in the U.S. housing and mortgage markets. As a consequence of these unexpected developments, many of the forecasts and assumptions S&P used in its ratings analysis of certain mortgage-related structured finance securities issued over the past several years have not been borne out. There is no doubt that had we and others anticipated these extraordinary events, we would not have assigned many of the original ratings that we did. (McGraw 2008: 3)

Conclusion

London does not need an industrial base in order to be a centre for the realisation of profits. Neither does the UK. Profits can be realised outside the nation where they are generated: so it was with the profits from South African gold and diamond mines which were partly realised in London; for the Indian cotton tea and cotton crops; and for the US railroad building enterprises. All these and many other ventures were partly financed by London and the profits partly realised in London. For as long as London could calculate risk and return, and access wider sources of capital for realisation it has been able to operate successfully as a centre of realisation of profits, first locally, then nationally and then globally.

By the nature of financial mediation it cannot consistently do so. It is successively drawn into speculations which have little regard for the generation of profits, only their realisation. It looks increasingly to the price of financial instruments, latterly called financial products, rather than the underlying ability of those instruments to faithfully represent the generation of profits in extraction, agriculture and/or production. Bankers extend credit on these inflated instruments of fictitious capital and some of this credit is used to drive prices yet higher, seemingly confirming the value of the instruments. There comes a point, due to fraud, an external event such as war or the realisation by one or a group of traders that there is no profit generation backing up the realisation and the bubble bursts. From the South Seas Bubble through the demise of Polly Peck and to the collapse of 2008, such is the cycle. How far the financial class in London can retain or extend its ability to realise profits is often governed by its relations with the state, as we shall see in the next chapter.

References

Aldcroft, D.H. (1993). *The European Economy 1914-1990.* Third edition. London Routledge.

Andréadès, A. (1966). *History of the Bank of England.* London Frank Cass and Co.

Ashworth, W. (1960). *An Economic History of England 1870-1939.* London: Methuen and Co.

Blakey, G.G. (1997). *The Post-war History of the London Stock Market.* Third edition. Shalford: Glos Management Books 2000.

Cain, P.J. and Hopkins, A.G. (2001). *British Imperialism 1688-2000.* Second edition. London: Longman.

Chandler, G. (1964). *Four Centuries of Banking as Illustrated by the Bankers, Customers and Staff Associated with the Constituent Banks of Martins Bank Limited*, vol. 1. London: Batsford.

Cottrell, P.L. (1994). 'The Historical Development of Modern Banking within the UK', in Manfred Pohl and Sabine Freitag (eds) *Handbook on the History of European Banks* Aldershot: Edward Elgar.

Healey, E. (1992). *Coutts & Co 1692-1992.* London: John Curtis.

Hobsbawm, E.J. (1968). *Industry and Empire*. London: Pelican.

Holt, R. (2001). *Second Amongst Equals: Chancellors of the Exchequer and the British Economy.* London: Profile Books.

Jones, E. (1995). *True and Fair: A History of Price Waterhouse.* London: Hamish Hamilton.

Kindleberger, C.P. and Aliber, R. (2000). *Manias, Panics, and Crashes: A History of Financial Crisis.* Fifth Edition. New Jersey: John Wiley & Sons.

Kynaston, D. (1991). *Cazenove & Co: A History.* London: BT Batsford.

Kynaston, D. (1994). *The City of London Volume I: A World of Its Own 1815-1890.* London: Pimlico.

Kynaston, D. (1995). *The City of London Volume II: Golden Years 1890-1914.* London: Pimlico.

Lavington, F. (1934). *The English Capital Market.* Third edition. London: Methuen.

Marr, A. (2008). *A History of Modern Britain.* London: Pan.

McGraw (2008). *Annual Report 2008,* available at http://www.mcgraw-hill.com/about/annual_report/ar2008.pdf, accessed 12 March 2011

Miller, D.M. (1970). *Bank of England and Treasury Notes 1694-1970.* Newcastle Upon Tyne Minerva Numismatic Handbooks Number Six.

Morgan, E.V. and Thomas, W.A. (1969). *The London Stock Exchange*. New York: St Martin's Press.

Morgan, K.O. (ed.) (2010). *The Oxford History of Britain.* Oxford: OUP.

Officer, L.H. (2009). 'Purchasing Power of British Pounds from 1264 to Present,' MeasuringWorth, available at http://www.measuringworth.com/ppoweruk/, accessed January-May 2011.

Plumb, J.H. (1950). *England in the 18th Century.* London: Penguin.

Porter, R. (1990). *English Society in the Eighteenth Century.* London: Penguin.
Postgate, R. (1955). *Story of a Year 1848.* London: Jonathan Cape.
Rose, D. (1997). *The Real Meaning of Money.* London: HarperCollins.
Smith, G. (ed.) (1945). *Addison and Steele and Others: The Spectator.* London: Dent.
Stephens, L. and Lee, S. (1917). *Dictionary of National Biography.* Oxford: OUP.
Tett, G. (2009). *Fool's Gold.* London: Little, Brown.
Thomas, W.A. (1986). *The Big Bang*. Oxford: Philip Allan.
Treasure, G. (1969). *Who's Who in History*. Oxford: Basil Blackwell.
Webb, G.H. (1987). *The Bigger Bang, Growth of a Financial Revolution*. London: Waterlow Publishers.
Weinreb, B. and Hibbert, C. (1983). *The London Encyclopaedia.* London: BCA.
Whitaker, J. (1899). *An Almanack for the Year of Our Lord 1900.* London: Whitaker.
Wright, R.W. and Pauli, G.A. (1987). *The Second Wave: Japan's Global Assault on Financial Services.* London: Waterlow Publishers.
Wolmar, C. (2009). *Blood, Iron and Gold: How the Railways Transformed the World.* London: Atlantic Books.

Chapter 6
Opening and Closing Spaces for Fictitious Capital: The State and Finance Capital in London

Richard Sharpe

Introduction

London is a place of financial mediation and, as the capital city of the United Kingdom, the location of political mediation. Its role as an international financial centre and as the centre of the state leads to a series of alliances, compromises, and partial victories and defeats for both interests: the political and the financial. The power of the state can open opportunities for London as a centre of financial mediation; the state can also close opportunities. Financial interests have the options of resistance, accommodation and/or reinvention. The spaces created and closed are not only market spaces: they are also physical spaces. These two spheres of the state and finance are, generally, geographically separated in London. On the one hand is Westminster, the home of the legislature along with Whitehall (the executive), and the judiciary lies a little further to the east around the Strand. Then we have a single word for the location of London's financial powers: the City – although, as we shall show, it is not confined to the geographical 'square mile' of the City.

The relationship between these spheres of political and financial mediation has changed significantly since the seventeenth century. We shall use the same structure of transitions as used in the previous chapter to explain and analyse these changes. The state changed the space in which financial mediation operated in London in the first transition from the 1690s to the 1840s with the repeal of corn laws and the adoption of free trade in the 1840s; it was the state which declared war in 1914 and ended the high point of Victorian/Edwardian profit realisation in London; it was the state that squeezed the space in which the London financial powers could realise profit with the election of the Labour Government in 1945; and it was the state, through successive Conservative governments, from 1979, that created the largest space for the realisation of profits since the previous high water mark of 'financialisation' in the late Victorian/Edwardian period.

The First Modern Circuit of Financial Mediation in London: 1680s-1840s

In the years preceding the creation of modern banking, wealthy individuals used the Royal Mint in the Tower of London to safely store their wealth until Charles I seized the contents worth £200,000 (£28.1 million in value in 2008 [1][Officer]) in 1640 to fund his war against Scotland. (Chandler 1964: 62) In 1640 it was possible for the executive to seize the property of the financial class. By the last decade of the seventeenth century, bankers established their own separate banking facilities. John Frame, for example, was a Lombard Street goldsmith who turned banker in 1690 (his company was one of the founders of Barclays.). Goldsmiths had strong boxes/rooms in which coin and plate could be safely held. In this early phase of the development of modern banking, the executive and legislative parts of the state gave the financial mediators the space in which to operate as legal entities through partnerships, Royal Charters and Acts of Parliament. A partnership could form itself, have its own rules and each partner would be liable for the full debts incurred by the partnership. If the operation sought limited liability for the founders, it secured this through an Act of Parliament or a Royal Charter. Since both of these, Charters and Acts, were expensive most ventures took the form of partnerships. These partnerships of London bankers lent to the monarchy, the aristocracy, to merchants and often bought and sold currencies on their own behalf.Sea shipping on the Thames could go no further than London Bridge making the pool below the Tower of London, a clear symbol of the executive's power and technically outside the City of London. The City banks were clustered around and along Lombard Street between the Royal Exchange and the Pool of London: money mediating both financially and physically between transport and trade. Produce bought and sold on the Royal Exchange was carried into London, which by 1702 had 40 per cent of England's maritime trade. The total tonnage and the number of vessels rose three-fold by between 1770 and 1776 (Porter 1990: 189).

Political changes in 1688 enabled London to draw ahead of rival centres of accumulation in the nation. The overthrow of James II in 1688 and the instalment of the Protestant Ascendancy with some City backing, called by Whigs "The Glorious Revolution", gave London the impetus to become the dominant centre for accumulation. Part of the new political settlement was, in effect, a constitutional monarchy ruling through a permanent Parliament, a change in the relationship between the executive and the legislature. There was also a change in the relationship between the judiciary and the executive with the executive's powers to control the judiciary diminished. These developments further focused political and financial interests in London, both the City and Westminster, with members of both houses of Parliament often in residence in the city when it was sitting. Banks located outside the City but still in the wider area of London, were either designated as "country banks", "West End banks" or "Westminster banks". One such was Coutts which was established by a Scottish goldsmith, John Campbell, in 1692. Its establishment in the financial circuit exemplified the expansion of the sector at this time. Campbell was backed by the Argyll family, heads of the Scottish

1 All contemporary values are calculated using the retail price index. See Addison's description of how the Royal Exchange brought together merchants from many countries equally, in the market, and benefitting England (Smith 1945: 212).

Campbell clan. The Argyll's had extensive land holdings in the west of central Scotland (Healey 1992: 3). From this they extracted rents and sold agricultural produce, the original source of their wealth. Some of this profit from agriculture was deposited in Scottish banks, some used for personal consumption in Scotland and to reinvest in agriculture. A further part of it was transferred to Coutts which used it to realise further profits – thus forming a circuit for capital a portion of which found its way into London's "country" banks.

Some of the funds transferred to London's "country" banks by the Argyll's and others were used for private consumption. Now that Parliament was a permanent fixture in the political settlement of 1688 and the monarchy no longer travelled the country but was settled, along with its executive officers, in or close to London, the grandees needed London houses as well as their country estates. Part of the rental income transferred to London was used to build a string of large houses in and close to London.[2] The merchants and financial interests of London also moved out of London, building and buying estates in the country as they grew richer on the accumulation produced by this circuit. They, in turn, kept in touch with the City and reinforced the circuit from agricultural production to accumulation centred in London. The continuing campaigns against Catholic France by Protestant William and Mary led to increasing demands for state loans. A group of merchants formed a bank, the Bank of England (BofE), with the express purpose of funding the state. They put their own money in and raised more through share offerings. They were paid a fixed interest by the state. BofE shares then became a financial instrument for speculation by other bankers.

The state had other means of raising money; all of which provided London's financiers with the opportunity to speculate on them. It issued "consols" short for consolidated fund, a combined debt certificate for the government. Consols were considered 'the very *best security* that a Bank can hold', according to a nineteenth century London banker (Kynaston 1974: 213). It also issued Treasury Notes. Another financial instrument was victualling bills for supplying the growing Royal Navy. And the state ran lotteries of debt: the debt would be paid off at random in a lottery. The state also raised considerable funds from custom duties through the Customs and Excise Commissioners on a range of goods including tobacco and alcohol. When these duties were changed, as they often were, London merchants would either profit or lose out. If the duty was raised, merchants holding stocks on which the duty had already been paid could raise their price in the knowledge that the next consignment of that commodity landed in London would carry the higher duty and therefore a higher price. If the duty was lowered, merchants holding stocks of that commodity would have to lower prices because the next

2 For example, Buckingham House, later Palace, was built for the 1st Duke of Buckingham in 1702-5; Chiswick House was built for the 3rd Earl of Burlington 1725-9; Devonshire House was built for the Duke of Devonshire from 1734-7; Argyll House was built for the 3rd Duke of Argyll 1735-7; and Chesterfield House was built for the 4th Earl of Chesterfield from 1748-9 (Weinreb and Hibbert 1983: 24, 102, 150, 154, 225).

consignment would carry a lower price and buyers need only wait until the new consignment was landed to buy at the lower price. In effect, therefore, by raising and lowering customs duties, the state was opening and closing opportunities for profit making. The various forms of financial instruments issued by the state were, apart from the bills of merchants training in London, the main space for speculation for London's bankers. The centrality of government debt funding, both directly and in supplies to the Navy, is shown by the accounts of Martins Bank for 1748: government stocks provided 37 per cent of profits; shares percent and the BofE 12 per cent (Chandler 1964: 133). There were other instruments with which London's financiers could speculate: the shares of private companies such as the Royal Chartered South Sea Company. The bursting of the South Sea Bubble in 1720 caused the state to intervene and restrict the space London's financiers could operate in. An Act was passed, the Bubble Act, which reinforced the powers of the state to regulate the formation of companies:

> It was the bursting of the South Sea Bubble in 1720 which killed off investment mania. Subsequent laws restricting company formation (a royal charter was required) nipped in the bud any possible stock market for industrial projects. Eighteenth-century industrial investments remained private, not corporate or speculative. (Porter 1990: 203)

In short, as Porter observed, the state intervened to regulate company formation. So the circuit of agricultural rents and income linking to merchant profits and government funding remained the central circuit for London's financial accumulation until the development of railway investment in the nineteenth century.

The fluctuations in this cycle of accumulation depended on battles won and lost – with the French and Spanish; harvests – good and bad; the access to new areas of the globe for extraction and markets; and the supply of silver and gold.[3] There was a decisive moment in the fight for the Reform Act of 1832 when parts of the London financial class used their financial strength to influence the state. An early attempt to pass a reform bill failed in Parliament and the Whig government collapsed. The Duke of Wellington, a Tory, tried to form a government which would block reform. Many London bankers supported reform. They knew that a run on the BofE would destabilise the Wellington government. One of them created a placard which he paraded around the City 'To stop the Duke, go for gold'; in other words present to the BofE its notes and demand gold. Even the power of Nathan Rothschild, close to Wellington since the funding of the campaign against Napoleon, could not stop it. He urged Wellington to allow some reform.

3 For example, Admiral Anson captured £600,000 (£71.7 million in 2008 value [Officer]) worth of Spanish gold and silver in the Caribbean in 1744 which was paraded through London on his return (Treasure 1969: 121).

Wellington preferred to let the Whigs reform and stopped his efforts to form an administration. The Whigs did reform (Kynaston 1994: 96-8)

The Second Circuit – Financiers and Merchants find a Policy in Free Trade: 1840s to 1914

The Charter for the BofE came up for regular renewal. It ran out in 1844 and the then Prime Minister, Sir Robert Peel, took the opportunity to curb the BofE's habit of issuing paper money well in excess of the deposits it had – in today's parlance to curb its policy of high gearing. Since the late 1830s the BofE had been criticised by one faction of the City for this habit, this was called the "currency" faction or school. Another school of thought, the "banking school" in the City had argued that banks should be free to issue what they liked and to take the consequences. Peel favoured the currency school and pressed his case in negotiations with the Bank. Other bankers, when they leaned of the strict "corset" which Peel was aiming for, generally favoured the BofE's position. Peel's measures involved – the separation of the BofE's note issue activities from its banking activities; a limit to the number of other banks which could issue notes; a fixed ratio between the notes issued and the BofE's bullion holdings; and a fixed amount of £14 million of notes which could be issued with the backing of securities. The bill became law with considerable support in Parliament despite the protests of some bankers who were Members of Parliament and members of the bankers' school. (Kynaston 1974: 126-9) Writing 30 years on, Walter Bagehot wrote: 'By that act the currency manages itself: the entire working is automatic' (Quoted in ibid.: 129). Kynaston calls the Bank Charter Act "one of the cornerstones of nineteenth century legislation" (ibid.: 126). The state took in the same year, 1844, a small step in expanding the legal area in which companies could act, while also imposing restrictions. The Joint Stock Companies Act of 1844 established a register of names for companies, their locations and their directors and internal roles. It required that shareholders should be presented with annual reports at Annual General Meetings (AGMs), but very limited ones compared to those required today. (Jones 1995: 48-49)

In times of crisis, when cash was in short supply because of lack of confidence in London's circuits of financial mediation. the BofE would negotiate with the government of the day to release the corset of the Bank Charter Act; in today's parlance to engage in quantitative easing. One such crisis was in 1847 when many London banks and merchants went down, including the trading companies of the then Governor of the BofE, two of its directors and a former Governor. After much discussion between the government and the BofE the former agreed to send a letter authorising the BofE to partly suspend the corset set by the Act. The news that the letter was to be sent was enough to restore confidence in the money markets (Kynaston 1974: 154-60). The same happened in 1857 with the letter of suspension enough to raise confidence after an American-triggered crisis; and again in 1866 during another crisis which, during this period, London seemingly experienced every decade (Kynaston 1994: 194).

A year after the passing of the Bank Charter Act another cornerstone of 19th century economic policy was firmly established which changed the space in which London's financial mediators could operate: the Corns Laws were repealed and the official policy became Free Trade. The failure of the potato crops, particularly in Ireland, gave the campaigners for Free Trade the issue they needed to press their case to success. The coming of free trade was not a single event. Tariffs had been lowered or abolished on timber, tea, sugar and other commodities before 1845. There was, in fact, a continuous battle between those advocating free trade and those advocating protection or, even, monopoly. The London financial class was split. Monopolists in trade, such as the East India Company with its monopoly of Indian tea, wanted continued protection. Others wanted free trade so that they could enter these markets (Kynaston 1994: 124-5).

The supporters of free trade fought successfully for the repeal of the Corn Laws in 1845, laws which, since the early 1800s, had set the price of corn, and they achieved the repeal of the Tudor Navigation Acts in 1849 which had restricted trade into England solely to English shipping. Free Trade was a broader policy than just focusing on trade: it also included commitment to a balanced government budget and a minimum state. As Morgan records, "'Free trade' of course meant much more than simply the abolition of protective tariffs. 'Free trade' or *laissez-faire* were shorthand terms exemplifying a whole philosophy of political, social and economic organisation" (Morgan 2010: 522). The state would step aside from interfering in the affairs of the market. The state would create an opened space in which profit generation and realisation could grow. In the mid-1850s the Government allowed banks to have limited liability, making the joint-stock bank a more attractive path to banking than partnerships. There was a burst of liquidity into the UK banking sector in 1853: Gladstone, then Chancellor of the Exchequer, decided to wind up the remains of the South Sea Company which led to up to £3 million (£224 million in 2008 [Officer]) to be made available for reinvestment. One stockbroker, Cazenove, recommended to its clients 16 stocks in which to invest their profits from the sale: eight UK railways; two North American railways; two European railways; three UK government stocks and one Canadian government stock (Kynaston 1991: 44). The policy of laissez-faire, the freedom of the individual to act as they wanted as long as it did not directly damage others 'created a situation in which opportunity marched with minimal control, and remained in force for almost a century until the 1948 Companies Act ended an era of *laissez-faire*' (Jones 1995: 49). Within the newly opened space of operations from the 1860s, London rapidly developed as an imperial centre for profit realisation.

How the state and London financial interests interacted in the Imperial era is shown by the debates over the policy towards Egypt in the 1880s. The London financial class showed its imperial face in 1882: pushing the then Gladstone government into occupying Egypt. In the early 1880s London investments poured into Egypt after the local ruler, under Turkish influence, was deposed. These investments raised the anger of Egyptians who "rioted". The *Economist* wrote "England has greater interests in Egypt than any other European Power, and those interests must be defended". There were frequent meetings in the City in favour of intervention or to stop the meetings of anti-interventionists. A banker wrote "I want to see England take Egypt and keep it". Gladstone said "the bondholders' interest would be protected". Alexandria was bombarded by the Navy; the country invaded; and the Egyptian army defeated. The bondholders were protected by the state in an imperial venture (Kynaston 1974: 336-40).

This influence on the policies of the state was reinforced by the members of London's financial class who were members of the legislature. As well as the members of the House of Commons who were part of the financial community, an increasing number of financiers were made Barons in recognition of the importance of finance to the Imperial state. Eleven were created barons from the mid-1880s including Rothschild, Schroder, Montague, Glyn, Loyd and Gibbs. They used their platform in the Lords to contribute to the opposition to Lloyd George's "People's Budget" in 1909 but did not press the opposition once the Liberal government threatened to flood the Lords with Liberal peers to drown the Tory opposition (Kynaston 1995: 494-502).

Increased tensions between Europe's imperial powers led the British Government to raise military expenditure towards the turn of the century. Government loans for armaments and communications rose from zero in 1870 to £50million in 1913 (Hobsbawm 1968: 239). Naval expenditure was the largest part of the budget. It was required to build new fleets based on the proposals of Admiral Fisher for "big gun" battleships. Naval expenditure was £10 million in 1875-84; and reached £40million in 1910. The armaments industry also needed more capital to build manufacturing capacity to fulfil the orders. The Naval Construction and Armaments Company (NCAC) in Barrow begun raising capital in 1888 and Vickers used London financing to take over its competitors (including the NCAC) making it, by 1897, the only company in Britain able to manufacture a battleship with armour, engines and guns. It raised £2 million in 1897 on the London markets (Kynaston 1991: 85).

Fisher's prediction that a major European war would break out six months after Germany completed the Kiel Canal proved correct in August 1914 (Massie 1991: 407).

War, the Battle to Regain "Normalcy" and War Again: 1914-45

The Stock Exchange was closed on 31st July 1914 after a turbulent few months of trading as a result of rumours of war. It opened again on 4 January 1915 with strict government regulations over new issues of stock in order to preserve capital for the war effort. The flood of new issues before the outbreak of war turned into a trickle (Kynaston 1991: 91-2).

At the end of the war London and the government wished to reinstate London's role as a central mediator for financial interests across the globe. The British Empire was at its zenith. German East Africa was allocated to Britain as were many offshoots of the defeated German overseas empire. These were added to the circuits of accumulation for London as British capital replaced German capital. At the same time the domestic economy changed as a result of the growth of domestic demand for consumer goods and housing. This led to some opportunities to accumulate from domestic economic growth but not always for domestic industrial capital: one quality issue for the Stock Exchange in 1928 was for Ford to build its new plant at Dagenham, East London, in which it raised £2.8 million (£126 million in 2008 [Officer]).

London was caught up in the turmoil of the early 1930s as a result of its international position. Although originating in the USA and spreading to continental Europe, the position of London as international lender caused the Wall Street Crash and subsequent crisis to eventually hit London as the demand for liquidity drained London of funds – in July and August 1931, £200 million alone left London. The state reacted with its most powerful weapon – sterling went off the gold standard in September (Aldcroft 1993: 72-3). By being one of the first and certainly the most important currencies to go off the gold standard, the state created the space for growth, combined as it was with a policy of low interest rates to stimulate consumption. This made the industries providing consumption commodities rather than primary industries a new source of profit generation. But the prices of raw commodities went into freefall cutting the profits of the merchants in London who dominated the world trade for tea, cotton and other primary commodities. The collapse of international trade and the world recession forced London to look elsewhere for accumulated profits. It turned inwards. 'The 1930s witnessed a fundamental shift in the London capital market away from foreign and towards domestic issues'. [4] The Treasury put restrictions on the flow of capital out of the Empire. By 1935 less than 40 per cent of issues were for overseas and the value of the international business was under one fifth of what it had been in the 1920s (Kynaston 1991: 143).

Reconstruction and Slow Growth: 1945-79

The BofE was one of the first parts of private enterprise nationalised by the Labour Government in 1945. This changed its role from being the bankers' banker to

4 These domestic issues included, in the order of their coming to market, Great Universal Stores; Ansells Brewery; Charringtons brewery; Raleigh Cycle Holdings; Yorkshire Amalgamated Collieries; the iron and steel companies Stewarts and Lloyds, United Steel, Dorman and Long, and Colvilles; Bristol Aeroplane; Blackburn Aircraft; Itas, a hat manufacturer; Joshua Tetley; Hoover; British Aluminium; Courage brewers; Eagle Oil & Shipping; and the Anchor Line shipping company (Kynaston 1991: 146-61).

being an instrument of government economic policy. The interest rate was no longer set directly by the BofE in relation to money markets: it was now a lever of wider financial management which was used to try to achieve different objectives at different times. The Labour government tackled reconstruction after the war, seeking to establish the welfare state, full employment even for the demobbed troops, stable growth and moderate inflation; all this 'in an atmosphere of perpetual crisis' (Holt 2001: 198). The 1945 Companies Act ended the laissez faire policy of government towards the disclosure of results. Group accounts consisting of a balance sheet and profit and loss were to be published; circulated to shareholders before the AGM and registered in public; audits would cover both; and the audits had to state that the accounts were a "true and fair view" of the underlying business; and the auditors used had to be a member of a short list of professional bodies. (Jones 1995: 235-6) The state was forcing London's financial interests to become more transparent in their reporting. Whole industries were taken out of London's circuits of accumulation by the nationalisation policy of the Labour Government from 1945 to 1951. These included civil aviation, the coal industry, transport, electricity supply, gas supply, the iron and steel industry which were nationalised in that order (Kynaston 1991: 191). This further increased the search by London for smaller companies not in these industries that could be plugged into the accumulation processes. The Labour government also adopted a cheap-money policy and held interest rates low, partly to lower interest payments on government debt and, under Chancellor of the Exchequer from 1945 and 1947 Hugh Dalton, because it sought to punish the rich who got less interest for their savings (Holt 2001: 33). But the Labour government could not, ultimately, keep the level of the pound at its fixed position to the dollar and devalued in 1949. This looked like an economic defeat but was, in fact, part of the foundation for the good times which followed to the benefit of the Conservative Government (Marr 2007: 134)

The City was lifted by the election of the Conservative Party to government in 1951. The first post-war bull market got under way. Blakey calls it a "popular" bull market. 'It was popular in the sense that investors were making money not out of shares in exotic companies from 'far away places with strange-sounding names' like Mexican Eagle or Wiluna Gold, but from shares in stores, breweries and motor manufacturers they came into contact with every day' (Blakey 1997: 37). The market continued to grow as did the economy; profits for motor manufacturers especially expanded.

The Conservative government under Churchill failed to be as radical in its acts as its predecessor. There was a plan in 1952, called ROBOT, which would have created a significantly better space in which London's financial interests could operate. The pound would be floated, in effect allowed to fall against the dollar; welfare spending would be cut back; and unemployment would be allowed to rise. This would have boosted reserves and stopped the chronic balance-of-payments crisis. 'It was nothing less than a free-market national coup', says Marr (131). 'It was the only example of such radical thinking for years to come' (ibid.). The plan was ditched and such a radical approach was not tried again until 1979. Instead, the Conservative government pushed up interest rates and raised the regulations to hire purchase, the main means by which motor cars and the consumer goods sold through stores were bought. The Conservatives kept pushing up the bank rate until it hit seven per cent in September 1957.

The core of the City of London looked much the same from the early 1950s through to the end of the 1970s. But successive governments, both Conservative and Labour, created space on the fringes which transformed the City: they allowed the Eurodollar market to be unregulated. The argument for this was that as long as these dealers were not operating in sterling, it did not matter. The first big Eurodollar loan out of London was negotiated between Warburgs and Samuel Montague with an Italian steel maker and the Belgium government. Then there was a deal by Hambros for a hydroelectric scheme in Norway and by others for the Austrian government followed by loans to Japanese enterprises. The success of this business brought in international banks who set up in London to take part of the action. Four Japanese banks entered London as did the USA's Citibank, Chase Manhatten and Merrill Lynch (Marr 2007: 422). By its benign neglect, the state created a huge new space for London to operate in.

But successive governments were, through their economic policies, trying to juggle so many factors that the result was 'stop-go': spurts of growth and then hard onto the brakes. This gave the London financial interests a turbulent and unpredictable environment in which to operate. Government policy was trying to achieve too many things at the same time: low inflation; high exports; the stable value of the pound; high employment; and raising the funds for government expenditure. Only when the Thatcher government ditched the aim of high employment and focused on inflation and getting government expenditure down were London's financial interests given the space in which to grow to successfully compete internationally again.

At the Top Again: 1979-2008

The Thatcher government, elected in 1979, opened up spectacular spaces for London's financial class through its economic policies and programme of privatisation of public assets. It started with a shock to London's financial interests: the abolition of exchange controls. 'Howe [the Chancellor] himself likened it to walking off a cliff to see what happened' (Marr 2007: 423). The message was clear: the City was going to be opened up and those parts which had been on the fringe, such as Eurodollar dealing, were going to come to centre stage and 'their ethos was going to be the guiding principles from now on' (ibid.).

During the 1980s, £29 billion was raised in sales of public land and businesses; 46 businesses left the public sector and entered the space in which profits could be realised in financial transactions. It started in small steps in 1981-2 with BP, Cable and Wireless and others. It spread to BT, British Gas, government-owned water utilities, electricity and onwards to include British Airways (Marr 2008: 428-9).

London's financial class absorbed them all as did many small shareholders for it was part of the privatisation programme to create a "shareholding democracy" to root the interests of the nation into the markets for their own shares. It failed: ownership slipped back to the established financial interests mostly in London. 'The failure to get a shareholding democracy properly rooted, despite endless Treasury initiatives to nurture it, is a more telling criticism of privatisation than the one most commonly heard at the time, which was that the assets were being sold off cheaply' (Marr 2008: 432).

Until 1986 the London Stock Market had evolved slowly from its origins at the Royal Exchange founded at the end of the seventeenth century. It had evolved into its own building and had its own structure of jobbers and brokers, its own fixed commission rates and its own monopoly of members. It was a clear example of the old money. The new Thatcher Government elected in May 1979 was, however, more dominated by the new money.[5] The Stock Exchange would be taken to the restrictive practices court and have to argue for its current structure and rules. After four years of building its defence the Stock Exchange, after talks with Government, announced that it would reform itself. It did so through a series of "little bangs" starting in July 1984 and ending with the "Big Bang" of the 27 October 1986 (Webb 1987: 93). Before big bang there was a feeding frenzy as large financial institutions bought up the smaller members of the Stock Exchange. The outcome was the abandonment of fixed commissions and thereby the introduction of competition for commission; the abolition of the distinction between jobbers and brokers and, therefore, more space for all to operate in; and the opening up of membership resulting in the infusion of domestic and foreign institutions directly in share dealing. This policy was adopted by the Labour Government of Blair and Brown in 1997 with the addition that the BoE would set interest rates, not the Government, against a target to control inflation.

Conclusion

We see from this brief history that the state has opened and closed spaces for the financial interests and institutions of London and, in turn, they have taken advantage of them, argued against them or repositioned themselves according to the restrictions. The state created the space for the early phase of accumulation in times of war as a result of its need for finance. In other times of war it closed the spaces in order, again, to raise funds for war. In times of peace it more often than not let the London financial interests operate as they wished, until the election of 1945. The sole purpose of the financial institutions of London throughout history has been to accumulate profit. There has not been a sole purpose for the

5 It included the likes of Cecil Parkinson from Metal Box and Parkinson-Hart Securities; Michael Heseltine who made his fortune in publishing; and Peter Walker who had been a junior partner in Slater Walker, the conglomerate famous for asset stripping.

state. Through most of the historic period outlined above, the state has not had to consider the democratic principles arising from a socially diverse electorate. It had, until the 1920s, only to consider the interests of a very narrowly defined social interest.

At the time of writing, the contention between the spaces to accumulate that is considered necessary for London as a centre of financial mediation and the space the state will allow it is, as it has often been, the central issue for the future of London as a global centre of financial mediation. In the past, the needs of Empire have been used by London financial interests to keep the space as open as possible. Now the needs of a globalised economy are being deployed. Yet the state has had to intervene heavily since the credit crunch to stop the failures of speculation at the top tiers of accumulation, identified in the previous chapter, from destroying the prospects of accumulation taking place elsewhere in the economy. The state is currently pressed into reviewing the spaces it should allow London's financial interests. There is no end to this contest, no stability, because there is no stability inherent in the process of capital accumulation.

References

Aldcroft, D.H. (1993). *The European Economy 1914-1990.* Third edition. London: Routledge.

Andréadès, A. (1966). *History of the Bank of England.* London: Frank Cass and Co.

Ashworth, W. (1960). *An Economic History of England 1870-1939.* London: Methuen and Co.

Blakey, G.G. (1997). *The Post-war History of the London Stock Market.* Third edition. Shalford: Glos Management Books 2000.

Cain, P.J. and Hopkins, A.G. (2001). *British Imperialism 1688-2000.* Second edition. London Longman.

Chandler, G. (1964). *Four Centuries of Banking as Illustrated by then Bankers, Customers and Staff Associated with the Constituent Banks of Martins Bank Limited.* Vol 1. London: Batsford.

Cottrell, P.L. (1994). *The Historical Development of Modern Banking within the UK* in Manfred Pohl and Sabine Freitag (eds) *Handbook on the History of European Banks.* Aldershot: Edward Elgar.

Healey, E. (1992). *Coutts & Co 1692-1992.* London: John Curtis.

Hobsbawm, E.J. (1968). *Industry and Empire.* London: Pelican.

Holt, R. (2001). *Second Amongst Equals: Chancellors of the Exchequer and the British Economy.* London: Profile Books.

Jones, E. (1995). *True and Fair: A History of Price Waterhouse.* London: Hamish Mamilton.

Kindleberger, C.P. and Aliber, R. (2000). *Manias, Panics, and Crashes A History of Financial Crisis.* Fifth Edition. New Jersey: John Wiley & Sons.

Kynaston, D. (1991). *Cazenove & Co: A History.* London: BT Batsford.
Kynaston, D. (1994). *The City of London: Volume I A World of Its Won, 1815-1890.* London: Pimlico.
Kynaston, D. (1995). *The City of London: Volume II Golden Years, 1890-1914.* London: Pimlico.
Lavington, F. (1934, third edition). *The English Capital Market.* London: Methuen.
Marr, A. (2008). *A History of Modern Britain.* London: Pan.
Massie, R.K. (1991). *Dreadnought: Britain, Germany and the Coming of the Great War.* New York: Ballantine Books.
McGraw (2008). *Annual Report 2008*, available at http://www.mcgraw-hill.com/about/annual_report/ar2008.pdf, accessed 12 March 2011.
Miller, D.M. (1970). *Bank of England and Treasury Notes 1694-1970* Newcastle Upon Tyne Minerva Numismatic Handbooks Number Six.
Morgan, K.O. (ed.) (2010). *The Oxford History of Britain* Oxford: OUP.
Officer, L.H. (2009). 'Purchasing Power of British Pounds from 1264 to Present', MeasuringWorth, available at http://www.measuringworth.com/ppoweruk/, accessed January-May 2011.
Plumb, J.H. (1950). *England in the 18th Century.* London: Penguin.
Porter, R. (1990). *English Society in the Eighteenth Century.* London: Penguin.
Postgate, R. (1955). *Story of a Year 1848.* London: Jonathan Cape.
Rose, D. (1997). *The Real Meaning of Money.* London: HarperCollins.
Smith, G. (ed.) (1945). *Addison and Steele and Others: The Spectator.* London: Dent.
Stephens, L. and Lee, S. (1917). *Dictionary of National Biography.* Oxford: OUP.
Tett, G. (2009). *Fool's Gold.* London Little, Brown.
Thomas, W.A. (1986). *The Big Bang.* Oxford: Philip Allan.
Treasure, G. (1969). *Who's Who in History.* Oxford: Basil Blackwell.
Webb, G.H. (1987). *The Bigger Bang: Growth of a Financial Revolution.* London: Waterlow Publishers.
Weinreb, B. and Hibbert, C. (1983). *The London Encyclopaedia.* London: BCA.
Whitaker, J. (1899). *An Almanack for the Year of Our Lord 1900.* London: Whitaker.
Wolmar, C. (2009). *Blood, Iron and Gold: How the Railways Transformed the World.* London: Atlantic Books.
Wright, R.W. and Pauli, G.A. (1987). *The Second Wave: Japan's Global Assault on Financial Services.* London: Waterlow Publishers.

Chapter 7
London's Financial Services: After the Credit Crunch

Daniel Ben-Ami

Introduction

Considering how much passion London's financial institutions have evoked since the credit crunch emerged in 2007, it is remarkable how little they are understood. The banks in particular are berated as 'greedy' and part of a giant casino, but that does not add any clarity to the discussion. Of course, most Londoners use financial products such as bank accounts, insurance policies and the like. But using such services only provides a momentary glimpse into the world of finance. Even those 300,000 or so Londoners who work in the sector (City of London 2011) are unlikely to have much contact with the financial world outside their own niche.

Part of the problem could be to do with the intrinsic complexity of the subject. There are various ways of addressing this. Perhaps the most obvious is to look at different types of financial institutions including commercial banks, investment banks, insurance companies and fund management groups. Another is to focus on different markets such as those in bonds, commodities, currencies, insurance and shares. A more abstract approach would look at the role of London as a financial centre – although this presents the difficulty of separating its several different functions.

The aim of this chapter is to identify how London has changed as a financial centre since the onset of the credit crunch in 2007. However, to achieve this goal it is first necessary to understand what London was doing before then. To achieve the preliminary task London's financial role must first be divided into its key component parts. Such an approach makes it easier to see how different types of institution, from banks to insurance companies, fit into the whole. Naturally it is not possible to relate all the complexities in such a short space. In any case it would probably require a PhD in mathematics or theoretical physics to understand some of the more arcane financial instruments being used. But it is not necessary to appreciate all the fine details to understand London's role in global financial mediation. It will then be possible to examine how London's financial role has changed over time and particularly since 2007. Although it is clear that the credit crunch and subsequent recession have had an impact, as has the associated hostility to finance, it is not easy to measure. Beyond the transition in ownership resulting from part-nationalisation of some banks, it is easy to exaggerate the changes.

One point on terminology: this chapter will use the term 'the City' (with an upper case 'C') as many Londoners do to mean London as a financial centre. Until two decades ago this was more-or-less conterminous with the 'Square Mile' of the old City of London. Since then the financial cluster has expanded in all directions but particularly eastwards to the Canary Wharf area of London's docklands.

The Great Go-between

Despite all the heated debate about the City, there is widespread agreement that it plays an important mediating role in the economy. It provides a way of channelling money from those who have more than they need at a given time to those who require it. By doing so it creates a relationship that, at least in principle, can benefit both sides. Financial institutions typically earn their revenue by taking some kind of cut from the transaction. In the words of Walter Bagehot, the editor of *The Economist* from 1860-77, the City is 'a great go-between' (Bagehot 1999: 11). Bagehot took the name of his classic study on the subject, *Lombard Street*, from one of the streets in the centre of the Square Mile. In the book he described how: 'Lombard Street is a perpetual agent ... between the two great divisions of England – between the rapidly-growing divisions where almost any amount of money can be well and easily employed, and the stationary and the declining districts, where there is more money than can be used' (Bagehot 1999: 12). Despite the national focus of this definition he went on to note that since the Franco-Prussian war of 1870-1871, the City of London had increasingly become a banker to Europe.

Banking is the best-known instance of the City as 'perpetual agent'. On the saving side, many people, such as those approaching retirement, may want to deposit money into high interest accounts. On the borrowing side, others may want loans for a mortgage or to finance investment in their companies. Banks, the intermediaries in the transaction, typically earn their revenue by charging higher rates to borrowers than they pay to savers. Although such textbook cases normally involve private individuals, it should be noted that the state played an integral part from the early days of the City. The Bank of England (abbreviated here as 'Bank') was founded in 1694 as a banker and debt manager to the government. The Bank of England Act of that year granted 'certain Recompenses and Advantages ... to such Persons as shall voluntarily advance the Sum of Fifteen hundred thousand Pounds towards carrying on the War against France' (Bank of England 1694, original capitals). In other words the Bank was originally an intermediary between private savers, some would say speculators, and the government as borrower. The Bank's role has changed several times since then, but it remains a central part of the City.

Although banking – more strictly, commercial banking, is perhaps the simplest form of intermediation, it is far from the only one. There are other conduits such as the stock market and the bond market. In these instances, the two parties at either end of the transaction are investors (usually institutional but sometimes private individuals) and companies. Typically, the financial institutions involved in setting up the transaction will receive a fee for their services. In relation to the stock market it is possible for companies to raise capital by issuing shares (also known as stocks or equities). This provides an alternative to conventional bank loans as a way for companies to obtain finance. The firms which issue shares are essentially selling a claim to their future earnings. After the initial issuance it is possible for investors in shares to trade them with others – the secondary market – and also for companies to buy back their own shares. The origins of the London Stock Exchange go back to about the same time as the Bank of England. Organised trading began in the coffee houses of London in the late seventeenth century. Throughout most of its history trading was done by 'open outcry' in which business was transacted on the floor of the Stock Exchange building. But since deregulation in 1986, known as 'Big Bang', trading in London has become fully electronic with traders sitting on the dealing floors of their respective institutions.

Although it is less well known to the general public, the bond market dwarfs the stock market (TheCityUK 2010). It provides a way for companies, usually larger ones, to raise money by issuing bonds (essentially IOUs) on the market. Bonds, like shares, can also be traded between investors on the secondary market. However, there are technical differences between the two markets. For example, whereas a share is essentially a claim on future earnings, bonds are a form of debt. Bonds generally have a fixed lifespan, i.e. they mature at a fixed date in the future, whereas shares do not.

Now that the roles of two of the key London markets are understood, it is possible, at least in broad terms, to understand what other types of financial institution do. For example, the activity of investment banks – which are not really banks in the traditional sense of the term – is closely linked to these markets. Among other things they advise companies on how to issue bonds or shares, facilitate the trading of bonds or shares, and participate in the merger and acquisition of companies. Typically they receive a fee for their services in contrast to relying on the margin between borrowing and lending.

Whereas investment banks are generally involved in the selling of financial assets to another type of institution, fund management groups are typically concerned with buying. Such groups manage large portfolios of assets, including shares and bonds, on behalf of their clients. Pools of these assets can take the form of pension funds, insurance funds, hedge funds, sovereign wealth funds and other types of portfolio. Nowadays the investment groups which manage such funds, known collectively as institutional investors, dwarf the direct holdings of financial assets by private investors.

So far the main forms of financial intermediation have been outlined. These can include traditional banking, where capital is channelled through banks themselves, or alternatively the siphoning of capital through markets in different types of assets. Whereas traditional banking is the domain of the commercial banks, the markets are more the terrain of the investment banks (the sell side) and fund managers (the buy side). Although all these activities are conceptually separate it should be noted that nowadays they can all be combined in large institutions. London-based

Table 7.1 Financial Services Employment in Central London (in thousands)

	City of London		Canary Wharf		City-type jobs	Total for UK June
	Fin. servs	Total	Fin. servs	Total		
2000	158	330	11	46	325	1,080
2005	135	306	47	87	327	1,060
2006	131	303	54	96	343	1,071
2007	135	312	57	105	354	1,078
2008	140	312	60	108	324	1,090
2009	–	–	–	–	305	1,020
2010	–	–	–	–	315	1,014

Source: ONS Annual Business Inquiry, *CEBR ONS Economic & Labour Market Review*.

financial giants such as Barclays, HSBC and Lloyds include all these activities and more, within their overall group operations.

Before going on it is necessary to outline one particularly important specialist form of financial activity: insurance. Although the insurance business is complicated, and there are different types of institutions, its main role is as a specialist form of risk management. It enables companies and individuals to protect themselves against risks when they are engaged in their activities. For instance, a ship owner might insure himself against his vessel sinking. Lloyd's of London, the world's largest specialist insurance market, is an important part of this business for London. In a sense the insurance company gives a particular twist to the role of mediator of capital. The individual or company who has taken out an insurance policy receives payment in the event of an adverse outcome they have insured against. The insurance company, or whoever has underwritten the insurance, makes the payment in such circumstances.

From this simple model it is possible to outline the key mediating activities of different types of institution in the City:

1. Commercial banking (including retail banking): intermediating in the movement of capital between savers and borrowers.
2. Investment banking: advising companies on activities in bond, commodity, currency, stock and other markets.
3. Fund management groups: the management of portfolios of assets such as bonds and shares; includes pension funds and hedge funds.
4. Insurance companies: specialist risk management institutions.
5. Associated companies: specialist companies in the City which, while not mediating institutions themselves, play a key role in assisting firms that are. These include the so-called City law firms such as Clifford Chance,

Table 7.2 Financial Services' Share of GDP in Major Economies (% Share of GDP)

	UK	US	Germany	France	Japan
1999	5.9	7.3	5.3	4.8	6.1
2000	5.2	7.5	4.2	5.1	6.1
2001	5.3	7.7	4.1	4.5	6.4
2002	6.6	7.9	4.4	4.8	6.8
2003	7.0	7.9	4.7	4.8	7.0
2004	7.0	7.8	5.1	4.9	6.8
2005	7.1	8.1	4.7	4.9	7.0
2006	7.7	8.3	4.5	4.9	6.9
2007	8.3	8.0	4.0	4.7	6.7
2008	9.0	8.3	3.6	4.6	5.9
2009	10.0	8.4	4.3	5.1	5.8

Source: TheCityUK.

Freshfields Bruckhaus Deringer and Linklaters, as well as accountancy firms such as PricewaterhouseCoopers and Ernst & Young.

6. State institutions: key to the life of the City, these include the Bank of England (responsible for monetary policy and financial stability), the Financial Services Authority (responsible for regulation, to be abolished in 2012), and the Treasury (the finance ministry, responsible for managing the government's finances).

Changing Role

This chapter has so far made the simplifying assumption that financial institutions are mere channels for capital. Either they are direct intermediaries themselves, such as the commercial banks, or they in some way assist the process of intermediation. However, financial institutions have long been complex and often large organisations in their own right. Often they have become important players in the domestic economy and, particularly in relation to global centres such as London, the international economy.

It is generally forgotten that the growing importance of financial institutions prompted an important theoretical discussion during the first wave of globalisation from 1870-1914. As trade and capital flows increased, the power and influence of financial institutions became more pronounced. Rudolf Hilferding, a socialist activist who in 1923 became Germany's finance minister, wrote about this in *Das Finanzkapital* (*Finance Capital*) which was first published in 1910 (Hilferding

1981). Hilferding's ideas were later taken up and adapted by Vladimir Lenin in his famous study of imperialism, first published just before Russia's October revolution of 1917 (Lenin 1963).

There is no space here to go into the historical debate but there is one important aspect that should be highlighted, since it is relevant to the current discussion. It is also an area in which the terminology, at least in English, has led to immense confusion. When Hilferding and Lenin referred to 'finance capital' they were not simply referring to financial institutions. Both made it clear that they were interested in examining the way that financial and non-financial institutions had become increasingly inter-twined. For Hilferding finance capital was 'capital at the disposition of the banks which is used by the industrialists' (Hilferding 1981), while for Lenin it was 'the merging of bank capital with industrial capital' (Lenin 1963). Lenin went on to argue that this merger led to the creation of a 'financial oligarchy' (ibid.). In any event the trend towards the globalisation of finance went into reverse in the decades following the First World War (1914-18). The succession of world war, Great Depression and Second World War (1939-45) broke many of the investment and trade linkages in the global economy. By the end of the Second World War the world economy, particularly in relation to finance, was much less global than it had been in 1914. As a result, financial institutions became correspondingly less important.

However, from the 1970s in particular, the trend towards the globalisation of finance has reasserted itself. Finance has one again become more international, and more important in relation to the rest of the economy. For instance, Adair Turner (then) Chair of Britain's Financial Services Authority (FSA), calculated in a 2010 paper that the total balance sheet of all banking entities in London (including foreign ones) reached about 500 per cent of UK GDP in 2007, compared with only 34 per cent in 1964 (Turner 2010: 20). He went on to observe that by the later date the banking system: 'was dominated not by the banks' relationship with UK households and companies, but with a complex mesh of intra-financial system claims and obligations' (Turner 2010: 20).

This can, at least in part, be taken as a sign that speculative capital is spending a lot of time flowing around within the financial system. Rather than financial institutions simply being channels for the movement of capital, they are involved in an elaborate circulation and manipulation of capital. This is still ultimately mediation but it is a more complex form than the direct transfer of capital from savers to borrowers or from investors to companies.

Another sign of the growing complexity of mediation is the comparison between the volume of business in the primary markets (companies issuing bonds or shares) and the secondary market (investors trading in these assets). For example, secondary trading on the London stock exchange was £2.342 billion in 2009. In contrast, new issues of shares, including the issuance of new shares by companies that were already listed, amounted to £82.6 billion (TheCityUK 2010). By this measure the secondary market was more than 28 times the size of the primary market in that year.

Since the 1980s another important factor has shaped London's mediating role. This is the increasingly risk-conscious nature of society: a heightened anxiety about all forms of uncertainty. In the financial sector this has manifested itself as a growing preoccupation with risk management and with devising instruments to achieve this objective. It has led to the creation of what I have previously called 'cowardly capitalism' (Ben-Ami 2001), in contrast to the widely held description of London as 'casino capitalism' (Strange 1986). In effect the whole of the City, not just insurance companies, has become a conduit for mediating risk as well as capital. As Andrew Freeman explained in his study of *The Risk Revolution*, 'Our improving understanding of risk is increasingly allowing the creation of securities with precise characteristics and payoffs' (Freeman 2000: 9). He went on to argue that technology: 'is making possible a revolution in our ability to shape securities so that they embody specific categories of risk and even specific risks' (Freeman 2000: 9).

Perhaps the most straightforward instruments for risk transfer are derivatives. Although these can be complicated in practice, they are generally conceptually simple. They are best seen as a form of insurance contract. Here is a hypothetical example to illustrate the point. On the one hand, a pig farmer might want to take out a derivative on pork bellies as a form of insurance against the price falling too much. On the other hand, a meat processing firm might want to protect itself against the price of pork bellies rising too much. By matching up these two sets of needs, through futures markets or financial institutions, it is possible, at least in theory, to benefit both sides. As usual the financial intermediary will take a cut from the transaction.

Of course in the real world, certainly in London, derivatives in agricultural commodities have become much less important than those linked to financial variables. It has become possible for companies to use derivatives to hedge themselves against adverse movements in currencies, interest rates, commodity prices and the like. It is also possible for speculators to bet on the market even if they do not have a stake in an underlying product, such as pork bellies or aviation fuel, to buy or sell. Nevertheless the principle still holds that such instruments are essentially ways in which companies and sometimes individuals can transfer risk between each other.

It is now possible to identify in broad terms the most important types of mediation prevalent in the City. London is centrally involved in the global circulation of capital. Ultimately it earns its revenue from taking a 'cut' from this circulation. But financial institutions are not simply conduits moving capital from one place to another. Their business is no longer mainly raising capital for companies seeking investment. Instead the convoluted circulation of capital has almost taken on a life of its own. This pattern is complicated still further by the additional mediating role of transferring risk. As well as transferring capital, the City is heavily involved in shifting risks between different parties.

Melded Capital

The final piece of the jigsaw harks back in some respects to the discussion before the First World War. There is, in a different form, an increased inter-locking of financial capital and non-financial capital. In today's context, perhaps it would be better captured by a term such as 'hybrid capital' or 'melded capital' rather than 'finance capital'. Not only is there a high degree of merger, but the non-financial firms involved in it, extend well beyond the industrial sector to include many service companies.

There are numerous ways in which such melding can take place. On the non-financial side, larger companies have expanded their financial operations and, in a closely related development, have become more preoccupied with risk management (Hunt 2003). Large firms such as BP, GlaxoSmithKline and Vodafone would be expected to be particularly developed in this area. Typically such activity is centred on their 'treasury' divisions: financial management operations within companies. In effect they are complex financial institutions, almost akin to investment banks, that exist within what are normally classified as non-financial companies. Among other things they can be involved in capital markets and funding (including debt and equity finance), asset management and risk management. Other forms of financial activity by non-financial firms may be even more apparent to consumers. The provision of consumer credit by retail and manufacturing companies is perhaps the most obvious example.

On the financial side, there are also many ways in which financial institutions get involved in other sectors. One of the most important is the holding of shares and bonds by fund management groups through vehicles such as pension funds. The largest British groups in this area include Invesco Perpetual, Legal & General and M&G Securities. In effect, most British public companies of any size are ultimately owned by institutional investors. With the increasing emphases on corporate governance, such investors are also becoming more involved in each company's strategic decision making. Therefore the City, with its complex mediating role, does not just involve financial institutions, at least as narrowly defined. The larger non-financial companies are also caught in the web of London's financial activities. So too, it should be remembered, is the state. The question now is, how much has this pattern changed since 2007?

The City since 2007

On much of what has happened in the City since 2007 there can be little doubt: the financial crisis came as a surprise to most, key banks were part-nationalised as a result, an economic recession followed, and there has been much talk of regulatory reform. How much all this has affected London's mediating role is more difficult to discern. Until the middle of 2007 everything appeared to be going well in the City. Gordon Brown, in one of his final utterances as Chancellor of the Exchequer (head of the UK Treasury), said in his annual Mansion House speech that the City had created: 'an era that history will record as the beginning of a new golden age for the City of London' (Brown 2007). He was far from alone in taking such a view. The Bank of England's Financial Stability Report opened its April 2007 issue with the words: 'The UK financial system remains highly resilient' (Bank of England 2007). It did go on to note the risks posed by problems in the surging American sub-prime mortgage market, but overall it was sanguine about these.

Soon afterwards several problems began to become apparent. Liquidity started to dry up in European credit markets as a result of global concerns. In Britain, Northern Rock, a medium-sized mortgage lender, was the first high-profile casualty. After a run on the bank the institution was nationalised in February 2008. At that point it was widely hoped that the Northern Rock debacle was a one-off event. But the worst was yet to come. The collapse of Lehman Brothers, a Wall Street investment bank, in September 2008 triggered a crisis that threatened the integrity of the global banking system. Two of Britain's largest banks were part-nationalised and other troubled institutions were subsumed within them. Within days of the Lehman crisis, Lloyds TSB had taken over the troubled HBOS banking group, which operated Bank of Scotland and Halifax. Bradford & Bingley, another mortgage lender, was nationalised and its operations sold to Spain's Santander. But further rescue packages failed to stabilise some of Britain's core financial institutions. Both Lloyds and RBS were brought into state ownership by early 2009. Such a move would have been unthinkable before the crisis.

The start of the financial crisis was soon followed by a global economic downturn. Britain's GDP dipped towards the end of 2008, falling 0.1 per cent over the year, before dropping by 4.9 per cent in 2009 (ONS 2010). Since then, at least at the time of writing (May 2011), it has experienced a weak and patchy recovery. Other developed economies also experienced a drop in output, although the downturn was generally more muted in developing countries.

There is also little doubt about the ferocity of attacks on the City by politicians, particularly on the subject of bankers' bonuses. Vince Cable, Secretary of State for Business and a Liberal Democrat, was perhaps their most vocal critic. At his party's autumn conference in 2010, in a characteristic turn of phrase, he declared that some people in banking were more culpable than militant union leaders:

> On banks, I make no apology for attacking spivs and gamblers who did more harm to the British economy than Bob Crow could achieve in his wildest Trotskyite fantasies, while paying themselves outrageous bonuses underwritten by the taxpayer. There is much public anger about banks and it is well deserved (Cable 2010).

However, beyond all the rhetoric, the reality of reform is more mixed. Although the coalition government has been relatively decisive in reforming state institutions, it has been much more cautious in relation to the private sector.

In June 2010, George Osborne, the incoming Chancellor, announced the new government's intention to replace the FSA as the main financial services regulator. A new Prudential Regulation Authority, to be part of the Bank of England, will regulate all banks, insurers and investment banks from 2013. There will also be a separate Financial Conduct Authority that will regulate conduct in financial markets and their infrastructure. Although this dual system may make regulation more complex, it is unlikely to alter the City's role fundamentally.

The government has been tentative towards private financial institutions, including the banking sector. Despite all the talk of radical reform, such as proposals to erect a regulatory divide between investment and commercial banking, at the time of writing no such measures have been activated. The new coalition government did appoint an Independent Commission on Banking which is due to publish its final report by the end of September 2011. But whatever the report says, it will not be binding on the government. In any event several years will have elapsed between the onset of the credit crunch in 2007 and the implementation of any such structural banking reform. Other sectors of the City are even less likely to face significant regulatory reform. To discover what has changed, it is necessary to look at the fine detail of recent developments.

In some respects state policy towards the financial system is, at least up to a point, contradictory. On the one hand, the banks have benefited enormously from loose monetary policy: low official interest rates and quantitative easing (essentially the state printing money). Their profits have been bolstered as they can obtain capital more cheaply while still lending it out at a relatively high rate. On the other hand, the British regulators, working with the Bank for International Settlements in Basel which sets the global standard, is tightening capital adequacy requirements for banks. In effect, the banks are being asked to keep more capital in reserve and therefore lend relatively less. The conflict here is mainly a temporal one. Although the banks have already been told to hold more capital, the requirements are scheduled to become progressively more stringent in a run-up to full implementation in 2019. It is also worth noting that the insurance industry is also being told to comply with a more stringent capital adequacy regime, known as Solvency II, imposed by the European Union.

Conclusion

Changes to the City since 2007 have, so far at least, been relatively marginal. They mainly relate to the relationship between the state and private institutions rather than the core functions of the City: Lloyds and the Royal Bank of Scotland were part nationalised; the Bank of England is taking over many of the regulatory functions of the FSA; the Bank has bolstered liquidity by keeping interest rates low and engaging in quantitative easing; but over the longer term tougher capital requirements are likely to push banks towards more conservative lending policies. The complex mediating role of the City that emerged before 2007 remains intact.

Financial institutions are still much more than mere conduits moving capital from those who have it in excess to those who need it. They have become substantial players in the convoluted manipulation and circulation of capital. The City's 'risk revolution', with the rise of a large market for instruments designed to transfer risk, has added another twist to the story.

Nor should the City be seen as confined to financial institutions narrowly defined. Both large non-financial companies and state institutions play an integral role. The lines between financial and non-financial as well as public and private have become increasingly blurred in the contemporary economy. In the most abstract terms the City remains what it has been for over three centuries: a mediator of capital. But the forms of mediation have become more convoluted and complex than ever before.

References

Bagehot, W. (1999). *Lombard Street*. New York: Wiley (First published 1873).

Bank of England, Reproduction of Bank of England Act 1694, available at www.bankofengland.co.uk/about/legislation/1694act.pdf, accessed 28 April 2011.

Bank of England (2007). Financial Stability Report, Issue 21, available at http://www.bankofengland.co.uk/publications/news/2007/050.htm, accessed 28 April 2011.

Ben-Ami, D. (2001). *Cowardly Capitalism*. Chichester: John Wiley.

Brown, G. (2007). Speech by the Chancellor of the Exchequer, the Rt Hon Gordon Brown MP, to Mansion House. available at http://webarchive.nationalarchives.gov.uk/20071001180823/http://hm-treasury.gov.uk/newsroom_and_speeches/press/2007/press_68_07.cfm, accessed 28 April 2011.

Cable, V. (2010). Vince Cable's speech to the Liberal Democrat conference, available at http://www.libdems.org.uk/speeches_detail.aspx?title=Vince_Cable's_speech_to_Conference&pPK=ce7d1681-e9c2-43bf-92db-2baa8fa77e4e, accessed 28 April 2011.

City of London (2011) statistics, available at http://www.cityoflondon.gov.uk/Corporation/LGNL_Services/Business/Business_support_and_advice/Economic_information_and_analysis/Research+and+statistics+FAQ.htm, accessed 28 April 2011.

Freeman, A. (2000). *The Risk Revolution and its Impact on Securities Markets*. Zurich: International Securities Market Association.

Hilferding, R. (1981). *Finance Capital*. London: Routledge (First published in German in 1910). Available at http://www.marxists.org/archive/hilferding/1910/finkap/index.htm, accessed 28 April 2011.

Hunt, B. (2003). *The Timid Corporation*. Chichester: John Wiley.

Lenin, V.I. (1963). *Imperialism: The Highest Stage of Capitalism* (First published in Russian in 1917), Moscow: Progress. Available at http://www.marxists.org/archive/lenin/works/1916/imp-hsc/index.htm#ch07, accessed 28 April 2011.

Office for National Statistics (ONS) (2010). Blue Book 2010 (national account statistics). Available at www.statistics.gov.uk/downloads/theme.../bluebook2010.pdf, accessed 28 April 2011.

Strange, S. (1986). *Casino Capitalism*. Oxford: Blackwell.

TheCityUK (2010). *Financial Markets in the UK*. November 2010. Available at http://www.thecityuk.com/what-we-do/reports/articles/2010/november/financial-markets-in-the-uk-november-2010.aspx, accessed 28 April 2011.

Turner, A. (2010). 'What do banks do? Why do credit booms occur? What can public policy do about it?', in A. Turner et al. *The Future of Finance*. London: London School of Economics and Political Science.

Chapter 8
The Apprentice: Realities and Fictions for the London Skyline

Iain Macrury

A concrete metropolis of unparalleled strength and purpose.

Introduction, Donald Trump (2004) *The US Apprentice*, Season 1 episode 1[1]

The human economy, then, is embedded and enmeshed in institutions, economic and non-economic. The inclusion of the non-economic is vital.

Karl Polanyi (1957), *The Economy as Instituted Process*, 146

Playing and Reality: *The Apprentice's* Fictitious Capital

In a book about 'fictitious capitals' this chapter explores London from perspectives afforded by looking at a highly popular[2] reality television-based presentation of the city. In its production, staging and narration, the BBC's *The Apprentice*,[3] broadcast in the UK since 2005, incidentally but forcibly, serially foregrounds London-as-cityscape (Figure 8.1). In particular both signature imagery and the show's unfolding events stage and are staged by *London*; presented in its guise as a hyper-modern global metropolis, signalled especially by mock up Canary Wharf offices[4] and framed and reframed throughout each episode by wide-angle panning shots of the city's iconic skyscrapers; the Swiss Re building (colloquially 'the Gherkin'), Tower42 (once the NatWest Tower) and with One Canada Square at

1 Trump is speaking against a backdrop of footage showing skyscrapers and the New York stock exchange – and in the relatively recent context of the September 11th terrorist attacks on New York's Twin Towers.

2 The Apprentice has been successful in growing a large prime time audience – topping 9 million in series 7, and with critical acclaim expressed in awards from the Royal television society and BAFTA. It has developed a range of subsidiary spin off shows including celebrity-based competitions and a *Junior Apprentice* programme aimed at young audiences.

3 The show is developed from a 2004 format launched in the USA with Donald Trump standing as the 'master'/'employer'.

4 (Fictive) location of the show's famous boardroom – and vantage point from which Sir Alan is imagined to survey the competition – alongside his trusty aides – Nick Hewer and Karen Brady (with former assistant judge Margaret less prominently involved in recent series.

Canary Wharf coded as the show's Head Quarters[5] set against London's growing clusters of surrounding financial-industry edifices. As Jonathan Freedland puts it in a 2006 review of the second series: 'London never looked so good' (Freedland: 2006). This is Marion Boyer's (1995) 'figured city' for the small screen.

The Apprentice's London is also a site of everyday commerce and business culture, ersatz arenas springing up in shopping malls and commercial offices with major parts of each episode requiring contestants to pit their wits on location, to 'get their hands dirty' in the reality show's business simulation tasks. Each episode samples an industry-based 'task' staging problems themed to refer to an array of commercial and professional areas of work; from selling rag-and-bone 'junk', to used car sales, to restaurant management, to market trading, to food manufacture and retail, to advertising and branding. These simulations are certainly in the register of 'game', serious as competitors become in pursuit of their goals. In genre terms the show has been cast as reality TV[6] (McGuigan 2008). Of course there appears to be little intention on the part of producers towards realism as such.[7] Instead a general understanding prevails in accord with genre convention, so that, telling and high pressured as the representative 'work' situations performed by the candidates might well be, the show is largely unconcerned with verisimilitude in relation to depictions of its work-themed scenarios.[8] In particular, while the show gives emphasis to 'city' locations there is no real engagement, no dramatisation of the major kinds of work undertaken in London's financial districts. Candidates might design a funny 'app' for an iPhone or seek to bake a better biscuit, but they are not tasked with derivatives trading or hedge fund management. This simple *trompe-l'œil* substitution – placing fictive concrete work in the spaces and places of actual abstract work – the real work undertaken beneath the city vistas on show can be examined as part of the shows appeal.

In the 'balloon debate' format typical of such shows, one by one and episode by episode the wannabe apprentices are removed from the game with Alan Sugar leading a panel and making a final evaluation before firing a candidate – that week's

5 One well known fiction in relation to the show's presentation is that the boardroom is in fact not located at Canary Wharf and that Lord Sugar's Amstrad offices are based in unglamorous Brentwood, an Essex-based suburb some distance from London's city-metropolis.

6 The show was invented by a producer who also made a US format called Survivor. The 'balloon debate' style pattern of competition and weekly ejection by some process of voting and/pr judgement is standard to the 'reality' format.

7 Other reality-style shows emphasise the fly-on-the-wall-exploration of working sites, notably airports and hotels. However, the surveillance aspect of *The Apprentice's* reality-TV commitments are fulfilled more fully in relation to emotional expose, framing the contestants 'seemingly real pain of failure and rejection for instance skilful editing juxtaposing hubris and incompetence, arrogance, tears, shame and shamelessness in contestants' self-presentations.

8 There is an extended debate about the accuracy and usefulness of the show's material as a resource in business education (Lair 2011; Wice 2006; Huber 2008).

'victim' is denied the winner's opportunity to become the master's apprentice and, formerly, to earn a 'six figure salary' or lately, to receive a £250,000 investment, a detailed format change reflecting a shift, post-crunch, as the show sought to endorse a more substantively entrepreneurial spirit for London and for Sir Alan – appointed entrepreneurship Czar in 2009. At the end of the series, one winner remains. He or she will be the apprentice.

Each episode is fronted by Sir Alan Sugar, presented partly as a quintessential London wheeler-dealer entrepreneur and partly as shrewd experienced business sage. Sugar is assertively *not* an establishment city figure, nor is there anything abstract about Sir Alan's to-the-point argot. Sugar's Hackney background, starting as a by-the-bootstraps electrical goods trader[9] is frequently mentioned in the show. His past stands as illustration and resource to warrant assertions and judgements about the rights and wrongs of business practice. Partly connected to the fame accruing to Sir Alan Sugar via *The Apprentice* (he had already been knighted in 2000) Sugar was offered his role of 'Enterprise Czar' by the New Labour administration in 2009 with an accompanying place in the House of Lords (Murray 2010). Couldry and Littler (2011) rightly point out the show's endorsement of neoliberal notions of 'charismatic' workplace leadership – embodied in Alan Sugar. This complementary reading of *The Apprentice* further asserts *place* as a key preoccupation – with London figured and refigured on screen accruing and evoking identifications and value in the process.

The Apprentice offers a particular and popular framing for London presented as a working capital. In terms made popular by Roland Barthes (1972), the show might be called 'mythic'.[10] Each episode offers up a fictive and poignant version of London-as-work-place – in the guise of light entertainment but with the underpinning structures of morality tale and moral trial. As such *The Apprentice* serves as an everyday media object, as a set of ritual (Couldry 2008; Couldry and Littler 2011) narrations and dramas which engage across media, and with the prime time TV show supplemented by subsidiary shows, a web site, a twitter feed and extensive cross media coverage.[11] The show, its coverage and its widely observed 'water-cooler' popularity together combine to produce a complex virtual-

9 Sugar's fortune emerged between from success in consumer electrical culminating in highly profitable partnerships with digital broadcasters and in computing – his company Amstrad has been a prominent UK High St. Brand. As Couldry and Littler (2011) observe: 'Sugar is indicative of the discourse of meritocracy which has become so central to New Labour government discourse, as the exhortations of Gordon Brown (ex-Prime Minister and Chancellor of the Exchequer) that schoolchildren should be more like Sir Alan in their entrepreneurialism, indicates' (Wice 2006).

10 Barthes famously described the mythologies surrounding everyday representations and practices in essays collected under the heading Mythologies (Barthes 1972;1979)

11 The show's official site can found at: http://www.bbc.co.uk/apprentice/. See also http://www.bbc.co.uk/programmes/b007qgcl for information on the sister show *The Apprentice You're Fired* in which 'The newly-fired candidate from The Apprentice receives a grilling in front of a studio audience'

serial media event each year (2005-2012 in the UK). This constitutes a fragile but engaging and extended conversation to obliquely cut across and illuminate more serious and deep rooted anxieties and reflections on London, value and work and on 'the city'.

In 2009 much anxiety about London and 'the city' was for instance elaborated through discussion of the social value of financial services, notably focussing on Financial Services authority head Lord Turner of Ecchinswell's comment that activity within the sector had become bloated and was of questionable social utility.[12] The debate set in train in 2008 continues to define the evolving image and reflections upon London-as-city and as site for economic productivity and social value.

This chapter proposes that one part of *The Apprentice's* popular appeal lies here – in the opening up of a casual reflective space through which anxieties and desires connected to the imagination of London-as-working-capital can emerge, alongside impromptu notions of value and judgements in these regards. All are fictionalised and dramatically played out on screen – and consumed largely in the Freudian mode of displacement.[13] *The Apprentice* appeals further as a media-based counter to a widespread and disorganised sense, that London, and in particular 'the City' is in many regards an abstract and peculiarly distant place whose productivities and fortunes are perceived to be increasingly delinked from the 'real' economy,[14] from consistently purposeful substantive activity and, even, from the political and moral economy of the capital city and the wider UK.

Critiques identifying London's abstraction are recently amplified through extended considerations of the banking crisis and its aftermaths. Certainly at a remove from formal public debate on the topic, nevertheless in its popular blend of light entertainment and reality format *The Apprentice* seems to engage with this

---

12 Lord Turner of Ecchinswell, an influential figure in the reform of banking rules in London and beyond, said that the City had grown 'beyond a socially reasonable size', accounting for too much of national output and sucking in too many of Britain's brightest graduates. 'I think some of it is socially useless activity,' he said, adding that the financial sector had 'swollen beyond its socially useful size' and seemed to make excessively large profits. Lord Turner named fixed-income securities, trading, derivatives and hedging as areas that have grown beyond socially optimal levels, adding that fund management and share trading might also have grown too big. *The Times*, 27 August 2009.

13 Classically Freud used the psychoanalytic term 'displacement' to describe a defensive organisation in the individual psyche whereby a patient might obsess, or otherwise direct attention away (via joking or parapraxis) from an object, person or idea that was troubling or traumatic and onto a focus that was psychically safe, less taxing, less disturbing – but perhaps still obliquely connected to the reality being avoided.

14 This delinking does not extend to the consequences of expanded debt in the aftermath of the governments numerous and substantial interventions to prop up banks' financial deficits in the wake of the crunch. A direct line can be drawn between this public expenditure and coalition policies drastically reducing welfare and public sector expenditure – with a knock on effect for national employment rates and general levels of public service.

debate both directly and indirectly. Thus before the launch of the fifth series in 2009 BBC controller Jay Hunt claimed:

> In the current economic climate, *The Apprentice* has never seemed more relevant. That emphasis on sheer hard graft seems more appropriate than ever before. (Holmwood 2009)

The 2009 series included a number of 'Buy British' tasks and a local regeneration project. As noted, subsequent series have replaced salary prizes with entrepreneurial investments.

Indirectly the show allows its audiences to symbolically offset 'the city's' abstract unintelligibility by offering up a peculiarly engaging mix of comedy, reality and fantasy in the form of a game: amounting to a drama of the city, for the city and staged and set up as a substitute for a London where work, meaning and value are sufficiently disturbed as to invite both refection *and* disavowal.[15] This presents viewers with a tabloidisation of business:

> Business culture is increasingly drawing on tabloid discourse to construct an image of itself as 'democratic', contemporary and cool (Littler 2007; McGuigan 2006)
>
> and the theatrics of *the Apprentice* are part of that shift. (Couldry and Littler 2011: 274)

This more dramatic business discourse functions especially in relation to the perceived 'abstraction' of the city, the show seeking to forge connections between the intelligible real-world commercialism figured in business tasks and in attendant reflections and evaluations, and the spaces and places of 'the city'. *The Apprentice* makes it easier to imagine continuities and connections between the algorithmic finance-industries inhabiting London's sky line offices, and the 'real' concrete commercialism of everyday trading, creativity and 'graft'. The abstract city-image is leant credibility in a screened association leveraging the affective 'reality' of the TV show and trading on its task-focused ethos.

Unreal City: Disembedded London

> In referring to human activities the term economic is a compound of two meanings that have independent roots. We call them the substantive and the formal meaning…The two meanings could not be further apart; semantically they lie in opposite directions of the compass. (Polanyi 1957: 139-40)

15 See footnote 12 above.

The Apprentice is usefully considered in the context of a broader argument about processes of ongoing and contemporary change and with a focus on London as 'fictitious capital'. The particular disturbance confronting and confronted in London here is *abstraction*.[16] Contemporary urban processes intensively played out across London in recent decades can usefully be understood under this heading. James Carrier (1998: 2) provides a helpful description of what he terms 'practical abstraction' a process he links both to Miller's (1998; Carrier and Miller 1998) conception of 'virtualism' and back to Polanyi's analysis of 'dis-embedding', noting, correctly, that many of the mechanisms whereby social processes become 'abstract' are delivered thorough shifts in practice – a dynamic historically in evidence as part of the emergence of modern societies.

> If abstraction can be taken as the removing of something from the social and practical contexts in which people previously existed, then one can talk about practical abstraction. That is, people can find that their practical activities have, for reasons beyond their control, changed in a way that make them more abstract: from the perspective of those who confront the changes, these practical activities have become removed from the contexts in which they existed. (Carrier 1998: 25)

Abstraction, as applied in this discussion, is both a matter of spatial as well socio-economic change, and, following Carrier (1998) can be said to have a practical aspect played out, for instance, in work cultures, as well as in the look and feel of London-as-place – in the built environment and practical managerial frameworks performing 'the city'.

Finance, London's dominant industry is, of course, susceptible to abstraction, dealing as it must with complex economic models and algorithms. But financial industries also and at the same time support real substantive needs and wants, for services related to the saving and investment of money, for housing, for structured borrowing, for inheritance and, lately for education, health and social care and so on. Indeed current debates about regulation and restructuring of London's banks[17] have revolved around a dichotomy seeking to protect High Street banking from

16 The identification of 'abstraction' here opens connections to a complex debate taking focus away from the main focus here. Certainly however there are key issues to flag up about the embodiment, location and performance of 'abstraction' in the social world. Carrier's account of abstraction as a practical process is helpful (Carrier 1998, see also Frith 1998 and Fine 1998) but it is useful to also note Miller's (1998; 2002; 2011) discussions of 'virtualism' which is linked to this concern with abstraction, and to a debate with Michael Callon (Miller 2002; Callon and Muniesa 2005) regarding the performance of markets and the conception of markets as practical-collective 'devices'. Thus abstraction should not be seen here as airy and un-located, even while its attendant practices and rationalities produce in realities and institutional relations and spatial effects of the kinds identified as 'dislocation' and 'disembedding' in much social theory.

17 Most UK banks are based in London – with one further important other UK financial centres in Edinburgh.

contagious relationships with investment banking. Advocates for better regulation hope that the 'lifeworlds' (Habermas 1987: 355) of ordinary savers and investors can be more effectively shielded from the volatility of the abstract global markets and the risks taken by banks, prone to risky mistakes linked to serially asserting and applying the formal logic of theoretical finance-driven market economics in the abstract– treating economic models as real and robust rather than as hypothetical and abstracted.[18]

The character and extent of finance's divorce from its former 'real' substantive referents; houses, capital investments and trading, savers' domestic financial concerns, and in favour of formal logical processes taken-as-real, 'treating the economic model of the market as though it were core to actual economies rather than a projection of economists' (Miller 2002: 219) can be said to determine the extent to which the practice of finance has become overly abstracted. As Boltankski and Chiapello (2005) write, describing an emergent and changing ethos in contemporary capitalist accumulation.

> The deregulation of credit markets, their de-compartmentalisation, and the creation of 'new financial products' have multiplied the possibilities of purely speculative profits, whereby capital expands without taking the form of investment in productive activity. (Boltanski and Chiapello 2005: vii)

Such abstraction-process are linked to related terms discussed in a number of chapters in this volume; especially financialisation (in particular), globalisation, extended commoditisation, 'time-space compression' (Harvey 1990) and deregulation – with London as a key network centre where these dynamics intensify and radiate. These processes are by no means total, defining or unitary.[19] Nevertheless they afford narratives framing a number of evident transformations experienced in London's recent and ongoing evolutions and crises, with parallel and interlinked crises extensive across the UK and globally.

This is not to say that London is 'abstract' as such. It retains its immanence, its multiplicities; its streets and scenes, its material and cultural resonance; cosmopolitan, productive, energetic and creative. And yet, in different places,

---

18 In relation to the notion of 'lifeworld', Jürgen Habermas observes that there is an ever present risk, namely, 'that the imperatives of autonomous subsystems make their way into the lifeworld from the outside—like colonial masters coming into a tribal society—and force a process of assimilation upon it. The diffused perspectives of the local culture cannot be sufficiently coordinated to permit the play of the metropolis and the world market to be grasped from the periphery (Habermas 1987: 355)

19 Frith makes an important criticism of over-arching narratives of change reminding that analysis must distinguish between confusing theoretical logics and narratives and the logic of practice. This applies in his notion of practical capitalism, a conception alert to the complex and multiple contradictions attenuating abstraction, globalisation, technological change and time-space compression (see Frith 1998: 162-3).

in differing registers London is marked by, sets out and displays a tendency to and deference towards this economistic abstraction. The extension of such abstracting logic into our structuring and experience of further spheres stands as both present condition and future threat (Miller 1998; 2002; Fine 1998; Carrier 1998). It is the model of efficiency and modernity, as per Ritzer's (1993) account of McDonaldisation, but it is also the target for reflective redress as we think about places, spaces and the development of contemporary city. *The Apprentice* is relevant in this context.

Apprenticeship: Dreaming the Substantive Economy

Part of *The Apprentice*'s attraction lies in its title and in its explicit but underlying theme. The name of the show 'Apprentice' alludes to a tradition of hands-on skills acquisition, an intimate social-relational process depending upon extended engagement with a master and with the social world of his work and craft – the workshop (Sennet 2008; 2006; Rule 1987; Carrier 1998) as a social context for economic productivity and relations. As Bauman observes:

> The very character of apprenticeship [is] an initiation into a totality of patterned existence of the closely-knit trade community. (Bauman 1982: 8)

Notionally, apprenticeship stands as counter to abstract market processes of selection and promotion structuring today's employment markets, predicated, as they are, on a modern discourse of 'careerism', 'personal branding', 'competition' and individuals' 'market value'.

Apprenticeship marks an era where some of the contemporary processes, linked to highly developed market societies, were far less extensive, and so did not so readily define individual 'value': a sociality where there was a demonstrable continuum between work, culture, family and community, place and the productivities in the application of skills and experience. In many ways redolent of the pre-modern, and finding its historical apogee in the proto-modern organisation of work, apprenticeship becomes rhetorically and nostalgically attractive as a traditional counterpoint to the hyper-modern realities of a risky, unsettling and marketised connection between work, self-identity, economy and society.

The Apprentice offers a notional and compressed version of apprenticeship as a prize, along with a large financial reward. While actual motivations in the show are multiple and complex, in the televisual poetics of *The Apprentice* and registered in the very title is the idea that the contestants seek not only to be contracted – to be paid the winner's salary. They want something more. The show also maps a journey from 'outside' Sir Alan's circle and inwards (project by project); it figures a promise of initiation and connection, to narrative and membership, to work and success framed not only by economic reward but by durable social engagement through work. The show valorises not just competitive and financial success but, also, instituted success. The atavism underwriting the show's title can be considered as a mass-mediated instance of social dreaming – with audiences' displaced desire reaching for 'apprenticeship', a rhetorical and compensatory emblem for the employment-sociality formally ejected from London's abstracted marketised economy and its casualised and volatile employment markets.

Foregrounding the Background: London, Place and Work

> According to Lao Tse, the reality of a hollow object is in the void and not in the walls that define it. He was speaking, of course, of spiritual realities. These are the realities also of the Canary Wharf Tower. The power of the void is increased and … with its supporting structure creates a portal to the sky … a door to the infinite. (Cesar Pelli, architect's speech at the opening of One Canada Square at Canary Wharf 1991)

The Apprentice is distinctive amongst reality shows in its studied consciousness of place. The place-based inflection stands as significant here in thinking about London. Put simply the aesthetic and presentational style of the show, redolent as it is with vistas traversing Canary Wharf, the financial districts of Docklands and, lately other numerous other iconic buildings,[20] works effectively to connect the show's discursive play and drama (around work, employee 'value' and values), with London underlined as space and place – as economic 'seat'.

It is commonplace to point out the ways in which cities 'star' in novels, film and lately television. 1990s drama *Sex and the City* is all about New York, as are Woody Allen's 1970s comedies (*Manhattan* and *Annie Hall* in particular). Inspector Morse is more or less a televisual hymn to Oxford. In each case the city-vision provides or implies an ethos – an urban style and a collection or collocation of subjectivities. It becomes both set and set *up*: an interruptive backdrop that sometimes supports and at other moments undermines characters' particular urbanity. So it is with *The Apprentice*. The show places its contestants 'on trial'; stuck in London traffic or in Sugar's putative Canary Wharf boardroom: do they fit in *this* city – are they at home *here* in and amongst these places? The city stands in the show as both obstacle to and destination for its competitive participants – as they negotiate the 'reality' contest.[21] Such London-based urban-imagery cut into

20 Such as 'The Gherkin' and Tower 42 and soon The Shard.

21 Numerous episodes unfold in which knowledge and ignorance of London is deployed by contestants seeking to solve problems. Much on screen time is devoted to contestants in taxis and hire cars shuttling between distant destinations around the London compass – and as they seek to return to the notional 'hub' Sir Alan's boardroom in Canary Wharf. And, finally, the lucky winner will notionally be installed at Sir Alan's side. Not in fact in the Canary Wharf Tower where so much putatively goes on – but at Sir Alan Sugar's

The Apprentice, like its musical score, drives the sense, the sensibility and the culture of events as they unfold.

London's city skyline is both figure and ground for the show. The opening shots, backed by Prokofiev's imposing 'Dance of the Knights' from *Romeo and Juliet*, comprise perhaps the most recognisable credit sequences in UK television. Sound and vision lend context, drama and affective charge to the business activities depicted. The same vistas have been foregrounded in recent years the context of anxiety and confusion about the 'content' and 'function' of some of London's buildings.[22] These have provided a spectacular stage and backdrop for narratives of economic success, but now (also) London's iconic skylines must signify and stand witness to news stories of grand-scale failures and to crises and decline. Spectacular architecture has become linked in the popular imaginary to over-speculation, abstracting de-control and market collapse.

Leslie Sklair (2005; 2006; 2010) has pointed up the iconicity of corporate buildings – part of a transnational vernacular for globalisation. As Sklair argues, global capitalism … mobilises the commercial potential of generic globalisation in the sphere of architecture as it does more or less successfully in all other spheres (Sklair 2010). A consequence of the financial crisis has been some uncertainty about the referentiality and value of such pervasive architectural iconicity – with knock on anxieties about the city-as-a whole[23] and underscoring more imminent and specific concerns regarding the commercial and market value of commercial property in London. To specify: the extension of anxieties about disembedding and abstraction outlined above extend into sentiment regarding the iconic built environment. The city risks losing the 'moral' value built into its aesthetic skyline – a 'hyper modern' skyline framing London and the city and tacitly affirming the coherence, the purposeful development and function of the (financial/global) cityscape.

The show's drama, staged by the city in this way, ends up offering up fictive work content for the city – and a framing, scripted sociality structured as game. The show populates the abstract city – the hollow abstract towers spreading across London's skyline – light heartedly but arrestingly figuring rituals of work, productivity, creativity as well as failure and ineptitude. This produces

---

real headquarters – until recently in Brentwood. On occasion contestants are taken 'global' with notable trips in past series to Morocco and to Paris.

22 TV and press imagery have continually featured the towers at London's Canary Wharf, the Swiss Re Building, widely known as 'the Gherkin' and Tower42, just as are framed in The Apprentice's vistas of London, along with a number of other banking head offices in London's financial districts. As finance-industry news spread to more frequently dominate front pages and news headlines in 2008-9 and subsequently, and with the credit crunch and its aftermaths demanding serial coverage and overview, the 'image' of the city – and attendant architectural imageries – has been very much in the frame for news audiences.

23 With The Shard soon to be added to the London skyline, a new tallest building for London, there is evidently a continuing confidence in the value of such structures in the reputation and the functional economic life of a global city like London.

Figure 8.1 The Apprentice dramatises individuals in competition, judgement, justification and business practice but it is also highly conscious of place – London's city skyline is both figure and ground for the show

Source: Photo courtesy of author.

an imaginary dramatic narrative of value, virtue, punishment and reward. Again the show answers an appetite – to apprehend London's *moral* economy. *The Apprentice* offers this up and framing punishment and reward in the imagined spaces of the city – and in a space where, as some have argued, judgement and justice have been suspended and deferred by abstracting market logics. Ethos is added to vista: affect to abstraction.

Moral Trial: *The Apprentice* as Modern Fairy Tale

> It is … no exaggeration to think that a society (or the state of a society) may be defined by the character of the tests it sets itself, through which the social selection of people is conducted, and by conflicts over the more or less just nature of those tests. (Boltanski and Chiapello 2005: 32)

The Apprentice is a moral fable tailored to a generation brought up on *Big Brother* and neoclassical economics. A further element to its imaginary encounter with the abstraction of disembedded market relations is the show's assertion of emotional-narrative engagement. While *The Apprentice* primarily invites the emotional enjoyment of competitive play – for viewers and participants – the structure of the format invites further analysis. A deeper component of the show's appeal lies in its structure as modern fairy tale – dressed up to conform to reality-TV's demands for cringe-making exposure, rendered comedic via slap-stick pitches and narcissistic assertions of success.

Couldry rightly compares reality TV to theatres of cruelty (Couldry 2008). If we are at a safe distance and the pain is largely self-inflicted, people under pressure are often funny or otherwise compelling – sympathy gives over to something else, especially on reality TV. Like much loved 70s classic *Fawlty Towers*, *The Apprentice* stages a painful kind of neurotic chaos. It exploits its frantic protagonists' confused eagerness to serve either the projected ethos of the master, or the embodied abstractions of market-competitive orthodoxy. Candidates become mini cartoon capitalists on the living streets of London or spluttering justifications in the boardroom. *On s*creens since 2005 and in a number of variants, this has provided one of the present generation's major workplace-comedy of manners. Like most comedy, *The Apprentice* is also, in the end, a morality tale.

The Apprentice's further appeal is to the affirmation of moral judgements – an attempt to link the abstract emotionally unintelligible world of city work, and to dramatise a process whereby 'good' is affirmed and embodied in one who triumphs, who *inherits*, in a narrative underpinned by the emotional register of a fairy story. Whoever devised *The Apprentice* format no doubt took inspiration from Roald Dahl's *Charlie and the Chocolate Factory* (1973) – another cruel theatre of selection and judgement. *The Apprentice* re-plays Willy Wonka[24] for Reality TV. The 'children', having won golden tickets to the mythic factory are presented to the master (Wonka/Sugar) passing through in a series of inventive scenarios: An ongoing moral trial, or, as Sugar likes to call his equivalent, 'a process'. They are given instructions and clues and we see them fail, one by one. Each is then unceremoniously ejected, weeping into their Blackberry, if not turned actually into one – remember Violet Beauregarde.

The annual crop of contestants readily personify the moral failings of childhood favourites; the greed of Augustus Gloop, the know-it-all-entitlement of Violet Beauregard, and, of course, spoiled 'daddy's girl' Veruca Salt: 'I want an Oompa Lumpa, and I want it now!' Pick any series and there are candidates who readily reference Dahl's modern-consumerist archetypes.[25]

---

24 If Alan Sugar makes an unlikely Willy Wonka, notwithstanding his sweet-toothed name, nevertheless Canary Wharf's towers suggest a credible great glass elevator (Dahl 1973b).

25 The most important Dahl character in all this has not yet been mentioned. Mike Teavee (TV) is a lesson to us all. He was the child for whom nothing mattered except that it was on screen. His fate was to be transmitted through a TV signal. Mike Teavee's efforts

The prize, as in Sugar's game, is a place at the master's side, the key to the factory. The master seeks an heir, an 'apprentice': the desperate heirs seek an inheritance – all the chocolate you can eat, or a £250,000 investment from Lord Sugar. A psychoanalyst might conjecture that the errant children in the chocolate factory are all also seeking more adequate father figures. It would be wrong to wildly extend that point to *The Apprentice* candidates. However, it is safe to conjecture that part of the show's appeal, if read psychoanalytically, stands in its offering some affirmation of and structure to contain a version of the 'good' in the city and in work, to construct from the process of elimination a further structure, also basic to the shows narrative – of *legitimation*: a way of reassuring ourselves and affirming that in 'the city' there remains an ethos supporting evaluations of good and bad – a moral economy as check and balance against an abstract market-place logics.

The provision of such a framework is especially attractive in relation to and in the context of popular anxieties about London-as-unintelligible city, the 'city' out of control and seemingly deferring regulation and (communal) reparation. As such this accounts for *The Apprentice's* further attraction – an attraction which of course might readily be cast as dangerously seductive – for the show does not invite real practical judgement. Instead it produces a light hearted fictive scene where judgement is applied satisfactorily and ritually, and in the seeming absence of a position to pass or enact judgement on real failures in the Square Mile.

Clash of Cities: *The Apprentice* as Legitimation

> It seems to us scarcely open to doubt that at an ideological level…capitalism will face increasing difficulties, if it does not restore some grounds for hope to those whose engagement is required for the functioning of the system as a whole. (Boltanski and Chiapello 2005: xliii)

The differences between TV shows and fairy tales are as illuminating as the comparisons between them. Thus the moral ground of *The Apprentice* is not as raw, not as comprehensive as in Dahl's fable. The show, pantomimic as it is, feeds into a more articulated morality play than Dahl's child's morality fable. The show does not simply, just pull out the 'baddies' and reward the good character – the one who passes all the tests. Instead the show tests the contestants and seeks to affirm a 'good' candidate, selecting and scripting an individual to embody a suitable ethos – a suitable version of business practice and capitalism befitting and connecting to the projected ethos of Lord Sugar and his corporation and his vision of a regenerated practical capitalism in the city. The show attempts to perform, or, rather, attempts to address an appetite for 'an ideological reconstruction [of

---

to become bigger by broadcasting himself made him very much smaller. Perhaps there is a lesson in there somewhere too?

business ethos] to demonstrate that the world of work does indeed still possess a "meaning"' (Boltanski and Chiapello 2005: 29).[26] The Apprentice amounts not to a critique of capitalism as such; far from it: but an exploration of variants within the differing scripts laid out in the show.

The show's format invites reflection: justification and the elaboration, in theory and practice, of competing 'scripts'. Versions of 'business' are hinted at. Differing ethos becomes personified in candidates; in Sir Alan, too; and with understated gravitas, in his 'eyes and ears', the experienced mentor/auditors Nick and Margaret, and lately Karen Brady. From within the series values begin to crystallise, emerging across the boardroom table and during tasks; between

Table 8.1 Ideal Types of business 'cities': Criteria for status and justification

Ethos	'city'	Justification of decisions and judgements made primarily in terms of...	Candidates/ commentary
Here the ethos depends upon a performative valorising of creativity, authenticity, artistry and so on. Also some valuing of religious purity/integrity etc.	The inspirational city	Authenticity and creativity. The scripts of romantic individualism, non-conformity and 'zaniness'. To what extent is there evidence of creative risk taking? It is carried credibly.	Candidates are often rejected for over-playing a creative approach and advertising creativity – as divorced from the hard sell approach favoured by sugar is mocked
Here status depends on respect for tradition, seniority and on enacting reciprocal dependencies allied to familial and generational structures. The 'great man' as elder, sage and protector	The domestic city	Respect for elders and continuity of concern with past values and approaches. To what extent does the candidate offer deference to the knowledge/experience of his elders?	Sugar asserts a discourse of respect, but uses his own biography to undermine candidates' assertions of entitlement and scripts of success linked to inherited privilege

26 Boltanski and Chiapello identify this 'appetite' not with TV programming but with the tracts of business books published in recent decades and which support their detailed analytic study of evolving business ethos. Their analysis is pre-empted by a helpful discussion of the 'globalization of reflexive business knowledge' by Nigel Thrift (Thrift 1998).

Table 8.1 (continued)

Here Status depends on the opinion of others. This is the city of 'celebrity culture' or, more soberly, of reputation systems and good conduct dependent upon 'the community view'.	The reputational city	The standing of the individual amongst members of important reference groups. What do peers, customers and other colleagues think of the candidate?	Sugar underplays aspects of his own celebrity, even as part of his cultivation of image. A notable failure in this regard was a 2010 candidate who announced himself as 'Baggs the brand' and who was ejected with an extra dose of scorn.
Here status is established via political power. How fully and how well does 'the great man' represent his constituency, his team, his firm and so on.	The civic city	The capacity to represent fairly, to subordinate their own views or aims within the task of representing and respecting the formal views of the group he or she might represent. Includes commitment to social justice as a guiding value	Few candidates emerge from political or public sector spheres and the show does little to support processes of democratic decision-making or social justice. One team failed a task, partly, for poor implementation of a charity-linked marketing scheme selling trainers (McGuigan 2008)
Here status is marked by wealth and acumen in the provision of commodities in the market	The commercial city	The profit motive. How much money has the candidate made. Was he or she successful in selling profitably?	This competent espousal of and performance conforming to version of capitalism seems to have a firmer success rate for candidates and 'winning' each week is often a matter of market competition – who made the most profit. Candidates who sell well and make good profits tend to thrive.

Table 8.1 (concluded)

Here status is primarily a matter of professional or other competence including efficiency and the capacity to 'graft'.	The industrial city	Expertise and technical skill. Was the candidate exhibiting know-how and applying expertise in the delivery of this or that task	A common trope in the shows find Sir Alan exposing failures on the part of candidates whose experience and CVs suggest they have expertise in certain areas – and then nevertheless fail in tasks themed to their 'home' industries. This, while well applied expertise is valued, Sugar rejects much expertise, but serially rewards and endorse graft. In the most recent series (2011) Sugar appointed an inventor, suggesting endorsement of this aspect of the accumulation process

Source: Adapted from Boltanski and Chiapello (2005: 24-6).

statements, judgements and justifications. Unstable and partial as these emerging scripts are, something engaging is transacted across the screen.

Boltanski and Chiapello (2005: 24-6) offer a useful typology here (Table 8.1). They understand the relationship between the various regimes of accumulation in terms of different 'cities'. Each 'city' (as they term it) identifies and is identified in the enactment of specific clusters of ideal typical values – underpinning a kind of regime validating 'success'. They describe these 'cities' as sites for justification (in terms of an appeal to ethos) of particular values affirming status and worth. The moral 'architecture' corroborating value and justification in specific moments makes for the character of 'the city'.

The show (and the reflective after show, where judgement and justification are picked over again and again in comedic mode), together comprise – and make a space for – a ritual enactment of an ethos for sense of 'the city'. The 'city' referred to and presented become, variously and at once, a purely thematic concept (e.g. domestic, reputational. commercial etc.) denoting a cluster of values, a specific location-in transition, i.e. the span linking 'The City of London' between the square mile and Canary Wharf tower so avidly traced in the show's imageries. For the audience, the city becomes also an approximation of an inner world of judgement, as the show affords moments demanding evaluative interventions on the part of viewers mobilising their adherence to this or that city, or, more likely, this or that hybrid combination of 'cities': a city of the mind and of aspiration. The show invites the private formulation via public discussion of 'the good city' – a private-public connection affirmed in the social media traffic that has surrounded the more recent series.

Sir Alan, for his part, appears to judge primarily in terms of the 'commercial city' – with some deference to 'the industrial city'. He is widely criticised for a narrow conception of what really counts in business and for an overly mercantile morality. Critique aside, Sir Alan is enacting an important ritual task in the cultural performance – presenting a version of the old to expose and test emergent and 'new' novice scripts. As Boltanski and Chiapello 2005 put it:

> The spirit of capitalism is transformed to respond to the need to justification by people who are engaged in the capitalist accumulation process at a given moment, but whose values and representations, inherited as a cultural legacy, are still associated with earlier forms of accumulation. (Boltanski and Chiapello 2005: 21)

The moral drama of the show –beyond a broad affirmation of and embodiment of the good apprentice in a winner – comes from a clash of generations and a clash of 'cities'. This clash is interesting in the context of the discussion of London as abstract city. To reiterate the world of work has become somewhat abstract, disembedded from framing scripts. It is lately at a remove from the sets of activities associated with previous regimes of accumulation; it is disconnected from established 'cities' i.e. the instituted regimes of accumulation and legitimating discourses that govern/have governed economic activity in the city-past. Ostensibly the show simply asserts a particular strand of capitalism. But what it also points to is an appetite for some framing, some social structure and moral-political governance of the market. Sugar, in person, cannot provide this. What *The Apprentice* points to, as media object, is a latent desire for a social-ethical frame for the city, for the market and for the people working day by day in those spaces and places.

Evident and widespread fascination with *The Apprentice* can be read as symptomatic of what I want to describe as a *virtual* movement – with the show affording not traditional critique, but a media space where anxieties and deficits in London's culture of work can be explored. This is in no way to say that the show is in any manner critical in its approach to business – again, far from it. As Couldry and Littler suggest 'neoliberal norms are both worked out and endorsed' (Couldry and Littler 2011: 270) and McGuigan (2008) finds engagements with 'cool' cultures in the show to serve mainly marketing ends.

However, in part, and as a general function of its status as entertainment-oriented media product, with a brief to engage audiences and to afford drama, and in part, also as a function of its narrative and meta-narrative structures, the show nevertheless affords a resource – an object around which emotive, moral and evaluative thinking can emerge. In particular *The Apprentice* has a specific salience in London, and that the specific presentation and execution of the show's format in its UK editions has tuned into the show's location – in the city – as a key underpinning theme.

Fictive and playful as it certainly is, *The Apprentice* has contributed a powerful set of imagery to accompany ideas about London – as a centre for business know how and entrepreneurial success. It locates a part of its appeal in a popular media-based image of 'London', in the space of, but in register counterpointed against the 'the city' and its discursive abstraction. This is abstraction of long standing, but that became lately 'real', in the sense of dramatically impacting news agendas, lives and livelihoods via the multiple unravelling of unstable financial mechanisms and in the collapse of fictitious dependences within the fiscal system, as described by Gillian Tett (2009) and others (Turner 2008; Nesvetailova 2010) in the immediate wake of the wake of the 2008 crisis.

There is a hint in the show's popularity of a need for a resilient institutional frame for London's economic life. As Polanyi writes:

> The instituting of the economic process vests that process with unity and stability; it produces a structure with a definite function in society; it shifts the place of the process in society, thus adding significance to its history; it centres interest on values, motives and policy. (Polanyi 1957)

Crucially this is a matter for governance and government, and not for 'leadership' and management styles as the show implies it might be. In the show's reality format, and as Couldry and Littler rightly identify, *The Apprentice* seems to assert commitments to the notion of individual corporate leadership. While such leadership has a place and a value, the city, London and the market require a process of social re-embedding to reconnect finance and the global-local flows of capital to the grounds of political, moral and community-linked governance – not least through a more stable connection between the jobs markets and education – and via real and not fictive apprenticeships. Then, again London might seem more real to more of its inhabitants and the excitement of energy of work will emerge, will be sought and found on the streets and in offices, institutions and work places – and not just on screen.

References

Barthes, R. (1979). 'The Eiffel Tower and Other Mythologies', trans. Richard Howard. New York: Hill & Wang.

Barthes, R. (1972). *Mythologies*. New York: Hill & Wang.

Boltanski, L. and Chiapello, E. (2005). *The New Spirit of Capitalism.* London: Verso.

Boyer, C. 'The great frame up: Fantastic appearances in contemporary spatial politics'. in H. Liggett and D.C. Perry, eds. *Spatial Practices*. Sage: New York

Boyle R. (2008). 'From Troubleshooter to The Apprentice: The changing face of business on British television'. *Media, Culture & Society*, 30(3), 415.

Carrier, J.G. (1998). 'Abstraction in Western economic practice'. *Virtualism. A New Political Economy*, Oxford: Berg.

Couldry, N. and Littler, J. (2011). 'Work, Power and Performance: Analysing the "Reality" Game of The Apprentice'. *Cultural Sociology*, 5(2), 263.

Dahl, R. (1973). *Charlie and the Chocolate Factory*. London: Puffin.

Dahl, R. (1973b). *Charlie and the Great Glass Elevator*. London; Puffin.

Freedland, J. (2006). 'What the Apprentice says about Blair's Britain: Only profit matters' *The Guardian*, Wednesday 3 May 2006.

Hird, C. (2007). Small Screen, *Prospect Magazine*, 135, June 2007.

Holmwood, L. (2009). The Apprentice tackles credit crunch as fifth series launches. *The Guardian*, Tuesday 17 March 2009.

Huber, N. (2008). The apprentice: Is it the real deal? *The Guardian*, Tuesday 27 May 2008.

Mandelson, P. (2008). speech by Rt. Hon. Peter Mandelson Monday, Secretary of State for Trade and Industry, CBI Annual Conference, Monday 2 November 1998.

McGuigan, J. (2008). 'Apprentices to cool capitalism'. *Social Semiotics*, 18(3), 309-19.

Hsin-Yi, L. (2008). 'Behind the Co-Construction of a Narrative of Survival and Success: A Rhetorical Analysis of the Reality TV Program "The Apprentice". available at http://libetd.shu.edu.tw/ETD-db/ETD-search/view_etd?URN=etd-0730108-034142, accessed 20 August 2011.

Lair, D.J. (2011). 'Surviving the Corporate Jungle: The Apprentice as Equipment for Living in the Contemporary Work World'. *Western Journal of Communication*, 75(1), 75-94.

Sklair, L. (2006). Iconic architecture and capitalist globalization, *City*, 10(1), 21-47.

Sugar, A. (2005). *The Apprentice: How to get Hired not Fired*. London: BBC Books.

Wice, H. (2006). 'The Real-life Business Apprentices', *The Independent*, 6 April: 4-5.

Chapter 9
A Tale of Two Journalisms: Counteracting Tendencies in London's Media

Andrew Calcutt

This chapter is made up of three parts: proposition; cross-examination; rebuttal.

My proposition is that the journalism now produced in London falls into two opposing camps. Though these journalisms are markedly different, each of them represents one of the two essential aspects of London today, namely, that aspect of London which exists for its own sake, and that other aspect in which London serves the world – the sense in which this city exists to meet demands that originate elsewhere.

A book concerned with the future of journalism would have to ascertain whether London's journalism can be so divided and yet remain a continuous entity. But there is little room for such considerations here. This part of the present book is primarily interested in London's formative relationship with its culture industries. Thus the main purpose of this chapter is to show how the dual character of journalism today is a construction of one and the same city; this will also reveal how the same city – London in its current iteration – is now answerable to two sets of demands, one mainly domestic, the other largely international. Conversely, showing how both journalisms belong to today's London will tell us more about the properties of each.

There is but one recommendation for the future of journalism in London, and this is confined to the very end of the chapter.

As posited in this chapter, London's two types of journalism are as follows:

1. Me–You Journalism, in which journalists and their readers relate to each other interpersonally, as members of the eponymous network identified in the publication title. Thus readers and journalists working on *Chat* magazine comprise the *Chat* network; the staff and readers of *Hello!* interact with each other to form the *Hello!* network; and so on.
2. Impersonal Journalism, which relates selected events that are perceived to make our world what it is; and seeks to account for them. This account is peopled by actors from these events, but they appear in it on account of their actions; not by dint of personality, or via a quasi-interpersonal relation to readers.

The first of these journalisms is distinct from the second in that it is essentially a process – not only in the sense that it occurs continuously (both journalisms do this), but also because its defining activity is to proceed with the relation between journalist and reader, utilising media content to establish and maintain this relation. Out of this process a network arises, with journalism as the means of connecting various users or networkers, including journalists, readers, and story participants, who may be either journalists or readers themselves. Photographs of journalists alongside their copy, inviting the reader to relate to them personally, are a strong sign of Me–You journalism.

While it, too, happens all the time, Impersonal Journalism is less like a network and more akin to a secondary form of production, in which journalists produce a limited account of selected, finite episodes in the production of the world. Its readers are asked to address themselves to the account so produced, and hardly, if at all, to the journalist who wrote it. In the *Economist*, where articles appear unsigned, the absence of by-lines is a clear indication of Impersonal Journalism.

Cross-Examination: The Mediating Role of Modern Journalism

But perhaps the 'two journalisms' described above, are only the two aspects which journalism as a singular whole, has always contained? Surely the role of journalism has been to contain the interpersonal and the societal within the same, representative object – the story, thereby enabling human subjects to contain within themselves the dual nature of their everyday existence? Accordingly, formative episodes from the history of journalism suggest that journalism has been there to mediate between our interpersonal selves and our parallel performance in the wider, impersonal world; also that, in the performance of its mediating role, journalism necessarily looks to each aspect and encompasses them both. Yet if journalism exists to provide a composite picture of the two aspects of our existence (the interpersonal and the societal), then the original proposition must fall, since it posits two separate journalisms which are opposite rather than complementary; contradictory instead of reciprocal.

The original proposition is put to the test in the following section of this chapter (the cross-examination), which summarises successive episodes in journalism's performance of just such a mediating role. That so much of its history has gone into the performance of this role, confirms the awkward suggestion that journalism mediates between the two polarities which are thus contained in it, rather than being polarised itself, as suggested (seemingly erroneously) in the opening proposition.

In London 300 years ago, the twin task of relating news and catalysing interpersonal relations was undertaken in publications of a new kind. These included the *Tatler* (founded in 1709) and the *Spectator* (1711). The founding editors of these titles, Joseph Addison and Richard Steele, promised to report '*quicquid agunt homines*' – whatever men do – as the *Tatler* announced on the front page of its launch issue, on Tuesday 14 April 1709; but they also established their titles as a kind of virtual reality in which avatars for some of London's leading social types (Andrew Freeport, merchant; Sir Roger de Coverley, squire; Will Honeycomb, rake) were seen networking with one another, having recently set aside their historic differences.

At the turn of the eighteenth century, less than 50 years after the end of the English Civil War, the effective suspension of class conflict *was* the top story of the day – the most important thing that (English) men had been doing. At this time, whatever they were doing (*quicquid agebant homines*, to paraphrase the *Tatler* in my own rusty Latin), they were not now fighting as Roundheads versus Cavaliers. In this early incarnation of London's journalism, relating the story of class compromise and idealising interpersonal relations between merchants and landowners, were largely the same thing. The identity of both these activities, which was itself actualised in journalism's simultaneous performance of them, could not have occurred any earlier, since it depended on the newly formed identity of bourgeois and aristocratic interests, i.e. their coalescence in the Glorious Revolution of 1688, when King James II was forced into exile and the British Crown was offered to a merchant prince (William of Orange). In the decades that followed, new relations between merchants and landowners were not only announced in the new journalism but also formulated in it. Thus the *Tatler*, *Spectator* and their contemporaries comprise the original instance of journalism as mediating activity.

The journalism of the day served to construct a mediating point between two parties – a third position that was critical of each and engaged with both. But this position was not only a product of class compromise and a function of consensus; it was also something to be enacted in relation to ideas, individuals and commodities alike.

In their attempt to launch philosophy into the coffee house, Addison and Steele championed John Locke (Price 1982: 174) and initiated critical thinking among a wider public; conversely, the initiation of critical thinking across London might be said to have rolled out what became known as the public sphere. In this context, ideas carried over from the Ancient World, which had lived separately for so long (like medieval monks in a row of cells, rarely speaking to one another), now became objects of continuous comparison; and the comparison of one idea with another also contributed to the creation of that third position from which to criticise both and engage with each. This same process, leading to a third position where judgement may be properly exercised, is equally discernible in Addison's treatment of individual behaviour as the object of comparative study and thus the subject matter of society (Steele and Addison 1988).

While Addison's preferred philosopher was Locke, his favourite place was the Royal Exchange in London (Mackie 1998: 203), possibly the largest emporium in the world, where all the world's goods were traded as commodities. In this place, as each commodity was scrutinised in a process of continuous comparison, in effect the whole world was being weighed in the balance, object by object. We need no further explanation for Addison's readiness to compare people and ideas, alongside commodities. Crucial to critical thinking and journalistic independence alike, the third position which he helped to disseminate into every aspect of London life, was based on the disposition of the merchant in the continuous process of choosing between one commodity and another, and at what price.

Journalism and mercantilism were twins of the early eighteenth century; each entailed the construction of a third position from which to compare the two entities which the third always alluded to, whether these entities were ideas, interests, individuals or commodities. Defined by the position which they took up between pre-existing parties, both journalism and mercantilism were mediating activities (Calcutt and Hammond 2011).

In the early eighteenth century, London was a merchant city – the largest in the world at that time (Brown 1991: 419-20). The city's writers and readers were so often involved in trade that the publications of eighteenth century London were written by merchants with merchants in mind; they were composed for the mercantile mind by the mercantile kind. Thus the writing contained in these publications also contained the mindset of the merchant: the mind of someone set to meet other men on equal terms; the same terms with which their commodities encountered each other on the Royal Exchange. Accordingly, Addison and Steele did not prostrate themselves in front of their subjects; neither did they treat their subject matter in such a way as to patronise it.

During the nineteenth century, however, London's journalism lost some of this early egalitarianism. Instead, it came to reflect the social position of the new cohort of professional journalists. By 1900, it was clear that most journalists considered the bourgeois and the aristocrat their social superiors, while working people were regarded as generally inferior. In mainstream press coverage, the latter were often shown acting according to habit or type, while the former were usually accorded free will. Thus the capitalist class was associated with consciousness and the proletariat with culture. Meanwhile, in addressing himself to both, the (male) journalist posited his own journalism as a mediating link between the two major classes. Journalism, as a way of seeing, seemed to confirm that each class had its own way of being – culture for the masses, consciousness for the elite; but since journalism was a way of seeing them both, by its supposedly consistent approach to their assumed differences, the ontologies of each class also came to be articulated, one with the other.

Similarly, social division was first represented, but also partially transcended, in the newly established distinction between newspapers and magazines, each with its characteristic content (*hard* news and magazine *features*), and distinctive orientation to the reader. This is not the same as the subdivision of newspapers into broadsheets and tabloids according to the social class of their readership. The distinction between magazines and newspapers, which was not consistently made until the second half of the nineteenth century, was also a product of capitalist development; but it was not derived directly from class antagonism. Instead, it grew out of the underlying distinction between particular, interpersonal relations and the general relation between capital and labour when jointly engaged in production. This latter relation is the further realisation of what had been the merchant's third position – engaged with both parties, but not contained by either – now transferred from the fixed gaze of the merchant in the marketplace to the dynamic combination of human activity and constant capital (machinery, raw materials) involved in production. This is the combination which creates capitalist society as something more than the aggregate of interpersonal relations.

In nineteenth-century Britain, as capital expanded beyond its mercantile base in London, taking hold of provincial production and thus constructing the first, modern nation (Rubin 1979), so its growth was matched by the growing number of people entering into a new and strangely impersonal relation with the anonymous actor that now employed them – productive capital. For the purposes of commodity production and capital accumulation, both parties to this relation – capital and labour – appeared to each other primarily as quantities of value (existing value in the form of capital, and potential value embodied in the worker's capacity to work), without a shred of personal quality on either side. Yet, before clocking in and after clocking out of the factory, those identified by their capacity to work – the proletariat, also lived another life comprised of interpersonal relations; hence their dual existence (first in the impersonal world of work, owned by capital; second, in their own world of interpersonal relations).

The development of this duality was indirectly represented in the consolidation of the two categories of (impersonal) newspapers and (interpersonal) magazines. Learning to read these publications, as the working class was largely able to do by the end of the nineteenth century, also meant learning how to categorise them.

Moreover, as the double life of interpersonal and impersonal relations was the characteristic experience of that class which became a majority in the new nation – the working class, so almost the whole nation came to be imbued with it. During the nineteenth century, the proletariat's double life was brought to bear even upon those who were not proletarian. Discernible in the simultaneous development of explicitly impersonal newspapers and intensely interpersonal magazines, this duality also made its presence felt in the further development of a wide variety of publications which formed a kind of axis between the two polarities.

There were other cultural influences which countered these trends – apart from maintaining its own press, for example, merchant capital also continued to impress itself on the cities in which it was located; but the cultural forms attuned to other, secondary aspects of capital, were obliged to give way to capitalist production and its impersonal manner of speaking – such was the dominance of the latter across the UK at that time; hence, also at that time, the higher status accorded to (impersonal) newspapers over (interpersonal) magazines.

Even though they were not accorded the same status, however, the two main components of print journalism – newspapers and magazines – continued to operate in tandem. Accordingly, in the late Victorian era, George Newnes built a London-based empire of magazines, including *The Strand* (named after London's famous thoroughfare) and *Wide World Magazine*, which drew down the British Empire to the level of personal experience and brought it into the parlour of respectable domesticity. Meanwhile, from their citadels in Fleet Street (adjoining the Strand), press barons such as the Lords Beaverbrook, Northcliffe and Rothermere developed a new form of popular, daily newspaper whose role was to bring the reader up the steps to a viewing platform, constructed in columns of print, from which to look out upon the whole world (and the mess of it) that human beings were making (a little less of a mess, allegedly, if they were lucky enough to be British). Thus magazines identified themselves by addressing the reader in a personal capacity. Meanwhile, the newspaper invited the reader's societal self to climb up and view the whole world from a more elevated vantage point – the point at which personal experience is reconfigured impersonally.

During the nineteenth century, the separate but simultaneous existence of interpersonal and societal relations prompted not only the separating out of (interpersonal) magazines from (societal) newspapers, but also the construction of 'the press' as a continuum of newspapers and magazines which thus drew a continuous line, i.e. they provided the mediating link, between societal and interpersonal relations. In social reality and its representation, the far reaches of each were increasingly distant from one another; but the existence of journalism in the space between these polarities, served to create an element of continuity between them. By the end of the nineteenth century, continuity between interpersonal relations and the societal relation was routinely constructed by the dissemination of news and features in the two wings (newspapers and magazines) of London-based popular journalism.

At the height of Empire, those who read newspapers over breakfast were expected to read magazines by the fireside of an evening. The possibility of the same people engaging with both varieties of journalism was given by their dual existence both on the plane of interpersonal relations and as a participant (directly or indirectly) in the general relation between productive capital and labour. In composing the first draft of history, journalism was asked to encompass both aspects of the double life of its readership. Furthermore, the double life of readers meant that, in order to engage them in their duality, each variety of journalism would have to be written with an eye to the other. Hence the two dimensions of imperial journalism – magazines and newspapers – were not only distinctive, they were also complementary; together they comprised a continuum.

The significance of this continuum, for society as for journalism, cannot be over-estimated. Edwardian Britain, perhaps the high point of capitalist production in the UK (if assessed both in terms of its own development and in relation to the output of other, advanced capitalist countries), only intensified the separation of interpersonal relations from the social relation between capital and labour – a form of separation expressed in the alienation of workers from their work, and while at work, in their alienation from life outside the workplace. Yet Britain's workers had no choice but to make the transition between home and work, interpersonal self and societal self, and to do it again each working day. Accordingly, various mediating mechanisms helped to effect that transition; and one such mechanism was the continuum stretching from magazines which inter-personalised society, to newspapers that socialised the interpersonal – always with the proviso that each must acknowledge the opposite, complementary process, just as journalism's mass readership – the daily worker – was also obliged to commute between both destinations.

On the surface, the continuum encompassed as much of the surface of the globe as was contained within the borders of the British Empire (approximately one third), so that Calcutta and Cape Town, Nairobi and Kingston, were all linked via London and its journalism. But the mediating activity of imperial journalism was not only a matter of bridging geographical distances; its underlying role was to bring about the death of distance between interpersonal relations and the societal relation. The continuum of different texts which professional journalists produced, served to produce the contemporary social context as a continuum. Yes, the continuum would have to be continually negotiated, but precisely because it was continuous, this meant that events contained within it did not appear disjointed or haphazard.

As journalists described all manner of events in their pieces, so the events themselves came to be all of a piece – the piece called Empire, or Progress, or that combination thereof which Kipling dubbed 'the white man's burden'. Enfolded within journalism, the jagged edges of human experience could become seamless; and the essential relation between capital and labour was seemingly less coercive.

These are only snapshots, but they suffice to show that the story of journalism in London is also the history of mediation. In the mercantile episode, journalism offered a mediating service between merchants, and between merchants and landowners. Furthermore, the creation, through journalism, of a critically engaged position from which to review existing objects (all things were objectified in the review process, including human subjects), was crucial to the construction of London as a new kind of city, in which the speculative attitude was essential to commerce and society alike.

In the imperial episode, London-based media continued to carry out this capital function, but they were expected to reach out beyond the city, as capital itself had moved beyond metropolitan markets to forge its own nation in the crucible of industrial production – the first nation of this kind. Across the new nation, and, latterly, throughout the empire named after it, journalism in particular was called to mediate between the two aspects of the human subject which arise from the simultaneous existence of interpersonal relations and the societal relation of productive capital to labour. It was partly through journalism (and other cultural forms such as the novel and the well-made play) that these two modes of existence were able to co-exist.

Though journalism remained concentrated in London throughout both episodes, what began as an extension of exchange, subsequently changed into a by-product of production. As part of this transformation, journalism's relation to the world beyond London also changed. In the early days of the *Spectator*, when capital had not yet taken hold of production, London was synonymous with society. Outside London and a handful of miniature merchant cities such as Norwich, Bristol and Edinburgh, there was really no such thing. Thus contemporary journalism was not only based in London; London was its major topic. But during the nineteenth century, the relation between the capital city and the provinces (provincial counties and, latterly, provincial countries which also looked to London), came to replicate the relation between capital and labour, in which neither party is fully actualised except in relation to the other. Accordingly, instead of being synonymous with one city (and a handful of smaller versions of it), journalism imitated the expanding relation between capital and labour by first nationalising and subsequently internationalising itself; though we should not forget that the expansion of journalism was also bound up with private ownership and stamped with national insignia – in this instance, the Union Jack. Now there was a whole world for London-based journalism to mediate.

On a global scale, the hemispheres of interpersonal relations and the societal relation were brought together, largely through mediating activity which took place in London. Lined with newspaper offices, Fleet Street was one of those indispensable *vertebra* forming the backbone of the nation, and the spine of Empire. Its substance was recognised as well as satirised in perhaps the most famous novel about journalists, Evelyn Waugh's *Scoop* (1938). The stature of this work of fiction rests not only on Waugh's comic writing, which is superb, but also on the serious nature of what he was writing about – the crucial concentration of mediating activity in London's Fleet Street.

Thus mediation, not polarisation, has been the essence of modern journalism. Even when popular publications were first subdivided into newspapers and magazines, these subdivisions adjoined each other in the same way that Fleet Street, the home of newspapers, opens out into the Strand, the street which gave its name to the most prestigious of magazines, and *vice versa*. Made up of different kinds of journalism, the integrated whole also comprised a mechanism for social integration; and the briefest history of journalism shows that compartmentalising it, as in the original proposition, is a category error.

Rebuttal: Separate Journalisms in a Divided World

Circulation figures for Britain's London-based newspapers have been in decline for half a century, with decline setting in around the same time as the end of Empire (OFT 2008: 20). This does not mean that the British population now consumes less media content than it did 50 years ago, nor that London is less central to national life. On the contrary, it seems that life in Britain is more media oriented than ever before, and London's continued centrality to media production suggests that it may command even more public attention. But the combination of declining interest in newspapers and rising engagement with media overall, does indicate changing patterns of behaviour among the domestic population.

Various explanations have been suggested for this. Some of the most influential can be summarised as: consumer culture; new technology; diminished attention span; or combinations of the above. But all three, and their various permutations, have been found wanting. The first simply projects its alleged outcome back to the beginning of the transition process, declaring that the effect is also its own cause; the second makes the mistake of investing man-made communications equipment with autonomous powers; while the third explanation takes the second account and, as if alarmed at its own inadequacy, turns it into a moral panic.

Not one of these accounts takes the current role of London into consideration, so it is hardly surprising that none succeeds in identifying the split personality of today's metropolitan journalism. But by locating London as a key site of mediating activity, this chapter has managed to account for two earlier episodes in journalism's history. By reference to London's mercantile and imperial past, it has been possible to show that the development of journalism was bound up with the performance of these historical roles; moreover, that the developing character of the former was largely determined by the evolution of the latter. For example, from the second of these episodes, it emerged that the original subdivision of journalistic activity into hard news and magazine features, both produced primarily in London, served to represent the different dimensions of contemporary experience as a seamless whole, with London as the construction site of this continuum.

However, the continuity which journalism provided between two sets of social relations occurring at the same time (interpersonal relations and the societal relation between capital and labour), is not necessarily continuous over time, i.e. it may not last forever, from one historical period to another. Accordingly, in the final episode of this essay, continuing usage of the same, London-based approach will suffice to show that London's changing relationship to the outside world, has also changed the character of locally produced journalism; notably in the growing tendency for London's journalism to compartmentalise itself. Furthermore, as these compartments have become more definite, by definition they point to the separation of our worlds, to increased estrangement between the two aspects of the double life of humanity, rather than their continued integration. It is also suggested that, if these developments are allowed to go unchecked, the integrating capacity of London's journalism can only be reduced along with confirmation of its own, internal boundaries.

In the imperialist epoch, as previously mentioned, it would have been plausible to assume that newspaper readers and magazine readers comprised one and the same readership, with identical people purchasing various London-based titles on different days or at different times of the day. Today the same assumption is implausible. Hence the regular refrain of journalism tutors that not even journalism students can be relied on to read newspapers. The young people of today, we are wont to complain, are more at home with the personal life of celebrities and the DIY celebrity facilitated by Facebook. Not for them the newspaper as a viewing platform on the wider world, constructed at the point where personal experience is reconfigured impersonally.

But if many young Londoners are giving up on the viewing range associated with newspapers, perhaps some newspaper publishers have already beaten them to it. Since the early days of the internet, they have championed the prospect of 'the Daily Me' – a diet of online news, digitally pre-digested to match the declared interests of individual readers (McGrath 1994: 27). This idea of representing the world I *want* to know about, is decidedly different from claiming to represent the world we all *need* to know about, in order to act upon it ourselves, in a more-or-less concerted fashion. Yet this last was the very idea that defined the modern newspaper; and in their readiness to move away from it, many titles which are still called newspapers, have effectively declared for the interpersonal role previously associated with special interest publications, i.e. magazines.

Some newspaper publishers have already acted on such inclinations, by turning much of what they do into a succession of magazines on media, science, culture, business, sports, property, travel, fashion, education and technology, etc. Of course, all national newspapers retain a capacity for general news coverage, alongside the list of interests particularised above. But in this general section, which has itself become one of a list of particulars, there is movement towards a mode of storytelling which no longer routes news through the impersonal terrain of truth and objectivity. Even these terms have been partly personalised and particularised in their conversion to 'truth' and 'objectivity' – the scare marks indicating that such qualities are not really general, as we once, mistakenly, thought they were; but only exist as particular claims pertinent to specific people.

In the modified mode of newspaper storytelling, the experience of some individuals is brought to other individuals (readers) by still more individuals (journalists) who also announce their individuality. This is news not only aggregated for 'The Daily Me', but also composed for me by the Daily You (the journalist), as if it were an email or a person-to-person phone call. Thus even the staple coverage contained in today's national newspapers has moved a long way towards the kind of interpersonal treatment previously associated with magazines.

Unfortunately, no one is benefiting from the tendency for British newspapers to become more like magazines – not even the UK magazine sector. When the nature of their relationship prompted each aspect of journalism to look to the other, both of them gained a degree of tensile strength. Now that much of this tension has gone, each aspect is enfeebled. Yet both newspaper and magazine publishers are convinced that only their current tactics can secure their market position. What amounts to the weakening of journalism, is passed off as the means of safeguarding it – a contradiction with echoes of that infamous, City-type misnomer: securitisation.

Why has so much of London's journalism allowed itself to become a lesser being? It is not that today's journalists are less grasping than before. On a personal level, many of them seem to be as ambitious as their predecessors. But if we accept that what London does determines what its journalism is, the explanation must be that London does less now than it used to.

After Empire, and the subsequent interlude in which most of Greater London's manufacturing sector went to the wall, London's increasing reliance on financial services and the surrounding business services sector, has prompted a whole way of life in which Londoners interact with each other in a continuous process resembling the interplay of so-called financial products (in reality, these are packets of value derived from production which has already occurred elsewhere). This is a particularly diminished way of life, with restricted access to the general relation between capital and labour, i.e. the impersonal relation which abstracts from personal particulars in the dual process of accumulating private capital and constructing capitalist society. Appropriately enough, this strictly personal way of life is adequately and accurately represented in a diminished form of journalism, which accounts for the world in the only terms with which its local readers are familiar – the same, interpersonal terms to which their way of life now tends to be confined. Moreover, as the inner life of London is increasingly restricted to one set of social relations (the interpersonal), so mediation between two sets of relations (the interpersonal and the societal) tends to become superfluous. For internal purposes, at least, Londoners are left with interpersonal journalism. This is journalism aligned to personal networks, which corresponds to the financial networks composed here in London; and it is reconciled to the recomposition of London in these terms, and on this narrow basis.

Thankfully, however, London's journalism also faces an altogether different set of demands. Partly as a result of its imperial heritage, and partly because the British Empire is no more, London-based journalism is highly prized in those other parts of the world where journalism's more expansive, mediating role is now much in demand. Moreover, if London's performance of this was originally wrapped in red, white and blue, by now the Union Jack has been re-drawn in the colours of the rainbow – rhetorically, at least; and journalism made-in-London no longer carries all the imperial connotations of its original colour scheme.

In this context, expanding economies which baulk at the political risks entailed in the full-blown development of indigenous civil society, can entertain the prospect of a global civil society, based in London and epitomised in its journalism. In response, some of London's most prestigious news organisations are now trading on this capacity and the expectation that others have of it. Thus the BBC World Service, previously the personification of Britain abroad (complete with an Ulster Protestant marching song as its theme tune), now advertises itself to a worldwide audience in the following terms: 'With more correspondents in more places than any other broadcaster, the BBC World Service gives you news and information with a truly global perspective' (BBC 2011).

This trailer is a response to demands which originate externally – outside London and beyond the journalism composed here for domestic purposes; nonetheless such demands have a beneficial effect on the internal life of London, including its journalism. While the local tendency towards personalisation is continually reinforced by the financial economy and its cultural equivalents, this tendency is counteracted by external demands for journalism with a broad perspective – the sort of perspective that can only be arrived at impersonally. In effect, those parts of the world which live by making objects instead of circulating money, are currently calling on London to objectify the world they produce; and at their insistence, this, secondary object – the *re-production* of the world in journalism – is not allowed to fall entirely short of its societal dimension. The effect of this external pressure has been to offset the degeneration of journalism in London, which could only have accelerated if it had been left entirely to its own, internal devices.

But London has lost an awful lot of that tensile strength between impersonal and interpersonal journalism. Most of the journalism that is processed here for domestic purposes, is too self-enclosed to have much bearing on its opposite number. Similarly, whereas a growing number of readers in the East are keenly interested in world affairs *and* the personal lives of Western celebrities, many of London's readers are now too narrowly focused, too interpersonally oriented, to be able to cope with both dimensions. In London itself, reciprocity between the two wings of one journalism has been largely lost, which means that, here and now (if not before now, and perhaps, even now, by no means everywhere), they really do comprise two journalisms marked more by their differences than their similarities; just as the financial economy is increasingly separate from the productive economy, the more it operates on its own terms, and its own terms alone.

In the mainly mercantile economy of today's London, perhaps there could be a return to the level of judgement contained in the pages of the *Spectator*, where Addison and Steele adjudicated on all manner of things, from people to ideas to commodities? Unfortunately, various factors are militating against the journalism of judgement and in favour of short-term calculation, instead. These include:

- The extent to which London's financial economy also depends on the exercise of calculation and the suspension of judgement;
- The large number of Londoners who resort to merchandising themselves in social media, where personal display is equivalent to a spectacle of financial products. There is little opportunity for them to trade in anything else, or to configure themselves in the image of anything else but trade;
- The concentric circulation of capital in today's trading economy, whereby capital tends to make a quick exit from the external world of production, moving ever more deeply into the thickening forest of financial 'products'. This inward movement makes for a similarly inward-looking mindset, in sharp contrast to the *out*look which predominated when, if only in order to accumulate, eighteenth century merchant capital was forced to look outwards, to new lands outside London and even beyond Europe.

Contrary to local experience, i.e. the spiral of finance and the vortex of personalisation, the wider reality is that there has never been more reason to look outwards from London. Nowadays, while value continues to pass through the portal of London in ever-larger volumes, so much of what is valuable goes on somewhere else (and comes from somewhere else again). If only it can regain more of the capacity to look both ways, inside and out, London remains well-placed to address the world as a two-way street. There is still a chance for London to develop the new iteration of journalism's third position. But if so much local bandwidth continues to be taken up with internal, interpersonal and increasingly narrow preoccupations, London may find that it is no longer able to meet the largely external demand for a wide-ranging account of world affairs.

My prognosis for London-based journalism is consistent with my earlier analysis of the variable effects of finance capital on the city playing host to it (see Chapter 4). When finance is well-connected to production, they both make a contribution to the life of capital; and the speculative attitude associated with finance, can make a particularly enlivening contribution to capital cities such as London, where, in the past, proximity to finance has even been good for journalism. But finance in isolation from production, has a kind of deadening effect, so that the culture of speculation then acts as a drain on the imagination and even the appetite for documentation. London's journalism, influenced by the relation between finance and production at any given time, once benefited from their interaction, has since suffered from their estrangement, but now has the opportunity to renew itself with a new story – the unfolding saga of East and West, and a new way of telling it.

If our city gets this story right, the world will see a much-needed improvement in the mediation of its two halves, and journalism may yet hear its new voice coming from a familiar stomping ground – London.

References

BBC (2011). Trailer for BBC World Service, broadcast on BBC World Service, 8 April.

Brown, R. (1991). *Society and Economy in Modern Britain, 1700-1850.* London: Routledge.

Calcutt, A. and Hammond, P. (2011). *Journalism Studies: A Critical Introduction.* London: Routledge.

Mackie, E. (1998). *The Commerce of Everyday Life: Selections from the Tatler and the Spectator.* New York: Bedford/St Martin's.

McGrath, P. (1994). 'The Daily Me', *Newsweek*, 6 June, 27.

Office of Fair Trading (OFT) (2008). *Newspapers and Magazine Distribution in the United Kingdom.* London: Office of Fair Trading.

Price, J.V. (1982). 'The Reading of Philosophical Literature' in *Books and Their Readers in Eighteenth Century England*, edited by I. Rivers. Leicester: Leicester University Press, 122-46.

Rubin, I.I. (1979). *A History of Economic Thought*, translated and edited by D. Filtzer. London: Pluto Press.

Steele, R. and Addison, J. (1988). *Selections from the Tatler and the Spectator*, edited by A. Ross. Harmondsworth: Penguin.

Waugh, E. (1951 [1938]). *Scoop: A Novel about Journalists.* Harmondsworth: Penguin.

Chapter 10
The Real Economy and the Regeneration of East London

Alvaro de Miranda

> For the future, Britain needs an economy with less financial engineering and more real engineering.[1]

> If the objective is to make the city a showcase, you have to hide everything that doesn't shine. The city turns itself towards the outside world rather than to its citizens.[2]

Introduction

The financial crisis severely shook the belief of politicians and policymakers in the financial services industry as a key component of the 'knowledge economy' and as the engine of the UK's and London's economic growth. This view had, until then, formed the consensus of both of the UK's main parties. Mandelson's statement was but one of many references made by politicians in the wake of the credit crunch about the need to address the requirements of the real economy. However, the proposals that have emerged with regard to East London regeneration policy as a result of the efforts to reorient policy in the wake of the financial crisis have, by and large, continued to follow the conceptual paradigm that governed previous approaches to regeneration. This chapter aims to critically examine the policy proposals that have recently emerged to develop the real economy of East London and provides an evaluation of their likelihood of success.

In the first section the conceptual assumptions common to all regeneration initiatives that have tried to address the effects of deindustrialisation are explored in order to show in subsequent sections how they still inform recent attempts to relate to the real economy. It is argued that three theoretical concepts underpin all such

1 Lord Mandelson, Statement to the House of Lords 27 January 2009 (http://services.parliament.uk/hansard/Lords/ByDate/20090127/mainchamberdebates/part005.html, accessed 20 June 2011).

2 Interview with magazine *Caros amigos* 12 January 2011 http://carosamigos.terra.com.br/index/index.php/noticias/1344-entrevista-carlos-vainer 30 April 2011. Carlos Vainer, Brazilian Professor of Urban Planning, answering a question on the likely impact of the 2016 Olympic Games on Rio de Janeiro (http://carosamigos.terra.com.br/index/index.php/noticias/1344-entrevista-carlos-vainer, accessed 20 June 2011).

initiatives- globalisation, inward investment and the knowledge economy. More recently, sustainability has been added to the dominant conceptual framework. The meaning of these concepts, insofar as they inform regeneration policy, is discussed.

In the second section, the relationship between innovation, the promotion of which is seen as central to enable the growth of the knowledge economy in the process of economic regeneration, to the real economy in general and, in particular, to manufacturing is examined. The historical changes that have taken place in East London, which transformed its economy from one based on highly innovative manufacturing to a largely deindustrialised wasteland, are analysed.

In the third section, the initiatives that have been associated with the policy shift towards the real economy are discussed. In particular the Mayor's proposal to turn the region into a Green Enterprise District and the more recent plan, announced by Prime Minister David Cameron, to build on the achievements of a cluster of start up technology-based companies in Shoreditch in order to develop a Technology City stretching to the Olympic Park, are described in the context of the dominant conceptual paradigm for regeneration analysed in the first section. The concluding section discusses the limitations of these policy initiatives, their implications for a possible resurgence of the real economy of East London and the likelihood of their success.

The Conceptual Basis of Regeneration Policy

The concepts of globalisation and inward investment are intimately linked in the way that they have informed recent economic development policy. The view that attracting foreign inward investment is the principal way in which the economic development of a region can be achieved derives primarily from an acceptance by policymakers of the globalisation thesis, that capital increasingly invests globally and that the most that national and regional governments can do is to make nations and regions visible and attractive to global capital. Political support for megaevents is based to a considerable extent on this view. Megaevents make regions and nations globally visible not only to capital, but also to tourism which is seen as an important component of the consumption-based regeneration policies which have become popular with what Poynter has described as 'entrepreneurial cities' (Poynter: 2006).

Publicity campaigns are sometimes run in association with megaevents to promote inward investment. Germany developed one such campaign when it hosted the 2006 FIFA World Cup. Explicitly entitled 'Invest in Germany', subtitled as 'Land of Ideas', the campaign used the supermodel Claudia Schiffer in an international poster campaign aimed at the world financial centres to create a supposedly attractive image for the country. One such poster was displayed in the City of London's Bank underground station. In it, Claudia Schiffer, wrapped only in the German flag is lying down in a suggestive pose under the prominent slogan

'Invest in Germany, Boys'. Although in poor taste, the poster is nevertheless an expressive symbol of the kind of thinking that underlies such policies, including their gender dimension. The widespread adoption of this approach sets up competition between nations and, more particularly, between regions for investment. In this way, paradoxically, capital becomes the customer and countries and regions, the suppliers/sellers.

The concept of the knowledge economy is related to deindustrialisation. There are a number of versions of this concept in the way it influences policy. In one, it is used to justify accepting deindustrialisation as a fait accompli and abandoning any form of state support for manufacturing. In this version, deindustrialisation is seen as a sign of modernisation and progress. The most advanced economy is said to be knowledge-based because economic growth and profitability come mainly from the development and sale of intellectual property rather than from the manufacture of physical goods. The theoretical basis of this thesis is said by Foss (1997) to be *New Growth Theory* (Lucas 1988; Romer: 1990). The thesis was taken up vigorously by the OECD (OECD 1996) and became the basis of UK policy following the publication by the UK Department of Trade and Industry of its 1998 Competitiveness White Paper (DTI 1998)

The official view became that an industrial economy is one based on routine, low skilled and boring jobs. The disappearance of these jobs is therefore not a problem if they can be replaced by high skill, knowledge-based jobs. These jobs are based on intellectual rather than manual labour. They involve the production of intangible rather than physical goods. It is the production of these goods that is driving growth in the modern economy and, therefore, the focus of policy has to be to encourage this form of production. Creative industries are seen as central to this drive and, until the credit crisis, the financial services industries were also viewed as central to the development of the knowledge economy. In June 2004, in a speech given in Canary Wharf entitled 'Creativity in the Knowledge Economy', Secretary of State for Trade and Industry, Patricia Hewitt, justified the choice of venue as 'a symbol of the vision and commitment to create a world leading cluster in a location where few thought it possible' (de Miranda 2007: 1).

Innovation and entrepreneurship are viewed as central to the development of the knowledge economy. The promotion of these, therefore, becomes one of the main aims of regeneration policy. However, there is a potential contradiction between inward investment and the promotion of local innovation and entrepreneurship which remains unrecognised in the regeneration policy literature. The wish to attract global capital to invest in the region is not necessarily compatible with the desire to promote local innovation and entrepreneurship. Global capital's reasons for investing in an economically depressed region are seldom related to the desire to use the region as a site for innovation. Their research and development activities are mostly located near to their decision making centres, or are placed in locations in which the particular areas of innovation in which they are interested already thrive. The potential problems this creates for regeneration will be illustrated later in this chapter when recent policy initiatives attempting to promote enterprise and innovation in East London are discussed.

The credit crunch led to the financial industries becoming discredited in the minds of the public. The view that it was necessary to differentiate between financial services and the 'real economy' became quite widespread and politicians felt the need to redirect their attentions to the latter, as the quote from Lord Mandelson that opens this chapter indicates. References to the 'real economy' have proliferated in the speeches of Prime Minister David Cameron[3] and, less frequently, of Chancellor George Osborne. The desire to promote the 'real economy' by policymakers has thus become widespread. However, what constitutes such an economy remains at best unclear. In the mind of Peter Mandelson, engineering appears central to it, with its implicit relationship to manufacturing. Even London Mayor, Boris Johnson, appeared to recognise the importance of manufacturing to the real economy when he called for an end to banker bashing by saying that he did not believe that reducing financial services would give a boost to manufacturing.[4] Manufacturing, however, is given little importance in the theorisation of the knowledge economy. The theory advocates a division of labour which separates geographically conception from production, giving economic priority to conception and relegating manufacturing production to the less advanced and less successful economies. There is, therefore, a problem in framing regeneration policy simultaneously in terms of a concept of a 'real economy' in which the importance of manufacturing is recognised and of a 'knowledge economy' in which the importance of manufacturing is downgraded. The resolution of the problem has been the attempt to promote high technology manufacturing which is perceived as being knowledge intensive. This, however, has its own problems as will be seen later.

Another issue that is unclear in regeneration policy is the relationship between production and consumption. Recent urban regeneration policies, as I have already referred, have mostly been consumption-based and tourism plays an important role in them. They tend to focus on commercial activities involving shopping or leisure. The concept of a productive economy plays at best a very secondary role in support of consumption. Yet production is, or should be, at the heart of a real economy. This includes both cultural production and the production of physical goods. However, manufacturing has hardly featured in the future visions of policymakers, a fact that is underlined by the virtually complete absence of commissioned research on the state of manufacturing in London.

Since the 1990s, another concept that has become a central reference point of economic policy in general and, therefore, of regeneration policy is that of sustainability. No policy is complete without paying at least lip service to the concept. Sustainability, insofar as it is used to frame regeneration policy, has

3 An example of this is a reference by Cameron to 'the need to get things right in the real economy as well as the financial world' in an interview with Adam Boulton for Sky News on the 12 October 2008, http://skynewstranscripts.co.uk/transcript.asp?id=615

4 Interview in the *Evening Standard* 5 January 2011

at least two dimensions. The first is the notion of environmental sustainability derived from the relative success of environmentalists in placing it on the global policy map particularly since the publication of the Brundtland Report (Brundlandt 1987) and its adoption by the UN Earth Summit in Rio in 1992 in Agenda 21.[5] Another sense in which sustainability often frames regeneration policy is in or via the notion of economic sustainability. In this context, sustainability refers to the capacity of a project that has been initiated with external support, usually public funds, to continue to exist and have beneficial consequences 'under its own steam' once the initial support has come to an end. This meaning of sustainability, when applied to mega-events, has something in common with what Blake, Poynter and MacRury (2007) have termed 'legacy momentum'. Sustainability has become a fundamental reference point for 2012 Olympic Games planning and post-crunch East London and Thames Gateway regeneration policy, as will be seen later in this chapter.

East London Creativity and Innovation in Historical Perspective

The notion that the old industrial economy was not creative and that creativity and innovation are a unique characteristic of the new or knowledge economy is belied by the history of East London which was the cradle of a great deal of invention and innovation from at least the middle of the nineteenth century, particularly in the electrical and electronic industries, but also in chemicals, and even in furniture design and manufacture.[6] Unlike today's knowledge economy view of innovation the inventor-entrepreneurs of yesteryear undertook local manufacture of the products they developed, using many raw materials imported from the colonies through the London docks. The process started in the 1820s with numerous inventions and patents in relation to India rubber and gutta-percha, particularly by the Hancock brothers (Thomas, Charles, and Walter), which led to several factories being set up in East London for the manufacture of the resulting products. From the 1840s the use of gutta-percha, the coagulated milk of the gutta-percha tree, imported from South East Asia through the London docks, in the insulation of submarine telegraph cables gave rise to a proliferation of competing and cooperating companies innovating and manufacturing on the banks of the Thames in East London, particularly Greenwich, Woolwich, and what is now known as Silvertown.[7] Amongst these companies was Siemens Brothers, established by the German born Charles William Siemens, in partnership with his brother, Werner

5 The Brundtland report defines sustainable development as 'development that meets the needs of the present without compromising the ability of future generations to meet their own needs'.

6 I have described this process in some detail elsewhere (de Miranda 2007).

7 The Silvertown name derives from the Silver family, father Stephen Winkworth Silver and sons Colonel H.A. and Stephen William Silver who set up the India Rubber,

Siemens, founder of the German Siemens company which is today Europe's largest electrical and electronic conglomerate. The degree of innovative activity during this period was such that one writer recently felt justified in describing the area in the middle and late nineteenth century as 'the forerunner of Silicon Valley' (Gannon 1997: 284).

In the last quarter of the nineteenth century and the first half of the twentieth, the East Thames and Lea Valleys also became the most important innovation centres in Britain for the electrical and electronic industries[8] as well as significant contributors to innovation in the chemical industries following the opening of the Beckton Gas Works in 1870. The East Thames and Lea Valley were the cradle of the wireless industry, following the establishment of the Chelmsford Works of the Marconi Company in 1898 from where the first radio broadcast that led to the setting up of the British Broadcasting Company took place in 1920. The thermionic diode, the invention which could be said to have been responsible for the birth of the world electronics industry, was patented by Ambrose Fleming, Pender Professor of Electrical Engineering at University College, London in 1904 and was the result of his collaboration with the Edison and Swan United Electric Light Company Ltd (Ediswan),[9] based on the Lea Valley, to which Fleming was consultant. The first diodes were manufactured at the Ediswan factory. Marconi set up in Chelmsford one of the first industrial research laboratories in the UK, initially as a department of the Chelmsford Works in 1912, later to become the stand alone Marconi Research Centre in 1922 (de Miranda 2007). Ekco, created in 1924 by Westcliff-on-Sea entrepreneur E.K. Cole, developed the first mains radio in the UK. Its radio and television factories in Southend employed 5,500 people by 1960 (ibid.).

Major technology companies such as Plessey, Ilford Ltd., English Electric, Marconi and Ediswan, were based and conducted research and development in East London and the East Thames Valley. The region played a major role in the inventions that led to the development of television. John Logie Baird, credited as the inventor of television, worked for a time at Plessey's in Ilford and conducted the first test transmissions from the roof of the plant. Ediswan developed the first commercial magnetically focused television cathode ray tube which was

Gutta Percha and Telegraph Works Co. which by 1859 had grown to such an extent that the area where its factories were located became known as Silvertown.

8 The Lea Valley also made a significant contribution to this. For a description of the Lea Valley contribution see Lewis (2010).

9 The Edison and Swan United Electric Light Company Ltd (Ediswan) was jointly founded in 1882 by the American Thomas Edison and the British Joseph Swan as part of a settlement of a patent suit in the British courts over who had been the inventor of the electric light bulb. Edison lost and Swan was declared to have the right to the patent. Ediswan set up its manufacturing plant in the Lea Valley. Ediswan It was in this factory that the first commercial magnetically focused television cathode ray tube was produced in 1936.

manufactured at its Ponders End factory from 1936. Ecko introduced the first portable television in 1955.

Three inter-related factors contributed to the deindustrialisation of East London. The first was technological change. This affected East London in relation to the docks, and to electrical and electronic manufacturing.[10] Containerisation of shipping cargo and the accompanying development of larger container ships that were unable to use the existing docks were major factors that contributed to the closure of all the London docks by 1982. The move from thermionic valve to semiconductor electronics which ushered the growth of Silicon Valley in California, and which British electronics companies were unable to keep up with, contributed to the demise of the high technology industry in the East Thames Valley.

The second important factor that contributed to the deindustrialisation in the region, already alluded to in the previous section, was the relative weakness of British industrial capital.[11] Practically all the high technology firms which operated in the East Thames Valley ended up in foreign hands. The process started in the 1920s with the sale of all the East London battery companies to American Chloride and was completed in 2005 with the sale of Marconi (not the original Marconi company, but GEC rebranded as Marconi) to the Swedish telecommunications company Ericsson (de Miranda 2007). All the foreign purchasers of the East Thames Valley technology companies maintained R&D and manufacturing activities in their home countries whilst those in the region closed down.

The third and possibly most important factor contributing to East London losing its high technology innovation and manufacturing was the change in the international division of labour which came to be described as the development of a new international division of labour (Fröbel et al. 1980). This involved the move of most low skill labour-intensive manufacturing from high to low wage countries, predominantly in East and South East Asia. Electrical and electronics manufacturing, which at its height employed several tens of thousands workers in East London, was labour intensive. Over time, as mass production processes developed, it also came to employ predominantly low skill labour. However, whilst this type of high technology deindustrialisation involving the loss of large numbers of unskilled workers affected also the high technology industries of other European industrialised countries, they were able to maintain their

10 Ford Dagenham, a major manufacturing employer in East London, also added greatly to the loss of manufacturing employment in the area. Technological change was a contributing factor through a process of automation. However, the major factor was a gradual process of restructuring its European operations culminating in 2002 when Ford finally abandoned body production and car assembly in Dagenham. (Donnelly and Morris 2003).

11 In the intense debate that has existed over the reasons for the decline of British owned manufacturing industry, one strand has consistently argued that the historical preponderance of finance capital and the City of London over industrial capital and the relative influence they have on the British State play a major role. See, *inter alia*, Van Helten and Cassis 1990; Hickox 1995.

innovation activities and some manufacturing in their home regions. Foreign firms which came to own British Thames Valley electronics and telecommunications companies such as Philips of the Netherlands, Ericsson of Sweden, Siemens of Germany, Alcatel of France still have their most important R&D laboratories and extensive manufacturing in their home countries.

The East Thames and East London manufacturing industries were embedded and clustered in an organic relationship with their locality; in contrast the next section reveals how the new initiaitives of recent years are not firmly embedded in the local economy, indeed they showcase the performance of productive enterprises based elsewhere in the world. London is consciously or otherwise reproducing the characteristics of a financialised economy even when it seeks to connect with the real economy.

The New Policy Initiatives

In the recent turn towards the real economy, two policy initiatives directed at the regeneration of East London deserve particular attention. The first is the Mayor of London's proposal to turn East London into a Green Enterprise District or Zone. The second is Prime Minister David Cameron's proposal to create a Tech City in the Olympic Park as one of the legacies of the 2012 Olympic Games.

The Green Enterprise District

The Green Enterprise District proposal was launched by Mayor of London Boris Johnson in May 2011 in a speech given at a Business and Sustainable Environment (BASE) Sustainability Conference in the newly opened International Convention Centre at ExCel. He said that the plan aimed to create up to 6,000 jobs and attract £140 billion pounds of investment to six East London boroughs (Hackney, Tower Hamlets, Newham, Waltham Forest, Barking and Dagenham and Havering). At the same time he announced that the centrepiece of the Green Enterprise District would be a Siemens Pavilion – an Urban Sustainability Education and Conference Centre to be built by the company on land owned by the London Development Agency (LDA) and Newham Council at the western end of the Royal Docks. The Urban Sustainability Centre would represent an investment by Siemens of £30 million and would be expected to house 230 Siemens employees, of which 50 would be new local jobs directly and in the supply chain. It would be an iconic building housing an exhibition and conference centre showcasing sustainable technologies. The Siemens Urban Sustainability Centre hopes to attract 100,000 visitors a year. The Mayor claimed that Siemens decision to locate its flagship centre of sustainability in London was a clear sign that it had confidence in London's ability to nurture and support eco-enterprises.

On the creation of the Green Enterprise District, Isabel Dedring, the Mayor of London's environment advisor, said:

> Creating an energy efficient society is a profitable enterprise as well as being good for the environment. The only way we will get the large scale carbon reductions and the associated energy savings required to tackle climate change is by using public sector funding to attract commercial investment.

This would be a means to … 'deliver the massive green job opportunities'. [12]

The concept of the Green Enterprise District was developed by the LDA on the back of previous initiatives, in particular the London of Borough Barking and Dagenham's regeneration plans for the Dagenham Docks area, the area left derelict and bereft of jobs by the withdrawal of the majority of the manufacturing activities of Ford whose workforce declined from about 24,000 in 1981 to less than 1,000 now. The factory had employed up to 40,000 people in the 1960s. The fact that Ford continues to manufacture in Dagenham Dock[13] and uses it as its main transportation hub, made the use of the consumption-based regeneration model unsuitable for the area.

In May 2001 the London Borough of Barking and Dagenham and the LDA appointed a team of consultants led by Scott Wilson to develop a Dagenham Dock Vision Implementation Strategy. The resulting report envisaged 'the creation of a best practice example of modern sustainable industrial development covering issues such as recycling operations, energy efficiency, 'green links' between businesses, transportation and waste minimisation' (*Dagenham Dock Vision Implementation Strategy Executive Summary* http://www.barking-dagenham.gov.uk/Regeneration/Dagenham/Documents/regen-dag-dock-vis-exec-sum.pdf accessed 20 January 2011). The main contribution to this strategy was the creation of a Sustainable Industrial Park (SiP) as an Eco-Industrial Park (EiP) conceived as 'a community of businesses that cooperate with one another to efficiently share resources leading to economic gains in environmental quality and equitable enhancement of human resources for the business and local community' (ibid.). The SiP aimed to 'showcase cutting edge sustainable technologies' and to create up to 1,500 jobs. The SiP's first tenant was Closed Loop London, a subsidiary of an Australian company, which offers recyclable plastic packaging solutions to clients such as Marks & Spencer. Its Dagenham Dock facility opened in 2008 to produce food grade recycled plastics. This investment was followed in March 2009 by UK waste management company Cyclamax, based in Monmouthshire, announcing its intention to build a 15MW facility to produce enough energy to supply 20,000 homes from waste. The centrepiece of the SiP, according to the London Borough of Barking and Dagenham (http://www.barking-dagenham.gov.uk/Regeneration/Dagenham/Pages/DagenhamDock.aspx accessed 20 January

---

12 http://www.sustainablegov.co.uk/central-government/built-environment/mayor-confirms-go-ahead-of-energy-efficiency-programmes-to-create-green-collar-jobs, accessed 20 June 2011).

13 Ford still manufactures around a million diesel engines a year in the Dagenham factory.

2011), is to be the Institute for Sustainability, whose aim is 'to drive innovative and collaborative demonstration projects that provide the knowledge, experience and practical solutions needed to deliver sustainable cities and communities' (http://www.instituteforsustainability.co.uk/about-us.html, accessed 20 January 2012).

Another important component of the East London Enterprise District proposal is the development of the London Thames Gateway Heat Network, a hot water pipe network planned to connect diverse sources of affordable low carbon heat to existing and new developments including hospitals, schools, apartment blocks and commercial premises. It aims eventually to supply up to 120,000 homes. It will be based initially on harnessing waste heat from electricity generation by Barking power station and complemented over time by a number of new conversion energy sources derived from waste technologies. It is intended that the heat from these diverse energy sources be captured and distributed via hot water pipes to properties to be used for domestic hot water and central heating, replacing conventional boilers. However, the proposal is based on the planned investment of £166 million of public funds by the LDA. In spring 2011 it was unclear what the effect of the cuts in public expenditure will be on the project.

The East London Tech City: Widow and Orphan

In July 2009 Matt Biddulph, co-founder of a Shoreditch- based start up company which developed an online service that lets frequent travellers share future travel plans, Dopplr, noticed that Shoreditch was home to a few technology companies and mapped them. There was a total of 15 firms, all based around the Old Street roundabout. In November 2009 *Wired* magazine followed this up with its own survey and published its results in February 2010. It mapped a total of 85 companies. (http://www.wired.co.uk/magazine/archive/2010/02/start/silicon-roundabout accessed 20 June 2011). In July 2010 Matt Webb, Managing Director of BERG, one of the Shoreditch companies mapped by *Wire* magazine, had accompanied Rohan Silva, senior special adviser to Prime Minister David Cameron on a UK trade mission to India. In a discussion in India, Webb asked Silva for ideas on how to support the development of the Shoreditch start ups saying that this was a better way to feed a recovery than expecting Tesco to create jobs (ibid.). This conversation seems to have been the catalyst for the rapid development of the Tech City proposal.

On 4 November, 2010, at an 'Innovation Future' networking lunch in the Truman Brewery on Brick Lane, David Cameron announced the coalition's ambition to transform London's East End into a world-beating technology hub. This was the initiative that became known as the East London Tech City. At the same time he announced the publication of the government policy document entitled 'Blueprint for Technology'. In his speech Cameron argued that if the creativity and energy of Shoreditch were joined to the promise generated by the Olympic Park, it would be possible to make London one of the great technology centres of the world. In the vision he created, the attractive consumption-led leisure facilities that the Olympic

Park would bring to East London would help to create a favourable environment which would be attractive to the knowledge workers needed to create the Tech City. He suggested that this was the mix of ingredients that had made Silicon Valley successful. He was, therefore, proposing the Tech City to be a hub that stretched from Shoreditch to the Olympic Park.

Cameron also announced that the government had persuaded a number of world leading technology companies to invest in the area. Intel would establish a new research lab in East London; Google would create an Innovation Hub; US computer networking technology monopoly Cisco would establish one of their new Innovation Centres in the Olympic Park; and Facebook would make East London a base for their Developer Garage programme. There would also be private finance available to the entrepreneurs. Vodafone would bring its Vodafone Ventures investment fund to London and Barclays would establish a dedicated new facility in East London to finance technology firms. Start up companies would be advised by McKinsey, one of the world's leading strategic consultancy firms. Also leading UK universities University College London and Loughborough University would work with the Olympic Park Legacy Company to build a bridge between academia and enterprise in the Olympic Park, whilst Imperial Innovations, the venture capital arm of Imperial College London, would advise on the creation of an 'accelerator' space by the Olympic Park Legacy Company for the incubation of start ups. However, in the same speech, Cameron also criticised previous government policies because they believed that it was possible to create a technology cluster 'from on high', whilst what was needed were policies that would build on existing organic growth.

A Post-Crunch Revival of the Real Economy of East London?

The policy initiatives to revive the real economy of East London represent a welcome reorientation toward increasing the role of production in the economy but the continuity in the conceptual basis of these regenerative policies creates serious contradictions which place in doubt their future success. The continued use of the theories of globalisation and inward investment as the main pillars of regeneration policy clashes with the desire to support organic growth of the local economy. The economic justification of the huge expenditure of public funds on the 2012 Olympic Games has always been that the visibility of the region to the world that the Games bring will attract the attention of global investors who will therefore be more inclined to invest in the region because by doing so they themselves will be kept in the eye of the world. In this way all the economic activities in the region acquire the nature of 'showcase' to the world. The use of the word 'showcase' in the policy documents and in the declaration and promises of politicians proliferates. Thus the whole region becomes a huge exhibition space with its window turned to the outside world. In order to guarantee that the attention of the world is maintained, all the activities that are promoted have to be described as 'world class'. The whole Green Enterprise District was conceived precisely in these terms. The models used by the original LDA/Design for London report putting forward the concept were not examples of previous success in developing a real economy but showcase initiatives such as the Eden Project, the Centre for Alternative Technologies in Wales and the Futuroscope in Poitiers, France, as well as historical examples like the Great Exhibition or 1851, the Empire exhibition of 1924 and the 1951 Festival of Britain (LDA 2009).

Undoubtedly all this has had its regeneration effects. The main reason why Siemens chose to build its Siemens Pavilion on publicly owned land in the Royal Docks as a showcase of its green innovation activities is not, as the Mayor claims, its confidence in East London's capacity to generate and nurture innovation, but most likely that it believes that the Olympic Games will add greatly to the world visibility of the region. By placing the Siemens Urban Sustainability Centre in East London, the company seeks to enhance the global image of the brand in the green technologies market where it hopes its future growth will occur. Siemens does not intend to carry out any innovation activities in East London, merely to showcase those developed elsewhere. In the same period as Siemens announced its intention to build the Siemens Urban Sustainability Centre in East London, it also declared its intention to create two new research and development laboratories in the UK, a Siemens Wind Power Research Centre at the University of Sheffield and a Centre of Competence for offshore grid connections in Manchester, both a long way away from London. Siemens is also not intending to carry out manufacturing in the East London Green Enterprise District. Its plan for developing new manufacturing activities in the UK is focused on building a new £80 million factory for the construction of wind turbines which it is looking to place somewhere on the East Coast of England. This strategy was announced in response to the Chancellor of the Exchequer's decision in the March 2010 Budget to allocate funding of £60m to a competition for land development (Siemens News Release 19 March 2010, http://www.siemens.co.uk/en/news_press/index/news_archive/siemens-to-build-wind-turbine-factory.htm, accessed 21 June 2011).

One problem with the consumption-oriented regeneration initiatives taking place in East London is that they can create few linkages to the local economy. The jobs they create tend also not to be the coveted knowledge jobs. A comparison of the projected headline economic effects of the planned Siemens investments in its East London Urban Sustainability Centre and in its wind turbine factory which is to be placed elsewhere will make the point clear. For £30 million, the Siemens Sustainability Centre is projected to create 50 new local jobs in the Centre and in the supply chain, a cost of £600,000 per job. Siemens' projected investment of £80 million in a wind turbine manufacturing plant is planned to create 700 direct jobs plus an unspecified number of additional jobs in the supply chain, a cost of £114 thousand per direct job, many of which will no doubt be highly skilled.

Overall, whilst the effort to revive the productive economy of East London through the concept of the Green Enterprise District undoubtedly constitutes a step in the right direction, a question mark hangs over its likely impact. Even at the headline level, the Mayor's aim to attract £140 billion in order to create 6,000 jobs is somewhat difficult to understand. The number of jobs that the initiative is intended to create is a small fraction of the number that have been lost through deindustrialisation at Fords alone. At an investment cost of over £23 million per job it appears to be a highly expensive, capital intensive enterprise with a very limited impact on employment. The success of the Dagenham Dock Sustainable Industries Park development so far has been limited. Its development plans are highly dependent on funding by the LDA and are likely to be greatly affected by public expenditure cuts.

The preoccupation with external image and 'world class' initiatives in order to continue to attract the attention of the world is also present in the Green Enterprise District proposal when it tries to address the prescriptions of the theory of the knowledge economy. The original LDA/Design for London report putting forward the concept of the Green Enterprise District refers to the need to bring to the district 'a faculty from a major internationally recognised university or consortium of universities, specialising in teaching and research around clean technology' (LDA/Design for London 2009: 7). It mentions as obvious examples University College London or Imperial College. As I have pointed out, the London Borough of Barking and Dagenham places the Institute for Sustainability at the centre of its Sustainable Industries Park. The Institute describes itself as 'an independent charity led by a world class board representing UK industry, academia and public sector set up to accelerate the delivery of sustainable cities and communities' (http://www.instituteforsustainability.co.uk, accessed 20 June 2011). The members of the board from academia are from Imperial College, University College London and Southampton University. The Institute is little more than another image building exercise aiming at a world audience, unrelated to any real activities existing in East London. It conducts no research and has a very small budget made up from public funds. Yet East London is home to several higher education institutions, most of which are post-1992 universities, who educate large numbers of local young people presumably in order to enable them to take up jobs in the knowledge economy. The University of East London has its own Sustainability Research Institute where actual research is carried out into sustainability issues. All other East London universities have strong links with the local population and carry out relevant research. Yet they are not given a significant role in the regeneration plans presumably because they are not considered 'world class'.[14]

The growing Shoreditch cluster of start up technology firms is indeed a very hopeful phenomenon contributing significantly to the development of a productive economy in East London. Cameron has recognised it as an organic phenomenon created primarily as a result of the availability of centrally located relatively cheap

14 The University of East London is mentioned in the 2009 LDA/Design for London report putting forward the concept of the East London Green Enterprise District as a possible partner for either University College London or Imperial College in the establishment within the District of an internationally recognised faculty specialising in green technologies.

warehouses in an area which is diverse and multicultural and where the diversity of the local population has created a mixed cultural and recreational environment conducive to creative activities. Yet, the initiative of the Tech City is in danger of turning this exciting development into another showcase for global capital. In the Prime Minister's eyes the only valid measure of the success of his project appears to be the extent to which global companies recognise and engage with it. It is the promises, unrealised in mid-2011, made by Cisco, Google, Facebook, Intel and McKinsey to come to the area that are seen to validate the Tech City project, rather than the concrete measures taken to ascertain the needs of the budding local productive economy and to ensure that those needs are met. David Willetts, Minister for Universities and Science, in an answer to a question in Parliament by East London MP Diane Abbott, measured the success of the Shoreditch start up firms by the fact that two of them had been sold respectively to Nokia and CBS for many millions of pounds (Hansard 9 March 2011). Yet the lessons that can be drawn from the historical fate of the high technology industry that existed in East London at the beginning of the last century seems to be that purchase of local firms by global capital is unlikely to contribute much to rooting innovation activities in the local economy. Also, there is no attempt to find ways in which the education and training of the young people of East London currently being carried out by the local educational and research institutions can be deployed to meet the needs of the new and developing productive economy. This would enable the local population to benefit by its future success. Instead the aim is to bring into East London and the Olympic Park world class universities with no existing links to the region.

There is a danger that the hype that results from focussing on attracting the attention of the world will be counter-productive to the organic development of the productive economy. East London estate agents are already using the Prime Minister's speech and the Tech City proposal in their advertising of properties in the area. This is likely to drive up property prices, whose relatively low level has so far been one of the reasons for the area attracting start up investment. A further problem with trying to regenerate by facing the global rather than the local economy is that every other region in the world is doing the same. There are innumerable regions trying to use the Silicon Valley model and the globalisation rhetoric to develop or regenerate their economies. This is likely to intensify the competition between regions and strengthen the hand of global companies in their search for extracting the best possible deal in their location decisions.

The sustainability discourse is equally being adopted by all countries and most regions in their economic development efforts. The concept is beginning to acquire a mythical dimension as the saviour of an ailing capitalist economy, a role that the concept of the information society played in the 1990s.[15] Siemens trying to reinvent itself as a green company and the Mayor of London's environment advisor's conviction that creating an energy efficient society is a profitable

15 For an examination of the role that the concept information society played in the 1990s, see de Miranda 2009.

enterprise as well as being good for the environment are but two expressions of this generalised belief. Such views will contribute to intensifying the competition between regions to attract global capital. Greater clarity about the relative role of consumption and production in regeneration, of the relative role of manufacturing and creative activities, less attention to the global and more attention to the locally embedded needs, as illustrated by the historical view of East London's production industries, just might produce a set of policies more likely to benefit the local population.

Bibliography

Blake A., Macrury, I. and Poynter, G. (2007). 'A Lasting Legacy?': A comparative study of the economic, environmental and social impact of the Olympic and Paralympic Games on four host cities for the Greater London Assembly. London: GLA.

Brundtland, H.G. (1987). *Our Common Future*. Oxford: Oxford University Press.

Donnelly, T. and Morris, D. (2003). 'Restructuring Ford Europe', *European Business Review*, 15(2), 77-86.

DTI (1999). *Our Competitive Future: Building the Knowledge Driven Economy*, White Paper Cm4176, London:DTI.

Foss, N.J. (1997). 'The New Growth Theory: Some Intellectual Growth Accounting' Department of Industrial Economics and Strategy Working Paper 97-2, Copenhagen Business School.

Fröbel F., Folker, J., Heinrichs, J. and Kreye, O. (1980). *The New International Division of Labour: Structural Unemployment in Industrialised Countries and Industrialisation in Developing Countries.* Cambridge, UK: Cambridge University Press.

Gannon, P. (1997). *Trojan Horses and National Champions*. London: Apt-Amatic Books.

GLAEconomics (2004). *London's Creative Sector: 2004 Update*, London: Greater London Authority.

Hickox, M. (1995). 'The English Middle Class Debate', *British Journal of Sociology*, 46(2), 311-24.

LDA/Design for London (2009). *Green Enterprise District: A Concept for East London* London: London Development Agency and Design for London.

Lewis, J. (2010). *Industry and Innovations: The Technological Revolution in the Lea Valley*. Faringdon, Oxon: LIBRI Publishing.

Lucas, R.E. (1988). 'On the Mechanics of Economic Development', *Journal of Monetary Economics*, 22, 3-42.

de Miranda, A. (2007). 'Creative East London in Historical Perspective', *Rising East* Online, 7, September, London: London East Research Institute (LERI), available at http://www.uel.ac.uk/risingeast/archive07/academic/miranda.pdf.

de Miranda, A. (2009). 'Technological Determinism and Ideology: Questioning the "Information Society" and the 'Digital Divide" in J. Burnett, P. Senker and K. Walker (eds) *Myths of Technology*. New York: Peter Lang.

OECD (1996). *The Knowledge Based Economy*, GD(96)102, Paris: OECD.

Poynter, G. (2006). 'From Beijing to Bow Creek', LERI Working Papers in Urban Studies, London East Research Institute, University of East London.

Romer, P.M. (1986). 'Increasing Returns to Long Run Growth', *Journal of Political Economy*, 94, 1002-37.

Romer, P.M. (1990). 'Endogenous Technical Change', *Journal of Political Economy*, 98, pp S71-102.

Scheffel, E. and Thomas, E. (2011). 'Employment and intangible spending in the UK's creative industries', *Economic and Labour Market Review*, January, London: Office of National Statistics.

van Helten, J.J. and Cassis, Y. (1990). *Capitalism in a Mature Economy: Financial Institutions, Capital Exports and British Industry, 1870-1939*. Aldershot: Edward Elgar.

Chapter 11
Energy

James Woudhuysen

Obsessions with CO_2 Obscure the Significance of Energy Supply

London consumes an enormous amount of gas to keep warm (especially to warm homes), electricity to power equipment (especially in industrial and commercial applications), and petrol to keep moving. The humbug about energy in London is also enormous. In line with Coalition government policy, rhetoric fastens on cutting emissions of carbon dioxide (CO_2), at the expense of assuring a reliable, cheap supply of energy for London's growing needs. In official documents, too, a reliable, cheap energy supply is subordinated to the higher goal of 'low carbon'.

The policy has not wavered since Mayor Ken Livingstone gave way to Mayor Boris Johnson in May 2008. In place of genuine innovation and investment in energy supply, we find 'showcase eco-projects', for which there has for some years been a worldwide fad (Pearce 2006: 2). While real data on energy supply and demand in London are hard to find, it is easy to see London's environmentalist gestures. For years after it was completed in 2002, admiration was lavished on Bill Dunster's BedZed architecture in Hackbridge, east London – zero-emissions houses, lined back-to-back, in a colourful pastiche of a pastiche. Today, we are supposed to wonder at charging points for electric vehicles – tall, black posts, their tops gleaming a lovely blue glow at night… but with no electric vehicles in sight.

London makes more than 40 per cent of the UK's general patent applications (Gurría 2009) and is relatively strong in university-based scientific research. In energy, London is the headquarters of energy regulators such as Ofgem, engineering institutions such as the Institution of Engineering and Technology (the largest professional engineering body in Europe, with 125,000 members), consultants such as Arup and Wood Mackenzie, and utilities such as Centrica. Yet for all such forces, London hosts no major, focused, open or continuous debate about its energy. Instead, the dogma continues that action around CO_2 emissions is logically prior to action around energy supply.

Here there is unanimity. For example, the first of two key Greater London Authority consultation documents misleadingly titled *Delivering London's Energy Future*, published in February 2010 and addressed to the London Assembly 'and functional bodies', lifted much of both its narrative and its data from a report by the City audit firm Ernst and Young – a report significantly titled *Prospectus for London, the 'Low Carbon Capital'* (GLA 2010a; Ernst & Young 2009). The GLA document has 70 mentions of the words 'sustainable' and 'sustainability', but many, many more of 'low carbon', 'zero carbon' and 'zero emission'. The document features pi-charts about the sources of CO_2 emissions, and time charts for the extent to which different measures will cut CO_2 in future (GLA 2010a). It represents a conscious decision *to count not energy, but carbon*. Indeed, the GLA celebrates London as 'the leading centre for carbon trading globally with over 75 per cent of the world's carbon trading desks', and, related to that, as 'the centre for the legal profession globally' (GLA 2010a: 42).

Here, under Boris Johnson, we meet two linked and special features of local government under New Labour: naturalism, and the target mentality. It is a green regime that Nikita Krushchev would perhaps recognise (Woudhuysen and Abley 2004: 20, 37). London policymakers, lobbyists and auditors are more interested in counting and cutting emissions of CO_2 than they are in creating a can-do culture of technological change and investment in energy supply. This also appears to be the attitude of the biggest supplier of energy to London, EDF Energy – 'Britain's largest producer of low carbon electricity', and, for £8m, a fully branded sponsor, between 2011 and 2013, of the London Eye (EDF Energy London Eye 2011, BBC 2011). The company, a top executive reports, founded www.TeamGreenBritain.org to help people cut their energy use 'at home, at work and at school'. Its vision for London is 'a lower carbon Olympic and Paralympic host city' (Wynn 2011). It will display on the Web the energy consumed by the Olympic Aquatics Centre and the Velodrome. It will install 3,000 'smart' meters in the Olympic Athletes' Village. It wants 'to reduce the carbon footprint of the London Eye and of Tower Bridge' (EDF 2011).

Table 11.1 Final energy consumption, Greater London and UK, 2008, TWh

	Industrial and commercial	Domestic	Total non-transport	Transport	Grand total
Greater London	55	62.1	117.1	31.5	**148.8**
UK	582	534.2	1116.2	478	**1,606**

Note: Figures have been rounded.
Source: DECC 2011a.

In high places, obsessions with London's *wastes* in the shape of CO_2 obscure the significance of London's *needs* in terms of energy supply. On the GLA's website, 'Environment' is listed as one of its formal priorities. 'Energy' is not (GLA 2011a).

Table 11.2 Main components of London energy use, by sector and by energy source, 2008, TWh

Electricity, domestic	Electricity, industrial and commercial	Gas, domestic	Gas, industrial and commercial	Oil, industrial and commercial	Coal, domestic, industrial and commercial; Oil, domestic	Wastes and renewables, industrial and commercial	**Total non-transport**	Road transport	Domestic aviation	Rail	Domestic shipping	**Total transport**	**Grand total Total**
13.8	26.1	49.9	24.4	2.8	0.3	0.2	117.5	28.2	5.7	0.4	0.1	**34.4**	**152**

Note: Figures have been rounded.
Source: GLA/LEGGI 2010.

Overview of Recent Energy Demand

Over a recent winter in London, I paid about £300 for 2000 kilowatt-hours (kWh) of electricity, and a further £200 for 10,000 kWh of gas. Remembering that a terawatt-hour (TWh) is a billion kWh, London's use of energy breaks down, according to the Department for Energy and Climate Change (DECC), as demonstrated in Table 11.1.

As the grand totals for London and the UK show, London's final energy consumption amounts to about nine per cent of UK national energy use. Since London's GDP is about 20 per cent of UK GDP, London is, by UK standards, relatively efficient in the amount of energy it uses to generate its part of national wealth.

The Greater London Authority's *London Energy and Greenhouse Gas Inventory* (LEGGI) for 2008 (GLA/LEGGI 2010) breaks down London energy use by sector and by energy source in Table 11.2

Gas-fired central heating in the home, followed by vehicles and industrial/commercial use of electricity and gas, are the main sources of demand for energy in London.

GLA/LEGGI figures (2010) suggest that London's energy use has dropped off since 2004, and DECC figures (2011) agree after 2005. Indeed LEGGI also suggests that London energy use will decline a lot by 2015:

What made London's use less energy between 2004 and 2008? Between 2004 and 2009, there was little improvement in cavity wall insulation in London (ONS/DECC 2011: 53). However the question *of energy efficiency* – that is, how much buildings and machines are able to make of a given energy supply – goes further than that (Table 11.3)

Table 11.3 Energy use, London, 2004-2008, and as projected to 2011 and 2015; TWh

2004	2006	2008	2011	2015
162.9	155.0	151.9	143.3	135.5

Note: Figures have been rounded.
Source: GLA/LEGGI 2010.

Rises in Energy Efficiency won't Depress London's Demand for Energy

Before now, Boris Johnson has written: 'Recession or not, this will be remembered as a new Victorian Age' (Johnson 2009). But the Mayor should know his beloved Victorian era better. In that time, William Stanley Jevons (1832-1885) trained and later professed at University College London. Jevons, derided by Marx and Engels as one of the founders of the marginal utility school of economics, wrongly anticipated the advent of what today would be termed 'peak coal'. But on one thing he was right: increases in the efficiency with which energy is used lead to a *greater* demand for energy, not a smaller one. Jevons wrote: 'It is wholly a confusion of

Table 11.4 Fuel poverty in London, thousands of homes

2003	2004	2005	2006	2007	2008	2009
108	119	120	254	309	328	402

Note: Figures have been rounded.
Source: DECC 2011b.

ideas to suppose that the economical use of fuel is equivalent to a diminished consumption. The very contrary is the truth' (Jevons 1865). Other things being equal, a bigger energy bang for a buck will lead to more use of energy, not less.[1]

Even if they happened (and they didn't), improvements in the energy efficiency in London's buildings look like an improbable source of lower energy demand in London, Nevertheless, what Johnson calls his 'palatable, commonsense approach' dictates that Jevons, and what is often termed 'the rebound effect', should be disregarded. Instead, as we shall see, RE:NEW, the Mayor's programme to insulate the capital's draughty housing stock and so raise its energy efficiency, is the centrepiece of Johnson's drive to reduce London's demand for energy.

Perhaps relatively warm winters[2] and a switch out of expensive gas and petrol explain the drop in London's energy demand between 2004 and 2008. The principal sectors contributing to the decline in energy use in London, after all, were gas, domestic (a 5.4 TWh decrease, 2004-8); gas, industrial and commercial (4.0 TWh), and road transport (1.8 TWh) (GLA/LEGGI 2010). Since gas prices in general track oil prices, the run-up to a price of $145 a barrel of oil in July 2008 seems to have had a deterrent effect on demand for energy.

Perhaps more Londoners spent more hours in workplaces or on the move, and fewer hours racking up energy bills at home. A more persuasive factor behind the drop in domestic gas usage might be that poorer Londoners felt compelled to save energy. It is true that the official category of 'fuel poverty' – officially taken as a situation in which 10 per cent or more of a household's income goes on maintaining a satisfactory heating regime – is rather dubious (Woudhuysen and Kaplinsky 2009: 10). However, the reported increases in fuel poverty in London are rather suggestive:

1 The Jevons perspective is no ancient piece of esoterica: not long ago, it was the subject of a long, careful and supportive article in the *New Yorker* (Owen 2010).

2 At the Meteorological Office's station at Heathrow airport, the mean daily minimum temperature between January 2004 and December 2008 never fell below 1.7°c (Meteorological Office 2011).

By the measure of fuel poverty, more Londoners than ever face energy bills that loom appreciably large in their outgoings. That may explain, in part, the drop in domestic gas use in London between 2004 and 2008.

The Question of Peaks

The drop in energy expended in road transport is small, but interesting. In recent years, the doctrine has grown that many countries in the West, including the UK, have met '*peak car*', in the sense that passenger-kilometres travelled have tended to stagnate (Millard-Ball and Schipper 2010, Goodwin 2010, Crabtree 2011). Indeed lower energy use on London's roads might be part of a wider trend toward the greening of London, as people turn to bicycles and to public transport. Perhaps, too, households and organisations don't want to burn gas the way they used to. With Britain set for slow growth for years to come, could even London have reached *peak energy demand*?

Not so fast. If we take road transport, it would be premature to call a peak. Although car ownership in London stagnated at below 0.5 per adult between 1992-4 and 2002-3, the figure is projected to rise to 0.53 per adult by 2026 and 0.56 per adult in 2036; with growth in London's adult population, the number of cars may rise from 2.942 million to 4.103 million, 2009-2036 (Whelan, Crockett and Vitouladiti 2010).

It is foolish to see peaks everywhere. As the International Transport Forum of the Organisation of Economic Cooperation and Development has noted, the rate at which car transport demand and transport expenditures increase with income is slowing in the West; but it is 'not at all obvious that continued income growth will no longer lead to more car transport'. When factors such as road building, income, age and population growth are taken into account, it would be 'excessively risky to base projections in rich countries on an assumption of saturation alone' (International Transport Forum 2011: 24-9).

The example of peak car should serve as a warning. Before the development of shale gas in the decade just passed, some worried about peak gas; before Japan endured Fukushima, some worried about peak uranium. Some people feel that the Earth's population will, sooner or later, reach its limit. But London does not live in a world of what the best-selling Californian Richard Heinberg calls *Peak Everything* (Heinberg 2007).

London Will Need Lots More Energy, Which is Getting Dearer

The GLA/LEGGI projection of a 10 per cent cut in London's energy demand between 2008 and 2015 is suspect. Even more suspect are two more statements by the GLA. The February 2010 *Delivering London's Energy Future* opined that in 2025, a quarter of London's total energy demand, *sans* transport, would 'amount to around' 29 TWh (GLA 2010a: 65). Then, in an October 2010 variant of *Delivering* designed for public consultation, 29 TWh magically became 23 TWh (GLA 2010b: 103). Now: this projection of 92 TWh for total non-transport demand for energy in 2025 compares with a figure of 117 TWh in 2008. The GLA believes, then, that in 17 years London can lower its 'stationary' demand for energy by 27 per cent.

How very convenient, how easily done! But despite the dip in London's demand for energy over 2004-8, the GLA's low-energy future will never arrive. De-industrialisation of London cannot go much further, denying the city further energy savings from this process. The London service sector is unlikely to lower demand much more than it has done: between 1970 and 2003, the UK service sector kept level its lowish demand for energy (House of Lords Science and Technology Committee 2005: 20). Despite poor prospects for the UK economy, London's GDP, which is the largest among European cities, will likely grow a fair bit between now and 2025: Citigroup, for example, projects that it will reach \$821bn, from a 2008 base estimated by PricewaterhouseCoopers as \$565bn (White 2011, PricewaterhouseCoopers 2009: 22). Last, the number of households in the capital is set to rise by 15.5 per cent between 2006 and 2026 (Holmans and Whitehead 2011: 3).

Now, UK policy on energy usually exaggerates CO_2 emissions from the residential sector. However in London, gas-fired central heating has a special salience. In 2009, London also had the lowest proportion of cavity wall insulation and loft insulation anywhere in England (ONS/DECC 2011: 52-3). The city has a slender industrial base and a relatively high population density. As Table 11.1 showed, these factors make London homes use, in aggregate, more energy than do London workplaces, which is the inverse of the picture for the UK as a whole.

Warmth isn't the only thing in the home. Between 1990 and 2010, the electricity consumed in UK homes grew by almost 27 per cent (DECC 2011c). Especially in London, which has a large middle class, the number of gadgets in each home continues to rise. Also, TVs are getting bigger, and so demand extra energy.[3] Not many houses look like being built in London. But more and more people will cram into the capital's tight, aging property and make a full and proper demand for heating and electricity. Between 2004 and 2008, rising population may have done little to raise London's demand for energy. But in the future, rising population could well join other factors ensuring that London will need lots more, not less, energy.

The issue is an immediate one, because energy capacity takes time to build. In *Delivering London's energy future* the GLA (2010b) notes that, by 2020, closures of old nuclear plants, and of coal and gas plants failing to comply with EU norms, mean that London's share of the electricity demand not met by national supply could be about 0.576 TWh. But by 2020, too, we are reassured, RE:NEW, the Mayor's home insulation programme could cut electricity demand by 0.756 TWh, 'plugging London's potential energy gap and around ten per cent of the national energy gap' (GLA 2010b: 9-10). But this is silly. Insulating London's homes won't

3 Between 2010 and 2011, indeed, the average size of a new television screen in the UK grew by three inches (Warman 2011).

lower *electricity* demand, which is what the GLA insists on boasting about. Worse, the GLA estimates that by 2015-6 Britain's national energy gap could run to 43 TWh (GLA 2010b: 27). So even if RE:NEW achieves its energy saving of 0.756 TWh, that is 1.34 per cent, not 10 per cent, of the national energy gap.[4]

Altogether, serious power cuts may hit London sooner rather than later. But there is another question: how much might energy in London cost? The general trend must be upward. Today the inflation of energy prices is a feature of worldwide general inflation. Perhaps a debt-fuelled world economic crisis may curb the price of petrol and diesel. However the 2011 White Paper (DECC 2011d) is set to force London households, businesses and other organisations, like the rest of Britain, to pay more for their gas and electricity (Lyons 2011). In a dear city like London, energy will not just be weak: it will also be dear.

Energy Security and Energy Metabolism

The first objective of the October 2010 *Delivering London's energy future* (GLA 2010b: 8) is 'to reduce London's CO_2 emissions to mitigate climate change'. The second is to make energy an instrument for other goals: that mysterious thing, the 'low carbon sector', could benefit London with 'an annualised average of 14,000 (gross) jobs per year, and £720 million of Gross Value Added (GVA) per year' (GLA 2010b: 9).

Ensuring that there is a *secure and reliable* energy supply for London comes third behind all this (the fourth objective merely reinforces the first: 'To meet, and where possible exceed, national climate change and energy objectives'). Moreover the Mayor's 'vision' for 2025 here is one of energy *autarchy*. By 2025, we are told, London 'will become its own powerhouse. Over a quarter of London's energy demand will be met from low or zero carbon local sources' (GLA 2010b: 7). Given its utopian hopes in lowering London's future energy demand, how realistic, then, is the GLA about meeting that demand from local sources?

For well over a century, large pieces of civil engineering have made and brought heat and power to Britain and to London. Indeed, London has always imported most of its energy as coal, gas, oil and electricity (UCL 2011: 4). There is nothing strange about this. As the *Digest of UK Energy Statistics* notes, 'the UK has traded fuels such as oil and gas regardless of whether it has been a net exporter or importer. In 2010 the UK imported more coal, crude oil, electricity and gas than it exported; however, the UK remained a net exporter of petroleum products' (DECC 2011e: 12).

Shamelessly, however, the GLA (2010b: 26-7) raises the alarm – not about *reliability* of energy supply in the sense of *sufficiency*, but rather about *security of energy supply* in the sense of *geopolitics*. 'An ever-increasing number of experts',

4 Confidence in the GLA's projections of energy demand is not improved by its repeated, if delightful, reference to 'Terra Watt hours' (GLA 2010a: 27, GLA 2010b: 64).

it reports excitedly (though it does not say who), ‘are pointing to the threat of peak oil; the notion that we have reached, or will soon be reaching, the maximum rate of global oil production, to be followed by a sustained decline in future production’. Of the UK, it says:

> [O]il and gas production from the North Sea has peaked and is falling steadily. The UK is once again a net importer of oil and gas where not too long ago it was a net exporter. The diminishing stock of domestic oil and gas means that the UK is becoming increasingly reliant on foreign energy sources. Given the volatility of the relatively few countries with most of the world’s oil reserves … [I]nvesting in domestic low carbon energy solutions would therefore help to protect London’s businesses and residents from being held hostage to soaring global energy prices. (GLA 2010b: 26-7)

This discovery of Londoners being hostages is hardly new. In both the UK and the US, fears of dependence on overseas sources of oil have a long history (Woudhuysen and Kaplinsky: 78, 83-4). But with the GLA oil and gas security are held up as a call not just for *energy conservation*, but also for a *renewables-based energy supply that is local to London*. What is forgotten is that innovation can create new, powerful, reliable and cheap sources of energy supply outside London – a tidal barrage on the Severn Estuary, for example. Meanwhile, new oil has been found off Brazil, Africa, and India; and the discovery of shale gas has made one energy specialist proclaim that the Americas, not the Middle East, will be the world capital of energy (Jaffe 2011).

The planet now has a world market for natural gas – something that benefited Japan after Fukushima. Globalisation cannot be wished away. So exactly why should the Executive Summary of the October 2010 *Delivering* open with the goal that, by 2025, London should generate ‘its own low and zero carbon energy’ (GLA 2010b: 7)? Yes, there are losses in transmission in electricity supply, but the GLA’s paranoia about the outside world goes way beyond that. In energy, dependency on technology and on international sources is a fact of life. London should build ‘its own’ energy supply only with techniques, at the scales and with the costs that make sense.

The GLA wants less dependency on outside energy. But it also wants London, by 2025, to have ‘the lowest carbon footprint per person of any big city in the world’, to have a lower citywide footprint, and to have neighbourhoods lower their ‘wider carbon footprint’ (GLA 2011b: 7, 40, 151). From one side and the other, the Authority offers an old staple of environmentalism: the city as *vulnerable-but-greedy parasite on outside energy resources*, and also the city as *energy-consuming organ of pollution*.

This is a generous vision of the city. We can expect to hear more about urban metabolisms in future, for London (Pearce 2006: 1), China (Shang et al. 2010: 1865-1879) and throughout the West (Troy 2012). We have seen that energy ‘security’ is a completely utopian quest, given the world’s international division of labour in energy. In the same way, naturalistic interpretations of cities and London that use the metaphor of metabolism – chemical reactions in biological organisms – are completely irrational.

Dreams and Realities

The GLA (2010a) has endless lists of dreams. Below, in brief, are four of the main dreams, together with the tortoise-like progress being made toward each one.

1. Through RE:NEW, 'the largest programme ever of its kind in London', the city will insulate 1.2 million homes by 2015 and all dwellings by 2030 – even though a preliminary series of technical trials and demonstration projects had, by 2010, reached just 9,000 homes (GLA 2010b: 13). Funding for RE:NEW was set to end in 2012.
2. Through RE:FIT, 'developed with the support of the Clinton Climate Initiative', London will improve energy efficiency in public sector and other kinds of workplaces – even though, by 2010, measures had been completed in just 10 fire stations, 10 police stations and 22 buildings run by Transport For London (TfL). Total annual savings were just £1 million a year (GLA 2010b: 170-1).
3. Supply, for perhaps £5-7 billion over 15 years and presumably under the leadership of the private sector, 25 per cent of the capital's energy, by 2025, from decentralised sources: primarily combined heat and power (CHP) systems based on gas, biomass and – especially – waste (GLA 2010b: 119-20). There are 197 mentions of the word 'decentralised' in the October 2010 Delivering. What is really meant is tiny. Over 15 years, even £7.5 billion is just £500 million of investment a year – hardly enough to build up to a quarter of the capital's energy supply. Furthermore GLA modeling shows that most of the famous 23TWh delivered by decentralised energy sources in 2025 is meant to come from what are termed 'medium scale', 'small scale' and 'microgeneration' projects. Here capacities, respectively, are just 40MWe[5] (enough electricity for up to 20,000 homes, public buildings and commercial sector consumers, and costing up to £100m), 3MWe (3000 homes, £10m) and 50kWe (one home) (GLA 2010b: 101-3).[6]
4. Within all this decentralised energy, Britain's capital city should up the level of renewable energy use to '11.70 GWh of energy, or 12.8 per cent of London's total energy supply – half of the 25 per cent decentralised energy

5 MWe means megawatts of electricity, a megawatt being 1000 kilowatts. MWt means megawatts of thermal capacity, or heat.

6 Similarly, a 2009 report by London South Bank University found 94 gas-fired CHP installations 'committing' to capacities of just 20MWe and 74 biomass boilers committing to just 50MWt (GLA 2010b: 188).

> target' (GLA 2010b: 120). With its usual sloppiness, what the GLA actually means is 11.7 TWh. Here, we learn that 'the Mayor is taking specific action to stimulate the use of advanced waste conversion and hydrogen technologies'. However, the GLA has to admit that there are currently no advanced waste conversion facilities in London, adding only that the Mayor's aim is for something called the Food to Fuel Alliance to develop 'at least one exemplar anaerobic digestion facility in London by 2012' (GLA 2010b: 119, 121). As for hydrogen, the ambition here is to deploy a maximum of 150 hydrogen-powered vehicles, as well as six pieces of hydrogen refuelling infrastructure, by 2012 (GLA 2011b: 221, 224).

The GLA programme is not entirely ridiculous. For the transmission of heat, *Delivering* talks about the 23km London Thames Gateway Heat Network, which will stretch from the City through Barking power station to Kingsnorth power station (by 2025, equipped with fully operational carbon capture and storage) (GLA 2010b: 18, 117). It is true that the heat capacity of the Network is not specified; that it might save only 100,000 tonnes of the 44.7 million tonnes of CO_2 associated with London in 2008; and that, even in its construction phase, the Network will create not much more than 200 jobs (GLA 2010b: 8, 117). Yet though it is billed as 'the largest new decentralised energy development in Europe' (GLA 2010b: 14), it may actually be a sensible step forward. But for the GLA such a step is a rare one. The common, if paradoxical, themes in all the initiatives listed above are *low technological ambitions* and *overblown long-term goals*. Let's look at each of these problems in turn.

Low Technological Ambitions

The GLA bemoans the 'lack of available investment funds to research, commercialise and develop low carbon technologies and solutions' (2011a: 63), yet its technological plans are modest. It has no serious outlook on R&D or innovation.

First, the homes programme RE:NEW – 'a range of cost-free, easy-to-install measures' in February 2010 (GLA 2010a: 102), but 'pay-as-you-save' by October of the same year (GLA 2010b: 129) – begins with a 90-minute energy survey from an advisor on how to save up to £154 a year on energy and water. The measures proposed? They're about changing to low energy light bulbs, installing stand-by switches, insulating hot water tanks and draft-proofing (GLA 2011b).

Second, the insulation of homes and other buildings is a low-tech, low-wage, but highly labour-intensive affair. According to the GLA, drawing upon Ernst & Young, investment in residential energy measures by 2025 will be less than £266 million, but will generate more than 8000 jobs a year (2010b: 61). This amounts to an investment of just £2000 per job. There is nothing capital-intensive or technological about that.

Third, the GLA is wrong to boast that its waste-to-energy schemes around anaerobic digestion and gasification/pyrolysis involve 'advanced' conversion technologies. Anaerobic digestion (AD)[7] has been used since the 19th century, at least, yet capital costs are relatively high, given that outputs in UK plants rarely exceed just 3MW (Anaerobic-Digestion.com 2008). For London, AD will principally be based on food waste; yet if *all of the UK's domestic food waste* was sent for AD, it would only generate enough electricity for 350,000 households (Renewable Energy Association 2009) – and back in 2001, there were more than three million households in London (ONS 2003). Done with limited amounts of oxygen and steam, the gasification of biomass, a newer technology, also requires high capital costs. It is also a process of low efficiency (Digman et al. 2009).

Last, the GLA says that there are two other opportunities in renewables: biomass heat and power schemes that are 'large-scale', and 'the wide-scale deployment of small and medium-scale renewable heat and power technologies, such as photovoltaics, solar thermal systems, heat pumps' (GLA 2010b: 119-20). The ambitions here are revealing. In biomass heat and power, 'large scale' means something higher than a paltry 5MWe. And with microgeneration, we are back to the heady days of *Our Energy Challenge*, the microgeneration strategy of New Labour's old Department of Trade and Industry (DTI 2006). There is no accounting made for what has happened since then – because in Britain home CHP devices and solar panels, after all the assistance they have had from government feed-in tariffs, still only generate less than 160MW, from fewer than 57,000 households (Ofgem 2011). Instead, there are kind words for solar panels, put on small roofs of homes as much as the big roofs of workplaces. Odd, that: as the GLA notes, almost 50 per cent of London's homes are flats, 'which are logistically harder to retrofit [with solar panels] than a house' (GLA 2010b: 136).

Overblown Long-Term Goals

In terms of energy output, technology and scale, the GLA lacks ambition. But in terms of overall targets, it shows all its familiar utopianism. A candid passage in the February *Delivering* admits that some of the changes it wants 'may sound unrealistically dramatic'. Unabashed, it goes on: 'But decades ago, computers took up whole rooms and were only used by big corporations' (GLA 2010a: 13). This is interesting. Over the past 20 years, the pace of innovation in IT has often been impressive; but it was prefaced by decades of US state intervention to build the Internet, as well as years of research funded by the European Union to establish second-generation networks for mobile telephony. In these periods, the willingness to take risks in the cause of technological innovation was greater

7 In anaerobic digestion, various microorganisms break down organic materials in a sealed, oxygen-free vessel to produce what is known as bio-gas – a mixture, in the main, of methane and CO_2, in which the methane can be used as a fuel.

than it is today – even if it already did not begin to match the audacity of the first and second industrial revolutions of the 18th and late 19th century (Woudhuysen 2010: 21-3). Worse, innovation in fields such as energy has proved much more chimerical than that in IT.

Nevertheless, the GLA insists that the kinds of changes it wants 'are not just fantasy; they are already happening'. It continues:

> People can already get an energy cheque rather than an energy bill, because they are selling more energy into the grid than they are using. More and more proposals come through for pyrolysis and anaerobic digestion facilities to convert London's waste into fuel. London has more electric vehicles than any other city in Europe. We have four times the number of combined heat and power planning applications coming through than we did just a few years ago. We are delivering one of the largest home retrofit programmes ever seen in the UK. (GLA 2010A: 10)

Cheques coming in the post, proposals for waste-to-energy bagatelles, relative comparisons, planning applications: these amount to very little. But with Boorish Johnson and energy, hyperbole must rule – especially around housing, and around electric vehicles.

Patching up Every Home in London

Given that gas-fired central heating generates CO_2, officialdom's obsession with carbon dictates a truly Sisyphean labour to insulate London's homes. The labour will be endless, for London's homes are not the worst insulated in the UK for nothing. All GLA goals and targets here are especially suspect.

Flats are again a problem, because new cavity wall insulation, cladding and windows 'must often be installed for all flats in a building at the same time'. Worse, only 30 per cent of London's homes have lofts at all, 95 per cent of which already have some insulation. Transport snarl-ups, parking and congestion charges all make the work of insulation in London particularly costly. Above all, 70 per cent of London's homes are hard to treat, 15 per cent are the property of landlords (usually uninterested in insulation), and about 13 per cent are also in conservation areas, making them poor candidates for external cladding, All this, yet London is saddled with no fewer than 30 home insulation schemes (GLA 2010b: 136-7). To believe that the city will insulate 1.2 million homes by 2015 and all dwellings by 2030 is just fanciful. It would be easier to build new, intrinsically well insulated homes, than to try to push to the limit the policy of make do and mend.

Electric Vehicles: Pie-in-the-Sky

In 2012, all new buses entering service will be 'hybrid or better' (GLA 2010b: 225). This goal is achievable. But elsewhere we understand that, by 2025, London will not only become 'the electric vehicle capital of Europe' (though apparently it is that already), but will have achieved something else altogether: it will have 'left behind its reliance on polluting fossil fuels' (emphasis added). In practice this quite ludicrous goal simply means 1,000 vehicles joining the GLA fleet by 2015 and, by 2020, new charging infrastructure being rolled out to 'support' the introduction of 100,000 electric vehicles on London's streets. It is added, too that, uptake of electric vehicles in London 'is a Mayoral priority' (GLA 2010b: 7, 14, 199, 222, 224). Yet the Mayor's figures, which compare with three million cars in London at present, are pie-in-the-sky. In 2010 there were just 1,700 electric vehicles in London, and about 250 charge points. As the GLA admitted, although running costs are many times less than those of conventional vehicles, hybrid, electric and hydrogen fuelled vehicles have 'a significant upfront price premium' (sic) over the internal combustion engine (GLA 2010b: 208, 222).

Electric vehicles are commendable, but need enormous technological development if they are to succeed (Woudhuysen 2008, 2009). A sense of the related commercial barriers is given by the fact that, although the Coalition has put aside £400 million to subsidise consumer purchases of electric cars, as well as a network of charging points, just 2,500 electric cars had been bought in Britain by July 2011 (Millward 2011). And will their electricity really be the low-carbon sort?

'Supported' but Ignored by Boris: the London Array

Since the closure of Battersea Power Station's two coal-fired electricity units in 1975 and 1983, most electricity supply has been brought into London from outside the city. This will remain true with the completion of the wind-based London Array. Here, in keeping with national energy strategy, 175 wind turbines 20km offshore from the Kent and Essex coasts, in the Thames Estuary, should add to London and Kent a sizable 630 MWe of electricity capacity, amounting to 'the largest offshore power project in the world' (London Array 2011, Haider 2011). A partnership between Abu Dhabi Future Energy Company (popularly known as Masdar), Dong Energy (majority owned by the state of Denmark) and E.ON (Germany) will build the turbines.

In 2011, major controversy broke out about the costs and efficacy of Britain's belated and hurried rush for offshore wind power. The country's targets for offshore installation looked even sillier than in the past, given that wind speeds over its land mass in 2010 were, at 14.3kph, distinctly below the mean for the century so far, which lies at 16.9kph (Ross 2011). Despite the real problems with wind, however, it is possible to wish the London Array well. Whatever its cost, its formal capacity really *is* large scale, compared with all the other petit-bourgeois energy parades touted by the GLA. In the 250 pages of the October 2010 *Delivering*, however, the Array get just one line, in which it is mentioned that the Mayor 'also supports' it (GLA 2010b: 119). Clearly the Array is big and in the Estuary, like Boris Johnson's rather imaginative, energy-demanding proposal of old – for a new airport in the Estuary. Perhaps Johnson only ignores the Array because, unlike his airport, it is actually going to happen.

Conclusion

Unlike financialisation as a process, the machine production of energy has a clear material aspect to it. It is true that energy futures are traded in the City, and that energy utilities quoted on the London Stock Exchange concern themselves more with prices, business models and billing regimes than they do with keeping the lights on (Woudhuysen and Kaplinsky 2009: 428-9). Yet there is nothing ephemeral or fictitious about energy in the real world. One either has it, or one does not. Despite this, the two major GLA documents we have reviewed are hardly exercised by Britain's coming energy gap.

London officialdom is like Britain in its insouciance about energy. For seven months in 2011, the Treasury's newly established unit dedicated to infrastructure, Infrastructure UK, did not have a permanent chief executive – and when it did get one, he had a background with Deutsche Bank, HSBC and the Treasury's own much-loved Private Finance Initiative (Lynch 2011, HM Treasury 2011). No matter how many pounds Sterling or tonnes of CO_2 are crunched, there is no way that the GLA will countenance a future of higher demand for energy in London. This is a worry. Given London's enormous energy needs, one does not need recession, riot or war to make the machine production of energy *inadequate*. Just stupid policies can do that.

So will there be *enough* energy to keep buildings heated, lights bright and internal combustion engines working? Or, one day, will the computer screens through which the City makes a living simply flicker and die? There is no need to be alarmist. But a sufficiency of energy supply might properly be thought to be one of most immediate issues facing the metropolis. Mayor Johnson intends to lower CO2 emissions partly by 'reducing energy demand on a sector-by-sector basis' (GLA 2010b: 43), partly by decarbonising the supply of energy to London, and partly by shifting London motorists over to electric cars. The chart below, which the GLA took from Ernst & Young, shows the key role intended for energy efficiency measures in London's existing residential sector, whether the measures are 'basic' (cavity wall insulation and draught-proofing) or 'extra' (efficient boilers and solid wall insulation) (Ernst & Young 2009: 26-7, GLA 2010b: 61). Indeed, 'the long-term solution to fuel poverty is through improving the energy efficiency of London's housing stock' (GLA 2010a: 20). However, the equally 'long-term' prospect of electric cars is also the subject of some investment, as is apparent from Table 11.5.

Over the period 2011-2025, the total investment of £848 million proposed above amounts to very little. It will do little about the world's CO_2 emissions; indeed all the hostility to a new runway at Heathrow pales into insignificance when it is remembered that China alone intends to build 100 new airports by 2020 (Broadbent

Table 11.5 Projected GVA, investment and jobs through the Mayor's climate change mitigation programmes by 2025

	GVA (direct) pa (£m)	Jobs (pa)	Investment Total (£m)
Electric Vehicles	48	832	284
Commercial public buildings (BEEP)	49	847	24
Residential buildings basics	50	2,674	44
Waste (EW and recycling)	52	1,260	78
Residential buildings Microgeneration	78	1,675	68
Commercial buildings (BBP)	126	2,436	62
Residential buildings extra	176	3,785	154
Decentralised Energy	142	848	132
Total	**720**	**14,357**	**845**

Source: Ernst and Young (2009), Prospectus for London, the low carbon capital.

2008). Nor will £848 million do much for energy supply – were only Battersea Power Station ever converted, after nearly 30 years of disuse, to generate nuclear power at a capacity of 1000MW, the cost would be £1-2 billion or more.

In energy, London's government knows and cares only enough about innovation to back the no-tech sort (labour-intensive home insulation) or the not-yet-tech variety (affordable electric cars). Offering a fraudulent amalgam of utopianism, autarchy and low ambitions, the GLA prefers to change not technique or economy, but Londoners' behaviour. They must, it says, make 'sustainable procurement, transport and consumption decisions'. In the home, many of their future savings in energy 'will be enabled by smart metering and instant feedback on energy consumption', but will, we are admonished, 'also require a behavioural response' (GLA 2010a: 55). In the workplace, Londoners can expect to receive 'employee energy efficiency behaviour change advice' (sic) (GLA 2010a: 121, 124). On the road, there will be a push to improve driving technique on public transport vehicles, and to acquaint the general public with 'eco-driving' styles and environmentally conscious vehicle maintenance (GLA 2010b 216). Meanwhile, the Metropolitan Police has begun to test a system that 'monitors individual driving styles, behaviours, vehicle performances and use. To further encourage this, TfL and GLA group employees who drive for work will undergo eco-driver training to both reduce emissions and develop safer driving behaviour … Taxi and Private Hire Vehicle drivers will also be eligible for this training' (GLA 2010b: 248).

All the bluster for which Boris Johnson is famous cannot disguise the continuity that lies between New Labour's policy on energy (or, more properly, CO_2) and that of the Coalition. Over the years, in City Hall and Whitehall, the same civil servants still cut and paste the same shocking prose and the same fake numbers from the same estimable oracles in the City, and continue to preach the same authoritarian doctrines.

Theirs will remain a brilliant dance. Until, that is, the music stops.

References[8]

Anaerobic-Digestion.com (2008). *Anaerobic Digestion Plants in the British Isles* [Online]. Available at http://www.anaerobic-digestion.com/html/ad_plants_in_the_uk.html.

BBC (2011). London Eye to be Renamed in £8m EDF Sponsorship Deal. *BBC News London* [Online, 7 January]. Available at http://www.bbc.co.uk/news/uk-england-london-12138387.

Broadbent, M. (2008). 100 more Chinese airports by 2020. *Airport International*. [Online, 28 January]. Available at http://www.airport-int.com/news/100-more-chinese-airports-by-2020.html.

Crabtree, J. (2011). End of the road. *Prospect* [Online, 19 April]. Available at http://www.prospectmagazine.co.uk/2011/04/end-of-the-road/.

DECC (2011a). *Total Sub-National Final Energy Consumption 2005, 2006, 2007 and 2008* [Online: Department of Energy and Climate Change, 7 February]. Available at http://www.decc.gov.uk/en/content/cms/statistics/energy_stats/regional/total_final/total_final.aspx.

DECC (2011b). *Trends in Fuel Poverty, England, 2003 to 2009*. [Online: Department of Energy and Climate Change, 14 July]. Available at http://www.decc.gov.uk/assets/decc/Statistics/fuelpoverty/2182-trends-fuel-poverty-england-2003-2009.xls.

DECC (2011c). *UK Climate Change Sustainable Development Indicator: 2010 Greenhouse Gas Emissions, Provisional Figures and 2009 Greenhouse Gas Emissions, Final Figures by Fuel Type and End-User* [Online, Department of Energy and Climate Change, 31 March]. Available at http://www.decc.gov.uk/assets/decc/Statistics/climate_change/1515-statrelease-ghg-emissions-31032011.pdf.

DECC (2011d). *Planning Our Electric Future: A White Paper For Secure, Affordable And Low-Carbon Electricity* [Online: Department of Energy and Climate Change, 12 July]. Available at http://www.decc.gov.uk/assets/decc/11/policy-legislation/EMR/2176-emr-white-paper.pdf.

DECC (2011e). *Digest of United Kingdom Energy Statistics 2011* [Online: Department of Energy and Climate Change, 27 July]. Available at http://www.decc.gov.uk/assets/decc/11/stats/publications/dukes/2312-dukes-2011--full-document-excluding-cover-pages.pdf.

8 All websites accessed August 2011

Digman, B., Joo, H.S. and Kim, D-S. (2009). Recent progress in gasification/pyrolysis technologies for biomass conversion to energy. *Environmental Progress & Sustainable Energy* [Online, 17 February] Available at http://onlinelibrary.wiley.com/doi/10.1002/ep.10336/full.

DTI (2006). *Our Energy Challenge: Power from the People – Microgeneration Strategy* (Online: Department of Trade and Industry, March). Available at http://webarchive.nationalarchives.gov.uk/20080205151941/http://www.berr.gov.uk/files/file27575.pdf.

EDF (2011). *London 2012* [Online]. Available at http://about-us.edf.com/london-2012/providing-low-carbon-electricity-for-the-london-2012-games-85011.html.

EDF Energy London Eye (2011). *EDF Energy: A Unique View. A Bigger Vision.* [Online]. Available at http://www.londoneye.com/EDFEnergy.

Ernst & Young (2009). *Prospectus for London, the 'Low Carbon Capital'* [Online, 30 March]. Available at http://www.lda.gov.uk/Documents/Prospectus_for_London,_the_Low_Carbon_Capital_5608.pdf.

GLA (2010a). *Delivering London's Energy Future: The Mayor's Draft Climate Change Mitigation and Energy Strategy for Consultation with the London Assembly and Functional Bodies* [Online, Greater London Authority, February]. Available at http://www.london.gov.uk/climatechange/sites/climatechange/staticdocs/Delivering_Londons_Energy_Future.pdf.

GLA (2010b). *Delivering London's Energy Future: The Mayor's Draft Climate Change Mitigation and Energy Strategy for Public Consultation* [Online, Greater London Authority, October]. Available at http://www.london.gov.uk/sites/default/files/CCMES_public_consultation_draft_Oct%202010.pdf.

GLA/LEGGI (2010). *PivotTableEnergy* tab in Excel [Online, Greater London Authority, Area PivotTable Analysis in Data Analysis folder in Supporting Folders and Files, September 2010, LEGGI 2008 Database]. Available at http://data.london.gov.uk/datastorefiles/datafiles/environment/gla-leggi-2008-folders.zip.

GLA (2011a). Priorities [Online: Greater London Authority]. Available at http://www.london.gov.uk/priorities.

GLA (2011b). We're Making London's Homes More Energy Efficient Through RE:NEW. [Online: Greater London Authority] Available at http://www.london.gov.uk/priorities/environment/climate-change/energy-efficiency/homes-energy-efficiency-for-tomorrow.

Gurría, A. (2009). Restoring Growth in a Post-Bailout Era: The Crucial Contribution of Cities [Online: Organisation for Economic Cooperation and Development, 9 November]. Available at http://www.oecd.org/document/41/0,3746,en_21571361_44315115_44047593_1_1_1_1,00.html.

Haider, H. (2011). Masdar's London Array project due for completion by end 2012. *Khaleej Times* [Online, 10 July] Available at http://www.khaleejtimes.com/biz/inside.asp?xfile=/data/business/2011/July/business_July162.xml&section=business.

Heinberg, R. (2007). *Peak Everything: Waking up to the Century of Decline in Earth's Resources*. Forest Row: Clairview Books.

HM Treasury (2011). Leadership of Infrastructure UK. [Online, 26 July]. Available at http://www.hm-treasury.gov.uk/press_88_11.htm.

Holmans, A. with Whitehead, C. (2011). *New and Novel Household Projections for England with a 2008 Base – Summary and Review* [Online, Town & Country Planning Tomorrow Series Paper 11, May]. Available at http://www.tcpa.org.uk/data/files/2011_holmans__whitehead_paper.pdf.

International Transport Forum (2011). *Transport Outlook 2011: Meeting the Needs of 9 Billion People*. [Online]. Available at http://www.internationaltransportforum.org/Pub/pdf/11Outlook.pdf.

Jaffe, A.M. (2011). The Americas, not the Middle East, will be the world capital of energy. *Foreign Policy* [Online, 24 August]. Available at http://www.foreignpolicy.com/articles/2011/08/15/the_americas_not_the_middle_east_will_be_the_world_capital_of_energy.

Jevons, W.S. (1865). *The Coal Question: An Inquiry Concerning the Progress of the Nation, and the Probable Exhaustion of Our Coal-Mines* [Online]. Available at http://www.econlib.org/library/YPDBooks/Jevons/jvnCQ.html.

Johnson, B. (2009). If we work hard we can make London safer, fairer, cleaner. *Evening Standard* [Online, 5 January]. Available at http://www.thisislondon.co.uk/standard/article-23611354-if-we-work-hard-we-can-make-london-safer-fairer-cleaner.do.

LDA (2009). *Powering Ahead: Delivering Low Carbon Energy For London*. [Online, October]. Available on http://www.london.gov.uk/sites/default/files/powering-ahead141009.pdf.

Lex (2011). Biohazard: Barons of subsidy. *The Financial Times* [Online, 12 June]. Available at http://www.ft.com/cms/s/0/2748fa28-9523-11e0-a648-00144feab49a.html#axzz1VxGA0YkV (subscription required).

London Array (2011). *A Building Site 20km out to Sea*. [Online.] Available at http://www.londonarray.com/the-project/offshore/.

Lynch, M. (2011). Acting IUK chief exec resigns. New Civil Engineer. [Online, 18 July]. Available at http://www.nce.co.uk/news/business/acting-iuk-chief-exec-resigns/8617433.article (subscription required).

Lyons, R. (2011). How green politicking will deepen fuel poverty. *spiked* [Online, 14 July]. Available at http://www.spiked-online.com/index.php/site/article/10877/.

Meteorological Office (2011). Heathrow (London Airport) station data [Online]. Available at http://www.metoffice.gov.uk/climate/uk/stationdata/heathrowdata.txt.

Millard-Ball, A. and Schipper, L. (2010). Are we reaching peak travel? Trends in passenger transport in eight industrialized countries. *Transport Reviews* [Online], 2010, 1-22. Available at http://www.stanford.edu/~adammb/Publications/Millard-Ball%20Schipper%20Peak%20Travel%20preprint.pdf.

Millward, D. (2011). Electric car scheme fails to excite motorists [Online: *The Daily Telegraph* 20 July]. Available at http://www.telegraph.co.uk/motoring/news/8650005/Electric-car-scheme-fails-to-excite-motorists.html.

Ofgem (2011). FIT Installations Statistical Report [Online, 20 August]. Available at https://www.renewablesandchp.ofgem.gov.uk/Public/ReportManager.aspx?ReportVisibility=1&ReportCategory=0.

ONS/DECC (2011). *Annual Report on Fuel Poverty Statistics 2011.* [Online: Office for National Statistics/Department for Energy and Climate Change, July]. Available at http://www.decc.gov.uk/assets/decc/Statistics/fuelpoverty/2181-annual-report-fuel-poverty-stats-2011.pdf.

ONS (2003). *Census 2001: London.* [Online, Office for National Statistics, data released on or before 13 February 2003]. Available at http://www.statistics.gov.uk/census2001/profiles/h.asp.

Owen, D. (2010). The efficiency dilemma. *The New Yorker* [Online, 20 and 27 December]. Available at http://www.newyorker.com/reporting/2010/12/20/101220fa_fact_owen.

Pearce, F. (2006). Eco-cities special: Ecopolis now. *New Scientist* [Online, 16 June]. Available at http://www.neiu.edu/~rdpurtuc/Forum-Archive/ecoCities.pdf.

PricewaterhouseCoopers 2009. *UK Economic Outlook November 2009* [Online] Available at https://www.ukmediacentre.pwc.com/imagelibrary/downloadMedia.ashx?MediaDetailsID=1562.

Renewable Energy Association (2009). *Anaerobic Digestion: Energy Balance* [Online]. Available at http://www.r-e-a.net/biofuels/biogas/anaerobic-digestion/ad-energy-balance.

Troy A. (2012). *The Very Hungry City*. New Haven, CT: Yale University Press. Summary before publication available at http://www.yalebooks.co.uk/display.asp?K=9780300162318.

UCL (2011). *Long-term Forces and Factors Shaping London* [Online: University College London 2062 Commission, July 2011]. Available at http://www.ucl.ac.uk/london-2062/documents/2062-12July-2011.pdf.

Warman M. (2011). Televisions are getting bigger. *The Daily Telegraph* [Online, 17 August]. Available at http://www.telegraph.co.uk/technology/news/8706640/Televisions-are-getting-bigger.html.

Whelan, G., Crockett, J. and Vitouladiti, S. (2010). *A New Model of Car Ownership in London: Geo-Spatial Analysis of Policy Interventions* [Online, 11 October 2010]. Available at http://www.mvaconsultancy.com/publications/A%20new%20model%20of%20car%20ownership%20in%20London%20Paper.pdf.

White, G. (2011). London set for biggest boost in GDP growth says Citigroup. *The Daily Telegraph* [Online, 21 February]. Available at http://www.telegraph.co.uk/finance/economics/8336878/London-set-for-biggest-boost-in-GDP-growth-says-Citigroup.html.

Woudhuysen, J. (2008). The electric car conspiracy … that never was. *The Register* [Online, 1 January]. Available at http://www.theregister.

co.uk/2008/01/01/woudhuysen_electric_car and http://www.theregister.co.uk/2008/01/01/woudhuysen_electric_car/page2.html.

Woudhuysen, J. (2009). Who's afraid of electric vehicles? *spiked* [Online, 21 July.]. Available at http://www.spiked-online.com/index.php/site/article/7174/.

Woudhuysen, J. (ed.) (2010). *Big Potatoes: The London Manifesto for Innovation*. London: Thinking Apart.

Woudhuysen, J. and Abley, I. (2004). *Why is Construction so Backward?* Chichester: John Wiley & Sons.

Woudhuysen, J. and Kaplinsky, J. (2009). *Energise! A Future for Energy Innovation*. London: Beautiful Books.

Wynn, G. (2011). Quoted in EDF Energy's vision for a lower carbon London. *The Evening Standard* [Online, advertisement feature, 14 July 2011]. Available at http://www.thisislondon.co.uk/edf-energy/article-23955633-edf-energys-vision-for-a-lower-carbon-london.do.

Zhang, Y. et al. (2010). Ecological network analysis of an urban energy metabolic system: model development, and a case study of four Chinese cities. *Ecological Modelling* [Online] 221(16). Available at http://www.societalmetabolism.org/aes2010/Proceeds/DIGITAL%20PROCEEDINGS_files/PAPERS/O_117_Brain_Fath.pdf.

Chapter 12
Carbon Trading in the City of Undoing

Maxine Newlands

Introduction

The Earthrise image, captured by the Apollo space mission in 1969, is thought to have catalysed a great change in the way we perceive our relationship to Planet Earth. (Gore 2007; Dryzek 1997; Doyle 2007; Lester 2010) But the priceless profundity distilled in this picture, and the far-reaching, deep-seated reforms said to have been instilled by it, have somehow led to more of the same, short-term market-trading which makes London what it is today. Alongside every other form of debt (personal, corporate, institutional, national), in the London markets humanity's perceived debt to the planet is now traded in the form of internationally-sponsored permits to emit carbon; and these, in turn, have emitted further, secondary markets in carbon-trading derivatives. This chapter seeks to show how a sense of the profound has found its way into the lightweight world of financial intermediation, and to account for London's role in implementing this transformation. The chapter begins with a skeletal sketch of carbon trading and how it works, followed by a brief note on London's central position in this trade. The next section identifies various factors which have contributed to the development of international carbon trading, in London especially. These include: levels of international cooperation; state regulation and its relation to the market; the parallel rise of environmentalism and financial services; and the role of politicians and policy makers in translating the former into the latter. The concluding section is a kind of balance sheet which offsets ways in which carbon trading marks a radical departure for capital, against other aspects in which it represents the natural continuation of capitalist commodification.

Permits to Pollute

'Carbon trading' is the buying and selling not of carbon, but of permits to emit carbon dioxide, under licence from state or inter-state institutions. Initial permits are allocated to states and companies through either free distribution, auctioning, (Stavins and Whitehead 2009), or a mixture of the two, depending on previous and estimated emissions (Buchs, Bardsely and Duwe 2011). This approach is sometimes referred to as 'grandfathering', and can lead to windfall profits for firms by selling a large volume of their allocated permits (ibid.). Auctioning is a form of the 'polluter pays' scheme, by passing on the costs to the consumer, and generating a revenues stream for governments (ibid.). For example, the European Union Emissions Trading Scheme (EU ETS) covers 11,500 energy-intensive industrial sites which together account for almost half of the carbon dioxide emissions across Europe. Under the terms of this scheme, each member state bids for permission to emit a specified amount of carbon dioxide. At the end of the bidding round, the European Commission determines what will be the capped quota for each nation state; and each state subdivides its quota into permits allocated to individual enterprises. At the end of the year, every enterprise must show that its emission has not exceeded its allocation. But these allowances are also transferable between enterprises – at a price. A company that comes in over-target, 'must buy them from other companies or face legal penalities' (Stavins and Whitehead 2009: 230), but they can avoid any penalties, by buying-in additional allowances from other enterprises with allocation to spare (the enterprises may be in the same country or different ones). Hence the EU system is known as a cap-and-trade scheme.

There are other schemes intended to reward projects which reduce carbon dioxide emission from high carbon industrialisation. These are known as project schemes. They include Joint Implementation projects (JIs),[1] and Clean Development Mechanisms (CDMs),[2] both of which are facilitated by the United Nations (UN) and its agencies, operating under the terms of the Kyoto Protocol. Furthermore, EU cap-and-trade is now linked in to Kyoto-sponsored reduction schemes, so that projects which lead to emission reductions recognised by UN agencies (a credit in the carbon trading stakes), can be set against carbon emissions (a debit) in the EU. Thus a UN-recognised Assigned Amount Unit (AAU) for one tonne of carbon dioxide is commensurate with the EU allowance (EUA) for the same amount, and each is tradable against the other.

Whether within the terms of a single scheme, e.g. EU ETS, or across more than one scheme (EU ETS – CDM), trading often occurs through the good offices of a broker, whose intermediary role in this market – the market in pollution permits – is an extension of the familiar part played by City stockbrokers. Furthermore, in line with City tradition, the primary market in trading allowances and reductions,

1 The mechanism known as 'joint implementation', defined in Article 6 of the Kyoto Protocol, allows a country with an emission reduction or limitation commitment under the Kyoto Protocol (Annex B Party) to earn emission reduction units (ERUs) from an emission reduction or emission removal project in another Annex B Party, each equivalent to one tonne of CO2, which can be counted towards meeting its Kyoto target. Joint implementation offers Parties a flexible and cost-efficient means of fulfilling a part of their Kyoto commitments, while the host Party benefits from foreign investment and technology transfer. (http://unfccc.int/kyoto_protocol/mechanisms/joint_implementation/items/1674.php) accessed March 2001

2 CDM project activity might involve, for example, a rural electrification project using solar panels or the installation of more energy-efficient boilers. The mechanism stimulates sustainable development and emission reductions, while giving industrialised countries some flexibility in how they meet their emission reduction or limitation targets.

has been supplemented by secondary markets in futures and options thereof. In other words, there is not only a price on the emission allocation which turned out to be surplus to the requirements of Company X; you can also get a price on whether Company X is likely to under-use or over-utilise its future allocations – just like any other kind of derivative. Taken together, primary and secondary markets in worldwide carbon emissions are thought to have been worth US$120 billion in December 2009 (PWC 2011). A year later (2010) the markets had expanded by $50 billion to an estimated $170 billion (ibid.).

Centred on London

The bulk of EU ETS trading occurs on the European Climate Exchange, based in London. During the recession, the volume of trade continued to increase – from 2008 to 2009, there was a year-on-year increase of more than 100 per cent; but the value of these trades increased much less than the volume, in line with a 50 per cent drop in the price of EUAs. Having peaked at 30 euros a tonne in 2008, they fell to 8 euros in February 2009 before stabilising at around 15 euros in June 2010. (The CityUK 2010: 2) The primary market in CDMs also fell back, in line with the reduced pace of industrial production; but the secondary market did not (ibid.). To the contrary, when, temporarily, the banks all but closed down as the major source of corporate finance, more companies started to play these markets in the hope of raising capital. Primary markets were also distorted by recession-hit carbon emitters 'selling their allowance – gambling that they would be able to buy … back when customers returned' (Clover 2010).

In addition to hosting the primary and secondary markets of the European Climate Exchange, London is central to almost every aspect of carbon trading and related trades. The CityUK, the City of London's research facility, reports that: 'the UK is lead investor in CDM, accounting for 37 per cent of purchases in 2009'; also that London is 'a leading centre for energy brokers operating in carbon markets'. Prominent players include Thompson Reuters Point Carbon; Climate Change Capital, an investment company with funds worth US$1.5 billion, which advises investors on any 'financial opportunity associated with a low carbon economy';[3] and 'ICap Energy' – an energy brokerage company with assets of $202 million (in 2007). By 2009 the City of London housed '80 [per cent] of the world's carbon market broking companies and 75 [per cent] of all carbon trading desks' (Blake 2009).

London pioneered emissions trading instruments, and went on to reap the benefit. In 1995, the London Stock Exchange launched the Alternative Investment Market, putting London in pole position when carbon trading took off. There are other markets in various cities such as Paris and Chicago, but London's position

3 For more information, see http://www.climatechangecapital.com/about-us/company-overview.aspx, accessed May 2011.

remains unequalled (though the further proliferation of markets in Australia, China, India, South Korea and Switzerland, may call this into question at some point). The CityUK's report, which declares London the 'leading global centre in carbon markets', also points to 'the launch and management of carbon funds', and the presence of 'major verification agencies such as Lloyd's Register Quality Assurance'. London is central even to 'the provision of finance to the renewables market' (The CityUK 2010: 2).

It seems that carbon trading in its present form could not exist without London; conversely, London's position at the centre of carbon trading now forms an integral part of its financial services offer. This chapter now turns to consider various factors which led to the current formulation of carbon trading, in London especially.

High Levels of International Cooperation

The fact that EUAs are 'fungible' with UN-backed AAUs is not only the result of recent negotiations between policy wonks based in Brussels and those looking to Kyoto from UN headquarters in New York. It is also the outcome of decades of international economic cooperation, dating back to the Bretton Woods agreement of 1944 which ratified the dollar as the currency that other currencies would peg themselves to. At this same conference, plans were drawn up for the International Monetary Fund, with the capacity to rescue any capitalist country from a balance of payments crisis (and the power to set the terms on which the rescue would be carried out), and the International Bank for Reconstruction and Development, now part of the World Bank, charged with financing development projects backed by the United Nations. The latter began life as President Roosevelt's preferred title for the countries fighting the Axis Powers of Germany and Japan in the Second World War. Towards the end of the war, the UN was ratified as a general, international organisation (as defined by the winning side). Its first full meeting took place in San Francisco on 25 April 1945.

Two years later, the first General Agreement on Tariffs and Trade (GATT) was signed by 13 countries, rising by 1986 to a total of 123 signatories. These nations entered the final round of GATT negotiations (the Uruguay round) before this particular, anti-protectionist apparatus was reconfigured as the World Trade Organization (WTO) in 1993.

In these pages, there is no space to detail the slew of institutions which jointly comprised the international framework for geo-politics in the second half of the twentieth century. For the purposes of this chapter, cooperative institutions such GATT and the UN are notable for the contrast they make with the inter-war period of fierce rivalry between advanced capitalist countries, each one hell-bent on protecting its national economy and its respective sphere of influence. This orientation, and the course of action derived from it, culminated in the resumption of hostilities between imperialist powers in September 1939. Since the end of the

Second World War, however, competition between advanced capitalist economies has tended to occur in conference chambers rather than on the battlefield; and this tendency was confirmed in the early 1990s by the end of the Cold War and the demise of the non-capitalist Eastern bloc, led by the (now defunct) Soviet Union. Now the whole world was made up of nations united in capital.

Not that the tension between nation states has disappeared altogether; rather, the preferred means of addressing it – jaw-jaw instead of war-war – consists of trading one country's concern against another's in a process of lengthy negotiation. Thus 'international cooperation' turns out to mean a protracted process in which each nation's toxicity – the problems it manufactures for others – is offset against the geo-political problems which they, too, have produced while pursuing their own self-interest. In this way, the overall trend towards international cooperation, i.e. negotiated offsetting, has set the scene for recent developments in related fields such as international carbon trading.

(It is worth noting that carbon trading has not been adopted as a global solution to climate change. There is international agreement that climate change should be tackled, but only the EU and those that signed the Kyoto Protocol (notably the USA refuses to sign it, and India and China were excluded) have agreed to tackle the toxicity. Australia, India and the BRICS countries are currently running pilot schemes, but have yet to implement a carbon trading schema.

Public and Private

But the trade-off between nation states does not necessarily entail the conversion of sovereign assets and liabilities into privately owned credits and debits. This was clearly not the case in the post-1945 period, when the British economy, for example, was moving in the opposition direction, from private ownership to state ownership. In the heyday of 'public utilities', when fuel, water, telephony, health provision, steel and the railways had all been nationalised (and much of the housing stock was owned and run by local government), the privatisation of pollution was barely conceivable. Instead, there were proposals for a tax on factory smoke, centrally administered with revenue accruing to the state. If the spirit of those times were extant today, regulation of carbon dioxide emissions would almost certainly have remained in the hands of the state, rather than trickling down to the level of private enterprise in the form of carbon trading. However, as noted elsewhere in this book, by the 1970s public ownership and the political consensus associated with it, were seriously troubled. In Britain, the 1980s were characterised by a combined government-and-management offensive against the post-war social order, including a series of well-publicised privatisations which were said to represent a new era of 'popular capitalism'. Although such rhetoric is no longer in use, one of the legacies of the period is the widespread assumption that anything and everything can be privately owned and repeatedly traded. This is the assumption at the heart of buying, selling and brokering state-backed, privately-owned permits to pollute; and these activities are fully in line with the recently revised relation between capital and the state.

Making Good without Making Goods

As early as 1962, former US secretary of state Dean Acheson declared that Britain had lost an Empire but not yet found a role. In the 1980s, losing an Empire was one of Britain's qualifications for its newly expanded role in financial intermediation. In the eyes of other countries, the UK was more equipped to play the part of honest broker because it was less closely associated with the pursuit of its own, imperial interests. Furthermore, when the British economy took a decisive, financial turn in the second half of the 1980s, in relative terms it was also turning away from domestic manufacturing. Although, over the longer-term, the value of British manufacturing did not contract absolutely, productive activity shrank dramatically in comparison to its financial counterpart. Again, whereas British manufacturing interests were once burnt into other people's image of London, the City of London was now in a position to gain financially from losing this identity.

Above all else, London edged ahead of everywhere else (Frankfurt, Paris, Tokyo, New York) as the place where money could be expected to make more money without reference to capitalist production. As the City came to be further identified with fictitious capital, in productive terms London's economic activity became a kind of non-activity. Seen from the point-of-view in which production is what capital *does* (or is supposed to do), then the City of London became a sort of un-doing, where profits are taken but without anyone having to do what we were previously told, namely: make goods in order to make good. On the other hand, a setting such as this, where there are grounds for seeing production as a liability (it's messy, it's dangerous and it ties up money which could be turned to a quicker profit), would have a natural affinity to the prospect of charging producers to produce and trading in the charges levied against them. As we have seen, from the second half of the 1990s this prospect was actualised in the form of carbon emissions trading, which now forms an integral part of London's international prospectus.

If this gives some indication as to why London looks askance at production, and has no qualms about collecting the tax on producers, it does not explain why London's estrangement from production is now coloured Green. Again, there is no scope in these pages to chronicle the general rise of environmental consciousness. But this chapter is concerned with the projection of environmental thinking onto City trading screens. How did Green get there, given that, as late as the mid-to-late 1980s, greed was good, limits were for wimps, and the City's preferred colour was matt black.

Painting the City Green

At the international level, when in the late 1980s and early 1990s the United Nations seemed to draw back from the wider repercussions of environmental policy implementation, institutions such as the World Bank took the initiative. Thus, the geo-politics of the environment were soon translated into a question of economics

The UN had already sponsored the Montreal Protocol (1987), banning the use of chlorofluorocarbon (CFC), and Agenda 21, ratified at the Earth Summit in Rio de Janeiro, Brazil (1992). Agenda 21 set out 'the first draft of the 'Earth Charter', a vision for an environmentally sustainable planet' (Cox 2006: 78); but at this time the UN was more readily associated with managing the international response to environmental emergencies such as 'earthquakes, flood or famines' (Finger 2008: 45). Where the UN hesitated, the cluster of Bretton Woods institutions (see above) stepped in, and, according to Finger, began the process of translating the UN's environmental remit 'it into its own commercial logic', leading to 'gradual adoption and integration of the Rio process into World-Bank-led "sustainable development"' (Finger 2008: 51). Although the UN had been moving towards the setting of climate change controls, the IMF and the World Bank intervened, recognising that climate change problems could offer 'further opportunities of industrial development, investment, and overall economic growth ... using environmental problem-solving as one more argument for further technological and economic development' (Finger 2008: 51). Capital, represented by the IMF and World Bank, began to encroach not only upon the UN's position but also upon the nation state's role in addressing the impact of a high carbon economy, leading to the development new markets in line with the revised (market-ised) version of this role.

Developments at the international level chimed in with forward-thinking here in Britain. Plans for trading in emissions on a global scale were initiated in the UK by Michael Grubb (1998), who drew on an earlier, North American plan to address the problem of acid rain. Grubb identified that any decline in emissions would require a multilateral approach between nations, transnational companies and international institutions; if the mechanisms were restricted to individual companies, regional administrations or state government, they simply would not work. He proposed a new emissions trading scheme – realised, eventually as 'the buying and selling of pollutant entitlements' (Newell and Patterson 2010: 96) – which focused on a division of emissions between countries, through the system of 'contraction and convergence' first envisaged by the Global Commons Institute (GCI), a London-based enterprise. According to the 'contraction and convergence' model, if emissions are lessened in the largest polluting countries, while emissions allowances are increased for developing countries, this will create equilibrium in global emissions. Meanwhile, in the (then) bear pit of British politics, the convergence between environmental concerns and economic self-interest, was already receiving support from an unlikely source – Prime Minister Margaret Thatcher.

'Environmentalism' had been written into the Queen's Speech as far back as 1971 (McCormick 1991), and a new government Department for the Environment was established in the same year (DoE 1971). But the turning point came in 1986 when Margaret Thatcher took a new interest in climate change, at the same time confirming that both capital and the state were keenly interested in this area. Thatcher's 'green' speech (Anderson 2008) to the Royal Society (1988) set out plans to encourage business, working with science, to take on the responsibility of solving the problem of global warming. In her speech she focused on the 'absence of leadership on the international environment' (McCormick 1991: 65), suggesting that British business take the lead in developing climate change solutions. No doubt aware of recent moves by the IMF and World Bank, Thatcher stressed the need for international cooperation in tackling climate change and global warming, whilst reminding the world that none other than 'British scientists had discovered a thinning of the ozone layer over the Antarctic' (McCormick 1991: 104).

Thatcher's speech increased the media profile of climate change solutions, but perhaps to the detriment of scientists who were replaced by 'political actors', who 'increasingly sought to shape the agenda' (Carvello and Burgess 2005). Political parties came to realise that climate change solutions no longer meant 'conservation', but were increasingly linked to socio-political and economic issues. Thatcher was proposing a new level of convergence between science and industry which would equip British enterprise to solve a global problem and turn a pretty penny at the same time: 'Industry is becoming more scientific-minded; scientists more industry-minded. Both have a responsibility to recognise the practical value of the ideas which are being developed' (Thatcher 1988). In the event, her pronouncement encouraged corporate environmental strategies which did not lead to British technological innovation; instead they fostered a combination of green consumerism and the eventual development of financial instruments for the carbon emissions trade.

At the time, critics complained that Thatcher's proposals had the effect of devolving responsibility from state to business. Many questioned her sudden move towards environmental discourse. Former head of Friends of the Earth, Jonathan Porritt suggested that 'making statements on the international environment … involved far fewer policy commitments than statements on the domestic environment' (McCormick 1991: 66). Until the 'green' speech, Thatcher's administration had shown little enthusiasm for the subject. Talking about the Falklands War of 1982, she herself referred to climate change solutions as 'humdrum', compared to the excitement of having 'a real crisis on your hands' (Robinson 1992: 177).

The 'green' speech was given against the 'backdrop of drought in the United States and unusual weather patterns' (Grubb 1998: 1), at a time when environmentalism was slowly becoming more prominent in the media (Anderson 1997; Lester 2010). At the time, the speech may have served mainly to demonstrate

Thatcher's 'style of how the nation should be run' (Robinson 1992: 176). But it turns out to have been the signal for British business to think about doing business with environmentalism – though a decade of financialisation went by before the business plan, substantially re-written, was finally put into effect.

After Thatcher's resignation (1990) and the demise of the Conservative government led by her successor, John Major, the convergence of state and capital interests in search of solutions to climate change continued under successive New Labour and Labour governments (1997-2010). Meanwhile, global policy-makers arrived at further combinations of 'governance' and enterprise in a range of New Environmental Policy Instruments (NEPIs), including a series of variations on emissions trading. Tony Blair and Gordon Brown (prime minister from 1997-2007 and 2007-10, respectively) both used NEPIs to create a carbon-budget and reform energy markets. During their terms of office, there was much talk about a green bank.

A further tipping point occurred in 2005, when all three major parties, New Labour, Conservative and Liberal Democrat, incorporated environmental governance into their manifestos. The impetus for a new iteration of Conservative environmental policy came from Steve Hilton, a key advisor whose 'inspirations are the Green movement and the flowering of grass-roots politics' (*The Times* 2009). As an environmental strategist and a keen cyclist himself, Hilton encouraged party leader David Cameron to be seen on a bicycle and to include cycling as part of his public image. Under Hilton's guidance, in May 2006 the Conservatives launched their local elections campaign with a new slogan: 'Vote Blue, Go Green'. The campaign was a clear signal that the Conservative Party was co-opting climate change solutions as part of its political manifesto, and a further indication that party policy was shifting towards an environmental discourse. In this instance of '*themenklau* – the stealing of green ideas by grey parties' (Dryzek 1997: 189), climate change solutions were presented as central to Conservative language. This was reinforced with a new logo, dropping the blue torch for a green tree, and a media strategy featuring Cameron on the Norwegian fjords and cycling to the Palace of Westminster (April 2006). As the instigator of the 'Vote Blue, Go Green' campaign, Hilton was strategically shifting the Conservatives away from their traditional terrain, and edging into Liberal Democrat territory. The election campaign was an attempt to move the Conservative Party away from the 'sleazy' image of the 1990s, and beat Labour to the eco-vote (Jacobs 2010), with Hilton and Cameron seeking out the eco-vote especially in marginal seats.

In response, Gordon Brown was prompted to sponsor the UK's first Climate Change Bill (2007). Encouraged by David Miliband (former Environment Secretary) and Ed Miliband (at the time, Secretary of State for Energy and Climate Change), and special advisor Michael Jacobs (Jacobs 1991; Stern 2006), Brown took 'radical' steps to reduce carbon emissions and ensure that the Climate Change Bill was enacted. The Climate Change Act (2008) has formalised market-driven climate change solutions, focusing on the creation of new markets for NEPIs. In the past three years since the Bill became law, there has been nothing in policy terms – certainly not the formation of the Conservative-Liberal Democrat coalition government in May 2010 – to undermine the privatisation of environmental issues. Instead, the political discourse described above has enabled environmentalism, or a bowdlerised version of it, to be fully entered into the financial world of City trading.

Real Fictions

Does carbon emissions trading constitute a substantial response to the problem of man-made global warming? Or is it simply an example of funny money? A perverse response, in other words, to the Earthrise image and the proper recognition of humanity's place in the universe.

That the atmosphere, and our access to it, has been made into a commodity, complies with the essential logic of capital whereby even 'objects that in themselves are not commodities, such as conscience, honour etc., are capable of being offered for sale by their holders, and of thus acquiring, through their price, the form of commodities' (Marx 1974: 105). We should not be surprised, therefore, if the air we breathe now has a price tag; nor that the tagging is carried out in accordance with the current configuration of the market and the state. Their interaction was duly acknowledged in a Friends of the Earth report which identified carbon trading as the outcome of 'action by governments to create this new commodity – the right to emit carbon – and then to limit the availability of this right in order to create scarcity and therefore a market for it' (Clifton 2009). In this respect, carbon markets are no less substantial than any other aspect of today's society; conversely, just because carbon emissions have been commodified, does not make them any less real.

In other respects, however, carbon emissions trading has acquired an air of unreality. It seems particularly prone to specious or even fraudulent transactions. There were the oil companies who profited by selling on their surplus allocations to under-allocated hospitals and universities (Davies 2007); and companies such as steel manufacturer Corus which obtained emissions permits for development at their Teesside plant, then shelved their plans and sold on the unused permits for an estimated profit of £250 million (Clover 2010). There has been VAT fraud in spot trading of EUAs (The CityUK 2010: 2), followed by 'cyber-thieves' hacking into spot trading, prompting the (temporary) suspensions of the market and raising fears that 'the entire market structure in emissions trading was now compromised' (Stafford 2011). Once the third phase of ETS comes into effect in 2013, organisations with remaining permits will 'carry over 1.8 billion permits… obviating the need to buy any new credits before 2016' (Schiller 2011), thus making a mockery of the system. And this list is only indicative.

Aside from various abuses of the system, in its current formulation 'the entire market structure in emissions trading' has compromised technological innovation in climate change solutions. Capital which might, conceivably, have gone into the development of innovative technology, has instead been sluiced into the channels of financial intermediation. Thus 'the development of secondary markets involving financial speculators and complex financial products based on the financial derivatives model brings with it a risk that carbon trading will develop into a speculative commodity bubble' (Clifton 2009: 32). Even the sage of investment funds, George Soros, when interviewed in 2009, warned of the tendency to 'create another opaque market for derivatives, similar to those that helped bring the global economy to its knees last autumn' (Granfield 2009). With only a few years' hindsight, these warnings now appear to underestimate the City's capacity to undo the ostensible purpose of carbon emissions regulation.

However, it is somehow appropriate that the City of Undoing should be the place where the problem of climate change and the possibility of solving it, have been unravelled into the repetitive transactions of an expanding derivatives market. Carbon emission allocations are not, after all, a permit to produce; rather, they entitle the bearer to pollute, i.e. to do what comes naturally during the production process. But instead of socialising this unwelcome by-product, the current system marks our collective estrangement from production by privatising responsibility for pollution, and, thus privatised, finding a home for it in a City that is equally estranged from productive activity; indeed, it now lives not from production but by alienation from it. How appropriate, then, that these two strangers to production should pair up in the metropolis where capital enjoys a second life; living together in the fictitious capital of the world.

References

Anderson, A. (1997). *Media, Culture and the Environment*. London: UCL.

Atherton, B. (2010, 11 May). 'Shelved ETS funds clean energy programs'. Retrieved 14 April 2011, from http://www.abc.net.au/news/stories/2010/05/11/2896602.htm.

Buchs, M., Bardsely, N. and Duwe, S. (2011). Who bears the brunt? Distributional effects of climate change mitigation policies in *Critical Social Policy*, 31(2), May 2011, 285-307.

Buckingham, S. and Turner, M. (2008). *Understanding Environmental Issues*. London: Sage.

Blake, H. (2009). Copenhagen climate summit: London should be hub of global carbon market, says CBI. *The Daily Telegraph*. London.

Booth, A. (2009). Capitalism, Carbon Trading and Copenhagen in 'In Defence Of Marxism', Online at http://www.marxist.com/capitalism-carbon-trading-copenhagen.htm, accessed July 2011.

Carvalho, A. and Burgess, J. (2005). Cultural circuits of climate change in UK broadsheet newspapers, 1985-2003. *Risk Analysis*, 25(6), 1457-69.

Clifton, S. (2009). 'A dangerous obsession: A research report the evidence against carbon trading and for real solutions to avoid a climate crunch', Friends of the Earth available at http://www.foe.co.uk/resource/reports/dangerous_obsession.pdf, accessed July 2011.

Clover, C. (2010). 'Buying off Big Polluters looks Bad but it Works', *The Sunday Times* Newspaper, National Edition, 28 February, 21.

Davies, N. (2007). 'The Truth About Kyoto', the *Guardian*, 2 June 2007, 1.

Doyle, J. (2007). 'Picturing the Clima(c)tic: Greenpeace and the representational politics of climate change communication (1994-present)'. *Science as Culture*, 16(2), June 2007, 129-50.

Dryzek, J. (1997). *The Politics of the Earth: Environmental Discourses*. Oxford: Oxford University Press.

Finger, M. (2008). Which governance for sustainable development? An organisational and institutional perspective, in J. Park, K. Conca, and M. Finger (eds) *The Crisis of Global Environmental Governance: Towards a New Political Economy of Sustainability*. New York: Taylor Francis, 8.

Gore, A. (1992/2007). Earth in the Balance: Forging a new Common Purpose. London: Earthscan.

Granfield, P. (2009). 'Soros' Cap and trade vision an illusion' *The National*, 13 October, online at http://www.thenational.ae/business/soros-cap-and-trade-vision-an-illusion?pageCount=2, accessed July 2011.

Grubb, M. (1998). Corrupting the Climate? Economic Theory and the politics of the Kyoto. The Royal Institute of International Affairs; Energy and Environmental Programme, Chatham House.

IPCC (2007). Summary For Policy Makers. Climate change 2007: The Physical Science Basis. Q. a. M. Soloman. Cambridge, Intergovernmental Panel on Climate Change.

Jacobs, M. (1991). *The Green Economy: Environment, Sustainable Development and the Politics of the Future*. London: Pluto Press.

Jacobs, M. (2010). Personal communication. Meeting of the ECPR Environmental Politics and Policy Summer School, Keele University, June. Videocast of the presentation by Jacobs available online at http://www.cccep.ac.uk/Events/Past/2010/ Conference/Michael/Jacobs.aspx.

Kamdar, M. (2007). *Planet India: How the Fastest Growing Democracy is Transforming the World*. New York, London, Toronto and Sydney: Scribner.

Kirk, A. (2010, 27 April). 'Labor shelves emissions scheme'. available at http://www.abc.net.au/news/stories/2010/04/27/2883282.htm.

Lester, L. (2010). *Media and Environment: Conflict, Politics and the News*. Cambridge, Malden, MA, Polity Press.

Marx, K. (1974). *Capital: A Critique of Political Economy*, vol 1, Moscow: Progress Publishers.

McCormick, J. (1991). *British Politics and the Environment*. London, Earthscan Publications.

Newell, P. and Paterson, P. (ed.) (2010). *Climate Capitalism: Global Warming and the Transformation of the Global Economy*. Cambridge: Cambridge University Press.

Oels, A. (2005). 'Climate change governable: From biopower to advanced liberal government', *Journal of Environmental Policy and Planning*, 7(3), September, 185-207.

PWC (2011). Press release, available at http://www.ukmediacentre.pwc.com/content/detail.aspx?releaseid=3524&newsareaid=2 – May 2011?, accessed 8 June 2011.

Stafford, P. (2011). 'Carbon exchanges halt spot trading', *Financial Times*, available at htpp://www.ft.com/cms/s/0/5afe9982-2489-11e0-8c0e-00144feab49a.html#axzz1Wy19QYBT, accessed 3 September 2011.

Stavins, R. and Whitehead, B. (2009). 'Market-based Environmental Policies', in J. Dryzek and Schlosberg (2009). *Debating the Earth: The Environmental Politics Reader*. Oxford: Oxford University Press.

Soloman, S. et al. (eds) (2007). Climate change 2007: The Physical Science Basis. Contribution of Working Group 1 to the fourth Assessment Report of the Intergovernmental Panel on Climate Change.

Stern, N. (2006). Review on the Economics of Climate Change: Executive Summary. London: HM Treasury HMSO.

Thatcher, M. (1988). Speech to the Royal Society, Fishmongers' Hall, City of London, 27 September, available at http://www.margaretthatcher.org/document/107346, accessed 12 February 2011.

The CityUK (2010). *Carbon Markets 2010*. London: TheCityUK Research Centre.

United Nations (2002). 'Report on the World Summit on Sustainable Development, Johannesburg, South Africa, 26 August-4 September 2002', A/CONF 199/20 (reissued), New York: United Nations Publications.

United Nations (2003). 'Agenda 21: Earth Summit – The United Nations Programme of Action From Rio', April. New York: United Nations Publications.

United Nations (2009). 'Good governance in public-private partnerships', United Nations Commission on Sustainable Development (CSD), New York, United Nations Publications. Also available online at http://www.un.org/esa/sustdev/csd/csd16/PF/presentations/hamilton.pdf.

United Nations (2010). 'The Millennium Development Goals Report 2010', August, New York, United Nations Department of Economic and Social Affairs (DESA), New York, United Nations Publications. Also available online at http://www.un.org/millennium goals/.

United Nations (2011). 'Millennium Development Goals Indicators. The Official United Nations Site for the MDG Indicators', updated 2011. Also available online at http://www.un.org/millenniumgoals/.

UK Climate Change Act 2008 (c. 27), available at; http://www.statutelaw.gov.uk/content.aspx?LegType=All+Legislation&title=climate+change&Year=2008&searchEnacted=0&extentMatchOnly=0&confersPower=0&blanketAmendment=0&sortAlpha=0&TYPE=QS&PageNumber=1&NavFrom=0&parentActiveTextDocId=3539938&ActiveText DocId=3539938&filesize=273144.

UK Department for Energy and Climate Change website, UK Low Carbon Transition Plan (July 2009), available at http://www.decc.gov.uk/en/content/cms/publications/lc_trans_plan/lc_trans_plan.aspx.
Low Carbon Industrial Strategy (July 2009). available at www.hmg.gov.uk/lowcarbon [external Link].

Chapter 13
Music from the Storm Clouds: The Continuing Troubles of the Music Business

Andrew Blake

> London is an acknowledged centre for arts and culture and commercial creative industries, all of which make a vital contribution to London's economy. Not only is the sector a major employer and economic generator, with a turnover of over £18bn, it also plays an important role in terms of boosting the visitor economy and ensuring London's position as a global capital for creativity and commerce. (Mayor of London 2010a: 10)

Economic cycles do not function uniformly. Despite the positive rhetoric and political well-wishing which had surrounded the cultural and creative industries since the mid-1990s (of which the above quotation is a typical example), the music business was already in profound crisis well before the 2007-8 collapse of the financial services whose outcomes are the principal focus of this book. Music provides, therefore – perhaps paradoxically – a paradigmatic example of the need to rethink economic, social and cultural structures well beyond the orthodoxies of financial reform, and indeed beyond the orthodoxies of economic growth which drive them, in a city which has been called the music capital of the world, and which certainly seems the most musically active. The published draft (for public consultation) of the Mayor of London's 2010 cultural strategy, for example, made the following comparison between London and its principal rivals as global cities:

Table 13.1 Music Venues and Performances in Five Global Cities

	London	New York	Paris	Shanghai	Tokyo
Number of music venues	400	151	122	148	132
Music performances p.a.	32,292	22,204	3,612	11,736	7,419

Source: Mayor 2010a: 35 (taken from GLA 2008).

The document from which these figures were drawn, a 2008 Cultural Audit of the city published by the London Development Agency GLDA), reported that in 2000 the value of ticket sales for live music performances in London had been estimated at £381m, while the equivalent figure for the recorded music market was £345m (based on Laing and York 2001). Meanwhile, the LDA document reported, London is now home to two of the top five most popular music venues in the world: the O2 Arena and Wembley Arena. During its first half-year of operation (2007), in fact, the O2 became the third most popular venue in the world (LDA 2008: 75).

The Decline of the Music Business in the Digital Decade

In one vital aspect of music, however, London could make no such claim: despite the continuing global success of British pop acts in the 1990s and 2000s, it was not the centre of the recorded music business. Indeed, EMI, at the time of writing still (just about) in business as a 'major record label', and the only one based in London, provides a particular take on a cautionary tale which encourages us to think about the current state and probable future not just of the music business, but of the cultural and creative industries as a whole.

The crisis of the recorded music business emerged at the dawn of the millennium, due to a loss of control over copyright. How did this happen? The structural origins of the crisis are in the production by chemical and electronics corporations of machinery and media with which the domestic consumer can make copies of commercially recorded music. The first such device, recordable audiotape, was introduced in the 1950s; the most significant recent example is the humble MP3 file. This software technology allows the compression of large amounts of data, and so provided domestic users with the opportunity to store large numbers of songs and/or albums as computer files. Using software programmes such as Napster, which allowed them free access to files stored on other users' hard drives, people had become used to sharing music without further payment either to each other, or to artists, publishers, record labels or other rights holders. Young people became used to obtaining recorded music without payment (Alderman 2001; Laughey 2007).

The major record companies set about closing this new loophole, echoing previous campaigns against commercially available recordable media which had threatened their ability to control copyright (the compact cassette, DAT tape, recordable CD, and minidisc formats; and in each case the associated recording machines). Industry representative bodies such as the Recording Industry Association of America, and the British Phonograph Industry, sued everyone involved: they took action against the makers of file-sharing software such as Napster, Grokster and KaZaa; a representative sample of its end users, including in some instances the parents of computer-literate teenagers; and the internet service providers (ISPs) which had facilitated the sharing of music files. They insisted that legitimate sales of music online should be controlled through Digital Rights Management (DRM) software, which prevents the purchaser from copying the purchased files onto other media; and they lobbied governments to legislate for tighter copyright control. While this has happened, sales of CDs have fallen dramatically, sales of online MP3 files have not yet reached replacement level, and income from broadcasting and live music events has also fallen since 2008. In August 2011, for example, PRS for Music, which collects and redistributes royalties for recorded, live and broadcast music in the UK, announced a 4.8 per cent fall in overall annual revenue. CD sales had fallen by 7.9 per cent to £1.24 billion. While sales of music online – as digital files – were up 20 per cent to £320 million, their rate of growth was slowing dramatically (Sweeney 2011c).

The Literature of Crisis

The crisis of the past decade has been addressed in a great deal of writing about the music business. The literature ranges from angry denunciations of copyright, to polite guides to ways in which recording companies can avoid copyright 'theft'. Occupying most of the points on a continuum between over-theorised academic and under-developed popular writing, all writing on the subject shares a fascination with an industry in continual turmoil, perhaps in terminal decline, despite the massive affective hold its products still have on consumers.

While this is not the place for a comprehensive review of that literature, a thematic overview of some recent texts will provide a useful starting point for the subsequent discussion of the tribulations of record labels and other musical activities in London. Most of these texts revolve around the vexed question of the persistence of the early modern notion of copyright, as, still, refracted through the Romantic ideal of the individual composer producing 'works' for the marketplace (a viewpoint neatly encapsulated in Frith and Marshall 2004: 1-2), and the ways in which the music business uses this ideological and legal tradition to lobby for continued protection for its business model.

Some authors still claim that this model is benign. Ronald S. Rosen, for example, writes as a practising entertainment lawyer, working in the USA, who is in favour of the enforcement of copyright as a means to protect authors' rights and encourage 'the free flow of ideas for the benefit of the public at large' (Rosen 2008: 3). Andrew Sparrow (Sparrow 2006), a UK solicitor dealing in media law, provides a somewhat more neutral tone in *Music Distribution and the Internet. A Legal Guide for the Music Business*; but as the title implies, his book is a survival guide for those challenged by the legal pitfalls of operating in the new world. Both authors discuss the music industry's moment of panic in the early twenty-first century, followed by the strategic legal action taken against software companies and ISPs, and the many exemplary cases against individual downloaders and file-sharers: Sparrow claims that in 2005 alone, 14,227 such cases were brought by the music industry in 12 countries (Sparrow 2005: 74).

This legal attack on music lovers – plus the far wider availability of legal opportunities to download or stream music – is, these authors claim, having an effect. Not only are fewer people using the internet to share music files without payment to record companies, but online sales of music – especially of singles – are rising rapidly (Rosen 2008: 574; Sparrow 2005: 43; see also David 2010: 91-

2). Rosen claims that the popular success through widespread illegal distribution of the *Grey Album* (DJ Danger Mouse's 2004 'mash-up' of Jay-Z's 2003 *Black Album* and the Beatles' 1968 *White Album*) encouraged EMI to seal the first DRM-free deal with iTunes in March 2007), and then with Amazon in September 2007 (though this was without the agreement of the Beatles themselves or the availability of their recordings – the remaining Beatles made their own deal with Apple in November 2010). In December 2007 Warner also agreed to offer their catalogue DRM-free on Amazon. Rosen concludes that lower prices and DRM-free access should make legal downloading more commonplace (Rosen 2008: 570-4).

If Rosen and Sparrow are to be believed, then, the music business is over the Napster-led worst, and can look forward to a reasonably prosperous future making and selling recordings, much as it has done since the early twentieth century. Copyright control, enhanced by the recent term extensions, will continue to allow a culturally productive industry to defend its existing catalogues, and add to them by investing in new talent.

This is not the majority view among writers on the music business. Even those who, on balance, agree that some form of copyright is necessary, are wary of endorsing the industry's position. The second edition of Simon Frith and Lee Marshall's edited collection *Music and Copyright* (Frith and Marshall 2004) examines the issue from a number of complementary angles. None of the contributing writers is happy with the way in which existing copyright law operates; neither are they favourably impressed by the ways in which royalty-based contracts reward artists (or fail to do so). This contractual approach (and the contributing authors' scepticism towards it) applies to composers or performers in every field of musical endeavour: to the western orthodoxies of written music (which has a tradition of exploitation stretching back to the eighteenth century: even G.F. Handel, who was among the pioneer composers of commodified music for a bourgeois audience in eighteenth-century London, was ripped off by his publishers); to folk's collective and anonymised compositions, or to African-American performativity, as against those orthodoxies; to indigenous performers' recordings being sampled without the performers' knowledge or reward; and to the difficulties of obtaining credit or reward faced by synthesiser programmers and other contemporary electronic sound designers. Frith and Marshall note that 'as editors, what surprised us most … was the recurring scepticism about the effects of copyright … many of the authors concluded that the current copyright regime is of limited benefit to musical practitioners' (Frith and Marshall 2004: 15). Indeed so – and I speak from personal experience.

In *Peer to Peer and the Music Industry: The Criminalization of Sharing*, Matthew David summarises the key problem thus: 'study of the royalty system in the USA, France, the UK and elsewhere shows chronic failure to reward artists'. Most artists fail to recoup the advances paid to them by record labels in order to enable them to record, and are thus never paid any royalties at all (David 2010: 7; 124-5). David chronicles certain aspects of the music business's battle against the culture of file-sharing which had not previously received the attention they deserved. In particular David examines the discourse of the industry's propaganda campaigns – noting the mixture of hyperbole and sheer semantic overload as the music business tried to brand all file-sharing as 'piracy', despite the fact that most of it was intended precisely as *sharing*, rather than as commercial theft for resale; then further confused the issue by trying to associate file-sharing with genuinely criminal piracy activities (such as CD copying for sale at street markets), which, adding another level of *non-sequitur* confusion, allegedly funded international terrorism or people-trafficking.

Defending the Business Model

Arguing that such tactics merely further alienate consumers, David asks a really important question: 'does a dominant ideology only need to persuade the ruling elite, while the rest of society can be managed with the threat of punishment and the absence of a viable alternative?' (David 2010: 97). The success with which music business lobbyists have managed to make their case, would appear to answer the question in the affirmative. In Brussels, after vigorous music-business lobbying against the relatively liberal conclusions of a review led by the University of Amsterdam's Institute for Information Law, in 2009 the EU moved in favour of endorsing copyright term extension in sound recordings to 70 years, much as the United States Congress had done in the 1998 'Sonny Bono' extension (which granted term extension to 95 years). Meanwhile in Britain music business lobbyists (and others threatened by digital copying, including film companies and the FA Premier League) claimed that illegal filesharing, and the illegal streaming of live events, together cost UK creative businesses £400m a year in lost sales (Halliday 2011). This estimate persuaded the New Labour government, then in its last few months of office, to rush through legislation – the 2010 Digital Economy Act – whose severe copyright protection provisions ran counter to the liberal proposals made in the 2006 *Gowers Review of Intellectual Property*, which the government had itself commissioned, but whose recommendations the music business did not like (Gowers 2006).

Under the Digital Economy Act, rights holders would collect data about people believed to be illegally downloading music and/or film from filesharing sites, and ISPs will then have to match the rights holders' data against their customer databases, and send warning letters to those accused. The Act stated that repeat copyright infringers could be fined, and will have their internet access slowed, or even blocked altogether. When the incoming coalition government decided to abandon the latter, having taken note of the counter-lobbying from ISPs (who argued that the draconian aspects of the Act were unenforceable), the music business continued to lobby for unfettered access to records of individuals' use of the internet (Sweeney 2011a; Sweeney 2011b).

Changing the Business Model

Not all responses to the changing market relations of the digital economy have been so stubbornly reactionary. There were also some creative responses to this apparent problem of lost rights control – indeed, some of these innovations had helped to create it. From the late 1990s a number of electronics manufacturers developed small portable devices which could download MP3 files from their owners' computers. The most significant of these was Apple's iPod, launched in late 2001, whose associated operating system, iTunes, included an online store where users could pay for music and video tracks, and which could be used on Windows-based PCs as well as Apple products. These and subsequent innovations such as the iPhone and iPad, helped Apple, heretofore a niche player in the personal computer market, to achieve Microsoft-threatening global hegemony within a decade; sales of music through iTunes increased rapidly, with the 10 billionth song download announced in February 2010 (Apple 2010).

Other innovations included streaming services such as the Swedish website Spotify, which was launched with the agreement of all the major record labels and other rights holders, who provided use of their catalogues for the new programme (though the royalties paid per use were very small). In return Spotify allowed users to stream music to their computers and/or smartphones, rather than to download and store their favourite tracks; they could also purchase music through various internet links. Another innovative computer programme is Last.fm, currently based in London (though it originated in Germany, and has been owned since 2007 by CBS). Last.fm's USP is the 'scrobbler', a device which takes into account the user's listening preferences and suggests new music, giving them the opportunity to audition tracks by the suggested artists, as well as directing them to internet sites where that music can be purchased, and to upcoming gigs by the artists in question.

Meanwhile the internet, so feared by the major labels, had apparently helped to ensure the survival of smaller labels, by enabling them to offer their niche products to a global market. In 2004 dance and experimental electronic music label Warp (which was founded in Sheffield in 1989, but moved its offices to London in 2000) launched Bleep.com, the first online music download service to be developed from within the record business, and the first to offer DRM-free recordings, which were sourced from the Warp label and other London-based independent labels such as Rough Trade, Beggars Banquet, One Little Indian, Hyperdub and Ninja Tune (Young 2005: 129; and see in general on this Young: 2005 and 2006, and Chick: 2010). In other words, while the major record labels tried to defend their twentieth-century business model – itself based on far earlier notions of publishers' rights and individual creativity – a great deal of internet-based activity originating outside those major labels has tried, with some success, to ameliorate the perceived decline in music sales by changing the way the music business works, while incidentally promoting a transitional model of music retail including the continued sales of CD, and indeed vinyl, as part of this preservation of genres and subgenres for an enthusiastic and knowledgeable fanbase.

This relative success was imperilled by the August 2011 London riots, during which the Sony warehouse in Enfield, north London, was burnt down in an arson attack. Among the warehouse's principal clients was PIAS, the most important UK distributor for physical sales of recordings by the independent labels mentioned above, and many others. Warp, whose innovative, individualised packaging had helped to promote continued sales of CD and vinyl, responded thus:

> The biggest challenge for us is replacing Warp's extensive back catalogue spanning the last 21 years. We will replace as much of this as we can by creating new stock and replenishing where possible with stock from outside the UK. Unfortunately some releases may never be available physically again. (Murray 2011)

While the fanbase responded positively to this new disaster, it seemed that arsonists had struck a potentially fatal blow against the transitional model of online music retail; but that the legal downloading of music would continue to drive Warp's development as a strong independent label.

The Decline of EMI

In this context the recent history of London-based major record label EMI provides prime evidence of a business which, despite the intentions of some of its more forward-thinking employees, reached a point of existential crisis early in the new millennium because it simply could not come to terms with the new world of digital distribution. In 1994 Jeremy Silver created the first website for Virgin Records, then wholly owned by EMI; but his plans to use this to offer music for sale were frustrated as, in Silver's words, 'the EMI people were even less receptive to the idea of the internet business than the Virgin people – they were completely baffled by it all' (Southall 2009: 52). Four years later Silver was talking to a number of start-up companies about licensing EMI's music for sale on the internet – and taking upfront payments from these companies, many of which were backed by institutional investors – but there was still no enthusiasm within EMI for sale by download (Southall 2009: 89). As Tim Clark, manager of Robbie Williams, put it, 'in the late 1990s EMI, along with most of the record industry, lost the plot with digital technology' (Southall 2009: 126). So the company didn't think about how best to invest enough in new business models and positive ways in which to deploy downloading technologies, or indeed the impact which cherry-picking tracks would have on the future of that conceptual artefact of the 1950s, 'the album' (this concept was based, of course on a physical artefact: the vinyl 12-inch record revolving at 33 and 1/3 rpm, which could contain about 40 minutes of music).

As a result of this failure to make existing catalogues freely available for sale for significantly less than the physical equivalent, the way was open for Shawn Fanning's Napster file-sharing software to revolutionise the ways in which recorded music was accessed by a wide segment of music-lovers world-wide (Alderman 2001). Though the record industry then took legal action to close Napster (and the similar programmes which appeared as soon as it was closed down by the courts), the effect on EMI was clear. After two years of falling sales, in March 2002 the company's Swindon CD plant was closed, and later that year approximately 400 out of EMI's worldwide roster of 1600 artists were dropped from the label, including, infamously, 49 Finnish bands (Alderma 2001: 142).

There had already by this point been talks between EMI and American label Warner about a possible merger between the two, or the takeover of one by the other, and such discussions re-emerged in 2003, and again in 2006 and 2007 (Southall 2009: 201). By the latter point the newspapers were beginning to carry rumours of a buyout by a private equity firm. On 2 August 2007, a week after EMI had posted annual losses of £260 million, Terra Firma was confirmed as the new owner (Southall 2009: 207). As a result, on 18 September 2007 EMI ceased to be a public limited company, and was delisted from the London Stock Exchange.

Guy Hands, Terra Firma's new owner, had just lost out on the opportunity to acquire Boots the Chemists (which had been bought by another private equity firm, Kohlberg Kravis Roberts, in the week before the EMI takeover). But though he may well be a music fan – certainly he subsequently admitted to having paid well over the odds for the company- Hands gave every impression of treating EMI as yet another failing business, and the artists signed to the label as part of the problem. Chris Morrison, manager of Blur and Gorillaz star Damon Albarn, summed up the cultural and financial problems artists were having with the new regime: 'Hands needed to understand that artists hate the major record companies because they are paid less than they should be, they are dictated to, and the executives are paid more than they should be' (Southall 2009: 219).

Some artists, including Roisin Murphy, The Rolling Stones and Paul McCartney, left the label. Joss Stone sued for early release from her contract, and Pink Floyd sued for unpaid royalties, while EMI's star rock act of the 1990s, Radiohead, left and set up their own label. EMI had refused to rewrite their contracts to include payment for downloads, just as Hands was telling employees that the business had indeed been too slow to embrace digital distribution (Southall 2009: 220). So the newly-liberated Radiohead pioneered their own distribution system, selling their albums *In Rainbows* (2008) and *The King of Limbs* (2011) in a variety of formats (including, once the material was available for download, CD); in the case of the earlier album, internet purchasers were given the opportunity to name their own price, including nothing, for downloading the material.

At this point we return perforce to this book's metanarrative. Whatever the *cultural* issues in the new EMI regime, the *financial* problem with the deal was that, having 'paid' too much – i.e. borrowed too much, in this case from US bank Citigroup, to finance the deal, and having subsequently written off £1.2 billion of the sums borrowed in order to refresh the EMI balance sheets – Hands' private equity group was in no position to work the usual private equity asset-stripping magic. This would have involved, as well as the extensive staff cuts which were indeed made, selling off (or otherwise exploiting the financial possibilities inherent in) the back catalogue, and thus returning EMI to apparent profit.

Such operations are quotidian to the workings of the private equity 'leveraged buyout', in which a small group of people borrow money to 'buy' an existing, mature company which already generates significant revenue – enough to pay the interest on the sums borrowed, which can be set against tax liabilities, while they cut wage costs and parcel up the company into smaller units, some of which are sold on (Stowell 2010). However, this particular way of making money required the chimeras of economic growth to be in full vitality; they were moribund. London's finance capital juggernaut, including its private equity sub-cult alongside the troubled banks, had crashed. The company's losses mounted, and in early 2011, after legal action, Hands relinquished his ownership of EMI, which became the property of his original backer, Citigroup, which wrote off yet another £2 billion of debt in a further attempt to put the business back on an even keel, then agreed to divide the EMI group's holdings among the existing major record labels, selling the recorded music division to Universal, and the back catalogue to a consortium led by Sony. Should European competition authorities agree to these proposals EMI will cease to be the only remaining British major record label. Meanwhile opportunities for new UK artists continue to contract.

Keeping Music Live

Another attempt to rework the finances of the music industry has been by contracting artists principally for live performance rather than recordings; this too was perceived to be a threat to the recorded music industry, based as it was on the assumption that music fans would be prepared to spend the disposable income they no longer spent on buying recorded music on live performances by their favourites – an assumption which seemed borne out by rising demand for tickets in the middle of the decade (David 2008: 152, 158; Rosen 2008: 255). Responding to this trend, the world's largest concert promoter, Live Nation, began merger talks with the largest ticketing and artist management company, Ticketmaster. The deal, which was cleared by both US and UK competition regulators in 2010, would see the new company tempting top artists away from deals with major record companies.

There are clearly possibilities here, at least for professional artists with established reputations. For amateur, semi-professional and emerging artists, despite the boasted number of venues in London, legislative problems put a brake on opportunities for live performance. The 2003 Licensing Act had controlled the provision of live performance in venues with a capacity of fewer than 200 (the back room of a pub, say) by permitting only two, unamplified, musicians to perform. For bands with three or more members, and/or amplified music, the venue would need a specific, and expensive, entertainment license.

The 2003 Act had also given the police extended powers to control music events, and the Metropolitan Police had responded with the notorious Form 696, which asked event promoters to specify the type of music to be performed and the ethnic group most likely to attend. Campaigners saw this as at least potentially racist, and claimed that as a result events featuring genres such as drum'n'bass, UK garage, grime, or dubstep – each of which emerged in London before gaining worldwide significance and commercial as well as cultural success – were likely to be refused permission.

The coalition government which came to power in 2010 promised to modify the 2003 Act, specifically in order to permit the performance of amplified music in small venues, but seemed in no hurry to do so. As a result, a Liberal Democrat peer, Lord Tim Clement-Jones, introduced a Private Members' Bill to exempt small venues for audiences of up to 200 from the need to apply for an entertainment license, while reinforcing the rights of local residents by allowing conditions to be placed on, for example, the premises' hours of opening. At the time of writing this Bill had reached the Committee stage, and had broad government support. But in the meanwhile, again, opportunities for emerging artists have contracted.

Keeping Musicians Alive

Given these restrictions, alongside the conclusions of Frith and Marshall quoted above, it is unsurprising that relatively few musicians earn a living solely from performance and recording. A survey conducted in 2000 found that only 57 per cent of its sample of people who identified themselves as 'musicians', claimed that over half of their annual income was from any form of public music-making (Metier 2000; Blake and Jeffery 2001: 36). Some of these people worked outside music altogether between the gigs and recording sessions which meant so much to them; for the majority, however, most of their paid work was in music education and community engagement.

Education remains among the most important 'cultural industries' in London, and education in music is a vital part of that overall project. Schools, colleges and universities are joined in music education by a bewildering variety of public, social and private enterprises which offer tuition in instrumental, vocal and production techniques at all levels, from the most basic to post-doctoral research in the physiology of music performance and the neuroscience of music perception. The London-based national charity Youth Music, for example, hosts workshops and personal tuition, rehearsal spaces and performance opportunities for aspiring musicians in all genres – and from five years old onwards – while the privately owned Institute for Contemporary Music, also based in London, provides diplomas and degrees in instrumental and vocal performance. Each employs professional musicians, on part-time contracts, to teach, mentor and inspire their aspiring successors.

In doing so they are helping to fulfil one of the more admirable social ambitions of the Mayor of London, who wrote in early 2010 that:

> Music education can have a transformative impact on young people; enriching the mind, giving knowledge and understanding, teaching valuable skills and discipline, and importantly, providing a source of lifelong pleasure. As Confucius said 'Music produces a kind of pleasure which human nature cannot do without'. (Mayor of London 2010c: 3)

This is from the preface to *Making Music Matter*, a refreshing document which makes no concessions to the rhetoric of the cultural and creative industries. It enjoins all Londoners to engage with music as a public good, not a commercial enterprise. Rightly pointing to the patchy nature of music education provision across the London boroughs since the closure of the Inner London Education Authority's music service in the early 1990s, and to the subsequent plethora of short-term initiatives which can prevent the implementation of joined-up thinking about career development, the document signals the Mayoralty's intention to join up as many dots as possible across the charitable, private, formal and informal educational sectors in order to encourage all children to maximise their potential.

In other words, this aspect of the Mayor's cultural strategy is not about maximising profit, or box-ticking, or underlining one set of cultural norms about music and its practices as against others. It is not about providing workers for the knowledge economy, and it makes no claim that the only music which matters is that which is hedged around by copyright restrictions, so that a few dozen music business executives can remain on the high salaries to which they are accustomed. It is a proposal for the creation and maintenance of a culture in common – in the sense of encouraging all Londoners to be musical.

This vision, if realised, would take us neatly back to the ongoing crisis in the music business. It would confirm, rather than solve, that crisis; but it would do so in a way which is entirely positive. The new culture of the digital age is personal and performative, socially interactive, participative and collaborative: it is not necessarily professional or otherwise commercially viable, and it does not necessarily map identity on to work. Charles Leadbeater and Paul Miller have identified an emergent tendency to 'pro-am' activity in contemporary society. In other words, they have argued that activities done to professional standards by people who are not paid their principal salary for doing so, are increasingly important and socially beneficial (Leadbeater and Miller 2004). In many ways this has always been the situation of most musicians, and although the aftermath of the credit crunch is unlikely to hand out more opportunities for well-paid skilled musical work, there will still be numerous opportunities for music making at all levels. Whatever the future of EMI, music will remain something many people do, and most enjoy. We simply do not need a commercial, let alone a leveraged, model of the (recorded) music business in order to make music.

Assuming, then, that the current government does indeed act on its word and that more venues become available, a more avowedly *socially* musical London would have less need of a successful recorded music business, and indeed successful (i.e. well-paid, fully professional) musicians. It might nonetheless remain the music capital of the world.

References

Alderman, J. (2001). *Sonic Boom: Napster and the New Pioneers of Music.* New York: Perseus.

Apple (2010). Available at http://www.apple.com/pr/library/2010/02/25iTunes-Store-Tops-10-Billion-Songs-Sold.html, accessed 3 August 2011.

Blake, A. (2007). *Popular Music: The Age of Multimedia.* London: Middlesex University Press.

Blake, A. and Jeffery, G. (2001). 'The Implications of "The Value of Music in London" for Local and Regional Policy', *Cultural Trends*, 38, 35-40.

Chick, S. (2010). *Ninja Tune: 20 Years of Beats and Pieces*. London: Black Dog Publishing.

David, M. (2010). *Peer to Peer and the Music Industry: The Criminalization of Sharing.* London: Sage.

Digital Economy Act 2010, available at http://www.opsi.gov.uk/acts/acts2010/pdf/ukpga_20100024_en.pdf, accessed 2 March 2011.

Frith, S. and Marshall, L. (eds) (2004). *Music and Copyright*, 2nd ed., Edinburgh: Edinburgh University Press.

Gowers, A. (2006). *Review of Intellectual Property* http://webarchive.nationalarchives.gov.uk/+/http://www.hm-treasury.gov.uk/independent_reviews/gowers_review_intellectual_property/gowersreview_index.cfm, accessed 24 April 2011.

Halliday, J. (2011). 'Filesharing: BT and TalkTalk fail in challenge to Digital Economy Act', available at http://www.guardian.co.uk/technology/2011/apr/20/filesharing-bt-talktalk-digital-economy-act, accessed 4 March 2011.

Laing, D. and York, N. (2001). 'The Value of Music in London', *Cultural Trends*, 38, 1-34.

Laughey, D. (2007). 'Music Media in Young People's Everyday Lives', in J. Sexton, ed., *Music, Sound and Multimedia: From the Live to the Virtual.* Edinburgh: Edinburgh University Press, 172-87.

Leadbeater, C. and Miller, P. (2004). *The Pro-Am Revolution: How Enthusiasts are Changing our Economy and Society.* London: Demos.

London Development Agency (2008). *London: A Cultural Audit*, available at http://static.london.gov.uk/mayor/culture/docs/cultural-audit.pdf, accessed 3 August 2011.

Marshall, L. (2005). *Bootlegging: Romanticism and Copyright in the Music Industry.* London: Sage.
Mayor of London (2010a). *Cultural Metropolis: The Mayor's Draft Cultural Strategy, 2012 and Beyond.* London: Mayor of London.
Mayor of London (2010b). *Cultural Metropolis: The Mayor's Cultural Strategy, 2012 and Beyond.* London: Mayor of London.
Mayor of London (2010c). *Making Music Matter.* London: Mayor of London.
Metier (2000). *The Music Industry: Skills and Training Needs in the 21st Century* Bradford: Metier.
Murray, R. (2011). 'Warp Respond to Sony Warehouse Fire. UK Stock Devastated', available at http://www.clashmusic.com/news/warp-respond-to-sony-warehouse-fire, accessed 11 August 2011.
Rosen, R. (2008). *Music and Copyright.* New York: Oxford University Press.
Southall, B. (2009). *The Rise and Fall of EMI Records*. London: Omnibus Press.
Sparrow, A. (2006). *Music Distribution and the Internet: A Legal Guide for the Music Business.* Aldershot: Gower.
Stowell, D. (2010). *Investment Banks, Hedge Funds, and Private Equity: The New Paradigm.* London: Academic Press.
Sweeney, M. (2011a). 'Government scraps plan to block illegal filesharing websites', *The Guardian* online, 3 August 2011, available at http://www.guardian.co.uk/technology/2011/aug/03/government-scraps-filesharing-sites-block, accessed 4 August 2011.
Sweeney, M. (2011b). 'Illegal filesharing: Trade bodies demand government crackdown', *The Guardian* online, 3 August 2011, available at http://www.guardian.co.uk/technology/2011/aug/03/illegal-filesharing-trade-bodies-crackdown, accessed 4 August 2011.
Sweeney, M. (2011c). 'PRS for Music 2010 figures show revenues down 4.8%' *The Guardian* online, 4 August 2011, available at http://www.guardian.co.uk/business/2011/aug/04/prs-for-music-2010-figures, accessed 4 August 2011.
Young, R. (2005). *Warp*. London: Black Dog Publishing.
Young, R. (2006). *Rough Trade.* London: Black Dog Publishing.

Chapter 14
Farewell Nathan Barley? The Rise and Decline of the Freelance Creative

Graham Barnfield

When somebody told Peter Cook that he was writing a novel, Peter replied, 'Really? Neither am I'. (Nobbs 2003: 103)

Introduction

Credit represents a claim on revenues to be generated in the future. It creates no new value by itself, although borrowed funds can be productively invested. As an analytical category for explaining credit and similar mechanisms, fictitious capital identifies that which appears to generate wealth but is typically withdrawn from a different, productive department of the same enterprise or derived from another sector of the economy. These sources of credit may be used for investment to stimulate the 'real economy', but they also feed confusion about what constitutes a useful economic activity. Throughout the late 1990s, the City and the creative industries were both treated as engines of growth and as a counterpoint to manufacturing in the UK. However, whereas pundits were wary about suggesting that financial services would entirely replace manufacturing industries, claims made on behalf of the creative industries were far less inhibited.

Statements from the Department of Culture, Media and Sport (DCMS) asserting Britain's transformation from the workshop of the world to its design studio are, in retrospect, easy to deride. They act as reminders of an economic transition that never occurred. With much debate focused on the financial sector today, even the claims made for the virtues of creative industries have become more muted.

Raking over the ashes of 'Creative Britain', it is worth considering the ideological factors that drove large numbers of young people to long spells of unproductive activity in the creative industries. While the economic and governmental framework for this process is significant, it does not explain the underlying imaginative justifications for individuals becoming what at a stretch could be called 'fictitious variable capital': turning up, working in the cultural industries, yet going through the motions because no new value was being created. Explanations of current financial instability, most of them backtracking to sub-prime mortgages and Lehman Brothers, are two-a-penny; but there is little to explain the parallel rise (and partial fall) of the freelance creative. This is more than an academic question since some degree of faith in the transformative capacities of culture-oriented, high-tech start-ups is discernible not only in the 1990s but right up to the present day, albeit in the diluted form accompanying 'Silicon Roundabout' (in Hoxton, East London), the sale of Tweetdeck and the valuation of LinkedIn.

Since 2007 the financial services sector has faced increasing moral disdain, in ways which suggest an intuitive sense that it is unproductive, even parasitic. Accordingly, those paid to circulate fictitious capital have gone on the defensive. Similarly, and in contrast to the recent past, it is now more difficult for working in the cultural industries to be portrayed as inherently worthwhile or an unalloyed good. This chapter considers the relative fall in the stock of the 'creative', a particular type of London employee linked in to a wider economic cycle which seems to have been brought down along with the crash in financial services. Specifically, it suggests that the idea of 'fictitious capital' – freely applied to the financial services sector – could be usefully extended to the activities of individuals in the 'creative' sector too; here, in spite of its avowed 'creativity', the often unproductive character of cultural work has meant that effort was expended but little or no value was added.

The argument starts by sketching how certain genre fictions have treated 'Creative London'. Written retrospectively, they combined hindsight, satire and broad brushstroke stereotyping to map out 1990s trends in cultural self-employment (without the necessarily untidy detail of the actual process itself). Since this is a chapter concerned with motivation and imagination, it is legitimate to discuss the moments when various popular authors used their imagination to identify how these motivations played out.

But before going immediately ahead with this line of inquiry, it would be wise to consider just what, in employment terms, is meant by 'creative'. In the 1960s advertising industry, the word shifted from an adjective to a noun, as in 'legendary creative Jerry Della Femina', chairman of the Della Femina Travisano & Partners advertising agency (Dean 2010: vii). At this time, the term was only applied to people who wrote or drew the adverts. Three decades later, perhaps inevitably, given the (then) government's preoccupation with the 'creative industries', the term was generalised to include many if not most of those working in these sectors. However, in the recent post-credit crunch, post-New Labour period, the admittedly vague job title tends to be more closely allied to the performing arts sector (Clews and Clews 2009), and other adjoining areas. At the time of writing, one magazine has even looped the etymological loop by referring to a fictional freelance creative, namely, Nathan Barley, to make sense of the 'ambience' at Shoreditch advertising firm Mother – so 'trendy it's almost a *Nathan Barley* pastiche of a creative industry' (Jeffs 2011: 16).

A second ideological influence is that, amid the initial hustle and hype, the distinction between professional and amateur was becoming blurred. While this should not be the cause for a full-blown panic (Barnfield 2010), the increasing importance of User Generated Content led to confusion between paid work, hobbies and volunteering. Though his efforts seem to have little purchase today, here is how Bruce Robbins usefully outlined these distinctions:

> On the one hand, the professional is distinguished from the "amateur" by the fact that she or he earns a livelihood by the given activity. This gives "professional" negative connotations of self-interested, mercenary motive as opposed to the desirable alternative – historically based on and limited to the leisure of certain social classes – of disinterested love of the activity or subject in and for itself. On the other hand, professions are often distinguished from *other* ways of earning one's livelihood – that is, from "occupation" or "trade" or "employment" in general – as possessing a superior degree of learning or skill and/or public utility and also, whether for these reasons or not, a superior social prestige. (Robins B. 1993: 34)

At a conceptual level, an almighty muddle developed between professional and amateur, parallel to that between productive and unproductive labour. Confusion was intensified by the way that creative industries were seen both as virtuous places to work and as the key source of growth, generating worth and wealth in equal measure. By the time fundamentally redistributive and even parasitic activities were welcomed into this mix, and their outputs inflected through the peculiar aesthetic sensibilities of the age, a peculiar ideology had become firmly ensconced.

In the first part of this chapter, we look at how fiction writers came to grips with the rise of the creative, printing the legend but from a critical point of view. In the second part, we try to isolate some of the key themes that helped to foster an occupational identity for the freelance creative. Both sections indicate that the work of such employee-entrepreneurs was often unproductive.

Fictional Fictitious capital

Unlike Peter Cook's party guest, some writers do manage to complete their novels. The works of genre fiction considered below owe their inclusion here to their portrayal of the creative industries in the 1990s. Of course, this was not the first time that the creative industries had come under the novelist's microscope. A distinctive and critical subgenre of Hollywood novels was going strong within two decades of the first talking picture. Skilled exponents included Schulberg (1941/1992), Zinberg (1947), and Puzo, Hollywood being the setting for some of the most memorable scenes in *The Godfather* (1969). Howard Fast's *Max* (1982) even revisited the pre-Hollywood era, when New York City housed much of US moving image production.

Britain, home to a far smaller film industry characterised by production in West London and head offices in Soho Square, hardly seems fertile territory for a literary corpus grounded in cinema. However, public appetites for film-related gossip have been matched by the willingness of those working in the cultural industries to recast their colleagues and rivals as fictional characters. This has ensured a steady stream of publications, but not all novels with a 'creative' setting have sought to develop a critique of this working environment. For instance, while movie producer Christopher Fowler's *Soho Black* (1998) is plotted against a backdrop of a stressed executive involved in film preproduction, the occupational details are subordinate to the requirements of a supernatural thriller. Likewise, Toby Litt's *Corpsing* (2000) revolves around a television producer who is trying to uncover the identity and motives of his ex-girlfriend's murderer. As with Fowler, Litt's industry-specific social commentary tends to be submerged under the traits of the mystery-genre. 'Hollywood novels' and their transatlantic cousins are not always tales of the workplace.

Over time, however, the restructuring of the creative industries started to have more of an influence on their literary representation. When we are confronted with characters and fictional scenes which are nonetheless recognisable as the social types and settings of 'Cool Britannia', it means that the collective self-image of 1990s cultural producers was finally emerging in culture itself, albeit in a distorted form. A range of writers created plots and narratives that dealt specifically with the emergence of a particular type of labour in London: one with a socially useful – even virtuous – reputation despite its often unproductive outcomes. (In a further paradox, as the individual roles in the division of labour intrinsic to such work broke down, references increased to its glamour and wastefulness alike). The success of various authors in coming to terms with these changes also sets the scene for the second part of this chapter, which considers the emergence of the social 'fiction' of freelance success.

For an insight into how such writing worked prior to the blossoming of the 'creative industries' narrative, we turn to *The Quorum* by Kim Newman (1994). Newman's 1990s retelling of the Faust legend identifies the four major cultural industries which his 1970s sixth-form characters, following their gradual disenchantment with music and theatre, wish to break into: film, television, publishing (books and magazines) and comics.[1] It is striking that each member of the Quorum starts out comfortably dabbling in several sections of the mass media. Three protagonists are recognisable 'media types': Mark Amphlett, self-made, working class publisher of 1980s style magazine *The Shape*; Mickey Yeo, writer of comics and a Hollywood screenplay; and Michael Dixon, author and writer-producer of mid-market TV. In exchange for them victimising their upper middle class friend Neil – together, 'they'd always been a perfect diagram of the class

1 Comics have long supplied Newman with reading material. His inclusion of this industry might now seem dated, but the late-1980s saw the rise of the 'graphic novel'. Hinting at Newman's foresight into long-term comics industry economics, US corporations Marvel and D.C. are now largely reconstituted around IP portfolio management and as film studios, after a near-bankrupting commitment to publishing 'collectors' editions' for older readers.

system' (Newman 1994: 21) – the Satanic Derek Leech guarantees them career success across a range of media platforms. Thus Dixon seems to be tucked away in the late night television slots (of the kind facilitated by Channel 4's 'publishing house' model of broadcasting in the 1980s), while Yeo gets to be writer of *City Hammer*, a Hollywood genre picture, though he ends up searching in vain for his screen credit as the pact unravels and his cultural production is undone.

For members of *The Quorum*, the opportunities grasped are superficially a product of the novel's Faustian pact. Without what they call 'the Deal', '*Michael would have written a few decent books, cult successes. Mickey would be drawing the Dr Shade strip in the* Argus. *Neil would be assistant editor of* The Shape' (Newman 1994: 296-7, emphasis in the original). Sacrificing their friend to Satan means that the trio enjoys a fleeting burst of fame, punching slightly above its weight in the entertainment industries. Even allowing for the Faustian plot, the contrast between *The Quorum* and the Hollywood novel remains striking. Schulberg and others show their embattled protagonist(s) locked into a Fordist career structure, enduring humiliations in the hope of becoming a respected producer or studio head one day. In contrast, Newman's three careerists each develop a kind of sideways mobility across the cultural industries, by dabbling – with undeserved success – in multiple 'creative' activities.

Outside the novel's fictional remit, these career developments are also plausible due to the way that film, television and publishing all became 'open shop' employers during the years in which the story is set. Newman himself (Newman 1995) has written of his own freelance experiences over a similar period, moving from university and fringe theatre into soft porn, listings magazines and obscure publications catering for fans of particular film genres. His subsequent career output included novelisations of the Warhammer fantasy role-playing game using the pen-name 'Jack Yeovil', and a 2001 *Doctor Who* novella, appearing in the hiatus between the 'classic' series and its 2005 revival. Such work was coupled with a growing number of television appearances, while balancing different readerships as a monthly contributor to both *Empire* and *Sight and Sound* magazines. Not for Newman the Fordist 'job for life'; his personal account of freelancing presents his own long-term success as a pen-for-hire as a rarity for his generation. As teenagers, he reports, 'we were all going to be famous writers, filmmakers, rock stars; in our early twenties, we were all considering street-sweeping and teaching English as a foreign language in Saudi' (Newman 1995: 5).

Whereas Newman's present-day profile rests on his talent, The Quorum's fictional characters propel their careers forward using supernatural help. They vacate a position not dissimilar to that of their creator, and they view their greatest personal achievements in terms of status rather than aesthetics; yet at the height of their powers they remain relatively marginal figures. They do not use the Deal to strike out for success in, say medicine or industry, but in entertainment. (In contrast, Derek Leech's pecuniary preferences become clear when he announces 'an ambitious new development in the Docklands' [Newman 1994: 310]). The entertainers meet their contract-holding nemesis at the narrative fulcrum of the novel when, nearly two decades on from the initial pact, the Quorum members see their dreams unravel as they pay the devil his dues.

It would be churlish to criticise Newman for *not* articulating a perception of the creative industries that was to emerge largely after *The Quorum* was published. Significantly, not one of his characters has undergone much in the way of an apprenticeship or is a member of a trade union when his career is getting underway. All their tentative multi-tasking remains some distance from the full-blown hyphenated creative industries worker of the late 1990s, who was expected to be equally comfortable pitching to clients, designing a website or shooting on digital video. Newman captures the analogue era, post-Thatcher media type – and hype – with panache. Who would do the same for the 'self-facilitating media nodes' who appeared in the decade after *The Quorum* was published? Would their representations in fiction come any closer to grasping whether such people employees and entrepreneurs were engaged in productive or unproductive labour?

The fully fledged stereotype of the freelance creative took shape in a decade when class conflict was in decline. Seniority, the closed shop and a craft-based identity were eroded as UK film production, print and broadcasting were restructured along post-Fordist lines. Outside such workplaces, *perceptions* of the class system and social mobility moved away from the rigid diagram described by Newman under successive Major and Blair governments. Even the humble flat cap – erstwhile proletarian garb – made a fashionable comeback (Davenport 2002). Admittedly, Major's Britain 'at ease with itself' and Blair's 'young country' concepts were unsettled by class-based bugbears – 'elitism' (Major), 'unreconstructed wankers' (Blair) and 'the underclass' (both) – but such matters were mainly of concern to the creative industries in that they provided subject matter for screenplays and documentaries.

Author Jake Arnott worked through these themes in *truecrime* (2003), the final volume of his crime trilogy, *The Long Firm*. Each of the three books combines fictional protagonists with a mixture of composite characters based on real people and historical figures appearing under their own names. Previous volumes featured 'Harry Starks', a showbiz-fixated homosexual gangster echoing the Kray Twins, and 'Billy Porter', a version of real life cop-killer Harry Roberts. The first two novels – set mainly in the 1950s and 1960s respectively, but both concluding in the 1980s – were adapted into television period dramas. The final instalment, while reuniting many of the surviving characters, introduced a 1990s creative industries *milieu* to complement the underworld setting. More specifically, it mediates moments when film and publishing overlapped with organised crime, whether in reality or merely by repute.

One recognisable supporting character is 'Jez Scott', who comes from a privileged background and is committed to making a 'film noir' (Arnott 2003: 213). Scott's equally posh co-producer Piers steers the project so that it eventually becomes 'Scrapyard Bulldog', a 1997 East End gangster romp. Jez is dyslexic, well-connected and a fan of Quentin Tarantino (Arnott 2003: 220); he departs from the novel hearing the words 'You need a strong woman in your life. Someone older maybe' (Arnott 2003: 313). Roughly half way between the fictional release of 'Scrapyard Bulldog' and *truecrime*'s actual publication, one Guy Stuart Ritchie (film director) married Madonna, as if following the advice offered to his avatar in the *Long Firm* trilogy. The character Piers resembles Ritchie's well-to-do producer Matthew Vaughn, but he also manages to contribute to a lad-mag called 'Sorted' and spout postmodern academic verbiage in support of his business decisions. Arnott writes of his characters: 'Both of them belonged by birth to the media aristocracy' (Arnott 2003: 219), a description easily applied to both Ritchie and Vaughn. Likewise, what we learn of 'Scrapyard Bulldog' reads like a pastiche of *Lock, Stock and Two Smoking Barrels* (1997).

Increasingly drawn to the same *milieu* as Arnott's Ritchie figure is Gary 'Geezer Gaz' Kelly, a skinhead turned career criminal. His career draws on events in the memoirs of several purported underworld figures, including 'Dodgy' Dave Courtney, Bernard O'Mahoney and Carlton Leach, whose exploits were starting to appear in print in the 1990s, largely through the output of publishers John Blake ('true crime') and Milo Books (football hooliganism). Kelly, like O'Mahoney and Leach, is portrayed in connection to the real-life Rettendon Range Rover murders of 1995. These killings also appeared as the climax of three feature films (two of them made with public funds), and they were central to at least ten books. Virgin even published a collection of commentaries by a 'real-life gangster' which included a weirdly postmodern appraisal of the authenticity of the performance in *Lock, Stock* of the actor (and convicted criminal) playing a character allegedly based on him (Courtney 2006: 76-83). This strange cultural turn would have been improbable if not for the young creative's foundational myth of the British gangster film as intrinsically 'cool'.

Prior to New Labour, Kim Newman depicted ambitious yet mediocre amateurs using the supernatural to become ambitious yet mediocre professionals in the media industries. Roughly a decade later, Jake Arnott showed a sense of entitlement which put posh boys behind the camera and officially retired criminals in front of it. By writing a thinly fictionalised version of the *Lock, Stock and Two Smoking Barrels* phenomenon, he captured the peculiar overlap between the entertainment industries and anti-social activity. It would be easy to view Arnott's narrative as solely satirical, bringing 'stab and tell' publications to the readership of literary fiction. Introducing a 2004 screening of *The Lady from Shanghai*, Arnott dismissed 'doormen paid a pittance to liken their lives to the miracles of the Saints', yet his parody speaks accurately of a specific trend in the 1990s cultural industries. For the young freelance creative, refining a particular representation of blue-collar crime – nostalgic, ethnically exclusive, morally relativistic ('they only hurt their own kind') – seemed like a meal ticket. If nothing else, 'Creative Britain' produced a surfeit of British crime films (of varying quality).[2]

2 The present author appeared in four of them: *Police 2020* (1997); *Mr In-Between* (2001); *Plato's Breaking Point* (2005, [with my scene reshot without me]); and *Number One Longing, Number Two Regret* (2004, [in a feature credit as 'Woods' Guy']).

In works of fiction, filmmaking was presented as central to the typical freelance creative's career. In comparison, internet start-ups were neglected and made to look peripheral to 'Creative Britain'. Hindsight and experience tell us that the dot.com boom was a largely speculative activity, in which idle capital – insufficient to start a new round of capital accumulation – found its way into internet start-ups. In turn, with one eye on earlier developments in Silicon Valley, such companies became overvalued and their employees were issued stock options that made them into paper millionaires, while sections of academia flattered to deceive with their 'knowledge economy' discourse. Creative Britain fictions struggled to incorporate the dot.com era, leaving this significant economic development largely absent from literary representations of the British scene.

There were exceptions: *truecrime* depicts a supporting character, disgruntled Soho pornographer Wally Peters, complaining of cheap video cameras, user-generated pornography and 'this new computer thing, you know, this fucking Internet. Diabolical' (Arnott 2003: 264). One year on, an episode of Channel 4's uncomfortable sit-com *Peep Show* hinged on an internet entrepreneur seeking a soundtrack for his 'film *noir*-style' advertisement (Shapeero 2004). This latter storyline was a closer approximation to economic reality, in that the opportunities available to make film increased because, for the young entrepreneur, the direction of cash flow ran from internet start-up to film production, and not the other way. Would-be filmmakers engaged with a new DIY ethos that could build on the internet as a marketing tool, particularly following the example of 1999's *The Blair Witch Project* (Jones and Jolliffe 2000: 515). One consequence of the emergence of 'new media' was that filmmaking and internet entrepreneurialism were becoming more closely entwined.

Against this backdrop, it took an especially vicious fictional stereotype to nail the freelance creative. If the loose 'types' in Newman and Arnott somehow typified industry-wide changes, a satire devoted exclusively to media upstarts made a grim impact on their reputations. Launched in 1999, *tvgohome* was a website resembling the *Radio Times* and written, largely anonymously, by Charlie Brooker. It featured coruscating summaries of fictional television programmes, e.g. *Daily Mail Island*, while traducing genuine shows, often with a grain of truth. For instance, long-running Australian soap opera *Neighbours* was billed as 'repeated tomorrow lunchtime for the long-term unemployed'. The centrepiece of the fake listings magazine was 'Cunt', a fly-on-the-wall documentary following the misadventures of Nathan Barley, a Hoxton-based trustafarian and 'self-facilitating media node', who embodied the new media scene which briefly colonised parts of East London in the late 1990s. Its participants – fashionable, gadget-obsessed, middle class – typically lived off their parents while being formally self-employed as web-designers, DJs and makers of micro-budget digital short films.

Amid the sheer invective of each programme synopsis featuring Barley, it is easy to lose sight of the grain of truth in its accurate reflections on coolhunting in Hoxton and Shoreditch. Fashion-obsessed child-men churned out worthless viral video idents and flash animations, while equally pathetic show reels, demo tapes and screenplays festered under the beds in their loft-living, live-work warehouse conversion apartments. While their daily outbursts were facilitated by relatively inexpensive semi-professional digital equipment, the really big projects could be unleashed using parental or public funds. Brooker's own employment at *PCZone* magazine put him in a position to observe Nathan's 'type' up close, before setting up a fictional social *milieu* that spoke to the underlying realities of the dot.com boom. Almost inevitably, the geographical base of such activity became the home turf on which it was satirised. By the time the hyper-trendy 'Hoxton fin' haircut was being mocked as a 'Shoreditch twat', the game was up.

By 2005 the web-based parody had developed into a full-blown Channel 4 sitcom, with an expanded role for magazine journalists in the storyline and the input of Chris Morris, satirist and 'Tory anarchist' (Wilkin 2009). Nathan remained a 'technologically and sartorially over-accessorised self-styled webmaster' (Monk 2007), but his TV show looked more like a period piece (albeit with a recurring send-up of smartphones that was ahead of its time). In print, author Stewart Home continued to hammer targets like Nathan in such novels as *Down and out in Shoreditch and Hoxton* (2004), but increasingly the East London new media scene was in decline. In parts of public discourse, that same *milieu* was a synecdoche for Creative Britain.

Fictitious Variable Capital?

In all three of the main fictional accounts considered above, the rise of the freelance creative is grounded in a distinctive political economy. This is characterised by the horizontal career paths of individuals 'portfolio working' across different industries and media platforms in order to progress. Such movement is facilitated by the decline of craft consciousness as a competing ideological force. While salaries and bonuses in *The Quorum* seem to be paid for out of the (dubious) profits of commercial broadcasting and publishing, Arnott and Brooker show us cultural producers supported by family wealth and – in their dreams – lottery disbursements. As personal savings are frittered away, this sheer waste is ignored by its producers who see their work as intrinsically important. Seldom are consumers found in sufficient numbers to make the frenetic activity seem worthwhile. (In an exception that proves the rule, the success of 'Scrapyard Bulldog' in Arnott and of *Lock, Stock* in real life, identified some precious metals among the criminal debris.)

Each of the three creative industries fictions considered above ends by threatening to undermine the careers of its protagonists. Yet Jez Scott and the sitcom version of Nathan Barley continue to thrive, lacking any self-awareness of their parasitic relationship to niche markets driven by changing social *mores* (such as the 'cool' gangster film). In contrast, each active member of the Quorum finds his livelihood (and more) abruptly cut short as the novel concludes. All that remains are ephemeral traces to show that they even worked in the cultural industries to begin with: 'In remainder bookshops, in old magazines, in trivia quizzes, the Quorum had left marks … the comet-like crashes of three burning lights' (Newman 1994: 311). The remaining part of this chapter sifts through similar ephemera to work out how the myth of freelance creativity became so entrenched.

Reading the London creative industries against their representation in the local equivalent of the 'Hollywood novel' has its attractions, but limits apply. Checking for modulations in a literary subgenre is all very well, but it could be seen as a sideshow when recalling that much of the 'Creative Britain' discourse was closely associated with successive New Labour governments. A significant moment in this was the rebranding of the Department for National Heritage as the Department for Culture, Media and Sport (DCMS), a move made by the (then) Secretary of State, Chris Smith, 'because we wanted something more forward-looking, a name that captured more accurately the new spirit of modern Britain, that signalled the involvement of all' (Smith 1998: 2). New spirit, new media – the superficial correspondence of these concepts seems appealing.

Institutional changes which emphasised novelty were often indicted as an example of New Labour's 'Year Zero' approach to what went before. However, tracking back through Old Labour – or, specifically, the social democratic centre-right – shows that in an earlier era, the party's cultural policy was conceptualised in relation to state expenditure and its benefits. Post-war Labour figures saw arts patronage as an important mechanism for increasing the general levels of 'gaiety' in society (albeit backed by the welfare state). Such hopes for, say, the Festival of Britain (1951) anticipate the 'Ministry of Fun' nickname applied to the forerunner of the DCMS. Thus Roy Jenkins made *The Labour Case* (1959) by asking 'Is Britain Civilised?' One metric for answering this question was derived from levels of state expenditure, where a 'switch to a new Government policy of moderate generosity would make a world of difference to the whole climate of our culture' (Jenkins quoted in Diamond 2004: 119). Jenkins also welcomed the broader shift in cultural climate, which, writing on the cups of the 1960s, he could already see in prospect:

> Let us be on the side of those who want people to be free to live their own lives, to make their own mistakes, and to decide, provided they do not infringe the rights of others, the code by which they wish to live; and on the side too of experiment and brightness, of better buildings and better food, of better music (jazz as well as Bach) and better books, of fuller lives and greater freedom. (Diamond 2004: 122)

The contrast with Blairite authoritarianism aside, it is clear that post-war 'revisionist thinkers in Labour's history', as Diamond dubs Roy Jenkins, saw arts funding as intrinsically worthwhile, rather than an economic stimulant. Nor were such ideas confined to the political classes. Moving on through the decades, Harold Baldry's 1981 account of arts patronage treats pre-Victorian support for museums – snowballing naturally into the Council for the Encouragement of

Music and the Arts – as the precursor to British arts institutions in the 1970s. The book culminates in an overview of the non-professional scene, praising the work and enthusiasm of local amateur dramatics societies, which Baldry also saw as a prospective audience base for commercial theatre. Significantly, praise for hobbyists and unpaid volunteers does *not* lead Baldry to minimise – or erase – the key differences between professionals and amateurs.

On balance, the emphasis in post-war cultural policy owes more to intrinsic aesthetic values than to the creation of economic value. This is a sharp contrast to the 1990s 'creative industries' concept, imbued with reverence for the 'freelance creative' as a vehicle for wealth creation and representing a break with earlier, patronage-centred ways of thinking about the cultural industries. In Creative Britain, amateur and hobbyist outputs were often reclassified as 'new media' and 'user-generated content', meaning Nathan Barley's leisure activities could be dressed up as the useful work of a Small/Medium-sized Enterprise (SME).

It would be a mistake to treat the contradictory pressures of official policies as being the inspiration for the creative industries characters and 'historical types' populating various works of genre fiction. Directly linking Guy Ritchie and Chris Smith in analysis, is almost as incongruous as Noel Gallagher and Tony Blair really were, on the 'tops' night (Gallagher's description) when they partied together at Downing Street. The limitation in such sweeping linkages is that important, mediating steps are missed out. Nonetheless, the road from the DCMS into Hoxton, connecting government minister to freelance creative, has remained under continuous construction.

Under New Labour, two aspects of government documentation stand out as part of the wider creative discourse. The first of these, discussed above, is the sense that the creative sector's SMEs could play a regenerative role, in terms of both wealth creation and national identity. Secondly, when explaining more specific policies, the idea that creative industries were both leading the way *and* a special case was used to justify such initiatives as, say, a regime of tax breaks for the film industry which was unavailable to other enterprises. What they could not do was help to forge an occupational identity for young 'creatives'.

A full account of the links between cultural producers and regeneration would require a separate study. As a rule of thumb, regeneration is one domain where it would be wrong to treat freelance creatives – previously represented both as unproductive and unaware of it in the predominant manifestation of their occupational identity – as having no economic impact whatsoever. Hence official wish-lists which hanker for 'creative industries clustering' – often paving the way for 'creative industries quarters' in otherwise run-down urban areas. Behind this goal lay a more landlocked version of the belief that the 'importance of networks and clusters within the new environment has led to the creation of new territorial and virtual clusters of innovation, for example, Silicon Valley in California and New York's Manhattan's Silicon Alley … Knowledge can now thus be created in 'virtual' research communities that can gain intellectual capital through the participation of cross-national teams working through computer-based collaborative technologies' (Carlaw et al. 2007: 171-2). Whereas this newer formulation of the 'virtual clustering' model seems to lack any geographical anchor, in the 1990s it was *de rigueur* to talk of clicks *and* bricks.

With one eye on the Silicon Valley example, and the other on sustainable, brownfield-based regeneration, it was (and is still) hoped that bunching up creative types in sufficient numbers would (and will) act as an economic motor. Under their various labels – clusters, hubs, enterprise zones – geographically oriented strategies have produced mixed results. This prompted one Professor of Investment Banking to ask just how 'can governments be smarter about which sectors to back? This is an especially important goal given that in each new industry there are typically only a few 'clusters' or centres of activity. We might be sceptical whether smart selection is a feasible task for governments given how little success academics … have had in picking winners' (Lerner 2009: 130-1). Maybe the scope for creating Hoxton-style 'scenes' would be reduced without the assistance of some form of state-led incentives; more broadly, government involvement is itself no guarantee of regeneration. That creatives wanted decent places in which to work and play does not mean that they bought in to the official line on urban regeneration.

What happened in a handful of locations could be accurately described as bohemian gentrification, where leftfield SMEs rehabilitated office space which, in turn, found its way onto an increasingly speculative property market (Tellingly, both Newman and Arnott link the higher-earning opportunities of the new creative class to housing development). Moreover, the necessity of finding a physical space to work from – despite widespread mantras about the 'paperless office' – became entangled with wider social proclivities for using residential space as a financial instrument. The straightforward process of London households combining pragmatism and ambition in their choice of dwelling – 'a staging post on the way to achieving their more long-term aspirations' (King 2010: 54) – became reified as a desire to observe the price of one's own house rising. The preferred dwellings of the freelance creative may have involved loft-living and 'funky live-work spaces', but they still approached the market with the same pragmatism as any other London first-time buyer. Property speculators benefited from the subsequent improvements to their buildings, and from attendant changes affecting the wider neighbourhood and its reputation.

If Hoxton and Shoreditch seem one stage removed from the high-profile ventures generating NASDAQ listings and share floatations elsewhere, these districts were themselves subject to exaggerated economic expectations. Specifically, the notion of 'creative industries clustering' came to inform a strategy for urban regeneration based on encouraging the high density coalescence of 'creatives' in the same geographical area. In turn, this demographic shift on the ground was supposed to lead to 'new synergies', prompting growth, employment and regeneration. Urbanist Richard Florida (2003) supplied a scholarly gloss for the idea that cafes, cheap office space and like-minded people created a 'funky' environment for a version of trickle-down economics. However, working life itself was not fully synchronised with Florida's model. Writing of Aspen, Colorado, climber

Aron Ralston noted 'There's mostly an unspoken acknowledgement among the voluntarily impoverished dues-payers of our towns that it's better to be fiscally poor yet rich in experience – living the dream – than to be traditionally wealthy but live separate from one's passions' (Ralston 2010: 11). In short, the ascendant Creative Cities formula for regeneration relied heavily on unpaid or underpaid labour, coupled with a willingness to chase the dream.

If an important aspect of the whole 1990s creative story was chasing the dream, individuals' motivations for working in this way, often for negligible financial rewards, found expression in the belief that their cultural outputs were intrinsically important. Creative industries SMEs were encouraged to think of themselves as *uniquely* creative, in a discourse that was often short on specifics. For example, there was little consensus about *what* exactly cultural practitioners should be producing. When one critic eventually plucked up the courage to ask, 'What good are the arts', it prompted considerable debate (Carey 2005: 261-70) in the review pages of the quality press. This brief controversy reflected upon the utility and relevance of cultural production, loosely blending canonical texts, public cultural patronage and social inclusion. John Carey's intervention helped to frame the debate in terms tended to exclude the (by now increasingly unfashionable) freelance creative. Simultaneously, the cash conduits formed in the 1990s, whether for moving dot.com start-up capital with, or just basking in, the warm glow of a favourable tax regime, looked increasingly obstructed. The poster-boys and girls of Creative Britain were losing direction, with little in the way of a record of wealth creation to fall back on.

So just who were Shoreditch Man and Hoxton Woman? In the 'period pieces' considered earlier, the authors make frequent recourse to biographical materials and real events and institutions. A demographic change was under way, prompting Newman (b.1959) and Arnott (b.1961) to acknowledge their generation's cultural ascendancy. Born at around the time Roy Jenkins was asking if Britain was civilised, it was unlikely that they would stick to his formulations on arts policy in their 1990s writings. Unlike cultural practitioners of Jenkins's generation, both had also been through the experience of popular music and youth subcultures, dabbling in amateur theatre along the way. Bookended by punk rock (1976) and the 'Second Summer of Love' (1988), music with a DIY ethos informed their sense of immediate access to cultural production and institutions that coincided with the decline of older certainties. As these younger voices approached middle age, some of their peers were getting closer to the running the mechanisms of cultural arbitration and decision-making. One wag described this trajectory as going from 'my generation to regeneration' (Redhead 1990: 1).

Various UK think tanks and social forecasters identified how the 1990s freelance creative was being demarcated as a distinctive social type from other types of wage labour. Handy (1995) identified the emergence of 'portfolio people', for whom flexibility is a matter of pride – not exploitation – and money is not the only reward. Such entrepreneur-employees – sometimes labelled 'the Independents' – were also praised for working inside an 'environment that promotes openness, free speech, diversity and expression' (Leadbeater and Oakley 1999: 49). Granted, there were dissenting voices willing to highlight the problems of so-called flexibility (Sennett 1998: 46-63), but overall, think tanks were voices of optimism. Yet an early critic captured their isolation from the world of work, noting caustically 'It seems that more people are making a living writing about the electronic cottage than actually work in one' (Heartfield 1998: 10). If think tanks and forecasters conceptualised certain processes in certain workplaces in thoughtful ways, they also elevated their new categories over the more prosaic realities of work. Presenting young freelancers as a dynamo of regeneration, they were less adept at admitting to their marginal economic status.

Think tanks such as Demos may have had some influence on government policy – this is, after all, one of their roles – but they lacked much connection with the younger creatives, whose interests were more focused on new media and film making. Sometimes mediated through the comment pages, where perhaps the cross-generational message could get across, think tanks fed the web of meaning through which the attractions of pro-am cultural work were made explicit. In this context, the rise of the freelance creative was a phenomenon which inflated the social virtues of a type of often unproductive labour. As one observer put it, 'the special importance of those sectors of the economy that are artificially demarcated as 'creative' tells us more about attitudes to creativity in the rest of the economy than the actual significance of those sectors. It is the want of creativity everywhere else – whether in their spare time or in the aspiration to 'work at something really creative', by becoming a pop-star, artist, or style-guru' (Heartfield 2000: 16).

When we consider how such attitudes to work coalesced with other values and opinions, the reasons for demanding 'creativity' in such a peculiar form become murkier still. As Arnott indicates, one mystery of 'Creative Britain' is that it spawned a seemingly endless supply of crime and gangster movies, in quantities which only one other popular genre – the clubland film – could keep pace with.[3] As we see below, there was an economic basis for this trend, yet it was also rooted in shifting social *mores*. Consider Richard Tull, a Martin Amis character proposing a *History of Increasing Humiliation*: 'a book accounting for the decline in the status and virtue of literary protagonists. First gods, then demi-gods, then kings and great warriors, great lovers, then burghers and merchants … Then maniacs and murderers, tramps, mobs, rabble, flotsam, vermin' (Amis 1995: 129). Tull's map of literature's trajectory corresponds to real developments in popular entertainment. Given these wider attitudes, cultural practitioners' proliferating urban crime narratives found themselves pushing at an open door.

It would be a cheap shot to say that *Lock, Stock* and its imitators were simply the morbid symptoms of an amoral age, or to treat post-*Human Traffic* British clubbing films (*g-mt:*, *South West 9*, *Sorted*, *Clubbed* etc.) as the fever dreams of

3 The resurgence of British horror production occurred much later, partly encouraged by the highly profitable *28 Days Later* franchise (2002-present day).

adults who should have long since come down off their ecstasy high.[4] Of more concern here is the way that the occupational identity of the creative encouraged the largely wasteful activity of churning out critical and box office failures, facilitated by a production process which combined spare cash and voluntary labour.

One key text for seeding the desire for crime films within the creative 'community' would be *The Guerilla Film Maker's Handbook.* Despite being packed with excellent, practical advice for its aspirational readers, it could not endow them with talent. The authors use case studies of 16 named films that, through careful pre-production, cunning marketing, territorial pre-sales and exploitation of the home video market, either broke even or acted as calling cards for the subsequently successful filmmakers responsible (Jolliffe and Jones 2000: 450-521). All the case studies were of genre pictures; six of the 16 listed movies were set in either clubland or the criminal underworld, including *Lock, Stock and Two Smoking Barrels* and *Human Traffic* (worth $25,297,569 and £2.5 million in respective box office takings). It seemed that the 1990s had conspired to give real-life Nathan Barleys both a tool kit of administrative techniques (the *Handbook* contains 65 pages of templates of paperwork) and an official aesthetic – kinetically-edited, self-consciously cool – to work with.

The same conditions also supplied different types of labour. Despite the availability of relatively inexpensive digital cameras and editing software and the expansion of film school recruitment, the new type of creative still depended upon skilled artisans to get their films made. No doubt many technicians who had 'gone freelance', i.e. they had been made redundant from the established industry, were glad of the work. That there was a culture clash was demonstrated in 2000, when law school drop-out turned director/producer/writer Alexander Jovy (b.1971) was caught by a documentarist's camera, showing that his patient yet exasperated director of photography was obliged to explain to him the basic cinematic grammar of 'not crossing the line'. In turn, people from the reservoir of film industry volunteer labour at the 'Shooting People' website (www.shootingpeople.org) used its email bulletin to debate the merits of keen (and often independently wealthy) amateurs telling hardened professionals what to do.

Jovy's feature debut *Sorted* was not a financial success, grossing just £53,578 from its 134-screen October 2000 UK opening weekend; it had cost a reported $9 million to make.[5] Yet *Sorted*'s huge losses, offset only slightly by the secondary market in VHS and DVD rentals, were typical of much UK film production in this period. If this considerable wastage had come out of the private incomes of their wealthy directors and producers, it would be easy to chalk it up to experience. It

4 Pointedly, many of the club culture narratives converged with crime stories, largely thanks to the presence of bouncers and drug dealers within the 'night-time economy'.

5 Somewhat churlishly, Jovy went on to make the largely unseen 2009 TV movie *Being Danny's Dire*, mocking perennial mockney crime and clubland actor Danny Dyer, a staple performer in British genre pictures. Little wonder both Jovy and Dyer's careers invoke the lingering 'funky' odour of Creative Britain.

is more galling to read, in print or amid screen credits, of the UK Film Council's subsidy of such doomed projects or of the injection of public funds from the National Lottery. One does not have to support the austerity measures launched in 2010 to see such production as economically wasteful. Accompanying the direct subsidies was a tax regime designed to encourage film production, although some might say its main beneficiaries were accountants. Turning a loss-making film into a tax shelter – at one point even allowing for 'double-dipping' (where expenses could be written off against tax *twice*) – did little to raise the overall quality of UK film production. Needless to say, the quantity of films increased, although more than a few of these productions could count themselves lucky if they went straight to video.

Even with the Film Council abolished, aspects of this regime are still with us. Sticking with my use of ephemera to 'print the legend' of the freelance creative, one can see the actuarial triumphing over the aesthetic when looking at a forthcoming film's 'Offer Document', the prospectus used to raise production monies through the issue of shares. The example I am citing is for *Top Shelf* (Formosa 2009), a brochure styled to look like a 'top shelf' magazine in line with the proposed storyline – a 'blistering modern comedy, exploring each side of the sexual battlefield, with telling and hilarious consequences', apparently. The document's content seems fairly standard; indeed, it has to be according to the laws governing investment advice, in order to approach prospective shareholders. EIS Legislation, risk factors and rules on Gift Aid: all are carefully outlined. Formosa Films also seeks to reassure future partners by referring to the company's previous involvement in music video director Neil Thompson's watchable gangland/clubland/bouncers feature debut *Clubbed* (2008). Yet the document seems evasive on the topic of that film's actual financial performance: after costing an estimated £2 million, its January 2009 opening weekend grossed just £12,683 at the box office.

Such actuarial strategies are not confirmed to Formosa, but routine across the industry. For instance, Black and Blue Films – 'one of the UK's leading producers of high-concept, low-budget genre specific films' – offers similar investor benefits,[6] while combining gangster and horror stories with a familiar cast from Creative Britain's heyday. If, say, Jonathan Glendening's *Strippers Versus Werewolves* (2011) is not to your taste, it could be that you are judging it on aesthetic grounds or speculating about its future box office performance. It is less likely that its merits as a financial instrument would be considered. Director Uwe Boll is widely reviled (including a 364,572+ signature petition calling on him to retire immediately) for his pre-2005 use of German tax shelters to fund tedious video game adaptations. Yet away from the British-based blockbusters of James Bond and Harry Potter, funny money and fictitious capital rule the filmmaking roost.

6 http://www.blackandbluefilms.co.uk/investors.html

Afterword

As the caricatures and critiques flourished, the occupational identity of 'freelance creative' was evidently failing to inspire. It is unlikely that it will return to those glory days. Since its election in 2010, the Conservative-led coalition has been formally committed to a programme of deficit reduction, in which arts funding has fared badly. For the time being, some of the peculiar financial arrangements that served to subsidise amateur film making can just about survive. In a new decade of economic gloom, it makes sense to lay to rest the previous years of waste and confusion in pursuit of 'living the dream'. Yet the purpose of this chapter is not simply to analyse historically a cultural sensibility that is not to be repeated; nor would it be accurate to write up the experience as a 'warning from history'. High hopes in Tweetdeck, LinkedIn and Silicon Roundabout should lead to the sensible and necessary questioning and criticism of the myths that could bind a new generation to a bogus prescription for prosperity. At the time of writing, an unseemly row over internships underlines the importance of challenging glamorous public fictions that would commit young workers to years of unproductive activity.

References

Amis, M. (1995). *The Information.* London: Flamingo.

Baldry, H. (1981). *The Case for the Arts*. London: Martin Secker & Warburg.

Barnfield, G. (2010). 'Born Yesterday: By treating amateur journalism as a threat, the UGC controversy ignores history', *Proof*: Journalists Defending Journalism Set 1, the Scale and Origins of the Threat to Journalism January, available at http://www.proof-reading.org/born-yesterday, accessed 8 August 2011.

Carey, J. (2005). *What Good are the Arts?* London: Faber & Faber.

Carlaw, K. et al. (2007). 'Beyond the hype: Intellectual Property and the Knowledge Society/Knowledge Economy', in M. McAleer and L. Oxley (eds) *Economic and Legal Issues in Intellectual Property*. Oxford and Chichester Wiley-Blackwell.

Clews, A. and Clews, D. (2009). 'And I also teach: The professional development of teaching creatives', *Journal of Arts & Communities*, 1(3), 265-78.

Courtney, D. (2006). *Dave Courtney's Heroes and Villains*. London: Virgin.

Davenport, N. (2002). 'Doffing the cap to nihilism', *Sp!ked*, 15 January http://www.spiked-online.com/Articles/00000002D3AC.htm, accessed 1 August 2011.

Dean, W. (ed.) (2010). *The Ultimate Guide to Mad Men: The Guardian Companion to the Slickest Show on Television*. London: Guardian Books.

Fast, H. (1982). *Max*. New York: Houghton Mifflin.

Florida, R. (2003). *The Rise of the Creative Class*. New York: Basic Books.

Formosa Films (2009). *Top Shelf Offer Document*. London: Formosa/privately published.

Fowler, C. (1998). *Soho Black*. London: Time Warner.

Handy, C. (1995). *The Empty Raincoat: Making Sense of the Future*. London: Random House Business.

Heartfield, J. (2000). *Great Expectations: The Creative Industries in the New Economy*. London: Design Agenda.

Heartfield, J. (1998). *Need and Desire in the Post-Material Economy*. Sheffield: Sheffield Hallam University Press.

Home, S. (2004). *Down and Out in Shoreditch and Hoxton*. London: Do-Not Press.

Jeffs, L. (2011). 'Wish you worked here?' *ES Magazine*, 5 August, 14-18. http://www.thisislondon.co.uk/lifestyle/esmagazine/article-23975612-wish-you-worked-here.do, accessed 5 August 2011.

Jenkins, R. (2004). 'Is Britain Civilised?' reprinted in P. Diamond (ed.) *New Labour's Old Roots: Revisionist Thinkers in Labour's History 1930-1997*. Exeter: Imprint Academic (OP 1959), 112-22.

Jones, C. and Jolliffe, G. (2000). *The Guerilla Film Maker's Handbook*. 2nd edition. London: Continuum.

King, P. (2010). *Housing Boom and Bust: Owner Occupation, Government Regulation and the Credit Crunch*. London: Routledge.

Leadbeater, C. and Oakley, K. (1999). *The Independents*. London: Demos.

Lerner, J. (2009). *Boulevard of Broken Dreams: Why Public Efforts to Boost Entrepreneurship and Venture Capital Have Failed – and What to Do About It*. Princeton, NJ: Princeton University Press.

Litt, T. (2000). *Corpsing*. London: Penguin.

Newman, K. (1994). *The Quorum*. London: Pocket Books.

Newman, K. (1995). 'Tales of the Overeducated Unemployed: Learning to Write About Films for Money', *Movie Heaven*, London: EMAP, 9-15.

Monk, C. (2007). 'London and contemporary Britain in BBC3's Monkey Dust', *Journal of British Cinema and Television* 4(2), November, 337-60.

Nobbs, D. (2003). *I Didn't Get Where I am Today: An Autobiography*. London: Heinemann.

Puzo, M. (1969). *The Godfather*. New York: G.P. Putnam's Sons.

Ralston, A. (2010). *127 Hours: Between a Rock and a Hard Place*. London: Simon & Schuster.

Redhead, S. (1990). *End of the Century Party: Youth and Pop towards 2000*. Manchester: Manchester University Press.

Robbins, B. (1993). *Secular Vocations: Intellectuals, Professionalism, Culture*. London: Verso/Haymarket.

Schulberg, B. (1992). *What Makes Sammy Run?* London: Vintage Books (OP 1941).

Sennett, R. (1998). *The Corrosion of Character: Personal Consequences of Work in the New Capitalism.* New York: W.W. Norton & Co.

Shapeero, T. (dir.) (2004). 'Jeremy Makes It', *Peep Show* Series 2, episode 8; TX 19 November.

Smith, C. (1998). *Creative Britain*. London: Faber & Faber.

Wilkin, P. (2009). '(Tory) anarchy in the UK: The very peculiar practice of Tory anarchism. *Anarchist Studies*, 17(1), 22-44.

Zinberg, L. (1947). *What D'Ya Know For Sure?* New York: Doubleday.

PART 3
Mobility and Social Policy in London

Chapter 15
Overcoming the Limits to Travel

Alastair Donald

Introduction

Playboy, convict, financier and entrepreneur, had he been alive today Charles Tyson Yerkes would be a match for any of the current generation of high profile bankers in the scandal stakes. Born in Philadelphia in 1837, he was jailed for indiscretions related to colossal stock speculation before gaining a reputation for underhand dealings and political fixing. (Franch 2006) He was the inspiration for the ruthless Frank Cowperwood, protagonist in the trilogy of novels by Theodore Dreiser which concluded with *The Stoic*, based on the financier's time in London (Dreiser 1981).

Yerkes lived in London for just five years before his death in 1905. But in that short time, he was immensely influential in shaping the modern city through the network of construction and operating companies he set up to expand and electrify the London Underground system (Baker and Robbins 1974). A product of the Gilded Age, he brought financial muscle, ruthless deal making abilities, and political acumen. A sharp eye for engineering innovation meant he was perfectly at home in a city where generations of ambitious Victorians with a problem-solving mentality had already developed imaginative solutions to urban problems. Dismissed initially as a 'dreamer' who wants to 'convey all London about in tunnels' (Baker and Robbins 1974: 63), one of London's most insightful historians later described this rogue entrepreneur as the mastermind of an historic transport revolution unrivalled in its scope and complexity (White 2008: 12).

Today, a new transport 'revolution' is underway, and once again the denizens of finance are prominent. The *Cycling Revolution* (Transport for London 2010), launched in 2010, is, according to the London Mayor, a new dawn, a gigantic pedal-powered crusade heralding the 'cyclised' city (Bike Radar 2010). Helping open the gates to cycling's cleaner, greener, healthier, happier future is Barclays Bank, supplying 10,000 bikes for the Barclays Cycle Hire scheme in return for the *kudos* of association with a sustainable mode of transport that helps people lead 'active lives' (Barclays Bank Sponsorship). Barclays also earns the right to splash some bright blue paint around London's streets to create 12 'Barclays Cycle Super Highways', a paint job that is scheduled to take five years to complete (Barclays Cycle Superhighways).

It seems fair to say that Yerkes and his Edwardian contemporaries would not be impressed. In 1905, in the exhilarating *The Soul of London*, the modernist writer Ford Madox Ford made his way through lively and congested streets, fascinated and inspired by a city that reverberated to the sounds of trains, trams and the first motor cars. Of cycling, he declared: 'I have always found entering London by bicycle tedious and dispiriting'. As for walking? 'Well some tramps do it still, but I fancy the proceeding is no longer modern' (Madox Ford 1995: 30-1). At a time when London was alive with cranes operating high up in the hazy skyline and workers flooding in daily from the new suburbs and beyond, Maddox Ford was enthralled by this modern city with a big future, whose dynamism expressed itself through ceaseless motion: 'England is a small country. The world is infinitesimal amongst the planets. But London is illimitable' (Madox Ford 1995: 15).

By contrast, the common sentiment today seems to be that we move too fast and too far; that we have become too mobile. This sentiment is explicit in *Slow Down London*, launched in 2009 'to inspire Londoners to improve their lives by slowing down' (Slow Down London). Traffic jams, crowded trains and cheap flights seem to induce fear and loathing of travellers. Detachments of researchers are employed to analyse, quantify and hand down judgement on the supposedly overly zealous travel-appetites that are frequently associated with eco-destruction, failing communities, poor health, and (through congestion) declining economic competitiveness. At the same time, it is often these impacts of travel that transport policy is charged with resolving, to the detriment of improving mobility itself.

This chapter explores the voluminous transport debate. London certainly groans under the weight of various strategies claiming transport will help create 'the best big city on earth' (Greater London Authority 2010: 3). So how mobile are we already, and what, practically, are current strategies likely to achieve in terms of material improvements to mobility? To what extent should transport be a tool for resolving issues other than those related to moving people around? Is it mobility that's the problem, or the lack of it?

While engaging with the debate, this chapter's assessment is that London is now close to being immobilised by transport policy. It calls for a re-assessment of policy, so that the past, present and future benefits of travel are re-asserted. Mobility, this chapter concludes, is worth arguing for on its own account.

London: A city slowing down

In December 1996, a lorry became trapped in the Blackwall Tunnel running under the Thames to the east of London Docklands. With roadworks and bridge repairs to ageing infrastructure closing down alternative routes through the area, the result was an eight-hour gridlock that affected most of the east side of London, both north and south of the Thames (White 2008: 84). Earlier the same year, a Parliamentary Commission reported that vehicle speeds in central London had declined to a level considerably lower than the 12mph regularly achieved by motor driven cabs in

1904 (Department for Transport 2007). According to the acerbic assessment of planner Peter Hall, Londoners were 'stuck in a gluepot' (Hall 1989: 10-28).

As a national trait, traffic pessimism may soon rival gloomy predictions about the weather. Against this mood, it is important to recognise that gridlock was and is still fairly rare. Nevertheless, Hall's comment did capture a city seemingly beset by inertia when it comes to the building of infrastructure. From the 1960s, as new office developments in expanding suburban and metropolitan centres provided jobs outside the urban core, Londoners increasingly opted for the convenience of cars over public transport. Yet as the post-war boom in the UK economy subsided, so under-investment in transport became more pronounced. Between 1967 and 1996, the number of cars in London increased from 1.5 to around 2.7 million, but the plans for an 800 mile, £20 billion motorway programme were abandoned, with nothing to replace it on anything like the same scale. The M25 orbital opened in the mid-1980s, but operated at capacity almost immediately, seemingly only remedying previous under-provision. On the railways, the South East was largely unaffected by Dr Beeching's line-chopping axe (it fell to devastating effect on Britain's rural areas in the 1960s), but by merely sweating existing assets, the system and stock decayed. Underground, the Victoria and Jubilee Lines were welcome additions, but mainly benefited those going to the centre of London (and out again). Large areas of London and its ex-urbs remained disconnected from fast, convenient transport, especially if the journey was suburb to suburb – increasingly a feature of the metropolitan region as it became more complex.

It is interesting to note the upbeat tone of the most recent London Travel Report which highlights 'continued progress in improving many aspects of transport and travel', and asserts that public transport in London is benefiting from 'the longest run of sustained high performance ever recorded' (Transport for London 2010: 1 and 11). It is true that there have been some impressive transport improvements. The extension to the Jubilee Line sets new standards in station design; the Docklands Light Railway, a less impressive piece of infrastructure, nevertheless caters for 200,000 journeys a day; and the extended East London line has now reached Croydon. Some of the engineering is impressive, too. Many people will start their journey to the new Olympic Park from the refurbished St Pancras Station, travelling just seven minutes on new high speed track, before arriving at Stratford International Station, built to span a track 'box' big enough to accommodate three QE2 liners.

All are welcome improvements. But they really only make up for lost time, remedying some of the previous chronic under-investment. Furthermore, substantial expenditure – on rolling stock, station refurbishment, road and footpath repairs – is no doubt needed, and may make travel less arduous, but does little to *expand* travel opportunities. Almost 200 new S-stock trains without partitions between the carriages will make journeys more pleasant. But why have Londoners not been allowed air conditioned trains? The relentless weekend closure of many London Underground lines hints at patch-and-repair for years ahead – a struggle to modernise what already exists, without further expansion.

The bigger story is that the historic trajectory towards *expanding* mobility has stalled. As the dominant system shifted from walking to horsepower, then steam, electricity and onto the combustion engine, by the end of the twentieth century individuals in Britain had increased the distances they travelled to around seven times the levels of the mid-nineteenth century. On the whole, this was not necessarily because of more journeys, or even more time spent travelling. The key achievement was the ability to move faster, more efficiently, more reliably, and therefore further.

Over the last few years, the average time Londoners spend travelling has slightly decreased (Transport for London 2010: 65). That certainly may be something to celebrate. However, it is not a given that more commuting equals less happiness (Layard 2006). Londoners' estimated 68 minutes-a-day average-travelling time is not so onerous, and could anyway become more productive if long-awaited electronic communications were introduced underground (Brewster 2011), or if computer-guided cars ever materialise (Markoff 2010).

More importantly, in the past 20 years the historic advance in distances travelled has ground to a halt. In 2008, the distance covered by Londoners shows no improvement on 1991, averaging 15km per day (Transport for London 2009: 147). For those living in outer London, the gains are being reversed, and distances are falling. In line with the now widely accepted wisdom that society must reduce the 'need to travel' (Department of Transport and the Regions 1998: 8), many will be tempted to see this as a good thing – after all, why travel further than necessary, especially if the journey is likely to be tedious and/or uncomfortable? But as urban commentator Austin Williams points out, '*having* to travel is one thing, simply *wanting* to travel is quite another' (Williams 2008: 17). Having both the option to travel and comfortable means of taking up this option, is surely the most-wanted position to be in.

Historically, we did not absolutely need to get out of the village, but the ambition to lead better lives led us to do so. Material progress has come from the ability to create a more integrated, mobile world. Instead of worrying about *reducing* the need to travel, we set about realising better connections to our fellow human beings over greater distances – historic gains associated with more productive economies and greater individual freedom.

In this sense, just as financialisation is associated with a loss of drive in the 'real economy', so London suffers from reduced momentum towards mobility. Yet there is little in today's commentary on London travel to suggest that the current slowdown is viewed as a problem. To the contrary, in the most recent *Travel in London* report compiled by Transport for London (TfL), the growth of slow modes such as walking and cycling is highlighted as a major achievement (Transport for London 2010: 225-46).

The embrace of slowing down evident in *Travel in London*, reflects a broader cultural despondency with mobility. There is no longer the belief that the benefits of mobility will outweigh the problems it brings. Former Department for Transport scientist David Metz is dubious about mobility: 'we are becoming ever more mobile. But are we better off as a result?' (Metz 2008: 1) The answer for many is an increasingly emphatic 'no'. In a report on what he terms 'hypermobility', the academic John Adams starts with an admission that mobility can be liberating and empowering, before swiftly asserting we can have too much of a good thing. The hypermobile society, he says, is more dispersed, polarised, dangerous, anonymous, obese and crime ridden; but less free, convivial, culturally varied and democratic (Adams 2001: 4-6).

It is notable that contemporary campaigns around transport and urban space no longer present the case for increasing mobility but rather for reductions in it, for example by cutting flights (Plane Stupid), creating 'slow cities'(Slow Down London), or by 're-localising' economic and social arrangements (Hopkins 2008). Even those such as The Campaign for Better Transport who *appear* to argue for improvements, are really advocating reductions, e.g. by campaigning to persuade councils to drop their road schemes (Campaign for Better Transport).

It's in the context of a cultural disenchantment with mobility that transport policy needs to be considered. The Mayor's Transport Strategy starts with the question 'What is our objective?', which elicits the answer: 'It is very simple. It is to help get Londoners from a to b as quickly, as safely, as conveniently, and as cheaply as possible' (Greater London Authority 2010: 3). As a statement of the seemingly obvious aims of a transport system, this is as direct and straightforward as it gets, especially in the abstruse world of transport planning. But over the 400 pages that follow, a commitment to material improvements to help people move from a-to-b is subsumed under a series of environmental and social objectives intended to remedy the problems that mobility is assumed to create. The Secretary of State for Transport in the coalition government, Philip Hammond, captures current expectations of transport policy when he maintains that it should facilitate 'carbon reduction, fiscal discipline, economic growth, social justice and genuine localism' (Hammond 2010). Notable by its absence is a clear commitment to improving mobility.

The problem is that when fiscal discipline, saving the planet or creating community become the priority, the principle of increasing freedom of movement becomes at best compromised, or worse, is viewed as *conflicting* with the other priorities. The transport system is said to be 'an ecosystem in which competing interests must sometimes be balanced' (Greater London Authority 2008: 12). But when transport is seen in terms of closed feedback loops of an ecosystem, it follows that increased mobility will be sacrificed to seemingly more important objectives. Narrowing the roads and building more pavement space in the hope of supporting retailers and enhancing community, become more important than speeding up the flow of traffic. Indeed the roads are often narrowed with the aim of slowing down cars, with the aim of prompting drivers to adopt alternative modes of transport. And if building roads carries the 'danger' of inducing extra traffic (or 'latent demand'), and increasing emissions, then as junior transport minister Norman Baker once admitted, sometimes 'his brief … meant asking people not to travel' (Pickard and Rigby 2011). The effect of the cultural turn against mobility is that transport policy has effectively become divorced from commitment to the technical improvements which would expand it. While there are few ambitious programmes of infrastructural provision, seldom has there been more engineering of the financial, social and environmental spheres now associated with transport.

Financial Engineering

In an age when train passengers have become customers, guards have transmogrified into 'Revenue Protection Officers', and the most prominent signage within London relates to the charging mechanisms associated with congestion, parking and speeding, the transactional nature of the travel experience seems ever more prominent. The Oyster Card swipe system no doubt provides convenient access, but equally, the visibility accorded to its 'integrated revenue management systems and services' suggests the broader importance of financialisation in shaping travel.

In the nineteenth century, railway mania played a formative role in the City of London's reinvention as a specialist financial and commercial district with no room for a residential population. Indeed banks were often conjoined to railway ventures, while the multiplication of insurance companies took place at a time when the equation of speed with risk represented a minor Victorian neurosis (White 2007: 39). Over recent decades, as UK PLC has homed in on public subsidies to keep it afloat, a new 'railways mania' has emerged. This time banks, finance houses, consultants, accountants and City lawyers have been gorging on state-sponsored rail, construction and engineering programmes. Whereas rapid technological developments in transportation, energy delivery and communications once provided opportunities for the finance barons to make massive profits, today the entwinement of finance and infrastructure reflects the private sector's hunger for public money to offset its own lack of dynamism.

In urban infrastructure and across construction as a whole, a web of state-capital linkages has been created, including the much-criticised Private Finance Initiatives (PFI) and associated Public Private Partnerships (PPP), but also extending to the wider integration of the private sector with public commissions (Mullan 2002). One indication of this entanglement comes in the way that major projects such as Crossrail and Thameslink support new types of private sector firms such as 'specialist rail sector finance adviser' Quasar, which can command vast fees to manage delivery of what are really public services. Capita Symonds, a sub-division of Capita and the sixth largest multi-disciplinary consultancy in the UK with over 50 offices, works almost exclusively on large state sector infrastructure projects where feasibility studies, procurement and, eventually, construction, provide attractive returns (Capita Symonds). Whether feeding from the enhanced values created by public monies dedicated to station redevelopment, or, as in the Shard London Bridge (Lydall 2011), benefiting from public sector organisations relocating office space to projects that otherwise cannot make the values stack up, an un-dynamic economy is propped up by subsidy.

The coalition government has asserted its intention of 'moving away from the top-down command and control system that has characterised Government in Britain since the Second World War', (Hammond 2010). For many critics of PPP and PFI, this amounts to political gravy for private sector companies at a time of rampant neo-liberal markets (Whitfield 2006). Yet, as James Heartfield has pointed out, this is not a new private sector boom, but a growing, state-dependent economy of concessions (Heartfield 2009). The Metronet consortium, for example, secured a 30-year contract worth potentially £17 billion for the maintenance of Underground infrastructure, all with a 95 per cent government-backed guarantee to cover debt obligations. Consequently, when the company went into administration, it meant a bill to the Exchequer of up to £410 million (Pawyer 2002). Such are the ongoing tangles of this web that in 2011, Bombardier, a former member of the Metronet consortium, became preferred bidder for the latest £1 billion contract for updating of signalling (*Railway Observer* 2011).

According to Heartfield, the contracting out of infrastructure provision reveals a state shorn of confidence in its own ability to organise either wealth production or the associated delivery of public goods such as transport. A report by the National Audit Office makes clear that it was not so much commitment to market principles that led to the appointment of Metronet, but the Department for Transport's inability to prevail upon London Underground to deliver enhancement and maintenance projects to time and budget (National Audit Office 2009: 4). Even a shambolic consortium seemed a better bet. In the risk-averse world of infrastructure provision, the public sector avoids taking responsibility by pushing contracts out to the private sector, but at the cost of taking on the financial risks that the risk-averse private sector refuses to bear.

The latest financial instrument is Tax Increment Financing (TIF), which seems likely to be introduced in 2012 to encourage up-front finance for infrastructure, drawn down against an anticipated growth in business rates. Dubbed 'scary son of PFI' amidst speculation that deals will be kept 'off balance sheet' in public sector accounting systems (Watts 2011), TIF is modelled on US-style municipal debt issuance, which, ironically, back in 2003 was (then) Mayor Livingstone's preferred alternative to the Metronet PPP for London Underground.

TIF has been promoted as part of the coalition government's 'localism' agenda, with emphasis on the benefits of local growth incentives and devolving greater control over finance to local authorities. Alternatively, it can be seen as a way of expanding processes associated with financialisation into new areas. Just as initiatives such as PFI and PPP were extended from an initial focus on major transport infrastructure schemes to encompass schools, hospitals, prisons and courts, so TIFs effectively expand the state-capital links into new areas. Builders, project managers and businesses will be directed to new models of finance at a time when developers resist Section 106 agreements for even relatively minor infrastructure projects. Extending financial intermediation to a local level may prompt the proliferation of procurement, risk and cost management processes. But given that the cost of private financing is likely to be prohibitively high for all but the safest projects, the public sector is again likely to bear most of the risks (Sear 2011).

From the 'Greater Good' to Local Goods

According to Transport Secretary Philip Hammond, sustainable transport planned at the local level helps create the Big Society, distributing power back to 'individuals, families, communities and local government, devising solutions to our many challenges from the bottom-up, rather than from the top-down' (Hammond 2010). But how does this vision of sustainable transport fit with the need to reinvigorate a *metropolitan* economy?

Back in 1981, the London of Borough of Bromley protested that local ratepayers should be exempted from contributions to 'Fares Fair', a subsidy programme that reduced fares within Greater London. The benefits of 'Fares Fair' were widely exaggerated – the real problem then, as now, was chronic under-provision (Gosling). Yet when the Law Lords sided with Bromley, and subsidised travel collapsed across London, it was clear that the state lacked the vision and ambition necessary to defend the principle of the 'greater good' in the form of universal provision of cheaper fares. Since then, the 'greater good' has been reinterpreted to mean the need to make sacrifices. 'Real political leadership is always about persuading people to *forgo* things for the general good', argued one commentator commending the London congestion charge as way of creating sustainable travel behaviour by curtailing travel choices (Ashley 2004). The discussion of limiting travel not only revolves around shifting people out of cars and onto public transport, but also entails recreating social and economic interactions on a more localised basis. As one planner puts it, 'light' transport systems are not *per se* sustainable – only less unsustainable than commuting by car (Bradshaw cited in Thakara 2011). Therefore, argues design consultant John Thackara, it is necessary to create a shift from 'faster' to 'closer' in order to 'optimise local-ness' (ibid.).

To this end, the Transition Towns project promotes the idea that rather than travelling to 'external economies', the community is the scale upon which many goods are best produced and consumed. In South London this resulted in the 'Brixton Pound', which can only be spent in small, local suppliers rather than chain stores where the money would 'leak' into the wider economy (Hickman 2009). Given this limited edition local pound soon appeared for sale on Ebay, the creative types of Brixton were clearly not averse to a bit of financial speculation. Ironically, this new 'local' currency and the expensive organic cafes, boutiques and galleries it supports in a gentrified area of London, are made possible by the high levels of disposable income derived from London's position as a finance centre, and from credit in the form of increased levels of personal debt. The 'urban villages' are no less dependent on credit than the City.

Further out from the centre, many of London's suburbs are still characterised by low value back office functions, state supported public services and low grade retail. Also in outer London, the car continues to predominate, and here, too, the intention is to localise the economy through creating 'mixed use' centres. For Thackara, the sustainable solution to the transport problem is 'think more, move less', a sort of high-tech localism or 'cache and carry' as he puts it, where one should 'export the recipe and sometimes the production equipment, but source raw material and distribute locally' (Thackara 2011).

Retreating to this virtual village not only seems a fairly insular vision, but risks reinforcing the difficulties of realising a more productive economy in outer London where there are many successful business, but ironically they are often located outside the suburban 'town' centres in business parks mainly accessible by car. Furthermore, the suburban outer London economy is outperformed not just by central London but also by the towns and cities beyond the London green belt, partly because these attract more businesses by offering superior access to motorways, rail and airports. The relatively unproductive outer London economy is not so much in need of transport localism as trapped by it. The area is dependent on the state to create jobs and hindered from attracting more dynamic wealth creating businesses by the lack of ambitious infrastructure schemes which might otherwise overcome its inaccessibility to regional and global networks.

Good Behaviour

If transport provision is undermined by financial engineering, and constrained by localism and sustainability, then the final blow is that transport strategies are being reorganised around a moralising agenda of behaviour management. For example, it was notable that the first act of Mayor Boris Johnson on his election in 2008 was to ban alcohol on the tubes and buses. Rather than revealing, as Johnson argues, 'a mission that is at every turn to improve the experience of travel' (Greater London Authority 2008: 18), in reality the ban was a solution to a problem that did not exist. When Johnson somewhat hopefully suggested that the ban was 'being effectively enforced by the collective will of the public', it did however reveal how transport policy now seeks to win support for behaviour modification and interpersonal codes of conduct. The state may have few answers to the lack of dynamism in the economy and society, but it has an appetite for managing behaviour.

This appetite was already discernible in the introduction of the inner London congestion charge. It is hard to make sense of this levy in terms of the urban economy. Economists point to congestion on London's roads costing about £2bn each year (Greater London Authority 2010: 17), yet in the absence of a widely agreed definition of congestion, this can only be guesswork. What's more, when the charge was introduced in 2003, peak hour traffic in central London had already dropped around 40 per cent since the mid-1990s, indicating that this measure was not motivated by worsening traffic levels (Department of Transport 2007). Since its introduction the number of drivers has dropped by 70,000 (Milmo 2008) and only six per cent of commuters to central London now drive (Transport for

London 2010: 8). But charging people to drive – a policy which reduces choice rather than increases supply – still has not delivered improvements to the speed of traffic. Indeed, speeds have decreased by around seven per cent since 2003 (ibid.).

While the congestion charge was formally introduced to ration scarce road space, it is primarily a mechanism for apportioning blame. It ensured that driving became a moral – rather than a modal – choice (Pierce and Williams 2011). When Johnson scrapped his predecessor's ('vindictive') £25 charge for SUVs, he pointed out that it was not his job to punish the motorist by treating every car journey as a sinful act (Greater London Authority 2008: 11). Yet a 'sinful act' is precisely the way that driving is now treated. According to 'sustainable entrepreneur' Pooran Desai, driving disconnects people from society, so 'if we want happier communities, we should foster.... less mobility' (Desai 2008: 44-51). As developer of the high profile south London eco-estate BedZED, Desai was true to his word when he cut parking places in order to remedy 'car dependency' – a view of drivers as addicts, with policymakers and sustainable entrepreneurs cast in the role of saving them from their addiction. That Johnson now aims to offer a range of measures which 'help' people out of their cars by 'persuasion, not persecution' may be more subtle. Yet it is no less authoritarian. Rather it indicates that in some areas of policy, the blunt commands of the 'nanny state' are giving way to a 'nudge' towards cleaner, greener alternatives to driving.

For some Londoners, cycling is an enjoyable pursuit, and hopefully it will remain so. But in transport policy, the promotion of cycling as a means to create the Big Society is more than a little problematic. The *Guardian*'s design critic objects to Barclays smothering blue paint over London's public spaces in what may be 'the largest piece of corporate branding in existence' (McGuirk 2010). But the cycling revolution is not really about financial returns, corporate branding, or even the practicalities of providing bikes and spaces to ride them in. It is a project loaded with moralism (O'Neill 2010). Just as the congestion charge targets bad drivers, so cycling is intended to promote good citizens. 'The cycle-ised city is the civilised city', Johnson claims, while Barclays, Chief Executive Bob Diamond adds that: 'Citizenship is not peripheral to our business, but rather lies at the heart of what we do' (Barclays News Report 2011).

It is not clear why cycling should be considered civilised. Indeed, the fact that they are thus equated suggests a society that has lost sight of what civilisation means.Furthermore, it is questionable whether being bossed or cajoled into a saddle is the sign of a good citizen – a figure usually understood as an autonomous individual, capable of making his own choices. But amid fears of social atomisation, the 'Cycling Revolution' aims teach people how to behave and act responsibly, so that city streets become places 'where everyone respects each other's right to use the road, where they stick to the rules of the road, and where everyone recognises their duty of care' (Transport for London 2010). As ever, the authorities stand by ready to extend the rules and enforce responsibilities. In order to combat the previously unknown problem of the 'Lycra lout', the coalition government is now supporting a new offence of causing death by dangerous cycling (Walker 2011).

The figure of the cyclist fits with broader attempts to redefine responsibility at a time when society is often portrayed as out of control and lacking restraint. Taking responsibility for our health has been especially prominent, for example in public campaigns which highlight the dangers of lax behaviour related to smoking, drinking and what we eat. In this context, the cyclist – who takes physical exercise and looks after himself – is now viewed as virtuous. Accordingly, in recent years the well-established figure of the 'sustainable traveller' is now accompanied in policy documents by the 'active traveller' in the form of cyclists and pedestrians (Department for Transport 2011: 43-9).

The role now accorded to travel is consistent with a society that struggles to find a productive outlet for human talents. In the past, the point of travel was mostly to undertake activities once we got to the destination, whether to work with colleagues in a factory, meet with friends, or to see new places and participate in new experiences. To these ends, it was recognised that we needed to get wherever we wanted to go, as quickly as possible. Today, in an economy geared less to production, in a culture prone to prolonged deferment, the activities to be undertaken on arrival – the *point* of the journey – seem to have become less important. Instead, travel itself is the activity. Travel gives us identity and moral virtue, so long as we live by the code of the 'active traveller'.

Reclaim the Streets for Mobility

The overwhelming acceptance of the Cycling Revolution indicates the absence of any substantial debate about how London might be reshaped to deliver material improvements to mobility, i.e. on the tracks, in the air, and on roads, where four wheels dominate rather than two. But as long as increased mobility remains secondary to the delivery of fiscal, environmental or social objectives, even initiatives that purport to offer transport improvements will be subsumed by the moralistic, localising, immobilising culture that pervades policy development.

Take, for example, the Olympic Games, which have rightly been criticised for turning a sporting occasion into the Regeneration Games (Woudhuysen 2008). For an event also billed as the 'public transport Games' (Gibson 2011), some new infrastructure is being built, but trains and track come second to creating 'a (*sustainable) behavioural* transport legacy [author's emphasis]' (Transport for London 2010: 143). In this spirit, transport minister Norman Baker (Pickard and Rigby 2011) has encouraged firms to experiment with cutting commuting and business trips. Of course there's nothing wrong with companies cutting out wasteful trips. But Baker is really suggesting that business should be reorganised in accordance with new limitations on travel.

For Baker, rush hour is an 'insane concept'. He adds: 'It is crazy that we all travel on the same train on the same day at the same time. We should be able to spread the peak across different times' (ibid.). In this Malthusian transport policy, the message is there are too many of us, trying to do too much. Rather than creating infrastructure that accommodates working practices – recognising that businesses liaise across the course of a relatively defined working day – it encourages the re-orientation of working patterns (and individual lives) around the presumed limits to transport provision, and the assumed need to change individual behaviour. Without reclaiming the progressive concept of mobility and the idea that there are great benefits to moving as many people as around as freely as possible, then a mobile society, and especially mobile people – with their 'insane' desire to move around when they need to – will continue to be seen as a problem that must be contained.

Conclusion: Overcoming the Limits to Travel

One of the things that is lost amidst all the planet-saving, community-enhancing, citizens-creating chatter about the benefits of public transport, walking, and cycling, is that even in an expansive built-up region such as London, with a central area relatively well-served by public transport, it remains the case that overwhelmingly, the vast majority of travel is undertaken by car: 30.4 billion passenger kilometres per year by road versus 17.4 billion for all forms of public transport combined (Transport for London 2010: 7-8).

Whatever the problems that cars create, their convenience is remarkable; hence their widespread appeal. Yet rather than recognise this and aim to resolve the associated problems, transport strategy proceeds on the basis that choices will have to be constrained: 'The car will continue to have a role to play for journeys that cannot efficiently be catered for by public transport, walking or cycling, and the transport system will *allow* for car use where appropriate' (Greater London Authority 2010: 7, author's emphasis). This grudging attitude does not mean that provision will be improved; quite the opposite. In the Mayor's Transport Strategy, remarkably, out the 158 pages dedicated to Transport Proposals, which include sections dedicated to cycling, walking, river crossings, and even the 'Blue Ribbon Network', proposals for developing the road network merit just a single paragraph at the end of a section on road management. There we find out that 'Due to limited space, the approach taken in London is generally "to get more from the existing road network"' (ibid: 158).

Such a dearth of imagination, lack of vision and collapse of confidence in human ingenuity, reflects a society at an impasse. Back at the turn of the twentieth century when Yerkes arrived in London, within the memory of a single lifetime, the *pre-existing* Dickensian city had been largely transformed, adapting it to the spatial and mobility requirements of the early twentieth century. Today in the more dynamic East, in Beijing or Shanghai, modern underground networks, high speed train linkages, and new motorway systems are being built in and around existing cities; in the past London, too, learned to build under, over, and sometimes through what already existed. Admittedly, as in the demolition of slum areas such as St Giles, even then the aims were sometimes as much to do with social engineering as infrastructure. Nevertheless, transformation was pursued in the belief that improvements could be realised and social advances would result.

Today's improvements certainly should not be limited to roads. Investment in better public transport, underground and overground, is also vital. High speed links to the surrounding regions would provide long overdue recognition that London does not stop at the green belt, but is effectively, as H.G. Wells anticipated a century ago, a megalopolis covering much of southern England (Wells 1902). The danger is that by basing decisions for major infrastructure projects merely on the outcomes of cost benefit analysis and eco-audits, progress will be undermined for decades to come. Transport does not always pay its way, and it does create emissions; and megaprojects are today associated with excessive risk (Flyvbjerg, Bruzelius and Rothengatter 2003). But they can also bring positive changes in new and unforeseen ways.

In the current climate, critics of high speed rail may hold sway when they claim that there will be only diminishing [financial] returns, and billions will be spent to save only a few minutes on journey-times (Glaeser 2011). And even if environmental auditors are not immobilised by this particular criticism, there will always be someone to point out that 'it's better to take a high speed train than to fly. It would be better still not to have to make the journey at all and to have some peace and stillness in our lives' (Monbiot 2010).

Here, too, history offers a pointed contrast. In the 1830s when engineers were planning to lay the millions and millions of bricks that would result in railways running over Londoners heads, many thought it absurd that locomotives should cross the city at more than twice the speed of a stagecoach: 'we will back Old Father Thames against Greenwich railway for any sum', they cried (Wolmar 2009). But the railway was built in the end, because of an ambitious social climate, and belief in human ingenuity. To achieve the same today requires less of the current emphasis on potential environmental and other harms, and rehabilitation of the belief that increased mobility is a sign of significant social advance.

To achieve a transport system befitting London in the twenty-first century, there needs to be clarity of purpose in transport, starting with a restatement of the benefits of travel and a campaign to win support for freedom of movement and increased mobility. As long as transport is viewed as the means to realise non-transport objectives, then infrastructure construction will remain a *justificatory* process, in which even its advocates are always on the defensive about wanting more travel. On the other hand, having regained our conviction as to the benefits of greater mobility, the ingenuity of designers and engineers could be put to much better use, constructing systems that enable more people to get out of the urban village and take a good look at the world.

References[1]

Adams, J. (2001). 'The Social Consequences of Hypermobility', Lecture, Royal Society of Arts, 21 November 2001.

Ashley, J. (2004). 'It's time to call time on our cheap flight hypocrisy', The *Guardian*, 15 April 2004. Available at http://www.guardian.co.uk/news/2004/apr/15/comment.environment.

Baker, T.G. and Robbins, M. (1974). *A History of London Transport*, Vol II, The Twentieth Century to 1970. London: Allen & Unwin.

Barclays Bank Sponsorship: Frequently Asked Questions. Available at http://group.barclays.com/What-we-do/Sponsorship/London-cycle-schemes/Barclays-Cycle-Hire-FAQs#1231784879044.

Barclays Cycle Superhighways: Routes and Maps, available at http://www.tfl.gov.uk/roadusers/cycling/15832.aspx.

Barclays News (2010). Barclays publishes Citizenship Report 2010, 26 April 2011, available at http://group.barclays.com/News/Barclays-news/NewsArticle/1231787366491.html.

Bike Radar (2010). London's Barclays Cycle Hire Scheme Goes Live, 30 July 2010, available at http://www.bikeradar.com/news/article/londons-barclays-cycle-hire-scheme-goes-live-27224/.

Brewster, T. (2011). London Underground ditches mobile plans, ITPRO, 1 April 2011, available at http://www.itpro.co.uk/632434/london-underground-ditches-mobile-plans.

Campaign for Better Transport (2010). Roads to nowhere, available at http://www.bettertransport.org.uk/.

Department for Transport (2011). *Creating Growth, Cutting Carbon Making Sustainable Local Transport Happen*. London: Department of Transport.

Department for Transport (2007). Transport Statistics Great Britain, 2007, available at http://www.parliament.uk/documents/commons/lib/research/rp99/rp99-111.pdf.

Department of Transport and the Regions (1998). *A New Deal for Transport: Better for Everyone*. London: DETR.

Desai P. with E. Blake (2008). 'Is Happiness the Key to unlocking sustainability?' in Jane Wernick (ed.) *Building Happiness: Architecture to Make You Smile*. London: Black Dog Publishing.

Dreiser, T. (1981). *The Stoic*. New York: Signet.

Franch, J. (2006). *The Robber Baron: The Life of Charles Tyson Yerkes*. Champaign: University of Illinois Press.

Flyvbjerg, B., Bruzelius, N. and Rothengatter, W. (2003). *Megaprojects and Risk: An Anatomy of Ambition*. Cambridge: Cambridge University Press.

1 All websites last accessed 16 May 2011

Gibson, O. (2011). 'London's transport system ready for "extreme" demands of 2012 Olympics', The *Guardian*, 15 April 2011 http://www.guardian.co.uk/sport/2011/apr/15/olympics-2012-london-transport-system.

Glaeser, E. (2011). 'Our best plan for growth is to set our cities free', *Financial Times* 7 March 2011 http://www.ft.com/cms/s/0/d6074404-48f5-11e0-af8c-00144feab49a.html#axzz1MvvmYd00.

Gordon, I. (2006). *Future Growth in the Outer London Economy* (Revised and Updated Version), December 2006 http://www.westlondonalliance.org/wlaextranet.nsf/0/7A3010B12CF3BBBC8025725C00729A65/$file/FutureGrowthOuterLondonRevised_Jan07.pdf.

Gosling, T. (undated). *Blueprint for a Green London* http://www.bilderberg.org/farefare.htm.

Greater London Authority (2008). *Way to Go: Planning for Better Transport*. London: Greater London Authority.

Greater London Authority (2010). *Mayor's Transport Strategy*. London: Greater London Authority.

Hall, P. (1989). *London 2001*. London: Unwin Hyman.

Hammond P. (2010). Sustainable Transport, Speech, IBM START Conference: Business Summit, 10 September 2010 http://www.dft.gov.uk/press/speechesstatements/speeches/hammond20100910.

Heartfield, J. (2009). 'State Capitalism in Britain', *Mute,* 29 June 2009 http://www.metamute.org/en/content/state_capitalism_in_britain.

Hickman L. (2009). 'Will the Brixton pound buy a brighter future?', The *Guardian*, 16 September 2009. http://www.guardian.co.uk/environment/2009/sep/16/will-brixton-pound-work.

Hopkins, R. (2008). *The Transition Handbook*. Totnes: Green Books.

Layard, R. (2006). *Happiness: Lessons from a New Science*. London: Penguin Books.

Lydall, R. (2011). 'It's not quite what Wren had in mind', London *Evening Standard*, 12 January 2011 http://www.thisislondon.co.uk/standard/article-23913452-its-not-quite-what-wren-had-in-mind-shard-towers-over-st-pauls.do.

Madox Ford, F. (1995). *The Soul of London: A Survey of a Modern City*. London: Everyman, [1905].

Markoff, J. (2010). 'Guided by Computers and Sensors, a Smooth Ride at 60 Miles Per Hour', *New York Times*, 9 October 2010, http://www.nytimes.com/2010/10/10/science/10googleside.html.

Metz, D. (2008). *The Limits to Travel: How Far Will You Go?* London: Earthscan.

http://john-adams.co.uk/wp-content/uploads/2006/hypermobilityforRSA.pdf.

McGuirk, J. (2010). 'Boris Johnson's London Cycle Hire scheme flogs our birthright to Barclays', The *Guardian*, 27 July 2010. http://www.guardian.co.uk/artanddesign/2010/jul/27/boris-johnson-london-cycle-hire-barclays.

Milmo, D. (2008). 'Transport: London still gridlocked despite congestion charge', The *Guardian*, 7 August 2008 http://www.guardian.co.uk/politics/2008/aug/07/congestioncharging.transport.

Monbiot, G. (2010). 'What's not to like about high-speed rail? The case simply hasn't been made', The *Guardian*, 17 May 2010 http://www.guardian.co.uk/commentisfree/2010/may/17/high-speed-rail-policy-carbon-emissions.

Mullan, P. (2002). 'Propping up the Private', *Spiked-online*, 31 October 2002, http://www.spiked-online.com/articles/00000006DB07.htm.

National Audit Office (2009). *Department of Transport: The Failure of Metronet*. London: The Stationery Office, June 2009.

O'Neill, B. (2010). 'A "cycling revolution"? On your bike, Boris', *Spiked-online*, 22 July 2010.

Pawyer, V. (2002). 'Cameron's aid Metronet in tube bid', 18 February 2002, *The Lawyer* http://www.thelawyer.com/camerons-aids-metronet-in-tube-bid/103494.article.

Pickard, J. and Rigby, E. (2011). 'Plea to business on 2012 travel', *Financial Times*, 6 April 2011 http://www.ft.com/cms/s/0/5a8a7864-6079-11e0-9fcb-00144feab49a.html#axzz1MvvmYd00.

Pierce, D. and Williams, A. (2011). 'The Sanitized City', in A. Williams and A. Donald (eds) *The Lure of the City: From Slums to Suburbs*. London: Pluto.

Plane Stupid, http://www.planestupid.com/.

Railway Observer (2010). 'Bombardier Selected as Preferred Bidder for London Tube Major Signalling Upgrade' http://railwayobserver.com/index.php/mass-transit-systems/europe/248-bombardier-selected-as-preferred-bidder-for-london-tube-major-signalling-upgrade.

Sear, C. (2011). House of Commons Briefing Note: Tax Increment Financing, 7 March 2011 http://www.parliament.uk/briefingpapers/commons/lib/research/briefings/snpc-05797.pdf.

Slow Down London (2008). Living life in real time http://www.slowdownlondon.co.uk/about/.

Thackara, J. (2011). 'The Gram Junkies: In Transportation Design the Key Issue Is Not Speed, but Weight', *Design Observer*, 12 January 2011 http://changeobserver.designobserver.com/entry.html?entry=24178.

Transport for London (2009). *Travel in London*: Report 1: Key Trends and Developments.

Transport for London (2010). *Cycling Revolution London*. Greater London Authority/Transport for London.

Transport for London (2010). *Travel in London*: Report 3.

Walker, P. (2011). 'Death by dangerous cycling law gets government support', The *Guardian*, 10 April 2011 http://www.guardian.co.uk/politics/2011/apr/10/death-dangerous-cycling-law-government-support.

Watts, R. (2011). 'Meet Tif, scary son of PFI', *Sunday Times*, 17 April 2011.

Wells, H.G. (1902). *Anticipations of the Reaction of Mechanical and Scientific Progress upon Human Life and Thought*. London, Chapman & Hall.

White, J. (2008). *London in the 20th Century: A City and its People.* London: Vintage.

White, J. (2007). *London in the 19th Century: A Human Awful Wonder of God.* London: Vintage.

Whitfield, D. (2006). *Financing Infrastructure in the 21st Century.* London: European Services Strategy Unit, November.

Williams, A. (2008). *Enemies of Progress: The Dangers of Sustainability.* London: Societas.

Wolmar, C. (2009). *Blood, Iron and Gold: How the Railways Transformed the World.* London: Atlantic.

Woudhuysen, J. (2008). The 'Regeneration Games', *Battle in Print*, London: Institute of Ideas, 31 March 2008 http://www.battleofideas.org.uk/index.php/2011/battles/1132/.

Chapter 16
Immigration and London's Economy

Gavin Poynter

> I believe controlling immigration and bringing it down is of vital importance to the future of our country. That's why during the election campaign, Conservatives made a clear commitment to the British people … that we would aim to reduce net migration to the levels we saw in the 1980s and 1990s.
>
> Now we are in government, we are on track to meet that aim. We are controlling legal immigration – having introduced a cap on non-EU economic migrants. We are clamping down on illegal immigration. And we are getting to grips with the asylum system too. The UK Border Agency is now close to clearing the back-log of almost half a million asylum cases. Our action is working.[1]
>
> A major rethink of Government policy is required as the cap would have a significant negative and disproportionate impact on London. It will put the economic recovery at risk by creating skills gaps and placing London at a competitive disadvantage in the global competition for talent and inward investment.[2]

Introduction

The coalition government's commitment to control immigration through the introduction of a cap on the number of non-EU economic migrants entering the country, generated much debate in London. According to Prime Minister, David Cameron, in his speech delivered in Southampton in April, 2011, the government was seeking a new and more balanced approach to immigration. Whilst recognising the valuable contribution of immigrants to UK society and economy, it was necessary to re-assert government control especially over non-EU economic

1 *The Guardian* (2011) 'David Cameron on Immigration full text of the speech', *The Guardian*, Thursday 14 April 2011. http://www.guardian.co.uk/politics/2011/apr/14/david-cameron-immigration-speech-full-text. Accessed 12 May 2011.

2 *Immigration Matters* (2010) 'London Mayor Boris Johnson demands immigration cap is scrapped', *Immigration Matters*, 11 September, 2010, http://www.immigrationmatters.co.uk/london-mayor-boris-johnson-demands-immigration-cap-is-scrapped.html, accessed May 12, 2011.

migration, including large numbers of students entering the UK to study with poor quality educational providers. In the wake of the recession, it was important to enhance the job opportunities and improve the skills of the UK workforce and reduce the potential for tensions to rise within the UK's communities. Some of the loudest voices expressing opposition were Boris Johnson, the city's Conservative mayor, and employers including London First, an umbrella organisation of London-based enterprises, universities, the NHS and restaurant owners.

The immigration debate has a particular resonance for London. The city has long been the first location for migrants entering the UK and its cosmopolitan character, arising from success waves of immigration, makes it different to other British cities. This chapter examines the relationship between the development of London's economy and recent patterns of migration, drawing attention to the complex ways in which a global city has absorbed immigrants into an economy whose centrality to the international flows of finance capital has also generated significant inward flows of migrant labour to service the city. The chapter divides into three sections. The first identifies the three main phases of inward international migration in the post-1945 period. The second section briefly reviews political and social responses to each of these phases and, lastly, the contemporary form of London's labour market is discussed in relation to conceptualising London's status as a global city.

Recent Trends in Immigration

Migration into and out of London has several dimensions but the city's population has been shaped since 1945 by three main phases of inward international migration. First, New Commonwealth migrants came to London in the 1950s and 1960s. They were attracted to the UK by the prospect of employment in stable jobs where there were shortages of labour in industries such as transport and health. It was this wave of migration, particularly from the Indian subcontinent and the Caribbean, that laid the foundations of London's current population of black and Asian ethnic minority communities. This population grew from approximately 240,000 in 1961 to about 2 million by 2001 (Gordon and Travers 2006: 5). Discrimination, segregation and racial violence arose especially in periods of economic downturn, such as the early 1970s, and successive governments sought to curb immigration from the New Commonwealth countries over subsequent years. Settlement in Britain following the 1971 Immigration Act, for example, was only allowed if applicants were British passport holders and could demonstrate that they had a parent or grandparent who had been born in the UK.

A second phase of inward migration from overseas gathered momentum in the 1990s. Migrants arrived from several different continents and countries including regions of the former Soviet Union, Latin and South America, as well as mainland Europe and North America. The 2001 census recorded 47 communities in London with populations of over 10,000, a figure that was probably an underestimate given the inaccuracies arising from non-completion of census forms (Gordon and Travers 2006: 6). These included economic migrants employed in the leisure and tourism sectors as well as significant numbers of refugees and asylum seekers. The proportion of asylum seekers staying in London was higher than that for the rest of the UK when, in 2000, a dispersal policy to other parts of the UK was introduced. Estimates suggest, however, that the category referred to as 'irregular' residents (including asylum seekers and over-stayers) accounted for an estimated 440,000 people living in London in 2007, still around 70 per cent of the total 'irregular' population resident in the UK (GLA Economics 2008: 9).

A third phase of inward migration occurred in the first decade of the twenty-first century. In 2004 ten new states entered the European Union (EU). The citizens of these accession states secured the right to move to other EU areas; taking up initially a restricted right of residence in countries like Germany and France, and/or the opportunity to come to Britain, which was amongst the first to open its borders to those who were wishing to work. Precise evaluation of the total numbers of EU accession state migrants entering the UK has generated much debate, especially within those local authorities where accession state migrant workers settled. The calculation of EU migrant workers resident and working in the UK is primarily based upon the issuance of National Insurance numbers, since anyone seeking work in the UK's formal labour market must have one of these numbers. In 2005-6, for example, 662,000 foreign nationals secured a national insurance number in the UK for the first time (Audit Commission 2007: 6). A majority of these applicants came from the EU accession states, though a significant but smaller proportion came from non-European areas including Asia and the Middle East.

The speed and scale of inward migration from the EU accession states post-2004 surprised government and local authorities. In a period of ten years from 1996 to 2006, the percentage of foreign workers within the UK workforce rose from 3.5 per cent to six per cent. In 2007-8 the numbers arriving from EU accession states peaked at 332,000, dropping to 257,000 in 2008-9. While migrants from EU accession states tended to cluster in different parts of the UK, London remained the location in which most registrations were made. In 2008-9, for example, London accounted for a little over 40 per cent of the total UK registrations (Department for Work and Pensions 2009).

The picture of inward international migration to London has, however, two further, important dimensions. First, inward international migration must be balanced with outward international migration, producing in the jargon the net migration figure. Inward and outward migration figures are calculated by counting those people who move into or out of the UK for a period of one year or more. The data for international migration is based upon several sources but the main one is the International Passenger Survey (IPS), while the regional distribution of international migrants within the UK is evaluated using estimates from the Labour Force Survey (LFS). In the period from 1993 to 2000, London experienced a significant increase in the inflow of international migrants. In 1998, 45 per cent of all international immigrants coming to the UK came to London. By 2007, the percentage had declined to 28 per cent, still the largest regional share of international migration to the UK (GLA: 2010).

Second, and most importantly, the changing character of London's immigrant population over the three phases described here, must be set against the backdrop of the changes in the city's total population in the post-1945 period. London's population peaked in 1939 at 8.6 million. Throughout the post-1945 period the city experienced population decline – as low as 6.7 million by the mid-1980s (Buck, Gordon, Hall, Harlowe and Kleinman 2002: 140). Since then the population level has grown again, especially since the early 1990s, with mid-2009 estimates standing at 7.8 million and a continuing increase projected to reach 8.8 million between 2011 and 2031 (GLA 2010: 4).

The first phase of international inward migration from the New Commonwealth occurred when total population levels were in decline and in the decades that followed, New Commonwealth migrants have created families in the city giving rise to a relationship between past immigration and the rise in birth rates in the early-twenty-first century (Buck, Gordon, Hall, Harlowe and Kleinman 2002: 142; GLA 2010: 4). These factors have supported the underlying growth in the ethnic minority population within the city; with complex spatial locations of different minority ethnic groups taking place between inner and outer London.

Movement into London from other regions in the UK is characterised by a net inflow from one age group, the 20-29 year olds. There is a tendency for older people to be dominant in the outflow from London and young people to be dominant in the inflow, particularly in the period since the late 1990s (GLA 2010). The former category seeks family housing, better schools and more space by moving out; and members of the younger generation moving in seek employment consistent with their skills and qualifications.

In the post 1945 period, estimates provided by the Office of National Statistics (2010) indicate that out of a total of nearly 6.7 million immigrants who came to the UK, almost 2.5 million settled in London. The city provided, therefore, a first UK home base for 37 per cent of the total migrant arrivals in UK over the period since 1945 (Table 16.1). The distribution of new migrants entering London's local authority boroughs is set down in Table 16.2. Broadly, international migrants, for whom London is their first destination, tend to move into areas where there is an existing community with a shared culture and ethnicity. For example, the Bangladeshi community is concentrated in Tower Hamlets, while Hackney hosts large groups of black African and Afro-Caribbean communities. There is, however, recent evidence of some migrant families, especially those from the first wave of New Commonwealth migration, moving from inner to outer London, a process referred to by Butler and Hamnett as 'minority ethnic suburbanisation' (Butler and Hamnett 2011: 93).

In summary, the three main phases of international inward migration to London since 1945 have had significant social, economic and cultural impacts upon the city. The first phase of migration from the New Commonwealth began at a time when Britain's public sector, especially health, traditional manufacturing

Table 16.1 Migrants to the United Kingdom by Decade of Arrival

Area	Total	Pre 1970	1970-79	1980-89	1990-99	2000-2008
North East	112,000	18,000	10,000	12,000	14,000	59,000
North West	493,000	102,000	49,000	46,000	72,000	224,000
Yorkshire & Humberside	401,000	80,000	40,000	32,000	51,000	198,000
East Midlands	377,000	76,000	41,000	30,000	54,000	176,000
West Midlands	539,000	132,000	56,000	49,000	71,000	230,000
Eastern	543,000	114,000	57,000	49,000	73,000	250,000
London	2,502,000	377,000	246,000	273,000	562,000	1,044,000
South East	856,000	183,000	88,000	69,000	147,000	369,000
South West	336,000	93,000	36,000	31,000	50,000	127,000
Wales	136,000	30,000	12,000	12,000	20,000	62,000
Scotland	290,000	48,000	23,000	23,000	37,000	159,000
Northern Ireland	100,000	18,000	7,000	7,000	18,000	49,000
Total UK	**6,686,000**	**1,271,000**	**665,000**	**634,000**	**1,169,000**	**2,946,000**

Source: Office of National Statistics July 2010, Demographics, http://data.london.gov.uk/datastore/package/migrants-united-kingdom-decade-arrival, accessed 24 May 2011.

industries and transport sectors experienced labour shortages. The second phase occurred in the wake of de-industrialisation and the expansion of service industry employment in the late 1980s and 1990s; the third phase, particularly driven by migrants from the EU accession states, coincided with the years immediately pre-dating the credit crunch and subsequent recession. Throughout this period, successive governments have sought to balance policies associated with sustaining a relatively open economy for capital and finance, with the ethical and political issues that necessarily arise from that openness – the international movement of people. The next section examines some of these issues, particularly as they relate to the political rationale lent to policy responses by successive governments since the 1970s.

Immigration and the Responsible Society

> We need to understand the impact of immigration on individual people in specific types of job. And here, the picture is mixed. Richard Layard has argued that while skilled worker migration benefits overall employment, unskilled migration has the opposite effect, harming indigenous unskilled workers. So when it comes to the economic effects of immigration, I would summarize the position as follows. Broadly, immigration has a positive impact on our economy.

Table 16.2 Total Migrants to London Boroughs from pre-1970 to 2008

Area	Total
Brent	147,000
Ealing	131,000
Westminster	128,000
Newham	120,000
Barnet	101,000
Enfield	99,000
Lambeth	99,000
Harrow	96,000
Camden	95,000
Wandsworth	95,000
Redbridge	91,000
Southwark	91,000
Haringey	89,000
Hounslow	88,000
Kensington and Chelsea	88,000
Croydon	83,000
Tower Hamlets	82,000
Lewisham	81,000
Hackney	73,000
Waltham Forest	73,000
Hillingdon	71,000
Merton	67,000
Hammersmith and Fulham	63,000
Islington	59,000
Greenwich	56,000
Barking and Dagenham	46,000
Bromley	39,000
Richmond upon Thames	39,000
Kingston upon Thames	38,000
Bexley	26,000
Sutton	25,000
Havering	22,000

Source: http://data.london.gov.uk/datastore/package/migrants-united-kingdom-decade-arrival (data extracted to show total migrants over the period, with boroughs identified from highest to lowest recipients).

> But there are negative effects too, and any responsible population strategy must distinguish between them, avoiding a broad-brush approach in favour of policy responses that are appropriately tailored to the varying economic effects of immigration, and which seek to share the costs and benefits fairly.
>
> I come to a clear conclusion. Our current level of population growth and atomisation is unsustainable. Immigration is too high. Family breakdown is too high. Unsustainable demographic change makes it harder to build the opportunity society I want to see, where young people can get on the housing ladder and where everyone has more power over their own lives. It makes it harder to build the responsible society I want to see, with strong families, communities and public services. And it makes it harder to build the secure society I want to see, with our quality of life and our environment protected in equal measure.[3]

David Cameron's speech to an audience at the think tank Policy Exchange, in London in the autumn of 2007, set down the Conservative approach to immigration; an approach broadly reflected in the Conservative/Liberal Democrat coalition government's policies adopted when it came to power in May 2010. Immigration was directly linked to a number of social problems including shortages of housing, insufficient work opportunities for British people, environmental degradation and unsustainable population growth. Immigration controls were allied to sustainable development and the protection of the environment; a vision touched by the hand of Malthus and fused with topical concern for 'quality of life'. This section briefly locates current Conservative thinking in the setting of the major debates about race and immigration in London by relating these to the three phases of inward international migration into the city.

As with earlier waves of migration into the city in the nineteenth century, the new commonwealth migrants in mid-twentieth century London found work in low paid occupations and, because of residence requirements, found themselves excluded from council or public housing and forced into the often overcrowded living conditions in the private rented sector (Hamnett 2003: 121-2). As they experienced discrimination in housing and employment, so black workers and communities organised against them, in areas such as Willesden and East London; and their self-organisation put pressure upon trade unions, locally and nationally, to respond to discrimination in the workplace and to challenge racism in the streets of the city (Phizacklea and Miles 1980). In this context, racism was seen as a social problem to be addressed by the political demand for equality (Malik 2007).

The hollowing out of inner city economies and the rise of youth unemployment in the late 1970s and early 1980s, contributed to social unrest in several British cities, including London, Birmingham and Bradford, culminating in events such as the Brixton riots in 1981. In their response to these events, local authorities

3 David Cameron 'The Challenges of a Growing Population', 29 October 2007, http://conservativehome.blogs.com/torydiary/files/population.pdf.

developed policies designed to enable black and Asian communities to establish themselves within urban areas, through the creation of new forms of community relationships based upon the recognition of their own specific histories and cultures. Community policing was but one feature of the new social interventions undertaken, while equal opportunities policies and race relations advisory committees were formed to provide the institutional foundations for a significant change in social attitudes (Bridges 1981: 180-1). The Greater London Council, before its abolition in 1986, played a leading role in developing these local state policies. In the process, equality was redefined; no longer focused upon equal rights for all, it became synonymous with the recognition of the right to be different. By the early 1990s, the rationale for the new categories of ethnicity adopted by the UK census (1991), and supported by the Commission for Racial Equality (CRE), was captured in the following assessment:

> Beyond the symbolic value of those new categories, which testified to some degree of public recognition of racial and cultural differences and indeed a new element, namely, hybridity, the ethnicity question was seen as necessary by a variety of social actors in order to assess the real extent of diversity, segregation and inequalities. The logic behind the ethnicity question, therefore, paved the way for the extension and generalisation of ethnic monitoring, seen by some as a prerequisite in order to devise more efficient equal opportunity strategies. In 1991, the CRE asked for a reform of the 1976 Race Relations Act, in order to generalise ethnic monitoring and make it a legal obligation for employers.[4]

From the late 1980s, the focus of immigration and race relations issues shifted from the political to the cultural; the shift was spurred by de-industrialisation and other complex changes in social structures and institutions, as Malik has sharply observed:

> ... the political struggles that had dominated the fight against racism in the sixties and seventies had become transformed into battles over cultural issues. Political struggles unite across cultural and ethnic divisions; cultural struggles inevitably fragment. Since state funding was now linked to cultural identity, particular groups began to assert their identity ever more fiercely. The shift from the political to the cultural arena helped to entrench old divisions and create new ones.[5]

The second phase of inward international migration in the 1990s coincided with Conservative attempts under Prime Minister, John Major, to secure a Britain that

4 Latour, V. (2009). Multiculturalism Upheld, immigration, race relations and diversity management under John Major (1990-1997), Observatoire de la Societe Britainnique http://osb.revues.org/804; accessed 1 June 2011.

5 Malik, K. (2007) 'The failures of multiculturalism' in Almqvist, K. (ed.) The Secular State and Islam in Europe, http://www.kenanmalik.com/papers/engelsberg_mc.html, accessed 1 June 2011.

was 'at ease with itself'; an implicit critique of the confrontational Thatcher years of government in the 1980s. Multiculturalism was embedded into the policies and programmes of local and national state institutions, and the 'new cultural arena' identified by Malik, took shape. Partly as a response to international events – the first Iraq War, the Rushdie affair – and the expansion of ethnic monitoring of civic, public and private sector institutions, significant numbers of new ethnic minority associations emerged, especially amongst the Muslim communities of Britain (the Muslim Council of Britain, for example, was formed as an umbrella organisation in 1997 representing hundreds of local Muslim associations). At the same time, public debate concerning immigration focused primarily upon the rising numbers of asylum seekers entering the country, with legislation passed in 1993 and 1996 in an effort to reduce the flow.

Following its election in 1997, the New Labour government continued with legislative efforts to reduce the flow of asylum seekers and economic migrants, introducing seven parliamentary acts over the period 1997-2009. Legislative attempts to control Britain's borders were tempered however by a utilitarian view that migration, especially that from the EU accession states, was good for the economy (Home Office 2006), contributing much needed skills and filling vacancies:

> Accession workers are continuing to go where the work is, helping to fill the gaps in our labour market, particularly in administration, business and management, hospitality and catering, agriculture, manufacturing and food, fish and meat processing.

[6]Such a view contrasted starkly with attitudes to asylum seekers, especially where they were associated in the popular imagination with jumping the queue for social housing in areas such as East London. Whilst there was little evidence to support such assertions, a 'moral panic' was provoked and arguably legitimated in part by an article in the *Observer* by Cabinet minister, Margaret Hodge in May 2007. It seems that the new Labour government was trying to ride two horses at the same time – a utilitarian acceptance of the positive contribution that inward migration was making to the economy, and a systematic attempt to curb non-EU inward migration, especially that undertaken by the most vulnerable section of the migrant population – asylum seekers (Robinson 2009; Flynn 2003). In drawing distinctions between the positive economic contribution of some and the abuse of Britain's relatively open borders by others, the government sought to legitimise its commitment to multiculturalism while retaining its capacity to use immigration as an issue, on the grounds that it was a major cause of concern to the white working class. Implicit in such views within the (then) party of government, was a disdain

6 Home Office/DWP/HMRC/CLG Accession Monitoring Report 2004-6, 22nd August 2006, http://news.bbc.co.uk/1/shared/bsp/hi/pdfs/22_08_06_migrantworkers.pdf; accessed 2 June 2011.

for the attitudes of sections of its own traditional, working class support. In turn, this served to legitimate the party's retreat from its historic ties to class, and its embrace of policies designed to promote 'a new kind of British decency' (O'Neill 2010).

In the wake of credit crunch and recession, the Conservative-led coalition government pursued a similarly pragmatic, utilitarianism while extending its social logic to develop a population 'policy' and improve 'well-being'. Britain could no longer sustain the levels of net migration achieved in pre-crisis years, because neither economy nor society could withstand the levels of population growth and the adverse effects on the urban environment that this was likely to entail. The control of inward migration would be based in the post-credit crunch period on an acknowledgement of the 'limits to growth' achievable by the UK economy and justified politically by a rhetorical concern for social well-being. The implications of this policy approach for London's labour market is significant given the structure of its economy, its social diversity and its global status. The final section of this chapter addresses these themes, drawing upon recent attempts to theorise the position of migrant labour in the global city.

Streets Paved with Bonuses?

Compared to other regions of the UK in the late 1990s and early twenty-first century, the relatively dynamic economy of London created opportunities for immigrants to move into employment, some at the high end of the occupational structures spawned by the buoyancy of a highly financialised economy and the expansion of public services, and others, the majority, at the other end of the spectrum, in low skilled public and private sector service jobs. This tendency for migrant labour to be employed at the top and bottom of London's occupational structures has attracted extensive commentary, as it raises wider and complex issues about the role of migrant labour in global cities such as London. Sassen (1991) has argued that cities like London and New York have followed similar trajectories. The role of such cities in international financial intermediation and the provision of business services creates a new dynamic in occupation and pay structures. The gap between top and bottom widens and the middle tier of occupations tends to diminish; the wealthy professional and managerial class at the top employ low paid labour to provide the goods and services required to sustain its status and lifestyle. The global city, typically located in the northern hemisphere, attracts migrant labour, usually from the south, to fill many of the low paid jobs that arise in the city – jobs that local people will not do. However, in subsequent examination of this thesis, various authors have questioned its apparently compelling economic logic, subjecting it to empirical test.

In relation to London's working population in the 1990s, Hamnett and others (Hamnett 1994; Buck, Gordon, Hall, Harloe and Kleinman 2002: 151-3) have argued that there was an increase in the proportion of professionals in post-industrial occupations, but the proportion of unskilled service workers remained about the same, at around 10 per cent of the total workforce (Buck et al. 2002: 152). London did not follow New York's experience of polarisation, at least in part because of the existence of a different welfare system which tended to moderate the effects of low pay and reduce the potential for a significant expansion in low paid occupations. By contrast, May et al. have suggested that Hamnett's analysis may be relevant to the early 1990s, but following the wave of inward international migration in that decade and into the twenty-first century, London demonstrated the characteristics of a new kind of 'migrant division of labour' in which polarisation was taking place in complex ways:

> …state, welfare, labour market and immigration policies have come together to heighten the effects of labour market change in recent years and facilitate the creation of a new "reserve army of labour" in London; a significant part of which consists of foreign-born workers. [7]

This new division of labour did not confine migrant workers to employment in those industries directly servicing the executive and managerial class working in the finance and business services sector. May et al.'s (2007: 160-1) survey of migrant workers (341 interviewees, working in four broad industrial sectors) found them to be employed in occupations such as contract cleaning, home care, food processing and hospitality, with evidence of ethnic segregation by industry, a situation partly arising from workers securing employment through word of mouth, via friends and acquaintances with similar ethnic backgrounds. The survey also indicated that whilst many migrants could be characterised as unskilled labour according to their occupation while in London, their educational background and previous work record in their country of origin indicated that they were now employed in jobs far below the skills levels that they possessed. What they had in common, however, was experience of working in the formal rather than informal economy; and all were low paid, irrespective of the sector in which they were employed (May et al. 2007: 160-3).

These findings are broadly consistent with analyses derived from other reports which drew upon official survey data and other qualitative sources. A Department of Communities and Local Government (DCLG) report published in 2009, found that in the UK as a whole, the proportion of the migrant workforce employed in professional/managerial roles fell to 32 per cent in the period 2004-6, much lower than the 43 per cent recorded for 1998-2003 (DCLG: 2009); and another detailed study found that a significant proportion of migrant workers, especially from EU accession states, had secured temporary employment in industries in which there was considerable 'churn' or labour turnover (Work Foundation 2008).

---

7 May J., J. Wills, K. Datta, Y. Evans, J. Herbert and C. McIlwane (2007) 'Keeping London Working: Global cities, the British state and London's new migrant division of labour', *Transactions of the Institute of British Geographers*, 32(2), 151-67.

The May et al. analysis provides compelling survey evidence that is broadly consistent with the insights derived from yet further attempts to quantify migrant workers' employment position and contribution to the UK economy, undertaken by government and other sources over recent years (Home Office 2010: 1; Green A., D. Owen and R.Wilson 2005). Inward migration has undoubtedly provided important high level skills in areas such as science and technology, health and allied health, and corporate management. A majority of migrants, however, with the proportion rising over recent years, have taken employment in low skilled and poorly paid, often temporary, jobs across a number of industrial sectors in London (and in the wider UK). There has been polarisation, but London's experience of inward migration does not conform to a polarisation thesis that rests solely upon filling the unskilled jobs arising from servicing a financial and business class alone. The wealth arising from employment in the 'streets paved with bonuses' have accrued to a favoured few; for the majority of migrant workers, employment in the city has arisen from a more complex relationship to an urban economy driven by finance and business sectors, but also demonstrating high levels of dependence on public sector employment and the services procured by them.

The majority of migrant workers have filled the considerable gaps in the unskilled occupations that an unbalanced economy gives rise to. They have entered flexible and low paid employment where they have met the needs of all who live and work in the city. The financialisation of London's economy over recent decades has tended to facilitate inclusion in the formal economy but has also generated various forms of social and financial exclusion. Migrant workers experience reduced access to both state welfare support and personal financial services (Datta, McIlwane, Evans, Herbert, May and Wills 2006). Paradoxically, financial service institutions have only taken more of an interest in communities of international migrant workers in cities like London as these communities have been seen to represent a potential 'niche' in financial provision, such as the use of mobile phones to transfer money, rather than traditional bank/money shop transfer facilities:

> In the third report in its Mobile Payments Series, Juniper Research found that there is a significant opportunity for the providers and vendors of mobile money transfer services as the market takes off, beginning as soon as 2010. The study explores how mobile money transfer will transform the ability of the 'underbanked' population and migrant workers to make remittances, using their mobile phones as mobile wallets. [8]

8 Jupiter Research (2008) 'Juniper Research forecasts Mobile Money Transfers Opportunity for Service Providers to exceed $5bn by 2013', Jupiter Research http://www.izmf.de/download/Studien/JuniperResearch_MobileMoneyTransfer.pdf, accessed 1st June 2011.

Conclusion

Earlier chapters have explained how the development of London's highly financialised economy has social implications that extend beyond the tight boundaries of the City and Canary Wharf. The underlying trend has been a growth in social inequality in the city, a trend reinforced by the rapid absorption of the majority of recent migrant workers into a range of unskilled and low paid occupations. Whilst there is evidence of established families from the first wave of New Commonwealth immigrants moving on and up (Butler and Hamnett 2011: 230), the majority of second and third wave migrants have often found themselves working in low paid occupations and living in poor quality, private rented housing. Put simply, the migrant division of labour is a form of polarisation between the minority at the top and a majority at the bottom of the occupational spectrum, with very few in between. This pattern has served top-end employers, hence the protests of the Mayor and London employers against the imposition of quotas by the coalition government; and has also served the city at the bottom end, sustaining services in areas where low pay is endemic (Work Foundation 2011: 46).

The current, Conservative-led government's commitment to an interventionist population policy designed, it is claimed, to improve 'well-being', is more the product of ideology than evidence. Research has demonstrated that 'immigration between 1998-2005 contributed to a rise in real GDP of three percent' (Department of Communities and Local Government 2009: 28; Audit Commission 2007: 7; Riley and Weale 2006); that the employment of migrant workers at the lower end of the occupational spectrum has not displaced UK citizens from local labour markets – other complex interactions between unemployment, welfare structures and educational attainment are far more important; and that migrant workers had a marginal downward effect on wage distribution at the lower end of the wage scale, whilst creating additional significant value for their employers and the wider economy (Audit Commission 2007: 7; Dustmann, Frattini and Preston 2008). In brief, inward international migration into London and subsequent natural growth rates over recent decades have ensured that the city's population has expanded and is younger than many other British cities, providing a dynamism and diversity which has served to restore rather than threaten the social and cultural life of the UK's capital city.

As Robinson (2010) suggests, the public debate about international inward migration in the UK needs to move beyond the numbers. UK politicians have been playing the same sort of numbers game since the 1970s; meanwhile the world has moved on. The extensive interdependence of national economies, the position of mega-cities in the international circuits of capital, the uneven but rapid processes of urbanisation in all continents, and the emergence of regional 'open markets', have all gathered momentum in recent years; and all have made their presence felt on the streets of London. But it may well be that their social impacts are more readily acknowledged and addressed by people in the streets of London than by those in the corridors of power. Most Londoners, most of the time, simply get on with whatever and whoever life puts in front of them. If only public policy were more aligned to this and less focused on divisive concerns about population growth and cultural difference, there would be no reason to maintain double standards about the movement of labour.

References

Audit Commission (2007). *Crossing Borders*. London: Audit Commission.

Buck, N., Gordon, I., Hall, P., Harlowe, M. and Kleinman, M. (2002). *Working Capital*. London: Routledge.

Butler, T. and Hamnett, C. (2011). *Ethnicity, Class and Aspiration*. Bristol: The Policy Press.

Bridges, L. (1981). Keeping the lid on: British urban social policy, 1975-81 in *Race and Class*, Volume XX111, Autumn 1981/Winter 1982, Numbers 2,3, 171-86.

Datta, K., Mcllwane, C., Evans, J., Herbert, J., May, J. and Wills, J. (2006). 'Challenging remittances as the new development mantra: Perspectives from low paid migrants in London', *Global Cities at Work*, Working Paper No 5, London: Department of Geography, Queen Mary University, London.

Department of Communities and Local Government (DCLG) (2009). *Regional Economic Performance: A Migration Perspective*, Economics Paper 4, London: DCLG.

Department for Work and Pensions (DWP) (2009). National Insurance Number Allocations to Adult Overseas National Entering the UK, London: DWP.

Dustmann, C., Frattini, T. and Preston, I. (2008). *The Effect of Immigration along the Distribution of Wages*, Centre for Research and Analysis of Migration, Discussion Paper Series CDP No 03/08, London: University College, London.

Flynn, D. (2003). 'Tough as old boots? Asylum, Immigration and the paradox of New Labour Policy' A discussion paper. London: Joint Council for the Welfare of Immigrants.

GLA Economics (2010). *Economic Impact on the London and UK Economy of an Earned Regularization of Irregular Migrants to the UK.* Summary Report, London: Mayor of London.

Gordon, I. and Travers, T. (2006). *Race, Immigration and Community Relations in Contemporary London.* London: London School of Economics. Mimeo.

Greater London Authority (GLA) (2008). GLA Data Management and Analysis Group, Demography Update, 20-2008, November 2008, London: GLA.

Green A., Owen, D. and Wilson, R. (2005). *Changing Patterns of Employment by Ethnic Group and for Migrant Workers*, National Report, Institute for Employment research, University of Warwick, Coventry: University of Warwick, November 2005.

Hamnett, C. (1994). 'Social Polarisation in Global Cities: Theory and evidence, *Urban Studies*, 31(3), 401-24.

Hamnett, C. (2003). *Unequal City*. London: Routledge.
Hickman, M., Crowley, H. and Mai, N. (2008). *Immigration and Social Cohesion in the UK*. Joseph Rowntree Foundation, http://www.jrf.org.uk/sites/files/jrf/2230-deprivation-cohesion-immigration.pdf.
Home Office/DWP/HMRC/CLG (2006). Accession Monitoring Report 2004-6, 22nd August 2006, http://news.bbc.co.uk/1/shared/bsp/hi/pdfs/22_08_06_migrantworkers.pdf.
Home Office (2010). *The Migrant Journey*, Research Report 43, London: Home Office, September 2010.
Malik, K. (2007). 'The Failures of Multiculturalism', in K. Almqvist (ed.) *The Secular State and Islam in Europe*, Ax:son Johnson Foundation. http://www.kenanmalik.com/papers/engelsberg_mc.html.
May J., Wills, J., Datta, K., Evans, Y., Herbert, J. and Mcllwaine, C. (2007). 'Keeping London working: Global cities, the British state and London's new migrant division of labour', *Transactions of the Institute of British Geography*, 32, 151-67.
O'Neill, B. (2010). 'Turning migrants into Status Symbols', *Spiked Online*, 12 April 2010, http://www.spiked-online.com/index.php/site/article/8522/.
Phizacklea, A. and Miles, R. (1980). *Labour and Racism*. London: Routledge and Kegan Paul.
Riley, R. and Weale, M. (2006). *Immigration and its Effects*, National Institute Economic Review, Number 198, 4-9.
Robinson, D. (2009). 'New immigrants and migrants in social housing in Britain: Discursive themes and lived realities', *Policy and Politics*. Bristol: The Policy Press.
Robinson, D. (2010). 'Migration in the UK: moving beyond numbers, People, Place and Policy Online', 4(1), 14-18. http://extra.shu.ac.uk/ppp-online/issue_1_260410/article_4.html.
Sassen, S. (1991). *The Global City*. Princeton, NJ: Princeton University Press.
Work Foundation (2011). *Welfare to What? Prospects and Challenges of Employment Recovery*, London: Work Foundation, January 2011.

Chapter 17
The Housing Crisis

Penny Bernstock and Gavin Poynter

Introduction

The UK housing crisis is, perhaps, the clearest social expression of the failure of financialised capitalism. The housing market bubble exposed in the initial stages of the credit crunch simply revealed the weakness and folly of economies whose expansion rested on assumptions about rising land and property prices and expanding, debt-fuelled patterns of consumption. The financialisation of social life, outlined in Part 1 of this book, was, in significant part, justified in the UK by successive governments since the 1980s by their commitment to create a 'property-owning democracy'. This philosophy and the economic model on which it is based are defunct.

In this chapter, we summarise some key shifts that have taken place in London's housing market and the implications of these shifts for who is likely to be able to afford to live in the city in future years. We explore the nature of London's housing market and make comparisons with the rest of the UK. We then discuss changes in housing policy and their implications for lower earning households in the London area, and the challenges to providing affordable housing post 2007, through a case study of the Olympic Park We argue that private developers have failed to meet the social need for housing in London over recent decades while public sector led programmes of 'regeneration' have fared little better. The tensions inherent in these regeneration projects are highlighted by the Olympic case study.

A number of themes have been associated with London's housing crisis in recent years. In particular: the increasing gap between incomes and affordable housing; the ongoing growth in population and lack of available space on which to build new housing. These have resulted in a number of policy developments ranging from a move to building housing at increasingly higher densities; the inclusion of a substantial proportion of affordable housing in new private developments (through the use of S106 agreements) and the attempt to optimise the possibilities for housing in the regeneration of East London and the Thames Gateway.

London and the East/West divide

London has historically been marked by an East/West Divide with East London characterised by urban deprivation, disadvantage and a predominance of council housing, particularly in boroughs like Tower Hamlets. The regeneration of Stratford it is claimed is, in part, designed to close the gap between the east and west in terms of prosperity. London's success as a global city was linked to the regeneration of London Docklands in the 1980s that led to the construction of a new financial quarter in Canary Wharf and new housing districts located in riverside settings. However, this project has increasingly become synonymous with the view that physical regeneration alone may not bring community benefit and the Director of the Olympic Park Legacy Company, Baroness Ford, has highlighted the importance of ensuring that such development is not repeated at the Olympic Park.[1]

However, as London increasingly marks itself out as a global city of the twenty-first century, the tensions over who will be able to live in London are profound. Employment rates are the highest in London of any metropolitan area in the UK. However, these range from 42 per cent for those with no qualification to 85 per cent for those with a level 4 qualification or above (Focus on London 2011). Wage rates are polarised for these two groups with some of the highest and lowest earners in the country living in London. Similarly, as employment opportunities have grown in London their complexion has changed significantly. Inner London has seen a massive decline in manufacturing jobs and a substantial growth in business and financial services. Changes in employment have impacted negatively on the populations who had previously worked in manufacturing and related industries. The closure of the docks resulted in a 20 per cent loss in employment in the five Docklands boroughs. Moreover, as new opportunities have emerged in boroughs such as Tower Hamlets, they have drawn on wider labour markets to recruit staff (Simmie 2002).

Despite the recession house prices have continued to rise in London. London's position as a leading global city, underpinned by its location in the circuits of financial capital, and its significant growth in population has meant that demand for housing is high. A number of reports have highlighted the ongoing tension between a lack of space for new development and London's expanding population. However, this demand is not just fuelled by those people living and working in the city, but through the trend, initially, by individuals to invest in the private housing market stimulated by the growth in buy to let mortgages after 2001 and increasingly from global entrepreneurs capitalising on the recent demand as a source of investment (HM Treasury 2010). London has, since the crash of 2007, been an attractive proposition for foreign investment. A recent report by Savills observed that 16.5 billion pounds worth of foreign investment had been invested in London since 2007. Savills concludes that the increasing attractiveness of prime housing in central London has meant that London's housing market has more in

---

1 See, for example, Baroness Ford's contribution in the Newham local authority publication 'Olympic Legacy Lessons' (2010) at http://www.thebigopportunity.org.uk/uploads/4/0/0/1/4001782/newham_symposium_-_olympic_legacy_lessons_march_20101.pdf.

common with other global real estate, commodities and investment markets than the domestic UK housing market. The report identifies what it describes as a 'champagne effect' with British vendors selling and re-investing in more suburban locations, such as South West London (Savills 2011). The impact of niche housing markets owned by international capital has yet to be known but one can anticipate that it will further exacerbate the crisis of affordable housing. Indicative of this trend was the Athletes Village, located on the Olympic Park at Stratford, being sold in part to a business consortium, Delancey and Qatari Diar.

Despite declining house prices across much of the UK since 2007, the London Housing market is the only region to have experienced house price increases, especially over the last year (2011). However, actual sales continue to be significantly below 2007 levels and new build has declined considerably and continues to be below the 2007 level. Demand for property in the capital remains high and research has indicated that London has experienced the biggest increase in rental prices of anywhere in the country (GLA 2011).

The dream to achieve and sustain a property-owning democracy in London is rapidly fading for a number of reasons. Despite being the region in which most new housing has been constructed over recent decades, London's property market is changing, with a significant rise taking place in the private rental housing sector. This trend has been reinforced by buyers, especially first time buyers, being unable to secure mortgages on anything less than typically a 20 per cent down payment on the value of the property they seek to purchase; a situation arising directly from the prudence exercised by banks and other mortgage providers in the wake of the credit crunch. Despite modest improvements in the flexibility exercised by lenders in more affluent regions, such as London and the south east in the course of 2011, it seems highly unlikely that the restrictions on demand arising from decisions made in the finance sector may be eased in the foreseeable future.

In relation to supply, the picture is not much better. In 2010-11, a total of 105,000 homes were constructed in the UK, the lowest number since the 1920s. The outlook for 2011-12 is for a modest improvement, especially in the London region, but this improvement is from an historic low base and is likely to be difficult to sustain given the impact of austerity measures on demand (income levels) and supply (credit availability and business confidence). In this context, developers are likely to continue to hold onto land earmarked for housing development until they feel sure that new builds will secure future profits. The prospect of a democracy based on home ownership has rapidly receded; its pursuit has paradoxically increased social inequalities within cities like London over recent decades. The period during which rising asset values have accrued to existing property owners afforded them the capacity to consume in the present and invest for their future and the disparity in wealth between those who owned and those who did not has widened. Even public interventions in the housing market via numerous 'regeneration' schemes tended to reinforce this trend through the process of gentrification, especially in London (Hamnett 2008; Lees, Slater and Wyly 2003).

Unsurprisingly housing waiting lists have continued to grow in London and Shelter recently estimated that some 360,000 households are on waiting lists across the city. The lack of social housing has meant that many families have been forced to rent in the private sector and it is here that planned changes to housing benefit are likely to be significant. Chris Hamnett has predicted that changes to housing benefit in London may lead to up to 80,000 families on housing benefit in inner London being forced to move, thus further excluding low income households from inner London; this is coupled with proposed changes to social housing rents which will require them to be set at 80 per cent of market rents (Lloyd 2011).

The shift to encourage Registered Social Landlords (RSLs) to develop affordable housing based on a funding model charging 80 per cent of market values for rentals will also create real challenges to RSL's ability to develop in inner London. The East Thames Housing Group has undertaken its own research on the impact of these changes on rent levels – as they shift from social rents to affordable rents – and have concluded that 44.5 per cent would be unable to afford a two bedroom property and 65.1 per cent of families would be unable to afford a three or four bed room property without housing benefit (Hollander 2011). With a range of financial and policy pressures pushing low income households out of inner London, the real concern is that low income households will relocate to outer areas where there will be limited access to employment opportunities.

Prior to the housing crash of 2007 one key mechanism for delivering affordable housing was through the planning gain system. Indeed, it became clear that this was increasingly the source through which affordable housing was being delivered in England. However, both cuts in new build housing and concerns raised by developers about profitability are impacting on this as a method for delivering 'affordable housing'. For example, the Thames Gateway Development Corporation recommended in 2009 that in order to kick start development in the Thames Gateway, planning gain requirements should be scaled down (Dowler 2009) and, more recently, it has been claimed that developers have been renegotiating their planning gain commitments.

Wider concerns have been raised about the poorly specified nature of 'affordable' housing in London. Affordable housing tends to be split between housing for rent and intermediate housing, such as shared ownership (with these schemes in the past being associated with a failure to relate costs to incomes). The credit crunch has impacted on shared ownership schemes as prospective purchasers have experienced problems accessing a mortgage. Developers, however, have increasingly begun to compete with RSL's as providers of shared ownership housing in the wake of the economic downturn. A recent study has noted that the need for higher deposits has meant that purchasers who would previously have bought outright are opting for this type of housing and some housing associations have reported that households on lower incomes who had previously purchased shared ownership housing, were no longer able to (Burgess 2009). An analysis of the London housing market by the Mayor of London, published in 2009, also records that the new types of homes that were built over the preceding ten years were typically too small and not those required to meet the diversity of needs within the city (Mayor of London 2009).

London: Key Problems and Emerging issues

London continues to experience a housing crisis, though the types of policy solutions that may resolve it are not yet clear. In summary, the city experiences:

- An urgent need for new homes to be built
- High costs of purchasing housing
- Huge demand for affordable housing
- Overcrowding
- An ageing housing stock
- Speculative investment by overseas buyers at the high end of the market
- Changes to housing benefit and housing finance regimes governing the development of affordable housing
- High costs involved with developing London based housing projects
- Rising Private Sector rents
- Overdevelopment of one and two bedroom properties

The weaknesses inherent in private development projects, has tended to place the emphasis on public investment to meet social needs. In 2009 the Homes and Communities Agency (HCA) was established by central government to oversee housing development and regeneration. In London, the HCA regional board is chaired by the Mayor of London and the board has responsibility for £5 billion of investment in housing between 2008 and 2011. In turn, the Mayor and London boroughs have committed to the construction of 40,000 affordable homes across London over this period. As part of his draft housing strategy, the Mayor has engaged in negotiations with local authorities aimed at agreeing targets for affordable housing development in each borough. The five Olympic boroughs – located in the east of the city – have been earmarked by the Mayor to be recipients of a significant proportion of the social housing developments to take place. The five boroughs are Hackney, Tower Hamlets, Newham, Waltham Forest and Greenwich. They provide a useful measure of the role of public investment and state intervention in offsetting the acute housing problems facing the city, especially given the historic weaknesses inherent in private sector driven housing development and its continued troubles in the wake of the credit crunch.

Of the five Olympic boroughs, Waltham Forest's housing profile is closest to the profile for the rest of London and for England. Hackney and Newham have a higher proportion of local authority housing stock than the rest of London and England and Tower Hamlets and Hackney have a higher percentage of Registered Social Landlords (RSLs) compared to the rest of the capital and England. Excepting Waltham Forest, the Olympic boroughs have a significantly smaller percentage of dwellings that are owner occupied or privately rented compared to the rest of London and the average for England. Overcrowding in the five host boroughs varies between 18 and 38 per cent of households, compared to a London average of 7 per cent, with three boroughs having the highest levels of overcrowding nationally. Market conditions in recent years have priced many local residents out of the housing market within the boroughs, leaving many existing residents with little housing choice. The combined future effects of domestic population growth and the need for social housing reflected in currently high waiting lists has to be balanced with the anticipated movement of higher skilled workers into the area. These circumstances create tensions between the urgent housing needs of the existing community and the potential needs of higher skilled workers moving into the sub-region. These tensions are illustrated by housing developments taking place in and around the Olympic Park.

Case Study: The Olympic Park, East London

East Londoner's may be cautiously optimistic about London 2012's housing legacy. The financial and reputational risk associated with failure will ensure that a range of government and quasi-government agencies will work to secure a positive housing legacy arising from hosting the 2012 Olympic and Paralympic Games. However, there are a number of serious challenges that will need to be overcome to ensure that London 2012 delivers an inclusive housing legacy that acts as an example of best practice in urban regeneration, both nationally and internationally.

There is a tendency to associate the housing legacy with the new housing built on the Olympic park but this is just one part of the legacy. One of the early housing legacies of London 2012 was the compulsory purchase and subsequent demolition of 425 properties. Some of these properties provided student accommodation and the remainder were occupied by residents of the Clays Lane Housing Cooperative (all of this housing was low cost housing for rent). Thirty five long established Traveller families lived on two sites and they were also relocated. Many of these residents were reluctant to move. The first dimension of housing legacy then is the initial loss of social housing.

Part of the rationale for the massive investment in the Olympic project related to the accelerated development that would be achieved by bringing the games to this part of East London. In other words, the games would kick start regeneration. London won the 'games' at a time when the housing market was booming and had this continued it is likely that the pace of development would have accelerated. However, it is worth noting that the regeneration of the Stratford area was well underway. Plans for Stratford City and the construction of 4,850 homes, along with the largest retail centre in Europe (Westfield Stratford City) were approved in 2004, and were in part used to support the London 2012 bid. A large number of planning applications had already been submitted in the area surrounding the park.

Some commentators would argue that though these planning applications had been submitted the housing collapse post 2007 would have meant that these schemes would have stalled and the large public sector investment arising from London 2012 has meant that many of these schemes either have or are in the process of coming to fruition; the Olympic investment having sustained developers' confidence in this area.

It is also worth exploring the nature of this accelerated development. Take a ride on the Docklands Light Railway (DLR) from Stratford to Pudding Mill Lane and you will be surprised by the pace of development. Half-finished and newly completed towers, comprising mainly one and two bedroom apartments are beginning to dominate the landscape. Interspersed between these new developments we can see the old Stratford, the high rise towers and blocks of flats that are home to some of Newham's most disadvantaged residents. Research undertaken by Newham council identified Stratford as having the highest level of housing need in the borough; above average unemployment rates and below average incomes. The two biggest housing problems relate to children living in high rise flats and overcrowding. Much of the new housing proposed as part of the Olympic development will not meet their needs and is not accessible to them. Most new housing is for sale, a proportion is designated as affordable housing for sale through schemes such as shared ownership. However, research on affordability has indicated that these residents could only enter owner occupation if prices were very low and this is not the case, and therefore they are dependent on the small number of homes for social rent.

There is a stark warning here from areas such as the Isle of Dogs. This region underwent massive transformation in the 1980s and as each new scheme was developed it became clear that regeneration would be characterised by the influx of a new population as opposed to a transformation of housing opportunities for existing communities. On the Isle of Dogs as in Stratford, policy makers were keen to rebalance the tenure mix through an increase in owner occupation. Housing waiting lists grew and for those residents able to access owner occupation, it often meant leaving the area as prices became increasingly unaffordable. Many of these developments offered discounted housing to buy for local residents but for most this was simply not affordable. Policy makers have been keen to distance themselves from the social polarisation on the Isle of Dogs, but there are parallels that will need to be addressed if Stratford's residents and more generally people on low incomes are to benefit from the regeneration arising from the hosting of the games.

Rising Rent and House Prices

A number of studies have indicated that house prices in Olympic cities have increased before the games. A recent study exploring house price change in post codes near to the Olympic Park identified an average rise of 26 per cent between

2005 and 2010. However, Stratford had the lowest increase of all of the areas studied at three per cent. There is some concern that an oversupply of housing for sale may lead to a fall in the value of properties, and a lack of interest from private developers in investing in the area.

The overall trend in rental values in Stratford since 2006 has been upwards, though rent levels have fluctuated over time. Both Shelter and East Thames Housing (the former the leading UK housing campaigners and the latter a regional housing association) have expressed concerns about the potential impact rising rental values may have on existing residents, both in the long term and directly during the games. Two bedroom apartments in some of the new developments in Stratford are being marketed at around £350.00 per week, and the proposed housing benefit cap on two bed properties is currently being proposed at £290.00 per week. This may result in the exclusion of residents dependent on housing benefit (Bernstock 2010).

From the perspective of the government, rising land values and increased demand for land were crucial assumptions in bidding for the games. Lower land values may impact on legacy as resources are cut to compensate for lack of income, resulting in poorer quality housing and neighbourhoods. On the other hand, a fall in land values may result in more activity from Registered Social Landlords who are able to take advantage of this, though reforms to housing finance may make this latter option less of a possibility.

New Housing Developments at the Athletes Village and in the Olympic Park

When London won the bid it was claimed by Sebastian Coe that the regeneration would create between 30,000-40,000 new homes, much of which will be affordable and available to key workers such as nurses and teachers. These claims were not linked to any specific plans but simply the anticipated outcome of the accelerated development of the Lower Lea Valley. However, more concrete legacy proposals are now emerging for the Athletes' Village and the Olympic Park.

Athletes' Village

One key dimension of the housing legacy is the conversion of the Athletes village into housing after the games. Initial plans were for 4,000 homes and this was revised downwards to 2,800. It was argued that this was the result of concerns with regard to the density of the scheme.

It was envisaged that there would be private sector interest in developing this project, however, this interest did not materialise initially and in 2009, a funding package was agreed through a mix of grants and loans, and the creation of Triathlon Homes (a consortium of two housing associations and a design company) to purchase around half (1379) of these homes. The proportion of housing provided through Triathlon will all be designated 'affordable' housing, with around half of this for social rent and the other half for sale through a range of 'affordable' housing options.

Qatari Holdings and Delancey have now signed a £557 million contract to purchase and long term management of the village. They will own 1439 properties. Current plans are to rent these properties and they will form part of the first UK private residential investment fund. They have also purchased six adjacent development slots with the capacity to provide 2000 homes (ODA 2011). Whilst this enables the government to recoup revenue it is estimated that this has still resulted in a considerable loss to the public purse and it is not clear how this development will fit with plans for an inclusive neighbourhood. The pressure to create a desirable neighbourhood attractive to those willing to pay substantial rents may begin to shape the nature of the affordable housing, for example there may be interventions to ensure that more 'desirable' groups such as 'key workers', have access to the housing over the long term unemployed. Another concern relates to the intermediate housing, whilst initially designated as affordable housing, this may very quickly revert to being market housing reducing the amount of affordable housing available over time. Clearly in a depressed market, there will be pressures to limit the amount of control/regulation applied.

The Olympic Park

In October 2010 the Olympic Legacy Company published a revised and impressive master-plan for the area. It is now envisaged that 8,000 properties (down from 10,000) will be built on the Olympic Park, organised within five neighbourhoods, with a greater emphasis on family housing with gardens and improved design. This new housing will be located in parklands close to the river and within easy access of new schools and health facilities. The emphasis on quality is welcome, because good quality design will be an intrinsic factor in encouraging people to live into this area, and the family housing may provide improved housing opportunities for the many families in housing need in Stratford and beyond. The OPLC are also engaging with a new innovative agenda around ensuring that the housing legacy is enduring, through the use of mechanisms such as community land trusts that give ownership to communities in perpetuity.

However, the transformation from master plan to reality will be dependent on securing private and public investment and to date this has posed real challenges. As the games draw closer there are massive public sector cuts, a radical reorganisation of housing entitlements along with a new benefits and social housing funding regime and changes in the governance of the Olympic Legacy, with plans to relocate the OPLC within the institutional framework of the Mayor's Office and the Greater London Authority and reorganise the Homes and Communities Agency. The OPLC is clearly beginning to create a vision for the area and this will need to be sustained through to implementation. There are other challenges arising from the proposed new benefits and housing regime; underpinned by reduced housing benefits, higher rents, short term tenancies and less public subsidy. The bigger the increase in land values, the more expensive the housing, the greater the need for subsidy will become and without different funding mechanisms it will be difficult for those on low incomes and dependent on housing benefit to live in the new developments.

As the exact detail of the housing legacy begins to unfold in East London, the increased emphasis on affordability; design and family housing are welcome. There is also scope for thinking in far more imaginative and inclusive ways about a housing legacy that embraces social mix in its broadest sense e.g. age; disability; income and ethnicity. The challenge will be in implementation, in resolving the tensions between finance and intention, and ensuring that there are parties ready to take this vision forward. In Vancouver, there were high ambitions with regards to housing legacy, they too had a vision of a mixed community. However, they have had difficulty selling market housing, and it is estimated that the non-market housing was the most heavily subsidised in the world.

The idea of community land trusts, given in perpetuity for communities, provides one way of ensuring that those on low incomes have a long term future in this part of London, though this too will result in either increased subsidy or loss of income both of which may be difficult in these increasingly challenging times. In its bid application, it was claimed that the legacy would lead to: 'The regeneration of an entire community for the direct benefit of everyone who lives there', it remains an open question as to whether this aspiration will be realised.

Conclusion

Housing in London reflects both its position as a global city and its connections to finance capital. The low exchange value of sterling in the wake of the credit crunch has meant that international investors have shifted their portfolio to property investment in London. The purchase of the Athletes Village itself has come to embody this trend whereby housing in London and other global cities becomes an international commodity. If housing benefit reforms are pursued and there is the anticipated exodus of lower income families from London this will raise the spectre not only of what happens to these families, but also what will happen to the properties they exit from. A large number of properties available to let or sale may act to reduce prices in the capital making it more affordable or, more likely, they may become part of a piecemeal process of gentrification or part of the investment portfolio of domestic and overseas enterprises. The long term implications of large swathes of London being owned by overseas investors is yet to unfold.

The capacity for low income households to continue living in Inner London remains uncertain. The credit crunch and subsequent austerity cuts have unsettled traditional ways of providing affordable housing in the city. The recent trend of decline in home ownership is also indicative of the tensions between the current models of financing housing and the high costs of property. The trickle down approach to delivering affordable housing through planning gain is now defunct and there is a desperate need for new solutions that recognise that low income households have an entitlement to live in the city in which they work.

References

Bernstock, P. (2010). Living on the Olympic Park, will dreams become reality BBC News, 6 December 2010, available at http://www.bbc.co.uk/news/uk-11842549, accessed 20 August 2011.

Burgess, G., Grant, F. and Whitehead, C. (2009). 'Low cost home ownership and the Credit Crunch: A report on regional markets and competition with other developers', Cambridge Centre for Housing and Planning Research. Available at http://www.york.ac.uk/inst/chp/hsa/papers/spring09/Burgess.doc, accessed 20 August 2011.

Dowler, C. (2009). 'Gateway developers cut low cost homes, Inside Housing, 11 March, available at http://www.insidehousing.co.uk/news/regeneration/gateway-developers-cut-low-cost-homes/6503604.article, accessed 18 August 2011.

Focus on London (2011). 'Labour Market, Beyond Headlines', available at http://data.london.gov.uk/datastore/applications/focus-london-labour-market, accessed 2 September 2011.

GLA (2011). London Housing Market Report, Quarter 2, available at http://www.london.gov.uk/sites/default/files/Housing%20market%20report%20Q2%20 2011.pdf, accessed 20 August 2011.

Hamnett, C. (2003). Unequal City, London: Routledge.

HM Treasury (2009). Investment in the Private Rented Sector, London: HM Treasury. Available at http://www.hm-treasury.gov.uk/d/consult_investment_ukprivaterentedsector.pdf; accessed 1 September 2011.

Hollander, G. (2011). 'Benefit cuts to widen rich/poor divide', Inside Housing, 2 September 2011, available at http://www.insidehousing.co.uk/care/benefit-cuts-to-widen-rich-poor-gap/6517571.article, accessed 20 August 2011.

Lees, L., Slater, T. and Wyly, E. (2008). *Gentrification*. London: Routledge.

Lloyd, T. (2009). 'London Thames Gateway predicts ten year slump', Inside Housing. 20 May 2009, available at http://www.insidehousing.co.uk/ihstory.aspx?storycode=6504680, accessed 24 August 2011.

Lloyd, T. (2011). 'Affordable rent to drive up housing bill', Inside Housing, 2 September 2011, available at http://www.insidehousing.co.uk/tenancies/affordable-rent-to-drive-up-benefit-bill/6517294.article, accessed 20 August 2011.

Mayor of London (2009). The London Housing Strategy, draft for consultation, published May 2009, 21, available at http://www.london.gov.uk/mayor/

housing/strategy/docs/london-housing-strategy09.pdf, accessed 15 August 2011.
Olympic Delivery Authority (ODA) (2011). 'Olympic Village investor announced with plans for a new neighbourhood for London', Friday 12 August 2011. Available at http://www.london2012.com/news/2011/08/legacy-owner-for-olympic-village-announced.php, accessed 20 August 2011.
Savills (2011). 'The World in London', Available at http://pdf.euro.savills.co.uk/residential---other/the-world-in-london---summer-2011.pdf, accessed 28 August 2011.
Simmie, J. (2002). The Changing city, Population, employment and Land use since the 1943 Country of London Plan, Oxford: Oxford Brookes University, available at http://www.brookes.ac.uk/schools/be/staff/jamessimmie.html, accessed 1 August 2011.

Chapter 18
The Health Service of the Future

Justine Cawley

> Our ambition is to create the largest and most vibrant social enterprise sector in the world. [1]

> Nearly everyone recognizes that in the mature economies current health provision is becoming too expensive to maintain. There are rising costs associated with a growing elderly population, expensive advances in medical care and technologies, and a growing problem with lifestyle illnesses such as obesity. Put simply, we cannot afford to carry on as we are, unless we are willing to pay far more in terms of GDP for health or accept a lowering of standards, neither of which is politically or socially acceptable. The NHS has been asked to make £20bn in savings by 2015; this would require a productivity gain of 3 to 4 per cent each year, in a service that has become gradually less productive over the past decade. Professor John Appleby, chief economist at the Kings Fund is also quoted as saying "Improving productivity has to be the top priority if the NHS is to maintain quality and avoid having to cut services. Politicians will need to be honest about the scale of the challenge ahead and help the public to understand that some of their services may need to change in order to improve efficiency and maintain quality. [2]

This chapter looks at the forces that are changing the way we deliver health services and will pay particular attention to the two white papers on health 'Equity and Excellence: Liberating the NHS' which deals with health service reforms, and 'Healthy Lives-Healthy People- Our Strategy for Public Health in England'[3] which focuses on public health and will initiate the biggest change in this area for many decades. Whilst there is a long history of white papers on health which sound radical and call for drastic change, their effects are normally watered down in the implementation and the result is tinkering rather than wholesale change. However, the combination of the desire for change in the delivery of public services shown

1 Equity and excellence: Liberating the NHS Department of Health July 2010.

2 Laurance, J. (2010) 'NHS Ordered to Find Massive Savings', *Independent*, March 25, 2010. http://www.independent.co.uk/life-style/health-and-families/health-news/health-nhs-ordered-to-find-massive-savings-1927023.html, accessed 6 September 2011.

3 Healthy Lives, Healthy People: Our Strategy for public health in England Department of Health November 2010.

by the coalition government, as revealed in the big society agenda, allied to a severe lack of funds to enable 'carry on as usual' policies, means this is unlikely to be the case this time. We have an unusual coalescence of desire for change, allied to a financial imperative of deliverance with reduced funds, which means that we should expect radical changes in the way the health sector is run and how services are delivered with much greater weight given to public health in achieving health outcomes.

The eventual outcome of the reforms is unknown. There are huge barriers to any major change within the health sector which will be explored within this chapter. However, it is very unlikely that the health sector of the future will be seen as a linear development from the health sector of the present. The health sector is likely to be transformed in the wake of the credit crunch and subsequent recession and London's health services will be a key focus of these changes given the capital's concentration of health institutions, its high levels of employment in health and social care and a population in which health and well-being varies considerably both geographically and in relation to socio-economic status.

Equity and Excellence: Liberating the NHS

Most of the government's current aims as outlined in the White Paper 'Equity and Excellence: Liberating the NHS' flow from the previous Labour government's concerns addressed in the white paper 'Our Care, Our Health, Our Say'.

The main themes for the latest white paper are:

- Putting the patient and public first – patients should be involved in decision making (or their nominated carers) and be at the centre of the process;
- Increased choice and control – the patient should have choice in terms of the provider of services and much more control over their individual care.
- Patient and public voice – the creation of a new consumer champion 'HealthWatch' which will act as an advocate for patients and channel the views of patients back to the providers, to ensure the patient voice is central to commissioning and provision arrangements. HealthWatch will be local bodies organised under the auspices of the Local Authority;
- Improving health care outcomes – to deliver safer and more effective care provision. The main focus will be on what is best for the patient and this will not be driven by broader output targets. The NHS will move onto clinical targets as decided upon by clinicians and not top down targets decided by politicians;
- Developing quality standards – setting of standards for each part of the patient pathway, which will enable a better monitoring of the care provision;
- Creating GP Commissioning Consortia – the power of PCTs will be devolved to GP consortia, made up of local GPs and primary care professionals meeting together to decide upon local health care arrangements;

- Transfer of public health functions to Local Authorities – the public health function of the PCTs is to end, and the responsibility will be devolved to Local Authorities
- Freeing the NHS providers – it will be easier for providers from the voluntary and private sectors to provide health services which the NHS can commission. A new economic regulator will be appointed, to promote competition and regulate prices. The aim is to have a multiplicity of providers competing to provide health and social care services;
- Cutting bureaucracy – the amount of bureaucracy involved in the NHS is cut, with more emphasis on front line staff. This will inevitably lead to a loss of management jobs and an increase in assistant practitioner roles, as they are cheaper to employ than staff belonging to professional associations.

Most of the themes in the white paper are not particularly new but are a logical follow-on to the measures outlined in 'Our Care, Our Health Our Say'[4] (January 2006) such as the GP Consortia which come from practice based commissioning. Quality and safety, patient/public involvement and opening the market up to competition were also key themes. These would warrant a separate analysis which, unfortunately, is not within the remit of this short chapter. However, the recent white paper acknowledged the lack of funds and the need for health care provision to take into account what can be afforded. Thus, one can see a marriage of desire for reform allied to realism in terms of what the state can afford to provide. Another major change is the pace of reform and the language used i.e. 'Our Health, Our Care, Our Say' are fairly benign words, whereas 'Liberating the NHS' is much more dynamic and signals the desire for fundamental change and a rethink of objectives and cultures. Various government spokespeople and ministers, as well as current and previous senior management in the health sector, have been advocating the need for fundamental change and using words like imperative, 'no choice but to change', 'we cannot afford to carry on the way we are' and so on.

Although there is not specific mention in the white paper about hospital closures, it is an inevitable consequence and experts are in agreement that the NHS has moved on from the era when health expenditure by the government increased hugely and over 100 new hospitals were built. Lord Crisp, who was NHS chief executive in England from 2000 to 2006, said, in an interview with the BBC,[5] that the previous government should have been tougher when it had the chance and that we now have overcapacity in the hospital sector, 'We missed that opportunity (for fundamental change) and this government needs to grasp that. We can't keep services going just because there is a nice building'. Whilst, Katherine Murphy,

4 Our Health, Our Care, our say: a new direction for community services Department of Health January 2006

5 http://www.bbc.co.uk/news/health-14729191, an article by Nick Triggle 1 September 2011 'More hospitals need to close' accessed 1 September 2011.

of the Patients Association,[6] bluntly said 'What is the point of having brand new hospital buildings if there are not enough funds to treat people in them?'

Thus, despite the political fallout, some hospital services will be amalgamated and indeed some hospitals will close. The mantra is more care in the community and more effort into treating people at home and in outpatient services, often provided in GP settings, there is a recognition that the NHS has to find a better way of offering provision that meets needs and better address issues, such as the fact that the majority of NHS expenditure deals with the chronic needs of a small proportion of the population, with around 10 per cent of the population consuming 60 per cent of the NHS provision. The reality of provision has to meet the reality of demand and the financial resources available.

Healthy Lives-Healthy People: Our Strategy for Public Health in England

In addition to the White Paper 'Equity and Excellence: Liberating the NHS' a public health white paper 'Healthy Lives-Healthy People- Our Strategy for Public Health in England' has been published. This needs to be understood as showing the direction of travel for the NHS and how it is adapting to the post credit crunch world of diminished resources. The white paper focuses on the necessity to reduce health inequalities and states clearly that they are part of wider inequalities and are interlinked. It notes the importance of work in reducing health inequalities, to improving education performance and to changing adult lifestyle behaviours and choices. It states that changed lifestyle choices in adults could 'Avoid a substantial proportion of cancers, vascular dementias and over 30 per cent of circulatory diseases; saving the NHS the £2.7 billion cost of alcohol abuse; and saving £13.9 billion a year, the societal cost related to drug-fuelled crime'.

The report starts by saying 'This White Paper sets out a radical new approach that will empower local communities, enable professional freedoms and unleash new ideas based on the evidence of what works'. It sums up the new approach in four key phrases:

Responsive – owned by communities, shaped to meet their needs: this argues that centralisation has failed and that top down government has ended and from now on local government and local communities will decide how best to improve the health and wellbeing of their citizens, deciding what actions to take locally with the NHS and other key partners, without undue interference from the centre. This will be supported by a proposed public health outcomes framework and a 'health premium', which will incentivise local government and communities to improve health and reduce inequalities, while leaving them free to decide how best to do this.

Resourced – with ring-fenced funding and incentives to improve; this states that public health budgets have been squeezed and that prevention has not enjoyed

6 Ibid.

parity with NHS treatment, despite repeated attempts by central government to prioritise it. The Government will ring-fence public health funds from within the overall NHS budget to ensure that it is prioritised, although it will still be subject to the running-cost reductions and efficiency gains that will be required across the system.

Rigorous –professionally-led and focused on evidence; it states that 'The system has often let the workforce down. Public health professionals have been disempowered and their skills not sufficiently valued when compared with their counterparts in NHS acute services. We need to address the imbalance, so that prevention and public health enjoy true parity with treatment'. A new body 'Public Health England' will be set up to 'be a uniting force for the wider family of professionals who also spend time on improving people's lives and tackling inequalities'. There will be much more stress on the use of evidence in making decisions and best practice with information freely available to local bodies via enhanced use of Information and Communication Technologies (ICTs).

Resilient – strengthening protection against current and future threats to health. The paper states that the current system for health protection is fragmented with the system lacking integration and over-reliant on goodwill to make it work. The government intends to make accountabilities in the system clearer and create a new streamlined public health service to lead health protection and public health efforts.

The white paper argues that the reforms will seek to 'Balance the freedoms of individuals and organisations with the need to avoid harm to others, and we will use a 'ladder' of interventions to determine the least intrusive approach possible, aiming to make voluntary approaches work before resorting to regulation'. The proposed effects of the public health white paper are that prevention is going to be far more important, that public health is to be community and local government led, and that new solutions and ideas are to be encouraged. This programme of reforms has significant cost implications, as the prevention of ill health is obviously beneficial in terms of cost savings for intervention NHS services. Outcomes in terms of enhanced health and wellbeing are to be far more important than specific performance targets

The Big Society

The health reforms need to be seen in the context of the wider government theme of the 'Big Society' which in essence means communities and individuals taking more responsibility for their own wellbeing and that the state should not be seen as the sole, or even the best provider of services.[7] The idea of the big society pervades everything but is particularly relevant in terms of health and social care where

7 Ten Big Questions about the Big Society, Anna Coote, New Economics Foundation June 2010.

there has long been an implicit assumption that the state is both the commissioner and provider of services, and is the resource that the vast majority of people will use (the 'big government' model). Given the reduced central resources available, alongside increased demand for expensive health interventions, this state and society relationship in terms of health care, can no longer be afforded in its present format. Thus, to understand the future direction of health and social care, we need to consider the implications of the big society agenda.

The big society was a central Conservative election commitment, though it was not broadly understood. British Prime Minister, David Cameron, is deeply committed to the concept of the big society and given the stringent financial constraints, it is opportune. In many ways having less central funding available means there is an encouragement for innovation and lateral thinking.

The big society, when applied to health services, means that individuals and communities will be required to play a major role in identifying needs, deciding on provision and commissioning agencies to deliver. The delivery can be by many different bodies from micro agencies through to large hospitals, charities or private sector for profit groups. The only unifying factors are that the service is free at the point of delivery, that standards are maintained and that all provision is able to be monitored via readily understood standards of care and delivery. The long term effects of this are unknown, in that we do not know who will succeed in being the best providers and meet the commissioning needs, it may well be a goldmine for private health companies such as BUPA and/or lead to a blossoming of community based organisations and charities. However, what seems certain is that the logic of the big society and the health white papers is that we will not have a continuation of the big government, state down, supply led model of health care provision.

New Ways of Thinking

The influence of the ideas associated with the Big Society and the shortage of resources will, according to government, facilitate new ways of thinking about approaching how to deliver care and the structures required. Co-production is an example of this – involving service providers and users to design and develop services[8] – but here the analysis will focus on effective monitoring systems.

Given that the NHS is likely to have a multiplicity of providers, offering various services in new ways, it is essential that an effective monitoring system is in place and that standards that are readily understood and can be measured are used. The current system of monitoring and assessment will not fit this model of provision. It is necessary to measure outcomes and benefits and not simply those objectives that can be measured easily. The Social Return on Investment methodology

8 Co-production is described in detail on the Patient Experience Network website. See: http://www.institute.nhs.uk/share_and_network/pen/co-production.html (accessed 5 September 2011).

(SROI) may well be found to be the most suited.[9] SROI looks at all the return on investment, taking into account softer outcomes, and gives a much fuller picture of the benefits (or deficiencies) of programmes and operations. It can be applied in all areas and is particularly useful in determining the benefits from community involvements where outcomes such as raised self-esteem, social cohesion, reduced call on medical services and greater proclivity towards healthier lifestyle can be accounted for. These can have huge community impacts and financial benefits for the state but are currently seldom measured. SROI methodology complements the white paper's more generic approach to health by looking at the role of work and peoples lifestyle choices in obtaining good health outcomes and reducing health inequalities; health outcomes and not health targets being the key focus.

The importance of monitoring and being able to furnish full information is also driven by the advent of 'Social Impact Bonds'. Social Impact Bonds have been trailed in Peterborough Prison.[10] Social impact bonds are bonds that can be purchased by investors that yield a return based on the effectiveness of a specified service in achieving targeted outcomes e.g. a smoking cessation project. If the targets are achieved, the investor will make a positive return but they also run the risk of losing money. To have an effective bond system, it is essential that there is a reliable information stream both on the provider of the service and on how to judge the effectiveness of the service itself. SROI could be a very good way of assessing the effectiveness and extent to which a positive return has been achieved because it reports on the financial return for every £ spent.

Obstacles and Barriers

The government is rightly claiming that its measures are radical; the white paper 'Liberating the NHS' is accurate in its intent. However, there have been many unfulfilled revolutions in policy in the past; so what might be the potential barriers and obstacles that might divert or prevent government from achieving its desired outcomes?

The first, and perhaps major barrier, is vested interests and the inertia of a huge bureaucratic body like the NHS. The NHS has long been accused of being producer led and whether this is accurate or not, it is hard to achieve radical change in such a large organisation, with strong professional bodies, that are adept at calling upon public opinion in order to prevent change. This explains why public health, which has long been seen by neutral health experts as more important in terms of achieving long term overall health outcomes, has been starved of funds relative to hospitals and why the medical interventionist model attracts the publicity and lion's share of funding. It needs considerable persistence to take on the medical interventionist

9 Seven principles for measuring what matters E Lawlor, J Nicolls and E Neitzart – New Economics Foundation January 2009.

10 Available at www.socialfinacne.org.uk/work/sibs, accessed 3 September 2011.

lobby and anyone wanting to close a hospital or even to amalgamate A&E services to achieve greater efficiency, faces a huge backlash. The NHS Confederation itself has recognised the self-imposed NHS constraints 'If we operate, as sometimes has been the case, through benignly intended paternalism or misguided vested interest, we will not deliver the change needed. And that fact is that NHS leaders experienced in driving performance delivery are not always best placed to engage emotionally with the public or facilitate a social movement'.[11]

The second major obstacle relates to the potential lack of commitment and acceptance by stakeholders of the main thrust of the white papers and the overall big society agenda. Thus, even though the government may legislate and command, if it is to achieve the radical change it desires, it also needs to obtain buy in from the stakeholders involved. This includes local authorities (who are now central to public health), medical professionals, community groups, the relevant media, the broader public and major opinion formers. There are many people and groups who might obstruct practice on the ground and so regardless of what is aimed at, the achievements may be limited. Many people will simply say the new measures and intentions are just a way of saving money and doing less for people. If the emphasis is on community groups and local bodies having a much greater role, this may mean middle class areas with articulate and demanding residents benefitting more than poorer areas. Those who demand more and know how to argue for it will do better than the disempowered who are accustomed to simply accepting what they are given.

A third significant obstacle may be the lack of funds to push through change, allied to the inability of the present structure to reform and adapt. The structural and cultural change which is needed to achieve the government objectives requires considerable energy and persuasion and whilst a lack of funds may encourage innovation, it can also act as a barrier to achieving major change. For instance, Local Authorities will inevitably find it difficult to take on new responsibilities in an era of reduced central funding. Also new systems require some pump priming and the courage to spend in different ways. Reform can be expensive, even if it saves money in the medium to longer term.

Conclusion

We can anticipate that the movement towards health and social care services being provided by whatever body is most suited to achieve a particular objective will grow, and the allegiance towards the model of top down interventions will reduce. The role of state run health provider institutions will decline (although acute intervention services will of necessity still have to be provided by the state for the vast majority of people).

11 http://www.nhsconfed.org/OurWork/latestnews/Pages/Reducing-care-footprint-key-to-transformational-change.aspx An article by Mike Reid quoting Mike Farrar the ex-Chief Executive of the NHS Confederation. 22 August 2011, assessed 6 September 2011.

The eventual winners and losers in terms of providers is not as yet known, and it may well be that different areas will have very different models, with state run enterprises strong in some regions and charities and third sector bodies dominant in others. There is also likely to be major inroads into health provision by for profit groups, such as BUPA, who will have the economies of scale and administrative expertise to bid for and run major contracts, perhaps in consortia with other providers, as is common in major construction projects. The essential principle that services are free at the point of use will, however, not change, as it is too deeply imbedded in the British consciousness and fears about the privatisation of the NHS tend to ignore this reality. Certain services have always been paid for and there has been a gradual increase in paid for provision, such as dentistry. This may well increase but for the vast majority of people their health services will remain free with the provider whilst the way it is commissioned and used will change.

The major changes in the NHS are being driven by a combination of ideology and by the new financial realities facing the UK economy; the health sector of the future will not be the same as the one we have known for the last 60 years. The rest of the developed world, and in particular the mature economies of Western Europe, will take note, as they all have to grapple with similar problems of an aging population, more expensive interventions and less resources available. Whether the government achieves its 'Ambition … to create the largest and most vibrant social enterprise sector in the world', remains to be seen, but the implementation of these reforms will produce major challenges to its ideology and severely test its capacity to achieve significant public sector reform.

References

Department of Health (2006). 'Our Health, Our Care, Our Say: A new direction for community services, London: Department of Health, January 2006.

Department of Health (2010). 'Equity and Excellence: Liberating the NHS' London: Department of Health July 2010 http://www.independent.co.uk/life-style/health-and-families/health-news/health-nhs-ordered-to-find-massive-savings-1927023.html An article by Jeremy Laurence 25 March 2010, accessed 6 September 2011.

Department of Health (2010). 'Healthy Lives, Healthy People: Our Strategy for public health in England' London: Department of Health, November 2010.

Lawlor E., Nicolls, J. and Neitzart, E. (2009). 'Seven principles for measuring what matters', London: New Economics Foundation, January 2009.

Reid, M. (2011). Reducing care footprint is key to transformational change', (http://www.nhsconfed.org/OurWork/latestnews/Pages/Reducing-care-footprint-key-to-transformational-change.aspx, accessed 6 September 2011.

Triggle, N. (2011). 'More hospitals need to close', http://www.bbc.co.uk/news/health-14729191, accessed 1 September 2011.

Chapter 19
Hard Times for Higher Education: Knowledge Economy, Economies of Knowledge

Karina Berzins

Introduction

Higher education is an important industry in London and performs a significant role in its economy, attracting UK based and overseas students to diverse institutions. This chapter examines recent developments and, in particular, focuses upon higher education policy and the move towards the establishment of a quasi-market for higher education, before turning to issues around the capacity of the sector to sustain its international reputation and to provide educational opportunities for an expanding younger population living in relatively deprived areas, particularly of East London.

Many of the students who protested in November 2010 in the UK against the proposed new fee regime for higher education made the link between the Coalition government's austerity measures to combat the national deficit and the new increased fees. Slogans like 'Cut Trident Not Education' show that at least in the minds of the students, the new fee regime is part of the coalition plans to balance the books. However, this chapter argues that the proposed new fee regime is tied to previous government's policies on higher education, and that the deficit problem (brought on or at least worsened by the credit crunch and ensuing financial crisis) is not the only driver for the new fee regime. The new regime, coming from the *Independent Review of Higher Education Funding and Student Finance* (the Browne review) can be seen as a continuation of policy that extends back through Blair's government to Thatcher. These reforms to higher education have been prompted by a particular type of economic ideology which has been apparent in the sector for over 20 years, and positions higher education within consumerist ideology, and is heavily influenced by fears around international competition and the corresponding need to increase local skills.

Higher education policy today hinges on a number of imperatives which if not contradictory, certainly contain tension between them. Firstly, the policy is driven by the desire to maintain international competitiveness, to up-skill the local labour force, and to provide business with the skilled labour that it requires. International competitiveness also plays a significant part in the provision of world class research (including product spin out) that drives the knowledge economy. Secondly, there are imperatives around social mobility, and widening participation, although for government(s) the argument for education based social mobility often aligns with the former desire for economic uplift via a highly skilled workforce, and the benefits of widening participation initiatives are often presented in policy documents as *economic* benefits, rather than as wider social ones. Thirdly, more and more higher education policy highlights the role of the 'student-consumer' and maintains that higher education provision needs to be consumer led. Alongside this UK institutions do not only serve local populations, but also cater for an already strong, and ever increasing overseas student market, which is worth £2.5 billion from London based overseas students alone (About London's HE: Facts and Figures 2011). Fourthly, and particularly relevant in times of economic downturn, is the question of exactly who should pay for the system, a question that governments have been grappling with since the 1980s. To disentangle the above pressures on higher education it is useful to review the most recent history of higher education policy to see how this has led, in the end, to the establishment of a quasi-market for further and higher education largely outlined in the Browne Review, and amended by the current coalition government.

Higher Education: The Funding Gap

Between 1987 and 1997, there was a major expansion in student numbers in higher education. Participation rates more than doubled, increasing from 15 per cent to 33 per cent (Lunt 2008: 742). During these years funding per student fell 36 per cent, according to David Blunkett, who was Secretary of State at the time (Blunkett in Lunt 2008: 743). This trend has been common to many countries, and can be explained through 'Baumol's Cost Disease' as productivity in higher education has grown at a much slower pace than other sectors of the economy, which has forced the costs of higher education to rise over time. This is not unique to education, but is found in 'relatively labour-intensive parts of the service sector, reflecting in higher education that labour-displacing technical progress has so far been relatively slow, with little or no displacement of highly educated workers from the process of teaching and research. Hence, real expenditure per higher education student tends to rise over time…which, together with generally rising participation rates … creates funding problems for those countries with largely state-financed higher education systems' (Adnett and Tlupova 2008: 244). The increasing costs of higher education provision (per-student), coupled with increased numbers entering higher education meant that the system of financing (entirely state based) began to become unaffordable to government.

By the mid-1990s the situation became increasingly fraught and the potential crisis that emerged led to the establishment of the Dearing review of education which was begun under the Conservative government, and completed under New Labour. Dearing had cross party support, due to the increasing 'funding gap' in higher education and perhaps was fuelled by the 'Vice Chancellor's revolt' in 1995, where Vice Chancellor's threatened to introduce top-up fees if more funding for higher education was not released by government. The Dearing report contained a number of recommendations; however the most important was the solution for funding higher education, with the introduction of a student contribution towards fees. The result was the introduction in the 1998/1999 academic year, of a flat-rate fee undifferentiated by institution or course of study. Dearing had recommended that means-tested grants to cover living expenses be maintained – however these were discontinued under New Labour. The shift away from wholly state funded higher education to one where the students also made a contribution was by no means unique to England; for instance Australia had introduced the Higher Education Contribution Scheme in 1989, based around a graduate taxation system.

That the New Labour government introduced a student contribution to their higher education fees may have been controversial at the time, but this move certainly reflected the New Labour approach. Many have commented on the continuity between neo-liberal policies of the previous Conservative government and Blairite policies that shifted the Labour party away from the left. Tomlinson points out that '…much continuity derives from an acceptance and elaboration of Tory reforms post-1988; indeed a pursuit of some of these policies passed the point that Tory ministers had been willing to go. There was an acceptance of the Conservative faith in choice and competition, with education developing as a market commodity driven by consumer demands' (Tomlinson 2001, cited in Lunt 2008: 743). Indeed, New Labour's second term continued the marketisation of higher education, and the *Higher Education White Paper* of 2003, coupled with the *Higher Education Act* (2004) put in place the introduction of variable 'top up' fees of up to £3,000 from the 2006/2007 academic year which universities could charge if they entered into an Access Agreement with the newly formed Office For Fair Access (OFFA). *The Higher Education Act* (2004) was not universally supported in its initial proposal, and became law only through a second reading, after a number of concessions were made, targeted at students from lower income backgrounds. Due to these concessions the Bill obtained a slight majority of votes, with 72 Labour MP's voting against the Bill and 19 abstaining (White 2001, cited in Greenback 2006: 159). Under these arrangements there would be no up-front fees for students, who would take out a loan to fund their education, alongside a range of means-tested grants and bursaries. Despite the famous New Labour slogan 'education, education, education' and the ambitious plan to have 50 per cent of young people entering higher education, New Labour's legacy to higher education has been seen as 'a highly marketised HE system, in which global competitiveness has been the major driver' (Lunt 2008: 749).

Alongside the problems associated with how to fund higher education, issues around widening participation became increasingly important as western economies around the world developed sectors of high growth in areas that required a highly skilled workforce. This meant that the development of educated human capital was paramount to any nation wishing to maintain its position on the global stage.

Indeed Dearing also commented extensively on widening participation; with the initial recommendations of the report dominated by the topic (Greenbank 2006: 144). However it has been noted that the report deals with widening participation only at the initial stages of the student life cycle – enrolment in particular, but does not deal with widening participation in other stages – retention and progression. The concern over widening participation was not only based on the desire for a more socially mobile society, but can also be directly linked to concerns over international competitiveness.

The Leitch report on skills in the UK *Prosperity for All in the Global Economy – world class skills*, published in 2006 was in response to fears over the relatively poor performance of the UK against comparator nations (France, Germany, the USA) in terms of productivity. Coupled with this, the fear that the 'emerging' economies of China and India, more general globalising forces, and changes to the nature of the UK economy where more and more jobs require highly skilled employees (the emergence of the knowledge-economy), led to the report's recommendation 'that the UK commit to becoming a world leader in skills by 2020, benchmarked against the upper quartile of the OECD. This means doubling attainment at most levels' (Leitch: 2006: 3). The emergence of the knowledge economy (coupled with the decline in manufacturing and other labour intensive industry) meant that to achieve a highly skilled workforce, participation rates overall had to be increased. This, in turn, meant that those who had traditionally not entered university now had to be encouraged to do so, if UK plc was to sustain its global role. The tasks of *widening* participation and *increasing* participation in these years were, essentially, synonymous.

Not only was there an imperative to up-skill local populations, the revenue generated by overseas students became increasingly significant to the sector, particularly in light of the funding issues around educating local populations. In 1999, targets for international student recruitment were introduced to maintain the UKs competitive edge in this market, with further targets set in 2006. The UK is second only to the US in terms of market share of overseas students, however, commentators such as Lunt have noted that this position is increasingly threatened by 'high tuition fees, perceptions of quality, and the use of English language for teaching by other European universities, and the impact of the Bologna Process in Europe' (Lunt 2008: 747).

In 2009, the Browne Review or, what it was formally called, the *Independent Review of Higher Education Funding and Student Finance* was set up to find solutions to the continued problem of higher education funding. Here, the review proposes a radical reform of student financing, and again can be considered as a response to the need to improve international competiveness. Lord Browne's own foreword points out that 'our competitive edge is being challenged by advances made elsewhere. Other countries are increasing investment in their HEIs and educating more people to higher standards' (Browne 2011: 2). The Browne review proposes the largest changes in student financing whereby students will bear the entire costs of their tuition, as well as the costs of financing the system, via interest payments on their loans. The coalition government adopted most of the recommendations, amid much controversy (including a vote of no-confidence by Oxford academics in David Willets, the government Minister responsible for universities).

The *HE White Paper: Students at the Heart of the System*, published June 2011, outlines the changes to the new system of higher education financing, including the new thresholds for tuition charges, which were approved by Parliament in December 2010, permitting institutions to charge £6,000 a year for their undergraduate courses. However, they can charge up to £9,000 a year if they meet conditions on widening participation and fair access. The White Paper also points out that 'around 95 percent of full-time, first-time undergraduate students' (BIS 2011) will receive more support than they do now. While this might be true, the reason behind the increased support is that this will be necessary to meet the higher costs of their education. Chapter two of the White Paper 'Well-informed students driving teaching excellence' sets out how these reforms will improve the student experience. The policy informing this conceives of students as consumers of an expensive service, and this chapter discusses the expectation that the higher education sector will become more responsive to students (as consumers). Chapter three of the White Paper continues on the theme of students and outlines how the new system will support a better student experience. The chapter deals with issues around student engagement, student unions, student surveys, complaints and the role of OFFA.

Chapter four 'A diverse and responsive sector' outlines the way in which current government policy is striving to create a market based system for higher education and outlines possibilities for new providers to enter the market, the potential of higher education in further education colleges, and importantly, ways in which student numbers can be freed, whilst still maintaining the management of overall costs. While the White Paper posits the potential to un-cap student numbers, it does not provide any detail on this, aside from the proposition to allow 'unrestrained recruitment of high achieving students' who score the equivalent grades of AAB or above at A-level. Finally, the chapter turns to the potential changes in future to degree-awarding powers, allowing private providers to award degrees. The attempt to create a more competitive market in higher education (strictly speaking, a quasi-market due to the high levels of regulation and limits on student numbers) is articulated throughout the White Paper. It is not until chapter five 'Improved social mobility through fairer access' that the White Paper introduces the ways in which the new system's fee regime is dependent on institutions' strategies to attract students from lower economic backgrounds into higher education.

Details of the Payback System

Under the new system of higher education funding, students will pay for their tuition in entirety via a student loan that covers the full amount of their tuition costs, so that no student need pay upfront. Students will begin to pay back the loan in the first financial year after graduation, only if they are earning over £21,000. When they reach this earnings threshold, they will begin to pay 9 per cent of their loan (regardless of the *amount* of the loan) on earnings over this threshold. This means that if two students have loans of £27,000 and £50,000, and they are earning £25,000 per annum, they will *both* pay back 9 per cent. The fact that the repayment amounts are not based on the size of a learner's debt, but based on income – is key to the understanding of the new system. This means that enrolling in a £9,000 a year degree will not mean that learners will be out of pocket any more than if they enrolled in a £6,500 a year degree – the only thing that changes is the length of the debt repayment period. As these debts are effectively written off after 30 years anyway, choosing the cheaper option does not *necessarily* make good economic sense. It is for this reason that this new payback system acts in a similar manner to a tax, rather than a straight forward loan. Despite these monies being paid back to government like a tax, the debt is still a loan, and interest will accrue. This will begin as soon as the loan is taken out, and will be based on a sliding scale (depending on income) of zero per cent plus the rate of inflation (calculated on the RPI) to a maximum of three per cent plus RPI. This represents a significant shift in the way higher education is financed in this country. Although learners have been paying a proportion of their higher education fee contribution since 1998, this is the first time that they will be also paying for the financing of their higher education – in the form of interest.

Although the trend towards students bearing the costs of their tuition has had a long history, the credit crunch and ensuing recession certainly exacerbated the problem of higher education financing. That students should pay the costs of their education might be seen as a rational economic argument, considering that graduates earn more over their lifetimes than those without degree level qualifications; however, this masks the discrepancies in earnings between degree subjects (for example between law and education). High fee levels also threaten the social mobility agenda that forms a strong part of current policy on higher education. This is particularly important for London as a whole, with its uneven distribution of wealth, and East London in particular, where large pockets of areas suffer from multiple forms of social deprivation. While the government pushes its social mobility agenda, there seems to be little consideration of how, exactly, this might be achieved in a city where higher education institutions have declared their fees for 2012 toward the top end of the allowable amounts.

The 'London premium' (as it is being informally, and a little cynically, called in London higher education institutions) is based on the desirability of London as a place to study, work and live, however, for those Londoners already trapped in cycles of poverty, it might be the case that the London premium dissuades them from progression into higher education, thereby reinforcing the deprivation found in areas of the city. While we will not know the effects of the new fee regime on higher education applications until the 2012-13 cohort, the concern is that those from lower socio-economic groups are more debt adverse than other groups, and may not then aim to go into higher education.

Research findings in this area, from studies conducted both in the UK and internationally are conflicted. A research paper issued by BIS in 2009 examined the attitudes of young people toward higher education. Main findings include that cost concerns do exist, but overall attitudes to higher education are positive, with 55 per cent of 17-19 year olds believing they were likely to apply to go to university. Of course, this is not evenly spread amongst all groups of young people – those with level two qualifications were much more likely to want to apply to university – with 76 per cent wishing to do so. And within this 76 per cent there are further uneven distributions between groups. Those most likely to apply to go to higher education in this group are females, from Black and Minority Ethnic (BME) groups, from higher socio-economic groups and those who report positive school experiences. Young white indigenous working class males are the least likely to want to enrol (BIS 2009: 1). This research also found that 'those with the greatest aversion to debt are among those least likely to apply to higher education' (BIS 2009, 2). The BIS report moves on to two recommendations: firstly, increasing the supply of students, secondly 'reducing the leakage' of students who have the potential to enter higher education but are not currently doing so – namely those from lower socio-economic groups (BIS 2009: 2).

The economic arguments for students to 'pay their way' in higher education with the various fee systems in the past, and the new fee system being introduced, have all been twinned with measures to incentivise participation from 'non-traditional' students – generally those from lower socio-economic backgrounds and neighbourhoods. However the economic orthodoxy behind these arguments assumes that the actors in the system make rational choices about their time and financial investments in education. In fact,

> …the orthodox analysis is based on the supposition that participation decisions of marginal entrants are primarily rational investment decisions, sensitive to financial incentives. It further assumes that these potential students are well informed about these financial considerations, that is, they can easily acquire and interpret the information they require to make these rational investment decisions. In other words, it assumes that potential non-traditional entrants to higher education can calculate that their liability to pay higher tuition fees is more than offset by the combination of grant, loan, scholarship and/or bursary available to them. (Adnett and Tlupova 2008: 248)

In any case, while widening participation policies might be successful in terms of encouraging non-traditional students into higher education – little research has been done on how 'the labour market may also reward educational attainment differently for these different social groups' (Adnett & Tlupova 2008: 247). Professions that require graduate internships certainly favour those from higher socio-economic groups as familial connections have been found to be important in securing places. Also, many of these internships are unpaid, or low-paid, again favouring those from families who can afford to subsidise the living costs of this form of work, which are particularly high in London.

Conclusion

Within a quasi-market for higher education, the student-consumer occupies a position of power. While this may be good in terms of the ability to demand an increased quality of education from their respective institutions, there may well be ramifications for whole subject areas under this new regime. The continued demise of subject areas that are not seen to be directly linked to employment outcomes (and high enough salaries to justify the levels of student debt) may well be a very likely outcome. This approach leans towards placing the direction of 'the academy" in the hands of school leavers, who are encouraged to acquire skills, rather than an education. This is already leading to a situation where whole disciplines of study (philosophy, classics and other liberal arts) may atrophy as the knowledge economy is seen to demand hard skills which are directly linked to business and industry.

The effects of the new fee system on social mobility via education, and widening participation have yet to be felt although there has been an unprecedented rush by students to find a place in higher education for the 2011/2012 academic year, to get into an institution before the new fees come into effect. In actuality this may have been misguided for many students, particularly those moving into areas where employment outcomes with high salaries may not be forthcoming, as the payback system for the new fee regime is very progressive, and geared to lower income earners. While the new fee system may not affect student numbers overall, within this there are concerns that those students who are already hesitant about participation in higher education (such as those from low-income families) will be further alienated from the possibility of continuing their education.

This will affect many in London, and East London in particular where large pockets of deprivation still exist, and which have been sharpened by the recession. There are also unresolved issues for some Muslim students as the new system requires students taking out an interest bearing loan – forbidden under Sharia law. However, many of the risks to those who are hesitant about entering higher education will be offset by attendant changes to the education landscape. In particular the rise in school leaving age to 18 by 2015 may well alleviate some of the threats to higher education participation. With such a radical change to higher education financing, and the further marketisation of higher education it is as yet unclear what the overall effects will be. However, it is clear that those who were already at risk of not participating in higher education will be further alienated, and those who do aspire to participate may well become much more instrumental in their decision making about what subject areas they choose to study.

References

Adnett, N. and Tlupova, D. (2008). 'Informed choice? The new English student funding system and widening participation'. *London Review of Education*, 6(3), 243-54.

BIS (2009). 'Who is heading for HE? Young people's perceptions of, and Decisions About Higher Education'. London: BIS.

BIS (2011). HE White Paper: Students at the Heart of the System. London: BIS.

Browne Report (2010). *An Independent Review of Higher Education Funding and Student Finance – Report of the National Committee*. London: HMSO.

Department for Education and Skills (2003). Higher Education White Paper, London: DfES.

Department for Trade and Industry (DTI) (2002). White Paper on Enterprise, Skills and Innovation. London: DTI.

Dearing Report (1997). National Committee of Inquiry into Higher Education – Report of the National Committee. London: HMSO.

Greenbank P. (2006). The Evolution of Government Policy on Widening Participation. *Higher Education Quarterly*, 60(2), 141-66.

Higher Education Act (2004). London: HMSO.

Leitch Review (2006). *Prosperity for all in the Global Economy – World Class Skills*. London: HMSO.

London Higher (2011). About London's HE: Facts and Figures. [online] Available at http://www.londonhigher.ac.uk/294.html, accessed 31 August 2011.

Lunt, I. (2008). 'Beyond tuition fees? The legacy of Blair's government to higher education'. *Oxford Review of Education*, 34(6), 741-52.

PART 4
London's Future

Chapter 20
The Crisis of Fictitious Capital

Michael Rustin

London, in the age of 'fictitious capital' has become both the worst and the best of cities.

We have seen how much it has become the worst in the widespread riots that broke out in August 2011 in many districts of London, and in the demonstration through these disturbances of the extent of disaffection from the dominant social order of significant numbers of young people, and their implicit despair about their lack of a stake or viable future in society. At the time of writing, there is too little evidence available for a full understanding of these events.[1] But their location of origin in some of the poorest districts of London draws attention to the great and growing disparities of wealth and well-being that characterise the capital city, now likely to become yet worse as unemployment increases and public services are reduced or withdrawn. No understanding of the three nights' mayhem on the streets will be adequate which does not focus on social conditions in some inner city neighbourhoods where there is endemically high unemployment, especially among the young; poor educational outcomes; many disorganised families; significant racial disadvantage; a disproportionate reduction of youth services, and the prevalence of drug abuse and petty crime.[2] Wilkinson and Pickett's statistical demonstration in *The Spirit Level* (2010) that the higher the gradient of inequality, the greater the prevalence of social problems of all kinds, could scarcely have had a more forceful demonstration.

The riots began and were concentrated in areas of acute deprivation in the east and south of the city, though over several days they spread outwards, and found echoes in cities outside London. They had many different aspects. One of these was racial tension, especially between Afro-Caribbean youth and the police (but also between Afro-Caribbeans and Asians), despite the improvements in police-community relations that are said to have been achieved since the previous period of urban riots in the 1980s. One can view these events as a form of anti-social rebellion by black and mixed race youth in particular, provoked by their large-

---

1 For a thoughtful early response (10 August) see Compass's *Anatomy of a Riot*, http://compassonline.org.uk/news/item.asp?n=13301.

2 The Guardian reported on August 18 that 41 per cent of those charged by that date lived in one of the 10 per cent of the most deprived districts in Britain, and that 66 per cent of neighbourhoods where the accused live The Metropolitan Police reported that half of those who had appeared in court by that date were under 18.

scale exclusion from economic opportunities, and at their continuing exposure to discrimination. A second, overlapping aspect is inequalities of class, which especially press downwards on the young in the present circumstances of economic recession and growing joblessness. By no means only black and mixed-race youths were involved in these disturbances, indeed their ethnic dimension became less significant as the disturbances moved rapidly beyond their original locations into districts such as Ealing and Croydon. A third aspect, much commented on, is the opportunities which are now afforded to those wishing to defy authority by the spread of electronic means of 'horizontal' communication – the technologies of smartphones, messaging sites, and the like – which enabled extraordinarily rapid and fluid gatherings of crowds and mobs to take place. The same technologies which have facilitated political mobilisations in the 'Arab Spring' were also available as a resource in the summoning of youths to engage in battles with the police and in what Zoe Williams in *The Guardian* (9 August 2011) called 'shopping riots'. 24-hour rolling television news coverage must also have played its part in amplifying these disturbances – why would one even need a messaging site if the latest outbreak of trouble (for some perceived as opportunity) were being notified in real-time on television screens on BBC News 24 and Sky News? The outbreaks of flagrant looting of items from ransacked shops enacted a parody of the mainstream religion of consumption. If for the more prosperous, its rituals are located in vast new shopping centres like London's Westfield and Stratford City, (not least on Sundays) for those who feel excluded from mainstream consuming a different kind of ritual celebration was devised, a carnival of theft and destruction, through challenging conventional rules of behaviour not in merely symbolic ways, but through violent enactment.

The larger picture in which these events need to be located is one in which greed and rule-breaking have been shown to be endemic features of the contemporary social order. Bankers, Members of Parliament, tabloid journalists and the police have become successively incriminated. One can say that the street mobs of August were following many in more advantaged positions than themselves in helping themselves to what they wanted. Although public expenditure cuts seem unlikely to have so far had a very direct causal role in these events, nevertheless the reduction in already meagre services – including police as well as youth and young family services – to deprived communities carries its message of abandonment. And all this in the exact week which marked one year before the opening of the hugely expensive 2012 London Olympics, close by the scenes of some of the disorder. Who can know in such volatile and unpredictable circumstances (would any of this have happened without the initial provocation of the shooting of a black man by a policeman?) what images had a place in the minds of people in the grip of destructive excitement. Freud's understanding[3] of the loss of individual

3 Taking up earlier writing on the psychology of crowds, Freud writes of the irrationality of the group mind. 'A group is impulsive, changeable and irritable. It is led almost exclusively by the unconscious. The impulses which a group obeys may according

identity that can take place in the context of the emotional life of groups and crowds is highly relevant to these phenomena, which seem unlikely to have had any previously planned or organised basis at all. A broader breakdown of social ties in individualised and media-coordinated societies like ours seems to produce anarchic protest as one of its endemic political forms, as we saw on the fringes of the largely well-ordered student and public sector demonstrations months before the events of August on the London streets.

London of course has been at the centre of what the title of this book terms the epoch of 'fictitious capital'. Here is where the great gamble taken in the 1980s that in future the banking and financial sector, and not manufacture, should become the dominant sector of the British economy was located, and has been played out since. The principal elements in this strategic choice were the destruction of manufacturing and mining which took place during the recession of the early 1980s, culminating in the miners' strike of 1984-5, and the 'big bang' of financial deregulation which followed this in 1985. London and its surrounding region has seen most of the economic benefits of this phase of economic development. This has been to a considerable extent at the expense of the stagnation or decline of many formerly industrial areas in the north of the country,[4] and of the city's own increasing polarisation between the beneficiaries of affluence and those excluded from it. It seems obvious that the urban youth riots of August (which also took place in Nottingham, Manchester and Birmingham) were one expression of this growing contrast between wealth and poverty.[5]

---

to circumstances be jealous or cruel, heroic or cowardly, but they are always so imperious that no personal interest, not even that of self-preservation, can make itself felt. Nothing about it is premeditated. Though it may desire things passionately, yet this is never for long, for it is incapable of perseverance. It cannot tolerate any delay between its desire and the fulfillment of what it desires. It has sense of omnipotence; the sense of impossibility disappears for the individual in a group' (Freud 1921: 77). It is a mark of the moral panic of the authorities following this violent assault on property and propriety (of which the most frightening aspect was arson) that they chose to regard participation in this contagious behaviour as grounds for extra blame and punishment, rather than as a reason for mitigation at least for young people with no previous criminal history. One may speculate that the stance of some police, who appeared to be passively watching the ransacking of shops, was taken as a virtual licence to loot by some, and then as an experience of defencelessness and fear by those identified with the legal order.

4 A recent index of regional disparities was evidence reported in the *British Medical Journal* (16 February 2011) that the north–south mortality difference was the widest for 40 years.

5 Disparities of income, wealth and opportunities between different areas of London – between the east and west, and between the inner city and the suburban and exurban peripheries, are long-standing., Buck et al. (2002) provides an analysis based on extensive data of differences within London and their causes. Although in 2002 they found that London did not show the entrenched pattern of impoverishment and exclusion that existed in some US cities (sometimes in a racialised form), they noted risks of polarisation which

Although the Labour government defeated in the elections of 2010 endorsed the neo-liberal commitments of its predecessor to the free market, and to the rise of finance as the leading sector of the economy, it also sought to mitigate the unequal effects of this development, both through some fiscal redistribution to those on lowest incomes, and through the growth of the public sector and the substantial employment of people which followed from this. This intervention created a significant stake in this phase of development for public sector employees and others on relatively modest incomes, as well as for the super-rich beneficiaries of financialisation itself. There is a large segment of the population which finds its livelihood and prospects newly threatened by the present government's plans to contract public expenditure and its field of employment. Protests about the raising of university fees, and the withdrawal of government funding for many fields of study, and the great demonstration in protest against public sector cuts, gave evidence of widespread anxiety about these developments.

But in this period, the capital city has also been the scene of glittering developments. The soaring towers of the new financial district of Canary Wharf, built on the site of the former docks, are one striking symbol of this epoch, rivalled by the construction of many other spectacular buildings throughout London, whose symbolic aim is to flaunt new wealth and power. The classes empowered by the globalisation and financialisation of the British economy have given expression to their dominant position in the city through this showy architecture of offices and luxury dwellings.

There have also been broader spin-offs from this economic development. London has sought to establish a leading position for itself as a centre of metropolitan culture, with a conspicuous development of its galleries and leisure spaces of many kinds. If a city wishes to be a centre of global capitalism, it has become important for it to be a place where the rich and ambitious will wish to live and to visit. The sphere of competition in which the city has been engaged has thus had cultural as well as economic dimensions, one aspect of which has been the development of tourism as a major industry. The campaign to secure London as the venue for the 2012 Olympic Games (Poynter and MacRury 2009). was part of this strategy, one intended benefit being to finance the extension of 'metropolitan London' some miles to the east of its previous *de facto* boundary at Aldgate. 'Spectacles' like the Olympic Games are now the targets in a global competitive market, another kind of fictitious capital (Rustin 2009).

These developments have brought some benefit to many London citizens and visitors who have little part in the development of the financial sector. The sheer multiplicity of the capital city provides an enormous diversity of opportunities and

---

more recent developments, including the effects of the credit crunch, will have accentuated. Hamnett (2003) provides analysis of inequalities in London in the context of its transition from an industrial to a post-industrial city.

amenities of many kinds.[6] London remains a city of neighbourhoods, many with remarkable character. Inward migration and ethnic complexity is a source of great new life and energy in the capital. As Marshal Berman (1983, 2006) has argued, especially in relation to New York, the diversity and unpredictability which can make a city at times seem an edgy and dangerous place, are also the source of its creativity. Ubiquitous CCTV cameras notwithstanding, people are able in most of the city to walk freely in the streets, along Thameside and by canals, and in parks great and small. They are still free to visit many great museums, free of charge, although the closure of branch libraries and other local centres shows the present government's small regard for free public amenities. Of course there are also strong tendencies in contemporary cities like London for the enclosure of the most desirable spaces by means of price or gated seclusion. Coalition policy on the *restriction of housing benefits will increase the economic segregation of city housing*, amounting in Boris Johnson's phrase to a form of 'social cleansing' (How revealing it is that the Canary Wharf tower is virtually unique among buildings of its kind in providing no viewing space – open to the public rather than to selected invitees – from its summit, despite the huge flow of visitors which such attractions invariably bring). Nevertheless, despite these signs of an increasing polarisation of the city between its privileged and less privileged citizens, the capital provides a variety of delights to many who live or visit there. And despite the contrary evidence of the antagonisms displayed in the August disturbances, there is also a greater degree of ethnic integration and amicable coexistence than might have been expected at the time of the previous urban disturbances of the 1980s.[7]

The capital is not only richer than the rest of the United Kingdom, but continues to accumulate a disproportionate share of investments in future improvement and growth. Whereas one would hope that large projects would be a key means of redressing regional imbalances and inequalities, the current pattern of development is going to accentuate them. The scale of investment in transport currently under way in London – the major renewal of its Underground system, and the construction of Crossrail, and Thameslink – far exceeds expenditure on equivalent developments outside the capital region.[8] Even High Speed 2 will give priority to the capital, with the first phase of construction to knock a few minutes off the rail journey from London to Birmingham preceding by a decade the extension

6 On the global forces which create the diversity and contrasts of a 'world city' like London, which are both exciting and troubling from the point of view of social justice, see Massey (2007).

7 See Chapter 16 in this book and Murji, K. and Neal, S. (2011) 'Riot, Race and Politics in the 2011 Disorders' in Sociological Research Online, 16 (4) 24, November 2011.

8 However these transport investments will bring more economic activity to the capital and its region, valuable in a time of recession. See report at http://www.crossrail.co.uk/news/press-releases/crossrails-wider-economic-boost-to-london-south-east-revealed. Peter Hall (1989) argued for a London version of Paris RER rail system, which is now coming into being.

of the line to the North and Scotland. Why was it not decided to commence the construction of HS2 from the other end of the country?[9]

So here until the credit crunch of 2008-9 was a pattern of economic development in which London represented both the best – in its wealth and variety – and the worst – in its inequalities and in its growing privilege in relation to the rest of the country. But then came the crisis, and the evidence of the vulnerability and instability of the finance-capital led economic model on which Britain has been reliant since the 1980s.

The Meaning of the Financial Crisis of 2008 (and its Recurrence in 2011)

The decades from 1980 saw the triumph of neo-liberalism – a version of free-market corporate capitalism – in almost every sphere of Britain's life.[10] The 'class settlement' which had been achieved as a consequence of the national unity of the Second World War, and of the period of post-war reconstruction, ended in the prolonged deadlock and ultimate turmoil of the 1970s (Hall et al. 1978). The negotiated balance between public and private provision, and the partial economic enfranchisement of the organised working class into government through the influence of trade unions were rejected by Thatcher and her government as intolerable steps in what it saw as the direction of collectivism and 'socialism'. The mission of the governments of the 1980s was to reverse these concessions to collectivist norms and power, substituting for them the supposed sovereignty of individuals in the role of consumers. The diminution of trade union rights and powers, the privatisation of publicly owned enterprises, and the creation of 'internal markets' in public institutions not deemed capable of full marketisation were principal elements of this programme.

Despite the over-reaches of this governmental strategy by the Thatcher and Major governments (the Poll Tax and the financial crisis of 'Black Wednesday' being its worst moments) New Labour when it came to power endorsed and sustained much of the programme of neo-liberal reform, in the economy and in public services. New Labour had no serious plan to lessen the new dependence on the financial sector, and thus little capacity to diminish the dominant role of London and its region in the national economy. It reversed few of the Tories major reforms, and continued its programmes of 'internal marketisation' in the public sector. The most significant difference was that Labour had been elected with a commitment to restore and improve the quality of public services, through the

9 We may note also the vigour with which governments defend the interests of the City against regulation from Europe, compared with their refusal to contest such regulation when it concerns manufacturing contracts such as that of the train manufacturer Bombardier in Derby.

10 For a global account of this development not confined to Britain, see David Harvey (2010) and Joseph Stiglitz (2010).

investment of significant resources. The significant real effects of this commitment are now being seen as services and institutions fall into crisis following the implementation of 'deficit reducing' cuts in public expenditure.

However, what seemed for ten years or so to be a new equilibrium, between market-driven economic growth and compensatory public initiatives, has turned out to be deeply flawed. At the moment of its apparent triumph (the Cold War won, most of Eastern Europe brought within the domain of the market, internal political opposition to capitalism fragmented and weakened) the neo-liberal system imploded in the crisis of the banking system in 2008 (On neo-liberalism and the crisis, see Hall and Massey 2010, Hall 2011, Massey 2011, and Rustin 2009 and 2011). The hypertrophy of the financial sector had many symptoms. These included the invention of financial instruments so complicated that no-one could understand them, the lending of money to recipients (e.g. the sub-prime housing market) who were unable to service the interest on the loans, and the packaging and selling-off of bad debts in ways which merely concealed their real nature (Tett 2010). But perhaps the most important was the dissociation of money-making, impelled by waves of ostentatious greed for wealth, power, and reputation (of which the 'celebrity culture is a media reflection) from productive economic activity. Instead of being the source of finance for real investment, financial exchanges – the domain of the circulation rather than the investment of capital – became a substitute for investment. Thus transactions in financial markets – trading in currencies, shares, 'futures' – came in scale and money-value to dwarf the economy whose reality it was supposed to represent, reflect and support.

While this was going on, the 'real economies' for example of manufacturing in those nations most addicted to the free-market, financialised model of capitalism, were in serious decline. What had been initially the outsourcing of routine manufacturing assembly operations to low-wage economies in the then 'third world' has become the displacement of entire industries to what are now aptly renamed as the 'emerging markets' of the Asia and Latin America. And not only manufacturing, but also technical and consumer services. If one rings British Telecom to complain about a faulty telephone line in rural England, one may well be answered by an advisor speaking from Hyderabad, and equipped with the software to diagnose the fault from there. The only element left in Britain of its largest telecommunications company's repair services seems to be the local technician who has still to come and fix a broken wire, if indeed the fault is mechanical.

Dependence of an economy on its financial sector has many harmful consequences. The dissociation of exchange from production – especially where the exchanges have become virtual and electronic – has the effect that wealth is accumulated by people who need engage in no actual relationships with the producers of substantive wealth, and who develop no sustained commitment to the process of production. A mine-owner or ship-owner of old might have been a harsh and driving employer, but he nevertheless had to have some means of engaging with employees, coming to some kind of settlement with them which would lead them to work. Similarly, as Will Hutton (1996, 2011) has pointed out, finance-dominated systems of corporate governance have proved to be uninterested in the long-term development of enterprises. If all that counts is short-term profit and the share price, there will be little commitment to investment or the nurturing of corporate loyalty. Indeed it seems that the dissociation of 'virtual' company ownership from 'real' corporate responsibility has been a major reason for the relative decline of those economies, like those of the UK or the USA, most addicted to the neo-liberal, globalised, finance-dominated economic model, in contrast to industrial economies like that of Germany whose methods of corporate governance are different.

Now has arrived the second phase of this crisis of neo-liberal, or finance-dominated capitalism. It emerges that there has been little real recovery from the collapse into indebtedness shown in the 2008 crash. Entire national economies (Iceland, Ireland) have gone down with their bankrupt banks. Where governments rather than banks have become heavily indebted (as in the case of Greece and Portugal) the problem is where to find the resources to prevent default on their debts (with possible knock-on effects on the banking system akin to the collapse of Lehman Brothers). If one seeks to remove deficits by reducing expenditure, the consequence is liable to be a recession or full-blown depression. The consequence of this will be further to add to debt, since the tax and other revenues which might otherwise contribute to deficit reduction fall during times of contraction. This is the deep contradiction which the global capitalist economy now faces.

It seems that the counter-revolution against 'welfarism' and social compromise unleashed in the period of neo-liberal domination has had self-destructive effects. As the proponents of 'Keynesianism' and welfarism have argued, the strategies of compromise pursued or accepted by governments and manufacturing corporations in the1950s and 1960s were functionally beneficial to all parties, to the owners of capital as well as to those dependent on the labour. This is because there can be no sustainable production in market economies unless there is also consumption. Without sufficient demand, there can be no supply. And to sustain modern industries and their necessary economies of scale, consumption has to be on an inclusive, mass scale. No amount of luxury consumption, of the kinds advertised in the *Financial Times* 'How To Spend It' high-gloss supplement, can sustain a modern economy by itself. Inequality is, as Wilkinson and Pickett (2010) have persuasively argued, destructive of health, social cohesion and well-being. But it is also destructive of capitalist economies themselves.

We know that economies largely owned and dominated by states and their functionaries, such as those of the former Soviet bloc, largely lack the capacity to innovate or to meet the complex and varied needs of their citizens. We are also learning once again that economies largely owned and dominated by private capital, without the moral restraint, far-sightedness, and attention to the general good, provided by the power of democratic governments, are also liable to fail. We are now in the west experiencing the nature and consequences of that failure.

Resolving the Crisis: Problems and Opportunities

It seems likely that the system of neo-liberalism which has been in the ascendancy since 1980 is now in a state of deep crisis. The financial collapse of 2008 and the near-repetition in the summer of 2011, were extraordinary developments for a system that appeared to have defeated virtually all of its serious enemies (Although militant Islamism has been constructed by the West as its principal enemy in recent decades, and has been fought in several wars, the substantive threat it represents to the dominant powers has always been small, compared with the era of the Cold War).[11] A form of capitalism dominated by its financial sector appears unable to generate either the supply (in terms of competitive products) or the demand (in terms of incomes sufficiently broadly spread to sustain consumption) to achieve global competitiveness or sustained growth. The definition of the primary economic problems as those of fiscal deficits, and the choice of deflationary remedies to resolve these, seem likely to make a bad situation worse, in the USA, in the European Union, and in the United Kingdom.

Prolonged high unemployment, static or declining incomes for the majority, and contraction and deterioration of public services, are likely to be the economic concomitants of this situation. Politically, one would anticipate a period of prolonged political volatility and instability as governments of whatever hue struggle to maintain legitimacy and popularity among their electorates since they are unable to provide what their citizens desire and need. The situation is reminiscent of the earlier period of crisis of the 1970s, as a previous hegemonic structure – the post-war welfare settlement between classes and its balance between 'public' and 'private' claims on the economy – began to collapse from its own contradictions. In Britain, this was the period of governmental 'U-turns' (this phrase was invented to describe the reversal of the premature neo-liberalism of Heath's 'Selsdon Man' phase) of unexpected election defeats ('who governs Britain?' Heath demanded, in response to the first miners' strike, to learn that it would not be him), and of large-scale urban disturbances. These culminated in the 'Winter of Discontent' of 1978-9 which in effect drove Labour from power. The internal crisis in Britain was brought about by irresolvable conflicts over the distribution of power and wealth, as the earlier relatively consensual arrangements for conflict-resolution broke down. Trade union power (the image of trade union tanks parked on the lawn of 10 Downing Street lawn was a vivid one) was a particular focus of conflict and

11 In his recent book, Jason Burke (2011) estimates the deaths attributable to what he calls the 9/11 Wars (so far, in Afghanistan, Iraq and Pakistan). Of an estimated number of 100,000 military and 150,000 civilian deaths (the latter could well be an underestimate, and serious injuries are usually taken to be at least three times the number of fatalities) he reports that approximately 10,000-12,000 were from US or allied Western nations, including the 3000 Americans killed on 9/11. These numbers are large, but so is the disproportion between the casualties from western and other nations. For a summary by Burke, see *The Guardian* (23 August 2011).

anxiety. The system experienced major perturbations from outside. One dimension of this was the sharp rise in oil prices, as Middle East oil producers sought to increase their share of global wealth at a time of opportunity as petroleum was in high demand. Another was the delayed effect of unaffordable wars on levels of inflation – the Vietnam War ended only in 1975. Both the role of oil price inflation, and of unaffordable foreign wars, have their obvious analogies in the present crisis, in the rise of emerging economies such as China's to a pre-eminent position in the world, and in the misuse of resources to ill-conceived Middle Eastern wars.

In this situation, it seems likely that many governments will struggle to retain office, as incumbents in power (whether of centre-left or centre-right composition) face the discontent of electorates they have disappointed and disillusioned. It seems more likely than not that elections in France, Spain, Germany and Italy will lead to changes of government within a year, and President Obama has already suffered a serious electoral setback in the Congressional elections of 2010. One possibility is that the Coalition government in the UK will find itself under severe strain, as the impact of its economic and social policies make themselves felt, and will fail to survive to the end of its full electoral term.

But while one relevant narrative may be that of the instability of the 1970s, the Tories in the Coalition government have a different comparative model in their mind. This is the counter-revolutionary demarche of the 1980s, in which, in the Thatcherite view, the unresolved problems of a previous era were resolved by decisive reforms. The Coalition's belief that the early years of its own strategy of drastic reform (substantially to reduce the role of the public sector in the economy) will be difficult, but will eventually lead to success, takes as its model the experience of the 1980s Thatcher governments, which survived its early difficulties to enjoy 18 years in power. It should be noted however that it probably survived the 1982 Election only because it followed soon after Thatcher's victory in the Falklands War, and because the opposition was in complete disarray through Labour's schisms and the rise of the SDP. That government even sought to turn popular resistance to its policies to its advantage, always defining the primary issue (as in the Miners' Strike of 1984-5) as one of 'democracy' and law and order, rather than of economic deprivation and injustice. An affinity with the Coalition government's response to the August street riots is plain. It is uncertain which of these competing historical analogies with the present – that of the strife-torn 1970s, or of the decisive action followed by recovery of the 1980s, will prove to be the most prescient.[12]

Although there seems to be some agreement among politicians of all parties that a rebalancing of the British economy away from the dominance of the banking and financial sectors is desirable, there is no indication that anyone understands

12 The Lib Dems' version of this situation is yet different again. They must have seen the outcome of the 2010 election as a mandate for compromise moderation, with themselves as its guarantors and ultimate beneficiaries, via electoral reform. As for the Labour Party, we are yet to learn whether it will offer any substantial analysis of the crisis that came to its climax while it held office, and of any conclusions which might follow from this.

how to achieve this, or even if they do, has the will to do so. The Coalition's idea that if the share of public expenditure in the economy is reduced, the private sector will create sufficient new enterprises, especially in manufacturing, to replace it, seems to have little more than neo-liberal ideology to support it. Indeed in so far as deficit-reduction leads to economic contraction, it seems more likely to reduce productive investment than to increase it.

Furthermore, because the financial sector does remain one of the UK's more competitive spheres of economic activity, it seems that governments of any hue will be constrained to support its continuing large role, whatever improvements in regulation and risk-taking they may also seek to make. Thus there is no sign that the dominant role of London in the national economy, and the particular configuration which this gives to the economy of the capital, is going to change any time soon. What is lacking at the present are substantial and coherent alternatives to the economic strategy on which the British economy has been based since the early 1980s, changes of government notwithstanding. Even if it appears to the public that the Coalition government has solved few problems (or has even made them worse), and thus fails to achieve a second term of office, this itself does not signify that a major change in direction will occur. The question of what might be the necessary elements of such a change will be the final one to be addressed in this chapter.

Major changes to a failing economic model are not straightforward to achieve. The situation accords with the often-quoted formulation by Antonio Gramsci – 'The old is dying, the new is struggling to be born, and in the state of interregnum there arise many morbid symptoms'. What is most needed at this point is a conception of an alternative system, or indeed a debate about what such a conception might include. Several central problems can be identified.

The first of these is that of diminishing the central role of the financial sector in the economy, and to ensure that productive investment in real goods and services replaces what has become a parasitic economy based on speculation and gambling.[13] Various measures have been proposed to achieve this end, One of these is a 'transaction tax' (the 'Tobin tax' named after the economist who originated this idea) to reduce the profitability of currency speculation and make some part of this speculative flow available for more useful purposes. This idea has recently been endorsed by the leaders of France and Germany, though with what consequence is at the time of writing unknown. Others are measures to increase the transparency and accountability of transactions within the financial

13 The commitment of previous and the present government to greater private sector involvement in the former 'public sector' is another aspect of this parasitic form of capitalism, companies wishing their profits to be underwritten by state guarantees and subsidies, whatever their free market rhetoric. The Treasury Select Committee's Report on Private Finance Initiatives (PFIs) (August 19 2011) made this dynamic plain. http://www.parliament.uk/business/committees/committees-a-z/commons-select/treasury-committee/news/pfi-report/.

sector, to separate the retail and investment functions of banks, and to require banks to hold more capital as security to restrain their risk-taking. But the most substantial idea recently put forward to address the problem of insufficient real investment is Robert Skidelsky's Keynesian proposal (*The Guardian*, 21 June 2011, *Financial Times*, 31 July 2011) for the establishment in the UK of a state investment bank, with funding of £1 billion, which would be charged to invest in substantial economic development, including in infrastructural projects. This proposal overlaps with the ideas produced by the New Economics Foundation for a Green New Deal (http://www.greennewdealgroup.org) by which such investment would be concentrated on achieving the necessary transition to the low-carbon production and consumption of energy. It is becoming recognised that major infrastructural and other material investment underwritten by governments is the most plausible remedy for the present economic crisis. The problem is that the major element of 'socialisation' of the economy that this would entail is contrary to the ruling tenets of neo-liberalism.

These ideas have in common the recognition that government needs to be an active force in economic development, rather than merely an enforcer of market freedoms, or the provider of compensatory welfare provision. The inadequacy of the neo-liberal model of economic regulation has been revealed not only by the credit crunch, and by the current prospect of prolonged economic stagnation, but also by the contrast with the active role taken by governments in the rapid development that is taking place in 'emerging market' economies such as that of China.

The British government's current plan to diversify economic activity, away from the financial sector relies largely on creating space for private enterprise through the contraction of public expenditure, and through reducing the regulation of businesses. It seems a pious hope indeed that this goal will be accomplished by this means alone. The state needs to take a much more proactive role in providing and directing investment where it can be effective. Laissez-faire will not secure this objective.

One problem is that the kinds of information gathering and processing – concerned with alternative technologies, supply chains, logistics, potential markets, competing provision – on which large corporations routinely rely when they make major investment decisions is deficient at the larger level of nation-wide or region-wide economic policy. The dominant idea has long been that government and the quasi-autonomous Bank of England should confine itself to the regulation of economic activity at a macro-level, basing this on the analysis of aggregate economic data (rates of inflation, growth, the balance of payments and the like), and using the blunt instruments of fiscal and monetary policy alone. More direct economic interventions, for example to support major infrastructural investments in energy or transport, are justified only in exceptional cases where 'market failures' are deemed to occur, such as where there are major 'externalities' and where long-term benefits beyond the time-horizons of private investors are in question. The neo-liberal assumption is that below the aggregate level of regulation of supply and demands', free markets will appropriately determine the allocation of capital resources. Share prices (whose movements *are* meticulously mapped from minute to minute) are said to provide the information that is required to assess opportunities for profitable investment. Meanwhile it is reported (Polly Toynbee, *The Guardian*, 23 August, 2011 that banks lend to business only 5 per cent of their total funds, worth four times UK's GDP. This is the ruling model of economic policy-making in the Treasury, while the Department for Business, and regional economic development agencies including the Greater London Authority and the Mayor's office have a subordinate and indeed feeble role.

But the fact is that without a system of intelligence which monitors what kinds of economic activity are taking place where, what their developmental needs may be, whether they are growing or declining, and what they contribute to economic well-being, there is no prospect of advancing a 'post-financial' form of development. A quite different kind of data gathering and economic mapping is called for, which would enable the emergence and needs of new sectors and their interdependencies to be evaluated. On the periphery of government, there is recognition[14] that new priorities should be established, and that support for broad economic approaches (e.g. 'knowledge-based industries') or specific sectors (e.g. low carbon energy, nano-technology, and the 'creative industries') is needed, even though there is no clarity about how such support is to be given or how resources are to be found for it.[15] A step-change in the availability and dissemination of information on the 'real economy', and in the terms in which debate about economic policy is conducted, is the first necessary step towards a viable form of economic development. The London Mayor's office and the Greater London Authority have an important potential role in such a development. The 'evidence-based' policy-making on which governments have been insisting in fields of public provision such as health and local government needs an equivalent role in the larger economy.

Related to this is the inappropriateness of the dominant models of corporate governance for enabling the economic development that is needed to take place. There is an endemic gap between ownership and responsibility in the way in which corporations are now owned and managed, such that short-term benefits for shareholders and directors often outweigh long-term commitment to the well-being and development of enterprises. The inflation of directors' and top managers' salaries that has taken place in recent decades is a manifestation of this structural problem. In effect, a corporate elite is being permitted to manage major sectors of the economy largely for its own benefit, to the disregard of the interests of enterprises themselves, of the employees on whose labour companies depend,

14 There are informative reports to be found on the BIS (Department for Business Innovation and Skills) website http://www.bis.gov.uk/.

15 An argument which is often put against such investment, following the attempts at planning by governments in the 1960s and 1970s, is that governments are no good at 'picking winners'. But meanwhile the 'free market' has ruled over a period of 30 years of industrial decline.

and of their customers' loyalty. It appears that the largest rewards to managers are often given for asset-stripping, for turning into liquid money-value what had been substantial enterprises, through company closures and the sacking of employees. Hutton's proposal for the introduction of 'stakeholder' models of ownership and control, in which employees and representatives of the public good would have representation on company boards, and could ensure that wider issues of corporate development were made transparent and open to debate, remains an essential model for the reform of the economy. More inclusive and cooperative modes of management would also be likely to contribute to the lessening of the growing inequalities of this finance-dominated system.[16]

Finally, it has become necessary to redefine the larger purposes of economic activity, and to call into question the idea that the 'economic growth', as expressed in the mere expansion of monetary incomes and wealth, can any longer be an adequate measure of social well-being. This redefinition is all the more necessary as merely financial measures of benefit have invaded so many spheres of activity in which they were previously of lesser significance. For example, public goods – such as those education or mental health – which were once seen as largely intrinsic, are being reclassified in terms of the instrumental contribution they are alleged to make to the supposedly higher-order value of economic benefit. Many forms of welfare intervention – including for example the Improving Access to Psychological Therapies Programme (Layard 2006) introduced by the previous government – are rationalised by their supposed contribution to the labour market –the benefit getting ill people back into work.[17] Reforms to university fees are changing a system which was formerly based on an intergenerational gift of an education which the young were free to enjoy and use as they wished, into an explicit economic investment, by the self in the self.[18] Eighteen-year olds are now expected to decide whether to take out a mortgage on their own education, by

16 The success of the John Lewis Partnership (reported to be Britain's most esteemed retailer) is evidence that co-ownership models can and do work.

17 It seems likely that this economic argument by the original advocate of IIAPT, Richard Layard (2005, 2006), a progressive labour market economist, was significant in persuading the then government to take up his proposal.

18 Karl Polanyi in *The Great Transformation* (1944) compared market exchange with previously dominant principles of economic organisation – those based on reciprocity or what we might now term gift exchange, redistribution (through governments), and household autarchy. His analysis of the effects of free market system needs renewed consideration in the light of the current crisis. He wrote: 'The commodity description of labour, land and money is entirely fictitious. Nevertheless, it is with the help of this fiction that the actual markets for labour, land and money are organised.... The commodity fiction, therefore, supplies a vital organising principle in regard to the whole of society affecting almost all of its institutions in the most varied way, namely the principle according to which no arrangement or behaviour should be allowed to exist that might prevent the actual functioning of the market mechanism on the lines of the commodity fiction (Polanyi 1944: 72-3). Our concept of 'fictitious capital' has a significant precedent.

calculating what are likely to be its future benefits. This is happening as the earlier concept of a balance between 'public' and 'private' provision, each organised with its own somewhat distinct values and norms, has been eroded under the hegemony of neo-liberalism.

There are deep ethical problems with this marketised redefinition of the social good. It represents the triumph of a one-dimensional ideology, in which what cannot be assigned a precise monetary value is deemed to have no significant worth at all.[19] Such a world-view is in its own way as totalitarian as that of the postulated goods of state socialism, even though its ultimate beneficiaries are held to be not collectivities but free individuals exercising free choices. The problem is that in a world in which all values are monetarised, all differences become flattened out, and real choice is diminished, since all fields of life are subordinated to a common measure. 'How much is it, or he or she, worth?' becomes the dominant criterion of value.

One practical reason why this world-view needs now to be re-thought is that we may soon have to accept that growth in economically advanced nations such as the UK is unlikely to continue at the rates to which we have become accustomed in recent decades. Global resources of energy, food, and water cannot sustain the indefinite expansion of material production, and since the emerging economies of the world with their immense populations can legitimately claim priority in ensuring that the basic needs of their populations must be met, it is reasonable that 'advanced economies' should accept a reduced share of resources. Managing the 'withdrawal symptoms' of reduced economic growth might be easier if we began to redefine our measures of well-being.

Amartya Sen (1999) and Martha Nussbaum (Nussbaum and Sen 1993) have in recent years argued for an alternative means of measuring economic development and welfare, by substituting measures of human capabilities for those of money income. Sen has been primarily concerned with development in what used to be called the Third World, and with the priorities which should be followed in that context, but his ideas have a relevance to developed economies which needs to be elaborated. The Human Development Reports now produced annually by the United Nations, following the influence of Nussbaum's and Sen's work, measures comparative development by reference to indices such as infant mortality, life-expectancy, the availability of sanitation and clean water, years of education (specifically for women), etc. One can add other indices, such as the prevalence of human rights and free expression, the proportion of a nation's population, or sub-group of it, held in prison, etc. This approach leads to significant re-evaluation of nations' comparative achievement in terms of well-being and the development of human capabilities. Some poor societies turn out to have levels of infant mortality and life expectancy as favourable as those of rich ones (Cuba's comparable to those

---

19 Michael Walzer's *Spheres of Justice* (1983) argued for the necessary plurality of values in society, against different forms of imposed one-dimensionality.

of Canada, for example, while one rich society, the USA, leads the world in its rate of imprisonment, and disproportionately of its African American population.

We need to develop such a 'capabilities' approach, which measures well-being by reference to human experiences, not merely by income and wealth, and deploy this to re-evaluate the quality and development of our own society. In so far as conceptions of 'broken societies' and 'big societies' are more than a kind of political triangulation to divert attention from the effects of public spending cuts, they could be usefully informed by a 'capabilities' approach.

In advanced societies, what should follow is the importance of relationships as the primary condition and measure of well-being. Work is of value not merely because it produces economic value, but because it brings people together in a common task. Schools have their educative functions because of the relations which teachers have with children, and children with each other. Where schools are finding themselves having to compensate for jeopardised relationships in disorganised families, it is obvious that they need the additional human resources which can enable them to give support and understanding to their pupils. Vulnerable families of young children need centres which can support the stressful experiences of parenting. It is simply perverse to be reducing the numbers of youth workers, probation officers, and policemen, at the same time as societies face problems of alienation and hopelessness in deprived communities.

There has long been a fashionable neo-liberal idea that the 'real economy' of the market sector produces wealth, while 'public' agencies like schools, hospitals, theatres or libraries merely spend it. This is a misleading and confusing polarity. What is 'produced' in the interactions between nurses and patients, or teachers and pupils, is just as much a form of wealth as what is 'produced' in a factory or an advertising agency, and may well be of greater value. The organisation of 'production' – whether by market, state or voluntary co-operative – is one thing, and the definition of what of value is 'produced' by any of these means is quite another. Far from prospectively increasing the national wealth and well-being, the enforced contraction of public provision is visibly reducing it. It seems likely that in future there will need to be more and not less people employed in the production of public goods – including the good of creative labour itself – if well-being is to be enhanced.[20]

---

20 Increased efficiency in manufacture and many services (e.g. banking and retailing) has the effect of displacing human labour (We see evidence of this in the displacement of many local and specialist shops in London by supermarkets and on-line commerce). But in many 'human services' (e.g. education, health, social care, cultural production) there are few such economies to be achieved. More and not less human labour is required if quality is to be enhanced. As the 'Baumol hypothesis' explains (Bailey 1976) some economic activities inherently give rise to less gains in 'productivity' than others, and these are located in the production of social goods and thus in the public sector for material reasons. Enhanced social well-being requires that the economic benefits of the more 'efficient' sectors are

To move away from the era of 'fictitious capital' will require a great deal of change. Some of this needs to be at the level of conceptions, understandings and measures. We should be seeking to develop a society committed to the production of real goods, no longer dominated by the power of financial markets. The vitality of democracy, both in the governance of enterprises referred to above, and in society more broadly, is crucial, since it is only through democratic processes that support for the production of public goods can be sustained against the imperatives and ideologies of financial markets.

An essential political context in which reforms need to be developed and articulated is the capital itself. Here there is after all an elected Mayor and Assembly, with high public profiles, and the capacity to set new agendas. Local government has been enfeebled in recent decades, in the London boroughs as elsewhere, through the loss of some of its key powers (e.g. in education) through excessive central government regulation and target-setting, and because so much of its funding is provided by central government rather than through accountable local taxation for which elected authorities can be held to account.[21] Drastic public spending cuts are now forcing local authorities to take political responsibility for the consequences of decisions which are not of their making. Vigorous debate in the capital about the ways in which the quality of life is being worsened by the withdrawal of public services is essential, if the idea of public goods is to be defended. The August riots were a severe warning about what can happen where there is a serious political deficit in the capacity to address social problems.

The decision by the previous government in 2008 to allow, where there is sufficient public support, the establishment of 'community councils' (the metropolitan equivalent of rural parish councils) in London where they were previously prohibited offers an opportunity for a new kind of democratic regeneration.[22] Such community councils will have a budget raised from a small precept additional to council tax, and will be able to engage in specific local initiatives. One of their main benefits should be to make possible greater civil involvement and participation on issues close to citizens' immediate experience. This initiative is consistent not only with the broader measures of democratic enabling of the previous government (e.g. Scottish and Welsh devolution, Freedom of Information Act, and the London Mayoralty), but also with David Cameron's conception of a 'big' (i.e. more integrated and cohesive) society.[23]

---

transferred to the 'less efficient' ones concerned with the production of human goods, not sequestered by the very rich.

21 Simon Jenkins (2006) has been the most vigorous advocate of the significance of local government.

22 At the time of writing, campaigns to establish community councils were underway in the Queens Park neighbourhood of Westminster, and in the London Fields district of Hackney.

23 Jesse Norman (2010) makes the best case for the 'big society' idea.

The renewal of democratic institutions and practices are critical if there is to be a shift from a world of fictitious money values, to an appreciation of the value of human and social goods. It is a paradox that some of the reforms which need advocacy in London ought to aim to rebalance national wealth and power away from the capital and its region.

References

Bailey, E. (ed.) (1976). *Selected Economic Writings of William J Baumol*. New York University Press.

Berman, M. (1983). *All that is Solid Melts into Air: The Experience of Modernity*. London: Verso.

Berman, M. (2006). *On the Town: One Hundred Years of Spectacle in Times Square*. New York: Random House.

Buck, N., Gordon, I., Hall, P., Harloe, M. and Kleinman, M. (2002). *Working Capital: Life and Labour in Contemporary London*. London: Routledge.

Burke, J. (2011). *The 9/11 Wars*. London: Allen Lane.

Hall, P. (1989). *London 2001*. London: Unwin Hyman.

Hall, S., Critcher, C., Jefferson, T., Roberts, B.H. (1978). *Policing the Crisis: Mugging, the State and Law and Order.* London: Palgrave Macmillan.

Hall, S. (2011). 'The neo-liberal revolution' *Soundings*, 48.

Hall, S. and Massey, D. (2010). 'Interpreting the crisis' *Soundings*, 44.

Hamnett, C. (2003). *Unequal City*. London: Routledge

Hutton, W. (1996). *The State We're In: Why Britain is in Crisis and How to Overcome It* (Revised Edition). London: Vintage.

Hutton, W. (2010). *Them and Us: Why We Need a Fair Society*. London: Abacus.

Jenkins, S. (2006). *Thatcher and Sons: A Revolution in Three Acts*. London: Allen Lane.

Layard, R. (2005). *Happiness: Lessons from a New Science*. London: Penguin.

Layard, R. (2006). *The Depression Report: A New Deal for Depression and Anxiety Disorders*. London School of Economics. cep.lse.ac.uk/textonly/research/…/DEPRESSION_REPORT_LAYARD.pdf, accessed 10 May 2011.

Massey, D. (2007). *World City*. London: Polity Press.

Massey, D. (2011). 'Ideology and economics in the present moment'. *Soundings* 48.

Norman, J. (2010). *The Big Society*. Buckingham: University of Buckingham Press.

Nussbaum, M.C. and Sen, A. (eds) (1993). *The Quality of Life*. Oxford: Oxford University Press.

Polanyi, K. (1944). *The Great Transformation: The Political and Economic Origins of Our Time*. Boston, MA: Beacon Press.

Poynter, G. and MacRury, I. (2009). *Olympic Cities: 2012 and the Remaking of London*. Farnham: Ashgate.

Rustin, M.J. (2009). 'Sport, Spectacle and Society: Understanding the Olympics' in G. Poynter and I. MacRury (eds), *Olympic Cities: 2012 and the Remaking of London*.
Rustin, M.J. (2009). 'Reflections on the present: A conjunctural analysis of the present crisis'. *Soundings*, 43.
Rustin, M.J. (2011). 'The Crisis of a Social System'. *Soundings*, 48.
Sen, A. (1999). *Development as Freedom*. Oxford: Oxford University Press.
Stiglitz, J. (2010). *Freefall: Free Markets and the Sinking of the Global Economy*. London: Penguin.
Tett, G. (2010). *Fool's Gold: How Unrestrained Greed Corrupted a Dream, Shattered Global Markets and Unleashed a Catastrophe*. London: Abacus.
Walzer, M. (1983). *Spheres of Justice*. London: Martin Robertson.
Wilkinson, R. and Pickett, K. (2010 updated edition). *The Spirit Level: Why Equality is Better for Everyone*. London: Penguin.

Chapter 21
Toward a New Urban Economy?

Gavin Poynter and Michael Rustin

Introduction

This book commenced with a question posed by the Mayor of London, 'To the banker bashers I say, what's your ideal economic model?' The contributors have answered – not that which has driven the city's development over recent decades. The pervasive effects of a highly financialised economy, with its impacts upon arts, culture, creativity, employment and the very social fabric of the city makes it difficult it seems, even in the midst of a long downturn, for alternative social and economic ideas to emerge in response to a model that has failed.

By summer 2011, renewed fears about the global economy arose from a slowdown in growth in China, concerns about the US economy returning to recession and continuing crises in the Eurozone. In Europe, political leaders were divided over the ways to redistribute or reduce debt levels for countries such as Greece, with Germany reluctant to underwrite debts and its own and other European banks exposed to considerable losses if the write down of debts occurred. In London, bank shares fell dramatically in August, even those of institutions, such as Lloyds Group, that were not exposed to the problems in the Eurozone. There seemed 'no magic medicine' capable of healing the UK, US or the European economies; with the crisis containing in equal measure, economic and political dimensions, the former arising from the stubborn persistence of low/no growth and the latter from politicians' apparent incapacity to agree about what should be done to kick start it (Harding and Atkins 2011: 5).

This concluding chapter does not provide a magic medicine, as Michael Rustin has suggested in the preceding chapter, significant shifts are required in conceptions, policy and practice. It does, however, argue that for the patient to improve a full diagnosis is a necessary prerequisite for an alternative treatment to be found. London's future is intimately linked to the future of the international economy; its financial and business services will continue to perform a significant global role but restoring economic growth and balance to the domestic, urban economy of the city is essential. After reviewing contributors' analyses of how financial interests have shaped recent developments within London's economy and social and cultural life, the chapter concludes with some further insights into an alternative vision for its future.

Financialisation: The Rise of Melded Capital

Contributors to this book are not 'banker bashers'. As Daniel Ben-Ami has argued in Chapter 8, 'the City ... provides a way of channelling money from those who have more than they need at a given time to those who require it. By doing so it creates a relationship that, at least in principle, can benefit both sides'. This role as 'go-between' or mediator between different fractions of capital (including people as variable capital) is essential to advanced economies. It is when this activity and its attendant tasks, conducted in the sphere of circulation, becomes the motor of an economy and society that severe problems eventually arise.

Chapters in Part 1 explained the rising importance of financial services in London and the UK by reference to the structural problems facing Britain's, and by implication, other western economies. The challenges presented by the crises of mass production industries in the 1970s generated a response which took shape in the 1980s and which created a process of financialisation, a process conducted by financial and non-financial corporate institutions and facilitated by successive governments, especially in the USA and Britain. Since the 1980s, growth in economies such as the UK has rested increasingly on the financial sector securing portions of the surplus produced elsewhere (particularly in the East and China) and domestic wealth creation and consumption has heavily relied upon rising property prices, increases in private debt and the (consequent but superficial) buoyancy of the retail sector. And when these began to flag, successive governments, particularly the Labour government (1997-2010) sustained economic activity (especially in the regions outside the south east) by injections of public expenditure.

The apparent wealth of London and the south east provided a level of growth sufficient to support public investment and spending elsewhere (a support boosted by the financial instruments designed into public/private partnerships which in turn fuelled numerous regional regeneration projects). Public spending served to mask the underlying problems in the production sectors of an undynamic economy. But the domestic trade-off or settlement between Britain's richer and poorer regions has proved as unsustainable as those imbalances arising in the global economy. In short, the credit crunch and its continuing consequences have arisen from long term structural problems facing advanced western industrial economies, with successive credit (2007-2009) and debt (2009-) crises occurring as the manifestation rather than root cause of the problems now faced most acutely by several European economies and the United States. As Sean Collins has explained in Chapter 2, New York and London have demonstrated similar patterns of economic development over recent decades – a hollowing out of production, a disproportionate rise and dependency upon financial and business services and a tendency for employment to distribute between high and low skilled occupations. These trends have arisen from urban economies reliant upon circulation and consumption; drained, as Hudson has argued, of their productive dynamism. By contrast, as Hudson has convincingly explained in Chapter 3, the framing narrative for dynamic, contemporary Shanghai is that 'production matters'.

In exploring the process of the financialisation of the UK economy, contributors have explained the ways in which its attendant values have been absorbed into the cultural, political and social life in particular of London, its location of origin. Here it is perhaps useful to draw out three dimensions of financialisation discussed in Part 1. Firstly, Richard Sharpe identified the historic conditions that afforded London the capacity to establish its unique position in international financial mediation and, in particular, the importance of the state's role through successive historic phases in opening and closing the spaces for it to prosper. In so doing, Sharpe highlights an important feature of the most recent period – that successive governments, while espousing the virtues of 'the market', have constantly intervened to facilitate and mitigate the consequences of its operations; seeking to regenerate regions and deploying, as Daniel Ben-Ami outlines, state institutions such as the Bank of England, to assist increasingly in the 'management' of national economic affairs.

Secondly, Ben-Ami has highlighted how non-financial institutions have come together with the finance sector in a variety of ways to share risk and engage in capital markets, asset management and funding (debt and equity finance). In turn, financial services institutions have engaged extensively with other industries through the holding of shares and bonds by fund management groups, using vehicles such as pension funds to do so. This trend caused the Economist to note in 2004, that private equity firms were the 'new kings of capitalism' as they spent huge sums on buy-outs of established companies in a diverse range of industries; with, by that year, two in five of all workers employed in the UK private sector working for companies that had been invested in by a private equity firm (Bishop 2004). Ben-Ami calls this complex interweaving of financial and non-financial institutions the emergence of melded capital with all its consequences for corporate governance and for its tendency to encourage the seeking of short term gain at the expense of longer term investment in research, technology and machinery, the essentials of an economy that might retain a competitive productive sector.

Finally, the third feature of financialisation and linked to the melding of capital, has been what we have called, contra-Keynes, the financialisation of society – evidenced, in the everyday, by for example the extension of credit facilities to private consumers by a wide range of companies, including retail firms and manufacturing companies. This trend is also reflected in the development of Asset Backed Securities (ABS) by consumer credit card companies which, according to Montgomerie (2007: 13) 'served to augment the supply of credit available for consumer lending but also made profits and future credit contingent on a steady stream of persistent revolving debtors'. The expansion of credit to pump private consumption, in turn, has enabled the consumer to access hitherto illiquid assets, in the form of property, through loans secured on mortgages. Whilst levels of mortgage-based debt greatly exceed that of personal debt in nations such as the USA and Britain, together they have generated a cycle of economic activities that have rested upon the increasingly shaky foundations of circulation and consumption rather than production.

In sum, financialisation refers to a phase (broadly from the 1970s onwards) in western capitalism in which melded capital becomes a dominant feature especially of the economies of Anglo-American societies and through which an active state has created, in Sharpe's terms, the spaces required for financial and business services to flourish. In the UK, the state has also developed social policies and patterns of public investment that sought to mitigate the adverse effects of de-industrialisation on areas of Britain that were largely outside the wealthier region of London and its hinterland, the south east. The lightly regulated financial economy of the capital city represented in this period a stark contrast to the highly regulated, public sector driven economies of other UK regions. The state, through the policies of successive UK governments, has made a series of, in Rustin's terms, 'strategic choices' about the way it has addressed the geographical and social 'hollowing out' of urban communities and the relative decline of the production industries upon which they once depended.[1]

Whilst a previous phase of domination of what was then called finance capital, occurred in the late nineteenth century and reflected the growing international domination of western capitalism, the current phase denotes its relative decline in global affairs, particularly in its Anglo-American form and when compared to the productive dynamism of the economies of the East, especially China. Paradoxically, this relative decline has also provided the backdrop to London's

1 Academics and other commentators have referred to the trends identified here as indicative of the ascendancy of neo-liberalism as an ideology and political strategy (See, for example, Harvey D. 2005 A Brief History of Neo-Liberalism, Oxford:OUP). In its ideological formation, neo-liberalism firmly associates individual freedoms to the unfettered workings of the market, in its political expression its highpoint refers to the 1980s administrations of President Reagan in the USA and Margaret Thatcher in the UK. Its conceptual origins lay in the opposition to the post-1945 social settlement that witnessed the ascendance in the UK of Keynesian economics, the emergence of the welfare state and state planning. Its leading opponents were Friedrich von Hayek, Ludvig von Mises and Milton Friedman. Their writings, and the moral principles underpinning them, have often been cited, especially by left critics, as providing the ideological foundations for the recent phase of 'rampant' capitalism discussed in this book. Here, however, it is suggested that while the label neo-liberal has resonance in capturing the rhetoric of political and business elites, it obscures rather than enhances our understanding of the economics and the economic policy-making of this period. This is a time, as contributors to this book have revealed, that the state performs a critical role in the 'opening' and 'closing' of markets, where the state facilitates (and regulates) the engagement of finance with the individual consumer and where nations have developed different pathways in pursuing their industrial development. The 'neo-liberal' frame is not adequate to the task of explaining the different patterns of state intervention that have taken place in the UK and in the dynamic and less dynamic economies across the globe; in brief, it may neatly help to delineate a period of social transformation that commenced some 40 or more years ago but its explanatory capacity is largely confined to describing the shifts from 'public to private', 'state to market' and 'society to the individual' rather than examining the more complex questions arising from the changing nature of the inter-actions between them.

success as an international financial centre allowing it to become, in Michael Rustin's words, 'the 'best and the worst' of world cities.

The Culture of the City: The Best and Worst

> In culture as in finance, London's history cannot be separated from the world's. What makes it unique is its role in the international economy, above all world commerce. This explains not only its extraordinary financial resilience – persisting and extending as Tokyo, Paris, and Frankfurt fell – but successive reconstructions. First as a political, then a naval, then a commercial centre; next as a financial centre and then in decline as a glorified reshipment centre, transiently as an unexpected manufacturing base and finally, ending a prolonged postwar eclipse in New York's brilliant light, its comet-like resurgence as the latest world financial supernova.[2]

Freeman's cultural audit of London (undertaken through a comparison with four other world cities – New York, Shanghai, Paris and Tokyo) reminds us, albeit with a rhetorical flourish, of London's capacity to reinvent itself and by the first decade of the twenty-first century, to be considered as a leading world city for finance and culture – a status reflected in its attractiveness as a tourist destination, the construction of several iconic new headquarters for corporate institutions and the huge success reflected in visitor numbers to its museums, galleries and theatres. The 'comet-like' rise which Freeman records was achieved in a relatively short period and fashioned, as Rustin notes in 20, largely by, and in the image of, the classes who benefitted from the resurgence of finance and business services.

The resurgence of the city's economy in the period 1980-2008 and its connection to the success of its cultural life it seems reflects 'the best'. Redevelopments to the East, including Canary Wharf, have been accompanied by the emergence of new centres of entrepreneurship and the development of arts and creative quarters, mainly concentrated in the east of London and on the south bank (Montgomery 2008). Most significantly, however, the city over this period has restored and developed its major centres of art and performance – the most iconic perhaps being the creation of the Tate Modern in the Bankside Power Station. The coal-fired power station – designed by Sir Giles Gilbert Scott who also designed Battersea Power Station and Waterloo Bridge in the period of post-1945 re-development of the inner city – closed in 1981. The Tate Modern opened in 2000 and by 2010 had become the most visited modern art museum in the world, receiving just under five million visitors per annum.

But, as Calcutt, reminds us there is another dimension to the relation between the city's economy and its cultural life. Its best may also be an expression of

2 Freeman, A. (2008). London: A Cultural Audit, London GLAhttp://mpra.ub.uni-muenchen.de/9008/1/MPRA_paper_9008.pdf, 13, accessed August 20, 2011.

its worst. For Calcutt, the financialised economy has given rise to a financially-oriented culture – culture and economy do not merely inter-act, each is inside the other. In contemporary London, financial activities are distanced from the world of production; London benefits, as a 'glorified reshipment centre' from generating complex circuits within circuits of capital and is increasingly distanced from the sites of real productive activity. As its financiers parody the real world of production through the creation of innovative new 'products' (derivatives) so its arts, in this case contemporary music, tend to parody that which is and has been produced elsewhere, creating, through no little skill and imagination, a 're-mix culture' – in short an art of its place and time that expresses social alienation but cannot break its bounds.

Deploying a different conceptual frame to discuss the business models of the music industry and by implication those of the cultural and creative sector, Andrew Blake also draws attention to the loss of the socially productive role that such industries should play. From the decline of EMI through its disastrous leveraged buy-out to the adoption of music as an erstwhile contributor to the development of the knowledge based, creative economy, Blake shows how such business models and pragmatic, finance-driven designations of the creative sector, paradoxically, threaten to diminish its creativity and its capacity to enhance the work and social lives of Londoners. In his chapter, Barnfield too draws upon the creative industries to analyse the representation of the freelance creative in fiction and in government policy-making, revealing the precarious nature of the 'portfolio career' and providing sharp insights into the inflated status accorded to the pursuit of largely unproductive labour.

The relationship between the economy and the cultural life of London is a complex affair. In its formulation as the cultural and creative industries, 'culture' has been accorded a significant role by politicians, economists and cultural commentators. It would be churlish to deny the achievements symbolised by the success of the Tate Modern or the continuing international recognition afforded London's cultural 'scene', its delights, as Rustin has observed, contributing to the desire of the wealthy to live in the city and for tourists to visit it. But, for many others who live and work in the city, the spectacle it affords has been accompanied by the hollowing out of its social substance or, in Zukin's terms, its authenticity.

Financial Cycles, Roundabouts and Bi-cycles

Is London's real economy and infrastructure, its tangible world, being reproduced in the twenty-first century as simply images? Echoes of Debord's view 'that everything that was directly lived has moved away into a representation' (Debord 1977), seems to underpin the concerns expressed by Alvaro de Miranda in his chapter on East London's manufacturing industries and his analysis of recent policy initiatives that emphasise the developing of green technologies and high tech clusters of firms in the east of the city. De Miranda reveals the dynamic and creative character of manufacturing in the last part of the nineteenth and the first half of the twentieth century, especially the electrical and early electronic industries. He compares their dynamism and their embedded, organic relation to East London to the initiatives designed to re-kindle manufacturing industry in the area in the twenty-first century.

Whilst welcoming the national and local policy emphasis on developing new production industries (and the expression of support from government for e-entrepreneurs in locations such as 'Silicon Roundabout' in Shoreditch) de Miranda is concerned that East London may become a mere showcase for these industries rather than a site for research, development and production; a showcase that arises in large part from East London being the host to the 2012 Olympic and Paralympic Games. The pre-occupation with image and presentation of brand to the rest of the world during the great spectacle that is the Games may impede rather than contribute to these new high tech and green initiatives contributing to a genuine re-balancing of the local economy.

In his evaluation of transportation in London, Alastair Donald expresses similar concerns. Contemporary London is slowing down. The energy that underpinned the entrepreneurship and investment in rail, underground and roadways that transformed Dickensian London into a modern city has been lost. The impetus to enhance mobility as a prerequisite to support economic progress and modernisation has been replaced by an immobilising culture which is symbolised by the 'bicycle revolution' – a means of transport whose promotion is primarily designed, paradoxically, to meet non-transport objectives. In his analysis of the City's policies toward the energy sectors and energy supply, Woudhuysen reaches similar conclusions; energy policies pursued by successive national and city-wide administrations have failed to address supply issues and have spurned opportunities for innovative research and development, while focussing increasingly upon seeking changes in consumer behaviour. In their analyses of infrastructure development, energy creation and supply and the city's relationship to the productive 'real' economy, our contributors reveal the limitations of public policy interventions in contributing to the renewal of London's productive industries.

Toward a New Urban Economy?

In his discussion in *Cities in Civilisation*, Peter Hall noted that at particular times, particular cities experience periods of exceptional creativity, and some cities experience more than one (Hall 1998: 1-19). His inclusion of London in this category and his discussion of its 'capitalism rampant' period (roughly dating from 1980)is detailed and measured; its concluding question as to whether the city's regeneration, dependent on speculative development and financial services, could be sustained remained understandably unanswered (his book was first published in 1998). A little over a decade on, and following the deepest international financial crisis in seventies years, it would seem, as several contributors to this book have argued, that the answer is 'no'. Equally, few of us would deny that the city of speculation has also experienced a renaissance since the 1980s.

Whilst three cities to the East have, in 2011, entered the top five international financial service centres in the world (Singapore, Hong Kong and Shanghai),[3] New York and London have retained their respective positions as second and first. London's position reflects its strength in depth across different financial markets, its geographical location, the widespread dominance of English as the preferred language for business and the depth and expertise of its international workforce. In turn, the city has benefitted too from its international standing as a centre of circulation and communication, attracting inward migration and developing a cosmopolitan diversity as a world city rather than as a European city of commerce (Frankfurt), culture (Rome, Paris) or heritage (Vienna). This capacity for reinvention has perhaps achieved greater recognition or resonance with the rest of the world than it has within the city itself. London may rely increasingly upon the productive efforts of others but it continues to have an important role to play in the world economy, albeit as a successful go-between. But as successive contributions to this book have outlined, there have been considerable consequences to being at the heart of the process of financialisation, especially when, as Rustin calls it, the great gamble begins to unravel. There are different ways in which these consequences may unfold, contributing alternatively to what we have called the best and worst aspects of the city. To conclude we will explore each of these potential directions.

Negative Possibilities

The short-term prospect for the capital city is undoubtedly one of a probable worsening of the conditions of life for the majority, in part because of the contraction following the credit crunch itself, and in part because the remedies adopted by the Coalition Government to deal with its outcomes seem more likely to make matters worse than better. Sharp and sustained reductions in public expenditure will bear particularly harshly on the poor, and on those London boroughs where the public sector has taken a particularly important role in providing work, not least in replacing lost manufacturing industry. There is already a crisis in housing provision, through insufficient house building over a long period of time, but also because of the perverse effects of allowing housing to be become a dominant form of saving and indeed speculation, in part through the privileged tax status

3 See the Global Financial Services Index (GFSI) produced annually by Z/Yen Group: 'The GFCI provides profiles, ratings and rankings for 75 financial centres drawing on two separate sources of data – instrumental factors (external indices) and responses to an online survey'. http://www.zyen.com/index.php?option=com_content&view=article&id=23&Itemid=29

of owner-occupied 'main residences' over other kinds of savings and investment. Britain's investment in real estate has not been as crippling to its economy as has been the case in Spain, but it has detracted from productive investment all the same. And apart from the sheer issue of scarcity, we now see the likelihood of enhanced stratification and social segregation in the housing market, through the capping of housing benefits, the reduction of role of elected local government in the supply of housing, and the pricing- out of many London districts of citizens with low incomes. These developments will undermine one of the attractions and sources of vitality of many parts of London, which is the juxtaposition within quite small geographical areas of populations of different economic status and often of different ethnic origins.

The reorganisation of the school system – and perhaps before long the health system too – according to an ideology of competition and 'consumer choice' – will further exacerbate, if it continues, the social segregation of neighbourhoods, as differences made highly visible by competitive league tables and Ofsted Reports in the quality of what different schools provide give additional force to pressures for residential segregation and polarisation. The reality is that in a competitive market system, a tendency to growing inequalities as a consequence of market forces themselves can only be restrained by the redistributive and reparative actions of governments. The ideal of good free education and health being available to all, and of affordable housing being available throughout the city, were such attempts to restrain these tendencies. In so far as the present government has little commitment to these egalitarian values (as evidenced by Cawley and Berzins in previous chapters), but on the contrary places its confidence in the role of competition to enhance the quantity and quality of products of all kinds, one can expect inequalities to increase. At a time when contraction and heightened unemployment increases the need for compensatory public provision – early years services, policing, mental health services, youth services, for example – government is actively reducing support for them. Although the August riots in parts of London and elsewhere were to a degree contingent events, they should nevertheless be taken as a warning of potential dangers to come. In a parallel way, although a 'flash flood' in a geographical terrain may seem to be the result merely of a particularly intense rainstorm, it may also reveal long term a vulnerability to stress of an entire ecological system.

Often, crises accentuate economic developments which are already in process. Thus a recession may bring insolvency and collapse to sectors of an economy which in better times were just able to struggle along. Crises can be seen, from a Schumpeterian view, as 'gales of creative destruction', providing new opportunities for investment through the freeing up of resources of land, labour and capital. But the costs of what David Harvey has called such 'devaluations' of existing capital can be extremely severe for those directly affected by them (Harvey 2008). We already saw this in the rapid deindustrialisation which took place in the early 1980s, in which a process of technological evolution was rapidly accelerated by the deliberately deflationary policy of the then government, which was intent on resolving what it believed to be a serious crisis of governance in Britain. But this deindustrialisation affected for the worse, and in the long-term, many former areas of mining and manufacturing in north of England, in South Wales and in Scotland. A Tory Minister, in September 2011, described on the radio the removal of Britain's 'smokestack industries' as one of Margaret Thatcher's achievements, which offered a strange though perhaps revealing concept of achievement.

One ongoing development which we can now see, which may also be intensified by economic contraction, is the changing pattern of retail distribution in Britain, with high streets becoming 'hollowed out' as much of their trade moves to markets and shopping malls on a town's periphery, and in part to growing internet commerce. In more upmarket areas, an adjustment may take place, in which while 'useful' shops like greengrocers, butchers and bakers may disappear, they are replaced by a different leisure and tourism environment of bars restaurants and boutiques. But no such development is likely to take place in poorer areas – here the outcome of this tendency may merely be boarded-up shop fronts, just as its outcome in rural areas has often been villages with no shop at all. It might be thought not to matter that citizens obtain their goods and services in one way rather than another, but these developments probably do damage neighbourhoods by removing locations in which people naturally meet and associate. Such developments are the reverse of what one would wish to see if one took David Cameron's idea of a 'big (ie integrated) society' seriously.

Graham and Marvin, in their book *Splintering Urbanism* (2001), have described a tendency for the different economic and social functions of cities and urban areas to become more spaced out and separated from one another, as the advantages of scale, specialisation, and motorised access and parking, outweigh the earlier advantages of proximity. Out-of-town supermarkets and shopping malls are a prime example of this development, which is sometimes resisted by the people of towns who fear for their effects on town centres and on their sense of being a socially integrated community. This 'splintering' pattern has been very prominent in East London in recent years. Major investments have taken the form not, as in decades past, of the integrated development of entire towns (such as the New Towns) but rather of mono-functional complexes like that of Canary Wharf, London City Airport, the Dome at North Greenwich, the Excel Exhibition Centre, the University of East London's Docklands Campus, and now the Olympic Park and the Stratford City shopping centre. What characterises all these developments is their relative indifference to their local populations and their needs, since it is expected that most of their consumers or users and their employees will be recruited from non-local catchment areas. There was at one time the hope that the regeneration of the Thames Gateway sub-region would take such a comprehensive form. But such a pattern of development requires substantial public investment and a conception of planning based on values of social integration. Such concepts, as we pointed out in an earlier volume (Cohen and Rustin 2008) have never had a very convincing place in the Thames Gateway development, but they now seem likely to be definite casualties both of a climate of scarce resources and of antipathy to government interventions designed to counterbalance the effects of market forces. Some major public investments which are taking place – for example in transport improvements such as Crossrail and Thameslink – will generate nodes of growth along their routes, but these nodes are likely to be highly selective, reinforcing market-driven patterns of inequality although also contributing to aggregate wealth. Both of these routes do, after all, pass through the City, London's financial centre, and one of them will connect it with Canary Wharf too. It is notable that this 'splintered' mode of development in the Thames Gateway is taking place in a context of fragmented and weak forms of democratic governance, political authority, such as it is, being divided between many different agencies.

This negative scenario anticipates that the consequences of the credit crunch, and of the present government's strategy to recover from it, will accelerate some of the less desirable aspects of development which have been taking place in London in recent decades, while doing little to redress their negative effects. Nor on present evidence does any determined action seem likely aimed to redress the imbalances of development between London and the South East, and regions to the north and far west.

An Alternative: Reinventing London – Looking East

Is it however possible for London to reinvent itself once more and, in so doing, begin to address the social, cultural and economic 'distortions' arising from its recent past?

Reducing the influence of finance on society, requires a major reconceptualising of society itself. The UK economy has been woefully slow in emerging from the aftermath of the credit crunch and there were few signs of any global recovery evident in summer 2011. The widespread adoption of austerity measures in other western nations and the slowdown of economic growth in China and even in Germany in the summer of 2011, suggested to some commentators that the west may well experience over the coming decade a Japan-style scenario – high debt burdens, sluggish growth and a 'political response to the troubles (that) is confused and does little to alleviate pain' (Milne 2011: 5). Such circumstances contributed to Japan's 'lost' two decades (1990-2010) of slow/no growth; a situation that, by summer 2011, seemed a real possibility for several western economies and not just those on Europe's margins, such as Ireland, Greece and Portugal. To avoid 'lost' years, it is clear that the UK, and particularly London's economy, must take on a new trajectory of development.

East London provides a useful 'case study' or insight into these areas of potential development, which can exemplify both the negative and positive potentialities of this situation. London's east has certainly been the site of significant regeneration over the last 40 years, first through the Canary Wharf and Docklands development and, more recently, through the locating of the Olympic and Paralympic Games at Stratford. The area has become synonymous with international finance and business services, the 'spectacle' of mega event development, the building of new housing, the creation of a new shopping city (Westfield Stratford City, adjacent to the Olympic Park)[4] and significant improvements in transport infrastructure. Despite these interventions the area retains high levels of unemployment and worklessness, with some wards in East London experiencing extensive overcrowding and many of the new housing developments (in London as a whole and in the east in particular) containing the smallest houses of any major city in the western world:[5]

> Since 1980 there have been no mandatory minimum space standards for housing in the UK, ever since the famous Parker Morris standards for Space in the Home, which were drawn up in 1961, were abolished by Margaret Thatcher's government in 1980. This has led, in recent years, to London having the smallest new houses and apartments of any major city in the Western world—and this at the end of an era of huge economic growth and rises in living standards. A new apartment in London now is estimated to have up to 30 per cent less space than its equivalent of 40 to 50 years ago.[6]

The economic 'model' that has informed East London's renewal, has generated considerable benefits for some but has delivered very few real improvements to the lives of the majority of East London's residents. Despite the credit crunch and recession, Canary Wharf's expansion is set to continue with the development of Wood Wharf over the next 10 to 15 years[7] and with Westfield Stratford City attracting high profile retailers, there seems scope for the area to continue with 'business as usual'. This would reproduce the pattern of social development of the recent past into the future but with sharper social divisions arguably in sharper social forms as public spending is cut. It would reinforce the polarisation of employment between the higher and lower skilled and generate pockets of housing and home ownership that favours the gentrified development of specific areas and districts whilst creating, elsewhere large concentrations of social disadvantage.

---

4 The Westfield Stratford City Centre opened in September 2012. It is a 1.9 million square foot shopping mall, with 300 shops and restaurants set to open on the site and a 95 per cent occupancy rate achieved at the time of opening. See http://www.canarywharf.com/aboutus/Media/News/Wood-Wharf-Detailed-Plans-Submitted-For-First-Two-Buildings/

5 Boris Johnson published a new Housing Design Guide in 2010 that contained over 90 requirements for new houses, including improvements in size. It came into effect in 2011 for all properties funded by public money and is planned to be incorporated into the new London Plan, published in 2012.

6 Long, K. (2010) 'Boris the builder: the mayor's vision for London housing'. Evening Standard August 18, 2010 http://www.thisislondon.co.uk/lifestyle/article-23868332-boris-the-builder-the-mayors-vision-for-london-housing.do; accessed August 12, 2011.

7 On completion Wood Wharf is designed to provide an extra 4,900 square feet of office space, 25,000 jobs and 1,668 new homes of which 483 will be affordable homes for the local community.

Four important dimensions of a new trajectory for development are investment in infrastructure; the attraction and nurturing of new industries; the building of new homes and, finally, moving to much reduce those conditions that have given rise to a significant growth in social inequality. To achieve different outcomes for the majority of citizens of East London, and to demonstrate that alternatives to a financialised capitalism are possible, significant changes in the conception and practices involved in each of these areas of public intervention would be required. There would need to be investment in forms of production which generate skilled middle-level employment, rather than merely unskilled and transient work, but this itself would require shifting the balance of the economy away from the financial sector. There would be need to replace a housing market based on speculation on rising land values and on scarcity of supply by house building on a scale sufficient to meet social demand, via new experiments in funding and ownership such as community-based land trusts. Here is a prime instance of the need to replace the 'fictitious capital' of speculative values, with an economy in housing which is mainly valued for its actual use. The changes that are necessary, if further crises of the financial system are to be avoided, and if a sustainable pattern of economic and social development is to be developed, are far deeper than those now being contemplated in the dominant political discourse. We cannot here set out the terms for this necessary new debate.

We can, however, say that East London, which now, as in the past, is at the same time one of the most dynamic zones of the city, but also one of the poorest and most vulnerable, will provide an exemplary test of what pattern of development now emerges. Will it remain dominated by its connections to the financialised form of capitalism that has arisen in recent decades (symbolised in the march eastwards of the city's glass towers), or will it become a site in which that model is at the least, challenged both in conception and practice?

References

Bishop, M. (2004). 'The New Kings of Capitalism', *Economist*, 25 November 2004, http://www.economist.com/node/3398496.

Cohen, P. and Rustin, M.J. (2008). *London's Turning: The Making of the Thames Gateway*. Farnham: Ashgate.

Debord, G. (1994). *The Society of the Spectacle*. New York: Zone Books.

Freeman, A. (2008). *London: A Cultural Audit*, London GLA, available at http://mpra.ub.uni-muenchen.de/9008/1/MPRA_paper_9008.pdf, 13.

Graham, S. and Marvin, S. (2001). *Splintering Urbanism: Networked Infrastructures, Technological Mobilities and the Urban Condition*. London: Routledge.

Hall, P. (1998). *Cities in Civilisation*. London: Phoenix.

Harding, R. and Atkins, R. (2011). 'No magic medicine to heal global finances', *Financial Times*, 20-21 August 2011.

Harvey, D. (2008). The Right to the City, *New Left Review*, 53, September-October 2008.

Milne (2011). 'Japanisation becomes new watchword', *Financial Times*, 20-21 August 2011.

Montgomerie, J. (2007). Financialisation and Consumption, Working Paper No 43, Centre for Research on Socio-Cultural Change CRESC: University of Manchester, http://gesd.free.fr/montgo7.pdf.

Index

accountancy firms 119
Acheson, Dean 204
Adams, John 253
Addison, Joseph 148-9, 158
Agenda 21 165, 205
AIG company, collapse 19, 47
amateur, professional, distinction 229
anaerobic digestion 188
Apple corporation, products 218
The Apprentice BBC tv series 127-44
 and apprenticeship, notion of 134-5
 and banking crisis 130-1
 as Barthian myth 129
 business 'cities', ideal types of 140-2
 'business' versions 140
 Charlie and the Chocolate Factory, parallels 138-9
 as 'city' substitute 131, 142-3
 fictive work content 128, 136, 143
 format 128-9
 as Freudian displacement 130
 initiation trope 134
 London
  abstraction of 132-4, 144
  images of 144
  skyline 127-8, 136-7
 as moral fable 137-9
 as reality show 128, 138
Arnott, Jake, *The Long Firm*, trilogy 232-3
arts patronage, as inherent good 236-7
Asia financial crisis (1997-8) 44
Asset Backed Securities (ABS) 18, 339
asylum seekers 275
 see also immigration

Bagehot, Walter 91, 105
 Lombard Street 116
Baird, John Logie 166
Baker, Norman 259
Baldry, Harold 236-7
Bank of England
 Bank Charter Act 105-6
 bank rate 91-2, 110-11
 crises 88-9, 91, 105-6
 establishment 85, 103, 116
 Financial Stability Report 123
 lender of last resort 89
 nationalisation 94, 108-9
 Prudential Regulation Authority 124
 railway expansion finance 90
 role 29-30, 85, 116, 119
Bank for International Settlements (Basel) 124
bankers
 bonuses, attacks on 123
 Cable on 123
 Johnson on 1, 337
 partnerships, formation 102
banking
 commercial 116, 118
 Independent Commission on Banking 124
 investment 118
 retail, growth 91
banking crisis (1837-9), Marx on 1-2
banks
 business lending 329
 failures 83
 international, in London 110
 investment 117
 and retail functions, separation of 328
 state bank proposal 328
 limited liability 106
 rescue packages 123
Barclays Cycle Hire scheme 249
Barthes, Roland 129
BBC World Service 157
Bear Sterns bank, collapse 19, 47

Beethoven, Ludwig van, *Pastoral* Symphony, London performance 70-1
Ben-Ami, Daniel 338-9
Berman, Marshal 321
Bethnal Green 7
Biddulph, Matt 170
Big Society
  and Cameron 300, 333, 346
  concept 256
  and NHS reforms 299-300
biomass heat and power 188
Blake, Andrew 343
Bleep.com download service 218
Bloomberg, Michael 48-9
Blunkett, David 306
bond market 117
Boult, Adrian 73
Boyer, Marion 128
Bretton Woods agreement 95, 202
Brill Building, songwriting factory 75
  assembly line approach 76
British Empire
  and Elgar's 2nd symphony 73-4
  ornamentalism 74
Brixton riots (1981) 273
Brooker, Charlie, *tvgohome* website 234
Brown, Gordon 23, 207
  on the City 123
Brundtland Report (1987) 165
Buffett, Warren 48

Cable, Vincent 24
  on bankers 123
Calcutt, Andrew 341-2
Cameron, David 162, 164, 170, 174, 207, 267
  and the Big Society 300, 333, 346
  on immigration 271, 273
Canary Wharf 2, 8, 116, 118, 127-8, 135, 284, 320, 341, 348
capital
  melded 122, 339
  and financialisation 340
  sources 94-5
  see also fictitious capital; finance capital
carbon dioxide emissions 191
  Assigned Amount Unit 200
  Clean Development Mechanisms 200
  dogma 177-8
  EU Allowance 200
  reduction schemes 200
carbon trading
  abuses 208
  basics 199-200
  and climate change 203
  criticisms of 208-9
  markets 200-1
  origins 205
Carey, John 239
Carrier, James 132
Cayman Islands, US securities, holdings 22
CD sales, fall 214-15
Chicago School, of sociologists 3, 4, 58
China
  GDP, annual change (1990-2010) 21
  growth, slowdown 337
  manufacturing, as percentage of GDP 25
  US securities, holdings 21
  USA
  economic relations 61-2
  exports to 21
cities
  and the credit crunch 9
  cultural critique 4-5
  de-industrialisation 5, 6
  decline 4-5
  in fiction 135
  financialisation 6
  global 9, 53, 57
  and social change 5-8
  theorising 3-4
'City, the' 122-5
  Brown on 123
  definition 115-16
  mediation role 116, 338
  and the real economy 130
climate change
  and carbon trading 203
  commercial opportunities 205
  economic issues 206
Climate Change Act (UK, 2008) 207-8
Coalition Government (UK) 24, 222

and the credit crunch (2007-09) 344
economic policies 32-3
ideology 326-7
immigration, attitude to 276
Coe, Sebastian 290
Cold War, end 203
Collins, Sean 338
Commission for Racial Equality (CRE) 274
Companies Act (UK, 1948) 106, 109
congestion charge, London 189, 257-8
'Cool Britannia' 230
copyright
criticisms of 216
and individual composer paradigm 215
and the music business 214
term extension 217
Corn Laws, repeal (1845) 106
corporate elites, excessive salaries 329-30
Coutts bank 102-3
creative
class 6-7
meaning 228
'Creative Britain' 227, 233-5, 237, 239
and crime films 240-1
roots 236
creative industries 163, 342
claims for 227, 229
clustering concept 238
in fiction 229-35
and New Labour government 237
output, uncertainty about 239
and regeneration 237-8
creatives, freelance 235-6, 239, 243
and wealth creation 237
credit
availability, and financialisation 17, 339
and the 'real economy' 227
sources 227
credit crunch (2007-9) 1, 15, 32
and cities 9
and the Coalition Government 344
and economic downturn 20-5
and financial industries, discrediting of 164
and the housing market 17, 344-5
and London 68, 115, 322
origins 17-19, 338
and the 'real economy' 164
see also financial crisis
credit rating agencies 90, 96
Crossrail project 254, 347
currency speculation, Tobin tax proposal 327
cycling, London 249, 258-9, 343

Dagenham Docks
Institute for Sustainability 173
regeneration policy 169-70
Dahl, Roald, *Charlie and the Chocolate Factory*, *The Apprentice*, parallels 138-9
Dalton, Hugh 109
Darling, Alistair 23
David, Matthew, *Peer to Peer and the Music Industry* 216-17
de Miranda, Alvaro 342-3
de-industrialisation 345-6
cities 5, 6
East London 167
and financialisation 27
and the knowledge economy 163
Debord, G. 342
Dedring, Isabel 168-9
derivatives 342
example 121
Desai, Pooran 258
Digest of UK Energy Statistics 184
Digital Economy Act (UK, 2010) 217
Digital Rights Management 214, 216
Donald, Alastair 343
Dreiser, Theodore, *The Stoic* 249
Duncan Smith, Ian 31

East India Company 106
East London
de-industrialisation 167-8
development model 348
alternatives to 349
Green Enterprise District 162, 168-70, 172-3
higher education, student fees 312
industrial capital, lack of 167
industrial creativity, examples 165-7
investment 171

Olympic Park 288-9
'real economy', post-crunch revival 161-2, 171-5
regeneration policy 7-8, 168-71, 347-8
consumption bias 172
and local economy 172, 174
Siemens Sustainability Centre 168, 172
Technology City 162, 170-1, 174
technology companies, foreign purchase of 167
University of 173
Westfield Stratford City Centre 348fn4
as world showcase 171-2
see also Dagenham Docks
East Thames Housing Group 286
economic development, measurement 331-2
EDF Energy 178
electric vehicles 190
Elgar, Edward, Symphony No. 2, and the British Empire 73-4
EMI corporation
decline 219-21, 342
delisting from LSE 220
exit of artists 220
energy consumption
and energy efficiency 181
Greater London (2008) 178
UK (2008) 178
entrepreneur-employees 239
environmentalism
Thatcher government 206-7
UK political parties 207-8
Epstein, Jacob 41
EU, Emissions Trading Scheme 200, 208
Euro 12 countries, GDP growth (1950-88) 20
Eurodollars 94-95, 110
Eurozone crisis 337
exchange controls, abolition 110

Falklands War (1982) 206, 326
Fannie Mae and Freddie Mac, collapse 19
Fast, Howard, *Max* 229
Federal Reserve Bank 19
Festival of Britain (1951) 236
fictitious capital 32fn9, 86-7, 97, 204, 227-8, 319, 333
creative workers as 228
London as 67, 127, 132, 209
film production, UK 241-2
finance capital 120
decline 340-1
'real economy', distinction 31
Financial Conduct Authority 124
financial crisis (2007-11) 1, 322-4, 325-34
banks, rescue packages 123
government indebtedness 324
short-termism 324
see also credit crunch (2007-9)
financial derivatives, construction, and remix culture 75
financial mediation, *see under* London
financial sector
need for proactive state role 328
parasitism of 327
financial services
output, selected countries 26
share of GDP, major economies 119
Financial Services Authority 119, 124
see also Prudential Regulation Authority
financialisation
alternatives to 349
cities 6
and credit availability 17, 339
and de-industrialisation 27
drawbacks 16-17
and global imbalances 27-8
London transport 254-6
meaning 16
and melded capital 340
origins 16, 17
and public spending 338
and the 'real economy' 252
UK 25-6, 30, 32, 338-9
USA 43
Fleet Street, mediation role 154
Fleming, Ambrose 166
Ford, Ford Madox
on London 250
The Soul of London 250
Ford, Gerald 40
Fowler, Christopher, *Soho Black* 230

Frame, John 102
France
financial services
output 26
share of GDP 119
manufacturing, as percentage of GDP 25
Fraser, Steve, *Every Man a Speculator* 41
Free Trade policy 106
Freedland, Jonathan 128
Freeman, Andrew 341
The Risk Revolution 121
Frith, Simon, and Lee Marshall, *Music and Copyright* 216
fund management groups 117-18
futures trading 92

GDP
growth, selected countries (1950-88) 20
manufacturing as percentage of 25
General Agreement on Tariffs and Trade (GATT) 202
see also World Trade Organization (WTO)
gentrification 5-6, 7, 10, 238, 285, 292
Germany
financial services
output 26
share of GDP 119
GDP growth (1950-88) 20
manufacturing, as percentage of GDP 25
World Cup (2006), investment opportunities 162-3
Glass, Ruth 5-6
Glendening, Jonathan, *Strippers Versus Werewolves* 242
Global Commons Institute (GCI) 205
global recession 15, 28
globalisation 53
of finance 119-20
and regeneration policy 162
Graham, S., and S. Marvin, *Splintering Urbanism* 346
Gramsci, Antonio 327
Great Depression 75, 120
Greater London Authority
climate change mitigation programmes 192
Delivering London's Energy Future 177, 182-3, 183
criticism of 184-8
electric vehicles, goals 190
energy goals 186-7
utopianism 189, 192
home insulation 186, 188
problems 189-90
schemes 190
London Energy and Greenhouse Gas Inventory 180
RE:NEW homes programme 187-8
Greece, debt problems 24
Grubb, Michael 205
The Guerilla Film Maker's Handbook 241

Hall, Peter 251
Cities in Civilisation 343
Hammond, Philip 253, 256
Hamnett, Chris 286
Hands, Guy 220-1
Harvey, David 8-9, 345
Heartfield, James 255
Heath, Edward 325
hedge funds, emergence 96
Heinberg, Richard, *Peak Everything* 182
Hewitt, Patricia 163
higher education
access, widening 307-8
Browne Review (2009) 308-9
Dearing report 306-7
expansion 306
funding 306-9
and the knowledge economy 308
marketisation 307
new fee regime 305, 307, 330-1
Office for Fair Access (OFFA) 307
overseas students 308
payback system 309-12
policy drivers 305-6
productivity 306
and student-consumer role 306
young people's attitudes to 311
Hilferding, Roland, *Finance Capital* 119-20
Hilton, Steve 207

Hodge, Margaret 275
Home, Stewart, *Down and out in Shoreditch and Hoxton* 235
Homes and Communities Agency (HCA) 287
Hong Kong, Shanghai, rivalry 63
housing market
    and the credit crunch 17, 344-5
    USA, collapse 22, 47, 123
    see also under London
Howe, Geoffrey 96
Hudson, Alan 338
Human Development Reports (UN) 331
Hutton, Will 324

immigration
    Cameron 271, 273
    Coalition Government, attitude to 276
    migrants
        distribution of 271
        occupational distribution of 277-8
    New Labour government attitude to 275-6
    reduction, attempts at 275
    see also under London
Immigration Act (UK, 1971) 268
inequality, disbenefits of 324
insurance
    companies 118
    as risk management 118
intellectual property
    Gowers Report 217
    see also copyright
International Monetary Fund (IMF) 202
Internet
    and the music business 218
    and retail distribution 346
investment
    diversification 18
    inward, and regeneration policy 163
iTunes service 218

Jacobs, Jane 4-5
Japan
    economic problems (1990-2010) 347
    financial services, share of GDP 119
    GDP growth (1950-88) 20
    manufacturing, as percentage of GDP 25
    personal savings 95
    US securities, holdings 22
Jenkins, Roy 239
    The Labour Case 236
Jevons, William Stanley 180-1
Johnson, Boris 164, 168, 177-8, 180, 191, 193, 257, 268
    on bankers 1, 337
    on music education 223
Joint Stock Companies Act (1844) 105
journalism, London, *see under* London
Jovy, Alexander, *Sorted* 241
JP Morgan bank 19

Keynes, John Maynard
    General Theory 28
    on role of the state 28-9
knowledge economy
    and de-industrialisation 163
    and higher education 308
    and manufacturing 164
Kyoto Protocol (1997) 200, 203

laissez-faire policies 106, 328
Last.fm program 218
Lehman Brothers, collapse 19, 47, 123, 324
Lenin, V.I. 120
Licensing Act (UK, 2003) 221-2
limited liability concept 91
LinkedIn 228, 243
Litt, Toby, *Corpsing* 230
Livingstone, Ken 177
Lloyd George, David, "People's Budget" 107
Locke, John 149
London
    abstraction of, in The Apprentice 132-4, 144
    alienation 69-70
        and Amy Winehouse 77
        from production 76
    banking, growth 84-5, 88
    banks, international 110
    Beethoven's Pastoral, performance 70-1

bull market 109
Campaign for Better Transport 253
capitalist society, construction of 72-3
car
    ownership 182
    travel 260
carbon emissions trading, lead player in 201-2
Cars 2 film, location scenes 67
cavity wall insulation 183
community councils 333
congestion charge 257-8
and the credit crunch (2007-09) 68, 115, 322
credit expansion 86
cultural dimension 68-9, 341
currency, local 256
cycling 249, 258-9, 343
diversity 321
Docklands Light Railway 251, 289
docks closure 167
Egypt, investments in 106-7
electricity consumption 183
employment rates 284
energy
    consumption 178, 179, 180
    demand 180-4
    needs 178, 191, 343
    peaks 182, 185
    security 184, 186
ethnic integration 321
European Climate Exchange 201
exports/imports 84
as fictitious capital 67, 127, 132, 209, 319
finance, and production 69, 74-5, 159, 204
financial markets, crisis (1857) 90-1
financial mediation 83, 97-8, 112, 121, 344
    1680s-1840s 84-9; 101-5
    1840s-1914 89-93, 105-7
    1914-45 93-4; 107-8
    1945-79 94-5; 108-10
    1979-2008 96-7; 110-11
complexity of 120
institutions 116-19
financial services
    employment 118
    moral disdain 228
floatations 95
Ford on 250
foreign government loans 90
fuel poverty, increase 181-2
as global city 67
and the Glorious Revolution (1688) 102
Greater, energy consumption (2008) 178
housing market 283
    affordable housing 286-7
    Athletes' Village, legacy 290-1, 292
    buoyancy 284-5
    construction 285
    key problems 287-8
    Olympic legacy 288-9, 291-2
    price rises 289-90
    rental values 290
    space standards 348
    waiting lists 286
images of, in *The Apprentice* 144
immigration
    distribution by borough 272
    numbers 270-1
    occupational distribution 276-7, 279
    phases 268-9
    younger generation 270
investment
    foreign 284
    opportunities 92, 104
journalism
    impersonal 147
    interpersonal 157
    Me-You 147-8, 156
    mediating role 148-54
    and mercantilism 150
    short-termism 158
    types 147-8
Jubilee line 251
law firms 118-19
localism 256-7
London First 268
Mayor
    cultural strategy (2010) 213

transport strategy (2010) 253, 260
mobility 252-4, 343
music
performances 213
venues 213
newspapers, decline 154-5
Olympic Games (2012) 8, 165, 259, 318, 320
Olympic Park 251
phone-hacking scandal (2011) 68
Pool of London 102
population
decline 270
peak 270
sources 270
prospects 344
Protestant Ascendancy 102
public services, decline 333
and pursuit of profit 83-4
're-mix culture' 342
Registered Social Landlords (RSL) 286, 287
riots (2011) 68, 69, 219, 345
causes 317-19, 333
consumption aspects 318
crowd behaviour 318-19
risk assessment 85-6, 121
Royal Exchange 84, 102, 149
school system, competition ideology 345
skyline, in The Apprentice 127-8, 136, 137
'splintered' development 346-7
and state, role of 101, 103-4, 124
student market 306
takeover bids 95
Tax Increment Financing (TIF) 255
Thames Gateway 8, 165, 346
Development Corporation 286
Heat Network 170, 187
transport
alcohol ban 257
financialisation of 254-6
improvements 251
investment 321-2
Mayor's strategy 253, 260
slowdown 250-1, 343
travelling time 252
underinvestment in 251
Victoria line 251
see also City, the; East London
London Array 190
London Development Agency 168-9, 173
Cultural Audit 213-14
London Eye 178
London Stock Exchange 85, 90
Alternative Investment Market 201
'Big Bang' (1986) 96, 111, 117
boom and decline 93-4
origins 117
Long Term Capital Management (USA), collapse 96-7
Luxemburg, US securities, holdings 22

Macmillan Committee (1931) 29
magazines
Newnes' empire 151-2
newspapers
consolidation 151-3, 155-6
distinction 150
Major, John 207, 275
Mandelson, Peter 161, 164
manufacturing
and the knowledge economy 164
outsourcing to third world 323
as percentage of GDP, comparisons 25
and the 'real economy' 164
and regeneration policy 164
Marconi Research Centre 166
markets, primary, secondary 120
Marx, Karl, on London banking crisis (1837-9) 1, 2
Metronet consortium 255
Mexico, debt crisis 95
Miners' Strike (UK, 1984-5) 326
Montreal Protocol (1987) 205
Moody's credit rating agency 90
MP3 music 214
multiculturalism 275
music business
alternative models 218-19
crisis 213-15, 223
and copyright 214
literature 215-17
and the Internet 218
legal action, against downloaders 215

music education
  Johnson on 223
  varieties of 222-3
music performances
  global cities 213
  legal provisions 221-2
music venues, global cities 213
musicians, earnings 222
Muslim Council of Britain 275

Napster file-sharing service 214, 220
National Health Service (NHS)
  and the Big Society 299-300
  change
    obstacles 301-2
    proposals for 295-8, 303
  'Equity and Excellence: Liberating the NHS' (2010) 295, 301
    themes 296-7
  GP consortia 296-7
  'Healthy Lives - Healthy People' (2010) 295, 298-9
  monitoring systems 300-1
  'Our Care, Our Health, Our Say' (2006) 296-7
  and Social Return on Investment methodology 300-1
neo-liberalism 322
  ascendancy of 340fn1
  crisis 323, 325
New Econmics Foundation, Green New Deal 328
New Environmental Policy Instruments (NEPIs) 207
New Labour government 178, 236, 322
  and creative industries 237
  immigration, attitude to 275-6
New York
  music performances 213
  music venues 213
New York City
  'Black Monday' (1987) 43-4
  cosmopolitanism 37-8
  deindustrialisation 40
  diversification strategy 48-9
  education and health services 45-7
  employment 40
  by industry 45-6
  films about 44
  financial services 38, 41-5
    employment in 43-5, 47-8
  key industries 49
  manufacturing
    rise and fall 39-41, 48
    and social cohesion 41
    population 37
    port 38
    professional and business services 45-6, 49
    Securities and Commodities Contracts 44
    size 37
    trade 39
    see also New York Stock Exchange; Wall Street
New York Stock Exchange 38, 43
Newman, Kim 233
  The Quorum 230-2, 235
Newnes, Georges, magazine empire 151-2
newspapers, magazines
  consolidation 151-3, 155-6
  distinction 150
Norman, Montagu 93
Northern Rock bank, collapse 18, 123
Nussbaum, Martha 331

O2 Arena 214
Obama, Barack 326
Office for Budget Responsibility, UK 30
oil prices, rise 326
Olympic Games, London (2012) 8, 165, 259, 318, 320, 343
Olympic Park Legacy Company 171, 284
Osborne, George 124, 164

Palmer, Andrew 17
Paris
  music performances 213
  music venues 213
  nineteenth-century reconstruction of 9
Peep Show tv series 234
pension funds 122
Petrodollars 94
Plan B
  curatorial role 76

The Defamation of Strickland Banks 75, 77
Polanyi, Karl 131, 144
Porritt, Jonathan 206
Private Finance Initiative (PFI) 254-5, 327fn13
privatisation 110-11
UK 203, 322
professional, amateur, distinction 229
professionalisation, urban labour market 6
profit realisation, levels 87-8
Prudential Regulation Authority 124
Public Private Partnerships (PPP) 254-5
public spending, and financialisation 338
Puzo, Mario, *The Godfather* 229

quantitative easing 105
USA 28

racism 273, 274
radio manufacturing 166
Reagan, Ronald 40
'real economy' 20, 27
and 'the City' 130
and credit 227
and the credit crunch 164
finance capital, distinction 31
and financialisation 252
information on 329
and manufacturing 164
post-crunch revival, East London 161-2, 171-5
and wealth production 332
Reform Act (1832) 104
regeneration policy
conceptual basis 162-5
and creative industries 237-8
Dagenham Docks 169-70
and globalisation 162
and inward investment 163
and manufacturing 164
and sustainability 164-5, 175
and tourism 164
see also under East London
retail distribution
and the Internet 346
and town centres 346
Rio Earth Summit (1992) 165, 205
Ritchie, Guy, *Lock, Stock and Two Smoking Barrels* 233, 241
RMB (Renminbi) currency, convertibility prospects 62
Robbins, Bruce 229
Rosen, Ronald S. 215, 216
Rustin, Michael 337, 341

securitisation 18
of mortgages 47
Sen, Amartya 331
Shanghai
citizen education 57, 60
economic
development 56-7
prospects 51-2
Expo 2010 55-6
social role 57-8
Five Year Plans 55, 58
foreign investments 55
GDP 59
as global city 57
history 54
Hong Kong, rivalry 63
Hongqiao Central Business District 59-60
internationalisation 55-6
IT infrastructure 59-60
multinational companies 55
music performances 213
music venues 213
population 60
port, world's biggest 55
production 52, 58, 61
region, GDP 55
transportation 59
universities 64
and Yangtze Delta 63-4
Sharpe, Richard 339
'Silicon Roundabout' 228, 243, 343
Silva, Rohan 170
Simmel, Georg 3
Situationist International (SI) 4
Sklair, Leslie 136
Smith, Chris 236
social change, and cities 5-8
Social Impact Bonds 301

Social Justice Policy Group, *Breakdown Britain* 31
social unrest 273-4
social wealth 9
solar panels 188
Soros, George 209
South Sea Bubble
  collapse 86-8, 104
  as Ponzi scheme 87
Sparrow, Andrew, *Music Distribution and the Internet* 215
Spectator 148-9, 153, 158
Spotify website 218
Standard and Poor's credit rating agency 90, 96
state, role, Keynes on 28-9
Steele, Richard 148-9, 158
Stone, Oliver, *Wall Street* 43
student-consumer, and higher education 306
Sugar, Alan 128-9, 143
  'Enterprise Czar' 129
  persona 129
sustainability 205
  dimensions 165
  economic 165
  environmental 165
  and legacy 165
  and regeneration policy 164-5, 175

Tate Modern 341-2
Tatler 148-9
telegraph, impact 89-90
television, development 166-7
Thackara, John 256-7
Thames Gateway, *see* London
Thameslink project 254, 347
Thatcher government 110
  anti-collectivism 322
  environmentalism 206-7
Thatcher, Margaret 96, 206, 346
Thompson, Neil, *Clubbed* 242
Tobin tax proposal, on currency speculation 327
Tokyo
  music performances 213
  music venues 213
tourism, and regeneration policy 164
Transport for London
  Cycling Revolution 249
  Travel in London 252
Treasury (HMG) 119
Turner, Adair 27, 120, 130
Tweetdeck 228, 243

UK
  banking sector
    bailout 22-3
    as share of GDP 27
  Dept for Culture, Media and Sport 236
  energy consumption (2008) 178
  film production 241-2
  financial services
    GVA 25
    output 25
    as share of GDP 26, 119
  Financial Services Authority 30-1
  financialisation 25-6, 30, 32-3, 338-9
  GDP growth (1950-88) 20
  GVA, financial services 25
  immigration, distribution 271
  manufacturing
    GVA 25
    industry, decline 20
    as percentage of GDP 25
  Office for Budget Responsibility 30
  personal debt 31
  political parties, environmentalism 207
  privatisation 203, 322
  public ownership 203
  traded goods, deficit 25
  US securities, holdings 22
United Nations (UN), establishment 202
urban labour market, professionalisation 6
US Monetary Forum 18
USA
  China
    economic relations 61-2
    imports from 21
  economic recession 23, 47
  financial services
    output 26, 42
    share of GDP 119
  financialisation 43
  GDP growth (1950-88) 20

housing market, collapse 22, 47
industry GDP, as percentage of total GDP (1947-2010) 42
manufacturing, as percentage of GDP 25
mortgage market, unsustainability 9
quantitative easing 28
securities
China's holdings 21-2
top five foreign holders of 22
see also New York City

Vaughn, Matthew 233

Wall Street 44
Crash (1929) 108
as cultural icon 43
securitisation of mortgages 47
Waugh, Evelyn, *Scoop* 154
wealth production, and the 'real economy' 332
Webb, Matt 170
Weiner, Martin 6
welfarism 324
Wellington, Duke of 104-5
Wilkinson, R. and K. Pickett, *The Spirit Level* 317
Willetts, David 174
Williams, Raymond, *The Country and the City* 10
Winehouse, Amy, alienation 77
'Winter of Discontent' (1978-9) 325
Wired magazine 170
World Bank 202, 205
World Cup (2006), and German investment 162-3
World Trade Organization (WTO) 202
Woudhuysen, James 343

Yerkes, Charles Tyson 249-50, 260
Young, M. and P. Wilmott, *Family and Kinship in East London* 7

Zukin, S. 5, 10